THE
PRESIDENTS
SPEAK

THE
PRESIDENTS
SPEAK

*The Inaugural Addresses
of the American Presidents from
Washington to Nixon*

ANNOTATED BY **DAVIS NEWTON LOTT**

HOLT, RINEHART AND WINSTON
NEW YORK • CHICAGO • SAN FRANCISCO

THIRD EDITION

STEEL-ENGRAVED PRESIDENTIAL PORTRAITS ARE REPRODUCED THROUGH THE
COURTESY OF THE BUREAU OF ENGRAVING AND PRINTING, WASHINGTON, D.C.

Acknowledgments

Thanks are due to Mr. Donald E. Cooke, formerly
General Manager, John C. Winston Company, whose
initial enthusiasm helped transform this book from idea to
reality; to Mrs. Louise Waller for her counsel and unflag-
ging zest in completing the project; to Dr. James Barnes
of Temple University for his months of painstaking verifi-
cation of each date and fact; to Clara Grant and Robert
McKinley for their efforts in the initial preparation of the
manuscript; to my wife, Arlene, for her patience and help
in proofreading the final galleys; to Tibbie, Sue, Andrew,
Vicki, Christy, Laurie, Kathy, and Wendy for their encouragement and help in a hundred ways.

LIBRARY OF CONGRESS CATALOG CARD NUMBER: 71-80344

SBN: 03-081856-7

PRINTED IN THE UNITED STATES OF AMERICA

To the
American people,
from whom
our future leaders
must come.

FOREWORD

Shortly after the inauguration of President Eisenhower on January 21, 1957, Walter Winchell wrote in one of his columns:

> You could almost write a history of this nation
> by compiling an anthology of inaugural addresses.
> Many were eloquent—and a few had that special
> quality which made them ageless.

Grateful acknowledgment is hereby made to Mr. Winchell for the thought that led to the compilation of these addresses over the past two years. If the words of the addresses are not merely read silently, but are spoken aloud as they were originally delivered, the eloquence of our chief executives and the ageless quality of many of their phrases will be clearly demonstrated.

Speaking for myself, I have found it a stimulating experience to don mentally the heavy mantle of responsibility worn by each president and to feel the pressure of the problems—local, national, and international—with which each incoming chief executive was faced on his first day in office. This exercise in imagination, to me at least, brought each man down from his place on the pedestal of history to where he became as human and as real as though I had known him personally. Faced with these same problems, what kind of an address would you or I write? It is an intriguing challenge!

Besides its obvious use as a reference text, perhaps this book will help to humanize our history by providing a better understanding of the character of the men who have been chosen to lead our nation from its precarious inception to its present position as the last bulwark of freedom in a troubled world.

—D.N.L.

Santa Monica, California

CONTENTS

THE
PRESIDENTS
SPEAK

THE PRESIDENT

George Washington was the son of Augustine Washington by his second wife, Mary Ball. Washington's marriage to Martha Dandridge Custis, his military career, and his eventual success need no elaboration. After he resigned his commission on December 23, 1783, he retired to Mount Vernon. But his retirement ended when he was asked to attend the Constitutional Convention, at which he was elected to the presidency. He was notified of his election at Mount Vernon, April 14, 1789.

THE NATION

Once France had been humbled in 1763, England began to tighten her control over the American colonies and taxed the American settlements heavily to help pay for British war debts. The Tea Act of 1773 precipitated the Boston Tea Party which, in turn, brought reprisals from George III in a fresh series of laws known as the "Intolerable Acts." The First Continental Congress met in Philadelphia in protest. The Declaration of Rights was adopted on October 14, 1774.

From the Battle of Lexington on April 19, 1775, until the surrender of Cornwallis to Washington at Yorktown on October 19, 1781, an American victory was a rare thing. But when the peace treaty was signed in Paris on September 3, 1783, it began to look as though a new nation *had* been brought forth. Six years later, with the Constitution written and ratified, the presidential electors named Washington as president with John Adams as vice-president and the date of the first inaugural was set for April 30, 1789.

THE WORLD

In the middle 1700's profound changes were taking place—changes that were to play a vital part in a realignment of the balance of power among the nations of the world. For example, from 1764 to 1769 three important inventions continued the Industrial Revolution which had started with Kay's flying shuttle in 1733: James Hargreaves' spinning jenny, James Watt's development of an improved version of a steam engine, and Sir Richard Arkwright's spinning frame. The balance of power between nations was being changed in other ways, too. In 1754 the Seven Years' War (so-called in Europe because it started there in 1756) broke out in America between Britain and France, and ended February 10, 1763, with the signing of the Treaty of Paris. England was left the leading colonial power of the period.

THIS, THEN, is the condition of the world and the nation the last two weeks of April, 1789. Imagine yourself, if you will, as a thoughtful Washington, sitting down in your quiet study at Mount Vernon to prepare an address you must deliver April 30th in New York City. Although you have been almost as adept with the pen as with the sword, still it comes hard, this address, and during the trip from Mount Vernon to New York with wildly cheering crowds along the way you cannot help but feel uneasy over its reception. Indeed, when you reach New York you discard your original address, and with the aid of James Madison prepare a much shorter message. After the oath of office has been administered to you by Chancellor Robert R. Livingston of New York on the balcony of Federal Hall you listen to the thirteen-gun salute from the harbor as the Stars and Stripes are raised, acknowledge the adulation of the crowd, and retire to the Senate Chamber, where you take your seat until the Chamber has settled down. Now the entire Chamber looks toward you as you stand, settle your dark brown coat on your shoulders, adjust your spectacles nervously, and begin to speak in a low voice the words you have so painstakingly rewritten . . . .

George Washington

[1789–1793]

FIRST INAUGURAL ADDRESS, APRIL 30, 1789

Federal Hall, New York, N.Y.

Fellow-Citizens of the Senate and of the House of Representatives:

Among the vicissitudes incident to life no event could have filled me with greater anxieties than that of which the notification was transmitted by your order, and received on the 14th day of the present month. On the one hand, I was summoned by my country, whose voice I can never hear but with veneration and love, from a retreat which I had chosen with the fondest predilection, and, in my flattering hopes, with an immutable decision, as the asylum of my declining years—a retreat which was rendered every day more necessary as well as more dear to me by the addition of habit to inclination, and of frequent interruptions in my health to the gradual waste committed on it by time. On the other hand, the magnitude and difficulty of the trust to which the voice of my country called me, being sufficient to awaken in the wisest and most experienced of her citizens a distrustful scrutiny into his qualifications, could not but overwhelm with despondence one who (inheriting inferior endowments from nature and unpracticed in the duties of civil administration) ought to be peculiarly conscious of his own deficiencies. In this conflict of emotions all I dare aver is that it has been my faithful study to collect my duty from a just appreciation of every circumstance by which it might be affected. All I dare hope is that if, in executing this task, I have been too much swayed by a grateful remembrance of former instances, or by an affectionate sensibility to this transcendent proof of the confidence of my fellow-citizens, and have thence too little consulted my incapacity as well as disinclination for the weighty and untried cares before me, my error will be palliated by the motives which mislead me, and its consequences be judged by my country with some share of the partiality in which they originated.

Such being the impressions under which I have, in obedience to the public summons, repaired to the present station, it would be peculiarly improper to omit in this first official act my fervent supplications to that Almighty Being who rules over the universe,

Washington was 6'2" tall and weighed 200 pounds. Now, however, at 57 the drain of long years at war was beginning to tell on him—as he briefly mentioned in his opening remarks.

Washington foresaw the young nation's difficulties. He didn't feel quite so much at home in a statesman's role as president. He felt better as commander in chief. But he evidently believed that by appealing to his colleagues, he could eliminate a good deal of the internal friction that was even then becoming evident. This friction was eventually to cause the dissolution of the Federalist party, of which Washington was a member.

The thought in this passage would occur repeatedly throughout the addresses of Washington's successors, but would seldom be expressed with the eloquence commanded by Washington.

The "future blessings" to which Washington referred were soon lost sight of in the storm of party bickering that began as the new government was seated—a development of which Washington was evidently not insensible, judging by the appeal in the next segment of his address.

Washington here revealed the meat of his message: "party animosities." His was a blunt request to the members of Congress who would be directing affairs of government under his leadership. But this appeal was soon to be forgotten, as it became plain that the young government was stronger than even its creators suspected. Political office was found to offer unforeseen rewards besides those of "public prospect and felicity"—rewards for which no sacrifice was apparently too great for the ambitious.

In this passage, which begins with the words "the sacred fire of liberty," Washington's eloquence reached its peak.

who presides in the councils of nations, and whose providential aids can supply every human defect, that His benediction may consecrate to the liberties and happiness of the people of the United States a Government instituted by themselves for these essential purposes, and may enable every instrument employed in its administration to execute with success the functions allotted to his charge. In tendering this homage to the Great Author of every public and private good, I assure myself that it expresses your sentiments not less than my own, nor those of my fellow-citizens at large less than either. No people can be bound to acknowledge and adore the Invisible Hand which conducts the affairs of men more than those of the United States. Every step by which they have advanced to the character of an independent nation seems to have been distinguished by some token of providential agency; and in the important revolution just accomplished in the system of their united government the tranquil deliberations and voluntary consent of so many distinct communities from which the event has resulted can not be compared with the means by which most governments have been established without some return of pious gratitude, along with an humble anticipation of the future blessings which the past seem to presage. These reflections, arising out of the present crisis, have forced themselves too strongly on my mind to be suppressed. You will join with me, I trust, in thinking that there are none under the influence of which the proceedings of a new and free government can more auspiciously commence.

By the article establishing the executive department it is made the duty of the President "to recommend to your consideration such measures as he shall judge necessary and expedient." The circumstances under which I now meet you will acquit me from entering into that subject further than to refer to the great constitutional charter under which you are assembled, and which, in defining your powers, designates the objects to which your attention is to be given. It will be more consistent with those circumstances, and far more congenial with the feelings which actuate me, to substitute, in place of a recommendation of particular measures, the tribute that is due to the talents, the rectitude, and the patriotism which adorn the characters selected to devise and adopt them. In these honorable qualifications I behold the surest pledges that as on one side no local prejudices or attachments, no separate views nor party animosities, will misdirect the comprehensive and equal eye which ought to watch over this great assemblage of communities and interests, so, on another, that the foundation of our national policy will be laid in the pure and immutable principles of private morality, and the preeminence of free government be exemplified by all the attributes which can win the affections of its citizens and command the respect of the world. I dwell on this prospect with every satisfaction which an ardent love for my country can inspire, since there is no truth more thoroughly established than that there exists in the economy and course of nature an indissoluble union between virtue and happiness; between duty and advantage; between the genuine maxims of an honest and magnanimous policy and the solid rewards of public prosperity and felicity; since we ought to be no less persuaded that the propitious smiles of Heaven can never be expected on a nation that disregards the eternal rules of order and right which Heaven itself has ordained; and since the preservation of the sacred fire of liberty and the destiny of the republican model of government are justly considered, perhaps, as

[4]

deeply, as *finally,* staked on the experiment intrusted to the hands of the American people.

Besides the ordinary objects submitted to your care, it will remain with your judgment to decide how far an exercise of the occasional power delegated by the fifth article of the Constitution is rendered expedient at the present juncture by the nature of objections which have been urged against the system, or by the degree of inquietude which has given birth to them. Instead of undertaking particular recommendations on this subject, in which I could be guided by no lights derived from official opportunities, I shall again give way to my entire confidence in your discernment and pursuit of the public good; for I assure myself that whilst you carefully avoid every alteration which might endanger the benefits of an united and effective government, or which ought to await the future lessons of experience, a reverence for the characteristic rights of freemen and a regard for the public harmony will sufficiently influence your deliberations on the question how far the former can be impregnably fortified or the latter be safely and advantageously promoted.

To the foregoing observations I have one to add, which will be most properly addressed to the House of Representatives. It concerns myself, and will therefore be as brief as possible. When I was first honored with a call into the service of my country, then on the eve of an arduous struggle for its liberties, the light in which I contemplated my duty required that I should renounce every pecuniary compensation. From this resolution I have in no instance departed; and being still under the impressions which produced it, I must decline as inapplicable to myself any share in the personal emoluments which may be indispensably included in a permanent provision for the executive department, and must accordingly pray that the pecuniary estimates for the station in which I am placed may during my continuance in it be limited to such actual expenditures as the public good may be thought to require.

Having thus imparted to you my sentiments as they have been awakened by the occasion which brings us together, I shall take my present leave; but not without resorting once more to the benign Parent of the Human Race in humble supplication that, since He has been pleased to favor the American people with opportunities for deliberating in perfect tranquillity, and dispositions for deciding with unparalleled unanimity on a form of government for the security of their union and the advancement of their happiness, so His divine blessing may be equally *conspicuous* in the enlarged views, the temperate consultations, and the wise measures on which the success of this Government must depend.

In his reference to the fifth article of the Constitution, which provides for proposal of Constitutional amendments, Washington was attempting to divert rash action on the part of party hotheads, to whom the Constitution was still an imperfect instrument. Federalist party leaders had stated their desire for Constitutional changes, and Washington was plainly displeased.

Here again Washington made an indirect yet nonetheless frank appeal to those who would make political office a means of excessive "personal emoluments."

At the close of his address Washington once more stressed a desire for "enlarged views . . . temperate consultations, and . . . wise measures" instead of acts of personal aggrandizement. A noble appeal, it fell on deaf ears—as Washington was soon to discover when ideals ran headlong into reality.

THE PRESIDENT

Washington worked unceasingly to reconcile Jefferson and Hamilton, making both members of his cabinet: Jefferson as Secretary of State and Hamilton as Secretary of the Treasury. But Jefferson believed the Federal government was restricted to those powers specifically conferred by the states. In opposition, Hamilton was convinced the government was not limited to powers expressly declared by the Constitution but also embraced implied powers. Political peace between Jefferson and Hamilton was impossible despite Washington's efforts. Nevertheless, the public regarded Washington's first term of office successful and he was unanimously reëlected.

THE NATION

1789 was a busy year, with Congress creating the departments of State, of the Treasury, and of War. The Supreme Court was formed, with John Jay as Chief Justice. Within two years ten amendments to the Constitution (known as the Bill of Rights) were ratified by the states and became a part of the Constitution.

In 1790 the first U.S. census was authorized and revealed a population of 3,929,214. 1791 saw Congress pass the first internal revenue law: the tax of 20 to 30 cents per gallon on whisky and distilled spirits, a levy that was to culminate in the Whisky Rebellion. On March 4, 1791, Vermont became the 14th state to join the Union, with Kentucky following suit on June 1, 1792. As election time approached, Thomas Jefferson assumed leadership of a new party: the Anti-Federalists or Republicans as they soon became known because of their sympathies toward the struggling French Republic. In the election on December 5 Washington polled 132 electoral votes and was reëlected president; Adams received 77 votes and was reëlected vice-president, with Jefferson's candidate, George Clinton, receiving only 50 votes. Jefferson himself received 4 votes and Aaron Burr 1. The election was a triumph for Alexander Hamilton's Federalist party.

THE WORLD

As the eighteenth century began to draw to its turbulent close the eyes of the world shifted from America to France, where the revolutionary pot was fast coming to a boil. On July 14, 1789, armed mobs tore down the Bastille in Paris in revolt against the rule of Louis XVI and Marie Antoinette. On October 6th the royal family was removed from Versailles by an unruly mob. In 1792 France declared war on the antirevolutionary powers of Austria and Prussia. And in 1793 the monarchy ended January 21st, when Louis XVI, former king of France, was guillotined.

PICTURE YOURSELF once again in Washington's place. You have been reëlected unanimously to a second term as president—a fact that to you is indicative of the success of your policies and your efforts during the past four years. Despite the growing schism between Hamilton and Jefferson, you feel a satisfaction that you have been given another four years to see the new government even more firmly entrenched behind the protective bulwark of the Constitution. Thus you prepare your second inaugural address in brief form, feeling your policies are too well known to bear repetition, yet sensing that a veiled reference to your belief in the Constitution would be fitting. And on the day of your inauguration you stand before the assembled members of Congress in the Senate Chamber in Philadelphia to receive their ovation. When their applause has died down and the members have assumed their seats you clear your throat and begin to read ....

George Washington

[1793–1797]

SECOND INAUGURAL ADDRESS, MARCH 4, 1793

Senate Chamber, Philadelphia, Pa.

Fellow Citizens:

I am again called upon by the voice of my country to execute the functions of its Chief Magistrate. When the occasion proper for it shall arrive, I shall endeavor to express the high sense I entertain of this distinguished honor, and of the confidence which has been reposed in me by the people of united America.

Previous to the execution of any official act of the President the Constitution requires an oath of office. This oath I am now about to take, and in your presence: That if it shall be found during my administration of the Government I have in any instance violated willingly or knowingly the injunctions thereof, I may (besides incurring constitutional punishment) be subject to the upbraidings of all who are now witnesses of the present solemn ceremony.

In his second inaugural address Washington used few words but implied far more than would seem apparent at first reading. He neatly summed up his basic political philosophy in his closing phrase: an unswerving adherence to the Constitution.

Nowhere was this adherence better evidenced than in Washington's appointment to office of contemporaries toward whom he acted "with the best intentions and fullest determination to nominate to office those persons only who, upon every consideration, were the most deserving, and who would probably execute their several functions to the interest and credit of the American Union, if such characters could be found by my exploring every avenue of information respecting their merit and pretensions that was in my power to obtain."

His feeling for the Constitution seems best expressed in the farewell address to Congress, delivered September 17, 1796, only three years before his death. Washington said, "The basis of our political system is the right of the people to make and to alter their constitutions of government. But the Constitution which at any time exists till changed by an explicit and authentic act of the whole people is sacredly obligatory on all."

Inauguration of Washington

THE PRESIDENT

John Adams graduated from Harvard at the age of nineteen, and married Abigail Smith in 1764. The clarity of his resolutions opposing the Stamp Act in 1765 brought him into colonial prominence. During the war years Adams worked abroad vigorously. After the Treaty of Paris had been signed in 1783 he was recalled to America from England, where he was minister, and rewarded by election as vice-president.

THE NATION

As Washington's second term progressed, it became clear that despite differences between some members of the cabinet his administration as a whole was proving capable of governing the new nation with the consent of the governed. Courts of justice, the foreign service, post office, customs, internal revenue, civil service, the cabinet, and the Congress—all were functioning satisfactorily. Indeed, the growing pains normal to any young government were remarkable by their mildness, and had it not been for the brief Whisky Rebellion Washington's second term would have been unmarred. Another state was added—Tennessee entered the Union on June 1, 1796.

In the election year of 1796 the undercover struggle for control of the government was growing in intensity between the Federalists and the Anti-Federalists or Democratic-Republicans. Vice-President Adams assumed he would step into Washington's shoes and supposedly was unaware of Hamilton's backstage scheming to elect Thomas Pinckney to the presidency, keeping Adams relegated to the vice-presidency. But when the electoral votes were totaled, Federalist John Adams had been elected president by polling only three votes more than Jefferson, who was elected vice-president. This was an indication of the rising tide of Anti-Federalist Republicans, who would eventually engulf bickering Federalists.

THE WORLD

The Reign of Terror in France continued to occupy the attention of the world from 1793 until July 27, 1794. Finally the monster thus created began to turn on itself, culminating with the guillotining of Maximilien Robespierre, one of the twelve members of the Committee of Public Safety, executive authority in France. In other parts of the world important events were also taking place. The Cape of Good Hope was seized by the British in 1795. Catherine II, Empress of Russia, died in 1796. And in the same year the French Directory unwittingly wrote the first paragraph of a new chapter in world history by promoting a relatively obscure general to command an army for the invasion of Italy: Napoleon Bonaparte.

IT IS MARCH 4, 1797. For you, John Adams, this should be the greatest day of your life. But from the moment you arise, peer outside, and note the day is cloudy, gloomy, and bitterly windy, you feel no elation —only a growing disappointment. Your wife, Abigail, could not make the journey to Philadelphia and already you miss her steadying presence and ready wit. As you make your way through the narrow Philadelphia streets to the hall of the House of Representatives you notice furtive tears and sad faces. And when the time comes for you to enter the Senate Chamber to deliver your address you become keenly aware that the center of attention is not your own short, rounded, plainly dressed self but the still heroic figure of the aging Washington. Nevertheless, despite your inner conflict you begin to speak the thoughts you have set down in your harsh, angular hand . . . .

John Adams

[1797–1801]

INAUGURAL ADDRESS, MARCH 4, 1797

Senate Chamber, Philadelphia, Pa.

When it was first perceived, in early times, that no middle course for America remained between unlimited submission to a foreign legislature and a total independence of its claims, men of reflection were less apprehensive of danger from the formidable power of fleets and armies they must determine to resist than from those contests and dissensions which would certainly arise concerning the forms of government to be instituted over the whole and over the parts of this extensive country. Relying, however, on the purity of their intentions, the justice of their cause, and the integrity and intelligence of the people, under an overruling Providence which had so signally protected this country from the first, the representatives of this nation, then consisting of little more than half its present number, not only broke to pieces the chains which were forging and the rod of iron that was lifted up, but frankly cut asunder the ties which had bound them, and launched into an ocean of uncertainty.

The zeal and ardor of the people during the Revolutionary war, supplying the place of government, commanded a degree of order sufficient at least for the temporary preservation of society. The Confederation which was early felt to be necessary was prepared from the models of the Batavian and Helvetic confederacies, the only examples which remain with any detail and precision in history, and certainly the only ones which the people at large had ever considered. But reflecting on the striking difference in so many particulars between this country and those where a courier may go from the seat of government to the frontier in a single day, it was then certainly foreseen by some who assisted in Congress at the formation of it that it could not be durable.

Negligence of its regulations, inattention to its recommendations, if not disobedience to its authority, not only in individuals but in States, soon appeared with their melancholy consequences—universal languor, jealousies and rivalries of States, decline of navigation and commerce, discouragement of necessary manufactures, universal fall in the value of lands and their produce, contempt of public and private faith, loss of consideration and credit with foreign

In four paragraphs Adams neatly summed up the chaotic years of unrest and turmoil leading up to the Declaration of Independence and the Constitution.

[9]

nations, and at length in discontents, animosities, combinations, partial conventions, and insurrection, threatening some great national calamity.

In this dangerous crisis the people of America were not abandoned by their usual good sense, presence of mind, resolution, or integrity. Measures were pursued to concert a plan to form a more perfect union, establish justice, insure domestic tranquillity, provide for the common defense, promote the general welfare, and secure the blessings of liberty. The public disquisitions, discussions, and deliberations issued in the present happy Constitution of Government.

Employed in the service of my country abroad during the whole course of these transactions, I first saw the Constitution of the United States in a foreign country. Irritated by no literary altercation, animated by no public debate, heated by no party animosity, I read it with great satisfaction, as the result of good heads prompted by good hearts, as an experiment better adapted to the genius, character, situation, and relations of this nation and country than any which had ever been proposed or suggested. In its general principles and great outlines it was conformable to such a system of government as I had ever most esteemed, and in some States, my own native State in particular, had contributed to establish. Claiming a right of suffrage, in common with my fellow-citizens, in the adoption or rejection of a constitution which was to rule me and my posterity, as well as them and theirs, I did not hesitate to express my approbation of it on all occasions, in public and in private. It was not then, nor has been since, any objection to it in my mind that the Executive and Senate were not more permanent. Nor have I ever entertained a thought of promoting any alteration in it but such as the people themselves, in the course of their experience, should see and feel to be necessary or expedient, and by their representatives in Congress and the State legislatures, according to the Constitution itself, adopt and ordain.

Returning to the bosom of my country after a painful separation from it for ten years, I had the honor to be elected to a station under the new order of things, and I have repeatedly laid myself under the most serious obligations to support the Constitution. The operation of it has equaled the most sanguine expectations of its friends, and from an habitual attention to it, satisfaction in its administration, and delight in its effects upon the peace, order, prosperity, and happiness of the nation I have acquired an habitual attachment to it and veneration for it.

What other form of government, indeed, can so well deserve our esteem and love?

There may be little solidity in an ancient idea that congregations of men into cities and nations are the most pleasing objects in the sight of superior intelligences, but this is very certain, that to a benevolent human mind there can be no spectacle presented by any nation more pleasing, more noble, majestic, or august, than an assembly like that which has so often been seen in this and the other Chamber of Congress, of a Government in which the Executive authority, as well as that of all the branches of the Legislature, are exercised by citizens selected at regular periods by their neighbors to make and execute laws for the general good. Can anything essential, anything more than mere ornament and decoration, be added to this by robes and diamonds? Can authority be more amiable and respectable when it descends from accidents or institu-

The "literary altercation" is a pointed reference to the Federalist papers, a series of published essays clarifying the Constitution, supposedly written by Hamilton, James Madison, and John Jay. Although highly controversial, the essays nevertheless helped to crystallize public opinion in favor of ratifying the Constitution.

Adams referred to the years spent abroad, when he acted first as commissioner to France, then as minister plenipotentiary to negotiate a peace treaty with Great Britain, as commissioner to conclude treaties of peace with other European powers, and finally as one of the American Peace Commissioners who signed the Treaty of Paris, September 3, 1783. Adams then went to Holland as minister for a year, before being appointed by Congress as minister of the United States to the Court of Great Britain, where he served until called home in June, 1788.

Like Washington, Adams was a conservative Federalist, and also like Washington he felt a deep and unswerving "attachment and veneration" for the Constitution—a feeling to which he often alluded not only in this address but also in others delivered during his term of office.

[10]

tions established in remote antiquity than when it springs fresh from the hearts and judgments of an honest and enlightened people? For it is the people only that are represented. It is their power and majesty that is reflected, and only for their good, in every legitimate government, under whatever form it may appear. The existence of such a government as ours for any length of time is a full proof of a general dissemination of knowledge and virtue throughout the whole body of the people. And what object or consideration more pleasing than this can be presented to the human mind? If national pride is ever justifiable or excusable it is when it springs, not from power or riches, grandeur or glory, but from conviction of national innocence, information, and benevolence.

In the midst of these pleasing ideas we should be unfaithful to ourselves if we should ever lose sight of the danger to our liberties if anything partial or extraneous should infect the purity of our free, fair, virtuous, and independent elections. If an election is to be determined by a majority of a single vote, and that can be procured by a party through artifice or corruption, the Government may be the choice of a party for its own ends, not of the nation for the national good. If that solitary suffrage can be obtained by foreign nations by flattery or menaces, by fraud or violence, by terror, intrigue, or venality, the Government may not be the choice of the American people, but of foreign nations. It may be foreign nations who govern us, and not we, the people, who govern ourselves; and candid men will acknowledge that in such cases choice would have little advantage to boast of over lot or chance.

Such is the amiable and interesting system of government (and such are some of the abuses to which it may be exposed) which the people of America have exhibited to the admiration and anxiety of the wise and virtuous of all nations for eight years under the administration of a citizen who, by a long course of great actions, regulated by prudence, justice, temperance, and fortitude, conducting a people inspired with the same virtues and animated with the same ardent patriotism and love of liberty to independence and peace, to increasing wealth and unexampled prosperity, has merited the gratitude of his fellow-citizens, commanded the highest praises of foreign nations, and secured immortal glory with posterity.

In that retirement which is his voluntary choice may he long live to enjoy the delicious recollection of his services, the gratitude of mankind, the happy fruits of them to himself and the world, which are daily increasing, and that splendid prospect of the future fortunes of this country which is opening from year to year. His name may be still a rampart, and the knowledge that he lives a bulwark, against all open or secret enemies of his country's peace. This example has been recommended to the imitation of his successors by both Houses of Congress and by the voice of the legislatures and the people throughout the nation.

On this subject it might become me better to be silent or to speak with diffidence; but as something may be expected, the occasion, I hope, will be admitted as an apology if I venture to say that if a preference, upon principle, of a free republican government, formed upon long and serious reflection, after a diligent and impartial inquiry after truth; if an attachment to the Constitution of the United States, and a conscientious determination to support it until it shall be altered by the judgments and wishes of the people, expressed in the mode prescribed in it; if a respectful attention to the constitutions of the individual States and a constant caution and

Adams' reference to an election "determined by a majority of a single vote" seemed to be directed toward the recent election in which he had only a three-vote margin over Jefferson. Although it is generally assumed that Adams was not aware until after he took office of Hamilton's herculean under-cover efforts to have Pinckney elected, the thought expressed here would indicate otherwise.

Adams' eulogy of Washington was at odds with his private thoughts, as witnessed by a phrase in a letter written to his absent wife after the ceremonies were over. "He seemed to me to enjoy a triumph over me. Methought I heard him say, 'Ay! I am fairly out, and you fairly in! See which of us will be the happier!' "

[11]

The President-elect set forth his belief in strict adherence to the Constitution, as well as his complete political philosophy, in this long sentence—one of the longest to appear in any inaugural address.

Adams' reference to the esteem in which he held the French nation was to be forgotten only two weeks later, when he issued a proclamation to convene both Houses of Congress to hear a special session message. France and England were at war, and the French Directory felt the government of the United States was bound to them by the treaty of 1778. The French tried to provoke war between England and the United States. Failing this, they insulted Charles Cotesworth Pinckney, our envoy to Paris, and set out to capture our vessels. This caused Adams to deliver his message to Congress, disclosing diplomatic relations with France had been broken off. Although war had not yet been declared, it appeared imminent.

delicacy toward the State governments; if an equal and impartial regard to the rights, interest, honor, and happiness of all the States in the Union, without preference or regard to a northern or southern, an eastern or western, position, their various political opinions on unessential points or their personal attachments; if a love of virtuous men of all parties and denominations; if a love of science and letters and a wish to patronize every rational effort to encourage schools, colleges, universities, academies, and every institution for propagating knowledge, virtue, and religion among all classes of the people, not only for their benign influence on the happiness of life in all its stages and classes, and of society in all its forms, but as the only means of preserving our Constitution from its natural enemies, the spirit of sophistry, the spirit of party, the spirit of intrigue, the profligacy of corrupton, and the pestilence of foreign influence, which is the angel of destruction to elective governments; if a love of equal laws, of justice, and humanity in the interior administration; of an inclination to improve agriculture, commerce, and manufactures for necessity, convenience, and defense; if a spirit of equity and humanity toward the aboriginal nations of America, and a disposition to meliorate their condition by inclining them to be more friendly to us, and our citizens to be more friendly to them; if an inflexible determination to maintain peace and inviolable faith with all nations, and that system of neutrality and impartiality among the belligerent powers of Europe which has been adopted by this Government and so solemnly sanctioned by both Houses of Congress and applauded by the legislatures of the States and the public opinion, until it shall be otherwise ordained by Congress; if a personal esteem for the French nation, formed in a residence of seven years chiefly among them, and a sincere desire to preserve the friendship which has been so much for the honor and interest of both nations; if, while the conscious honor and integrity of the people of America and the internal sentiment of their own power and energies must be preserved, an earnest endeavor to investigate every just cause and remove every colorable pretense of complaint; if an intention to pursue by amicable negotiation a reparation for the injuries that have been committed on the commerce of our fellow-citizens by whatever nation, and if success can not be obtained, to lay the facts before the Legislature, that they may consider what further measures the honor and interest of the Government and its constituents demand; if a resolution to do justice as far as may depend upon me, at all times and to all nations, and maintain peace, friendship, and benevolence with all the world; if an unshaken confidence in the honor, spirit, and resources of the American people, on which I have so often hazarded my all and never been deceived; if elevated ideas of the high destinies of this country and of my own duties toward it, founded on a knowledge of the moral principles and intellectual improvements of the people deeply engraven on my mind in early life, and not obscured but exalted by experience and age; and, with humble reverence, I feel it to be my duty to add, if a veneration for the religion of a people who profess and call themselves Christians, and a fixed resolution to consider a decent respect for Christianity among the best recommendations for the public service, can enable me in any degree to comply with your wishes, it shall be my strenuous endeavor that this sagacious injunction of the two Houses shall not be without effect.

With this great example before me, with the sense and spirit, the faith and honor, the duty and interest, of the same American people pledged to support the Constitution of the United States, I entertain no doubt of its continuance in all its energy, and my mind is prepared without hesitation to lay myself under the most solemn obligations to support it to the utmost of my power.

And may that Being who is supreme over all, the Patron of Order, the Fountain of Justice, and the Protector in all ages of the world of virtuous liberty, continue His blessing upon this nation and its Government and give it all possible success and duration consistent with the ends of His providence.

In the summer of 1800, when Congress moved from Philadelphia to the new city of Washington, the north wing was the only finished part of the Capitol. A muddy road led down to a swampy area along the Potomac. Despite the dismal surroundings Congress convened in the fall. On November 22, 1800, President Adams delivered his Fourth Annual Message to the two Houses, meeting for the first time in their new Capitol building.

THE PRESIDENT

Thomas Jefferson was a brilliant man with many talents; he was a lawyer, architect, inventor, statesman, philosopher, musician, writer, and leader of men. In 1772 he married a widow, Martha Wayles Skelton, who died ten years later. Jefferson wrote the original draft of the Declaration of Independence, which was adopted, essentially as submitted, July 4, 1776. He served in many capacities in the new government. After a tie vote in the Electoral College between Aaron Burr and himself, Jefferson was elected to the presidency by the House.

THE NATION

Following the X.Y.Z. affair Adams found Washington's policy of strict neutrality increasingly difficult to maintain in the face of the rallying cry that swept the nation: "Millions for defense, but not one cent for tribute!" At Federalist insistence Adams appointed Benjamin Stoddert the first Secretary of the Navy. Stoddert at once organized the U.S. Navy, and the army was strengthened when Washington was recalled as commander in chief of the provisional army. War seemed inevitable, and had it come undoubtedly both France and England would have carved up the young nation. But, to his everlasting credit, Adams stubbornly refused to give in to the war mongers and managed to negotiate an unpopular peace with France in 1800. This split the Federalists badly. The passage of the ill-advised Alien and Sedition Acts virtually completed the dissolution of the party shortly after Jefferson's victory in 1800.

On December 14, 1799, Washington died at Mount Vernon. From the funeral oration delivered by Henry Lee before Congress at Philadelphia on December 19th came the immortal phrase: "First in war, first in peace, and first in the hearts of his countrymen."

The census of 1800 showed 5,308,483—an increase of 1,379,269 over 1790. On October 1, 1800, Spain ceded the Louisiana Territory to France. This was the beginning of Napoleon's schemes for a new French colonial empire, schemes that would affect America greatly.

THE WORLD

The turn of the century found France still at war with England, Russia, and Austria. In 1798 Bonaparte embarked on his frustrating and virtually fruitless Egyptian campaign. But on his return to France in 1799 he engineered a coup d'état that swept away the French constitution and placed him in power. Following this he defeated the Austrian army which had occupied northern Italy, and the Peace of Lunéville was signed with Austria in February of 1801, a month before Thomas Jefferson was inaugurated. Napoleon was now free to turn his full attention to England and Russia.

NOW, AS YOUR INAUGURATION DAY DAWNS, you feel a deep satisfaction. At last you, Thomas Jefferson, will be able to put into practice your ideas for a decentralized government responsive to the people's wishes, as opposed to Hamilton's belief in a strong central government controlled by the aristocracy. Although you are a slave-owning aristocrat yourself, still you have the common touch that has endeared you to the masses. And so you modestly walk with a few friends up muddy Pennsylvania Avenue to the unfinished Capitol, where, to your surprise, you learn the outgoing Adams has left Washington earlier that morning in a fit of pettiness that will be equaled by only one other president. Despite this unsettling incident your sense of personal satisfaction persists, as you stand before the assembled members of Congress and guests and in an almost inaudible voice begin your address which will amaze the nation because of its conciliatory rather than vindictive tone . . . .

Thomas Jefferson

[1801–1805]

FIRST INAUGURAL ADDRESS, MARCH 4, 1801

Capitol Building, Washington, D.C.

Friends and Fellow-Citizens.

Called upon to undertake the duties of the first executive office of our country, I avail myself of the presence of that portion of my fellow-citizens which is here assembled to express my grateful thanks for the favor with which they have been pleased to look toward me, to declare a sincere consciousness that the task is above my talents, and that I approach it with those anxious and awful presentiments which the greatness of the charge and the weakness of my powers so justly inspire. A rising nation, spread over a wide and fruitful land, traversing all the seas with the rich productions of their industry, engaged in commerce with nations who feel power and forget right, advancing rapidly to destinies beyond the reach of mortal eye—when I contemplate these transcendent objects, and see the honor, the happiness, and the hopes of this beloved country committed to the issue and the auspices of this day, I shrink from the contemplation, and humble myself before the magnitude of the undertaking. Utterly, indeed, should I despair did not the presence of many whom I here see remind me that in the other high authorities provided by our Constitution I shall find resources of wisdom, of virtue, and of zeal on which to rely under all difficulties. To you, then, gentlemen, who are charged with the sovereign functions of legislation, and to those associated with you, I look with encouragement for that guidance and support which may enable us to steer with safety the vessel in which we are all embarked amidst the conflicting elements of a troubled world.

During the contest of opinion through which we have passed the animation of discussions and of exertions has sometimes worn an aspect which might impose on strangers unused to think freely and to speak and to write what they think; but this being now decided by the voice of the nation, announced according to the rules of the Constitution, all will, of course, arrange themselves under the will of the law, and unite in common efforts for the common good. All, too, will bear in mind this sacred principle, that though the will of the majority is in all cases to prevail, that will to be rightful must be reasonable; that the minority possesses their equal rights, which equal law must protect, and to violate would be oppression. Let us, then, fellow-citizens, unite with one heart and one mind. Let us

Undoubtedly a reference to England rather than France.

Willingness to humble himself and abstain from ostentation while in office was part of Jefferson's carefully planned appeal to the people and made him extremely popular with them. Thus Jefferson succeeded in presenting the contradictory picture of an aristocrat with manners and ideals which appealed to the common man. One hundred and thirty-two years later a successor would combine similar qualities.

Despite the differences between Hamilton and Jefferson, it was largely due to Hamilton's sense of duty that Jefferson was made president after seven days of balloting had failed to break the tie between Jefferson and Burr. After 36 ballots Vermont and Maryland turned to Jefferson, and Delaware and South Carolina handed in blank ballots. This gave Jefferson 10 votes and Burr 4. Thus the Constitution was able to survive the almost fatal deadlock, until problems of a similar nature were eliminated later by the ratification of the twelfth amendment, September 25, 1804.

restore to social intercourse that harmony and affection without which liberty and even life itself are but dreary things. And let us reflect that, having banished from our land that religious intolerance under which mankind so long bled and suffered, we have yet gained little if we countenance a political intolerance as despotic, as wicked, and capable of as bitter and bloody persecutions. During the throes and convulsions of the ancient world, during the agonizing spasms of infuriated man, seeking through blood and slaughter his long-lost liberty, it was not wonderful that the agitation of the billows should reach even this distant and peaceful shore; that this should be more felt and feared by some and less by others, and should divide opinions as to measures of safety. But every difference of opinion is not a difference of principle. We have called by different names brethren of the same principle. We are all Republicans, we are all Federalists. If there be any among us who would wish to dissolve this Union or to change its republican form, let them stand undisturbed as monuments of the safety with which error of opinion may be tolerated where reason is left free to combat it. I know, indeed, that some honest men fear that a republican government can not be strong, that this Government is not strong enough; but would the honest patriot, in the full tide of successful experiment, abandon a government which has so far kept us free and firm on the theoretic and visionary fear that this Government, the world's best hope, may by possibility want energy to preserve itself? I trust not. I believe this, on the contrary, the strongest Government on earth. I believe it the only one where every man, at the call of the law, would fly to the standard of the law, and would meet invasions of the public order as his own personal concern. Sometimes it is said that man can not be trusted with the government of himself. Can he, then, be trusted with the government of others? Or have we found angels in the forms of kings to govern him? Let history answer this question.

Let us, then, with courage and confidence pursue our own Federal and Republican principles, our attachment to union and representative government. Kindly separated by nature and a wide ocean from the exterminating havoc of one quarter of the globe; too high-minded to endure the degradations of the others; possessing a chosen country, with room enough for our descendants to the thousandth and thousandth generation; entertaining a due sense of our equal right to the use of our own faculties, to the acquisitions of our own industry, to honor and confidence from our fellow-citizens, resulting not from birth, but from our actions and their sense of them; enlightened by a benign religion, professed, indeed, and practiced in various forms, yet all of them inculcating honesty, truth, temperance, gratitude, and the love of man; acknowledging and adoring an overruling Providence, which by all its dispensations proves that it delights in the happiness of man here and his greater happiness hereafter—with all these blessings, what more is necessary to make us a happy and a prosperous people? Still one thing more, fellow-citizens—a wise and frugal Government, which shall restrain men from injuring one another, shall leave them otherwise free to regulate their own pursuits of industry and improvement, and shall not take from the mouth of labor the bread it has earned. This is the sum of good government, and this is necesssary to close the circle of our felicities.

About to enter, fellow-citizens, on the exercise of duties which comprehend everything dear and valuable to you, it is proper you should understand what I deem the essential principles of our Government, and consequently those which ought to shape its Administration. I will compress them within the narrowest compass they will bear, stating the general principle, but not all its limitations. Equal and exact justice to all men, of whatever state or persuasion, religious or political; peace, commerce, and honest friendship with all nations, entangling alliances with none; the support of the State governments in all their rights, as the most competent administrations for our domestic concerns and the surest bulwarks against antirepublican tendencies; the preservation of the General Government in its whole constitutional vigor, as the sheet anchor of our peace at home and safety abroad; a jealous care of the right of election by the people—a mild and safe corrective of abuses which are lopped by the sword of revolution where peaceable remedies are unprovided; absolute acquiescence in the decisions of the majority, the vital principle of republics, from which is no appeal but to force, the vital principle and immediate parent of despotism; a well-disciplined militia, our best reliance in peace and for the first moments of war, till regulars may relieve them; the supremacy of the civil over the military authority; economy in the public expense, that labor may be lightly burthened; the honest payment of our debts and sacred preservation of the public faith; encouragement of agriculture, and of commerce as its handmaid; the diffusion of information and arraignment of all abuses at the bar of the public reason; freedom of religion; freedom of the press, and freedom of person under the protection of the habeas corpus, and trial by juries impartially selected. These principles form the bright constellation which has gone before us and guided our steps through an age of revolution and reformation. The wisdom of our sages and blood of our heroes have been devoted to their attainment. They should be the creed of our political faith, the text of civic instruction, the touchstone by which to try the services of those we trust; and should we wander from them in moments of error or of alarm, let us hasten to retrace our steps and to regain the road which alone leads to peace, liberty, and safety.

I repair, then, fellow-citizens, to the post you have assigned me. With experience enough in subordinate offices to have seen the difficulties of this the greatest of all, I have learnt to expect that it will rarely fall to the lot of imperfect man to retire from this station with the reputation and the favor which bring him into it. Without pretentions to that high confidence you reposed in our first and greatest revolutionary character, whose preeminent services had entitled him to the first place in his country's love and destined for him the fairest page in the volume of faithful history, I ask so much confidence only as may give firmness and effect to the legal administration of your affairs. I shall often go wrong through defect of judgment. When right, I shall often be thought wrong by those whose positions will not command a view of the whole ground. I ask your indulgence for my own errors, which will never be intentional, and your support against the errors of others, who may condemn what they would not if seen in all its parts. The approbation implied by your suffrage is a great consolation to me for the past, and my future solicitude will be to retain the good opinion of those who have bestowed it in advance, to conciliate that of others by doing them all the good in my power, and to be instrumental to the happiness and freedom of all.

Relying, then, on the patronage of your good will, I advance with obedience to the work, ready to retire from it whenever you become sensible how much better choice it is in your power to make. And may that Infinite Power which rules the destinies of the universe lead our councils to what is best, and give them a favorable issue for your peace and prosperity.

[17]

In this summation of Jefferson's essential principles of government he used the phrase so often attributed to Washington: "peace, commerce, and honest friendship with all nations, entangling alliances with none." Although this was also Washington's belief, it is Jefferson's adroit phrasing that has become so well known.

While filling the subordinate office of vice-president, Jefferson said, "The second office of the government is honorable and easy, the first is but a splendid misery."

Jefferson seemed to refer to Adams as an "imperfect man." Just prior to the inaugural he learned Adams had left the Capitol to avoid appearing at the ceremony. There had been only two presidents before Jefferson, and George Washington had certainly not retired as president with less reputation and favor than he had enjoyed previously. Thus it can only be Adams whom Jefferson so adeptly condemns.

Indeed, Adams had spent his last days in office nominating as many Federalists to official posts as possible; and John Marshall, Adams' Secretary of State, had signed as many of these commissions as he could before midnight, March 3, 1801. Between February 1 and March 3, 1801, Adams sent no less than 216 nominations to the Senate. After such a petty display Jefferson could hardly be blamed for a subtle riposte.

THE PRESIDENT

After startling the Federalists with the conciliatory nature of his first inaugural address Jefferson lived up to the philosophy of political moderation outlined therein. When the election year of 1804 arrived, his popularity was overwhelming. In accordance with the twelfth amendment to the Constitution, passed on September 25, 1804, barely in time for the election, Jefferson and George Clinton (his running mate who replaced the controversial Burr) were elected by a landslide: 162 electoral votes for Jefferson and Clinton to 14 for the Federalist candidates, C.C. Pinckney and Rufus King. His administration thus vindicated, Jefferson looked forward with eagerness to the start of his second term.

THE NATION

The specter of Napoleon failed to intimidate the growing Union. Ohio was admitted as the 17th state, March 1, 1803, and approximately 900,000 square miles of land were added to the nation in the Louisiana Purchase made during the following year. Nor was the young nation intimidated by the depredations of the Barbary pirates. In 1803 Jefferson sent Captain Edward Preble against Tripoli. Two years later peace was effected. Meantime the nation dropped the cloak of neutrality with which Washington had enveloped its foreign policy, and under Jefferson began swinging the bold sword of an aggressive nationalism that would not be denied.

In 1803 John Marshall, as Chief Justice of the Supreme Court, established the doctrine of judicial review in handing down his decision in the *Marbury* v. *Madison* case. This decision set the precedent for Supreme Court power to declare an act of Congress unconstitutional.

The death of Hamilton in his duel with Vice-President Burr was virtually the only jarring note in this prosperous period.

THE WORLD

Napoleon's defeat of the Austrian forces in Italy marked the emergence of France as a major world power. As First Consul, Napoleon spent the first two years of the nineteenth century in reforming and reorganizing the government. The revolution had left the French financial system in chaos, but stability slowly returned when Napoleon resumed specie payments, established a Bank of France, and set up a public works system. On April 30, 1803, he sold the Louisiana Territory to the United States for $15,000,000. Napoleon's next move was to have himself crowned Emperor of France, December 2, 1804, at Notre Dame.

IN THE WHITE HOUSE, sitting at your desk downstairs in your basement office while your pet mockingbird hops and flutters about the cluttered room, you read over your second inaugural address with understandable gratification. It has been a good four years, and you are beginning the second term with your enemies reduced to silence and the nation loud in its expression of confidence in the principles and policies for which you stand. In fact your policies of economy in government have been extremely successful. As your last official act, four days previously, you reported to the Senate and the House of Representatives that no occasion has arisen for making use of any part of a fund of $18,560, established for defraying the contingent charges of government. Accordingly, the entire amount has been carried to the credit of the surplus fund. Shortly before noon on March 4, 1805, you make your way to the Capitol building, and soon are reading aloud the closely filled pages written in your neat, slightly cramped handwriting . . . .

Thomas Jefferson

[1805–1809]

SECOND INAUGURAL ADDRESS, MARCH 4, 1805

Capitol Building, Washington, D.C.

Proceeding, fellow-citizens, to that qualification which the Constitution requires before my entrance on the charge again conferred on me, it is my duty to express the deep sense I entertain of this new proof of confidence from my fellow-citizens at large, and the zeal with which it inspires me so to conduct myself as may best satisfy their just expectations.

On taking this station on a former occasion I declared the principles on which I believed it my duty to administer the affairs of our Commonwealth. My conscience tells me I have on every occasion acted up to that declaration according to its obvious import and to the understanding of every candid mind.

In the transaction of your foreign affairs we have endeavored to cultivate the friendship of all nations, and especially of those with which we have the most important relations. We have done them justice on all occasions, favored where favor was lawful, and cherished mutual interests and intercourse on fair and equal terms. We are firmly convinced, and we act on that conviction, that with nations as with individuals our interests soundly calculated will ever be found inseparable from our moral duties, and history bears witness to the fact that a just nation is trusted on its word when recourse is had to armaments and wars to bridle others.

At home, fellow-citizens, you best know whether we have done well or ill. The suppression of unnecessary offices, of useless establishments and expenses, enabled us to discontinue our internal taxes. These, covering our land with officers and opening our doors to their intrusions, had already begun that process of domiciliary vexation which once entered is scarcely to be restrained from reaching successively every article of property and produce. If among these taxes some minor ones fell which had not been inconvenient, it was because their amount would not have paid the officers who collected

Jefferson's pride was understandable: his first term had closed after four years of remarkable progress, unmarred by serious setbacks and climaxed by his triumphant reëlection. One of the occasions to which he alluded was his engineering of the purchase of Louisiana, a transaction in which he deliberately exceeded his Constitutional authority.

Jefferson's first acts were to discontinue internal taxes, reduce the Army and Navy, slash the number of political patronage offices set up under Adams' administration, and greatly economize in the conduct of state affairs. A far cry from conditions of today, where taxation is virtually universal.

them, and because, if they had any merit, the State authorities might adopt them instead of others less approved.

The remaining revenue on the consumption of foreign articles is paid chiefly by those who can afford to add foreign luxuries to domestic comforts, being collected on our seaboard and frontiers only, and incorporated with the transactions of our mercantile citizens, it may be the pleasure and the pride of an American to ask, What farmer, what mechanic, what laborer ever sees a taxgatherer of the United States? These contributions enable us to support the current expenses of the Government, to fulfill contracts with foreign nations, to extinguish the native right of soil within our limits, to extend those limits, and to apply such a surplus to our public debts as places at a short day their final redemption, and that redemption once effected the revenue thereby liberated may, by a just repartition of it among the States and a corresponding amendment of the Constitution, be applied *in time of peace* to rivers, canals, roads, arts, manufactures, education, and other great objects within each State. *In time of war,* if justice by ourselves or others must sometimes produce war, increased as the same revenue will be by increased population and consumption, and aided by other resources reserved for that crisis, it may meet within the year all the expenses of the year without encroaching on the rights of future generations by burthening them with the debts of the past. War will then be but a suspension of useful works, and a return to a state of peace, a return to the progress of improvement.

I have said, fellow-citizens, that the income reserved had enabled us to extend our limits, but that extension may possibly pay for itself before we are called on, and in the meantime may keep down the accruing interest; in all events, it will replace the advances we shall have made. I know that the acquisition of Louisiana has been disapproved by some from a candid apprehension that the enlargement of our territory would endanger its union. But who can limit the extent to which the federative principle may operate effectively? The larger our association the less will it be shaken by local passions; and in any view is it not better that the opposite bank of the Mississippi should be settled by our own brethren and children than by strangers of another family? With which should we be most likely to live in harmony and friendly intercourse?

In matters of religion I have considered that its free exercise is placed by the Constitution independent of the powers of the General Government. I have therefore undertaken on no occasion to prescribe the religious exercises suited to it, but have left them, as the Constitution found them, under the direction and discipline of the church or state authorities acknowledged by the several religious societies.

The aboriginal inhabitants of these countries I have regarded with the commiseration their history inspires. Endowed with the faculties and the rights of men, breathing an ardent love of liberty and independence, and occupying a country which left them no desire but to be undisturbed, the stream of overflowing population from other regions directed itself on these shores; without power to divert or habits to contend against it, they have been overwhelmed by the current or driven before it; now reduced within limits too narrow for the hunter's state, humanity enjoins us to teach them agriculture and the domestic arts; to encourage them to that industry which alone can enable them to maintain their place in existence and to prepare them in time for that state of society which to bodily com-

Jefferson's idea of a "pay-in-full-as-you-go" fiscal policy was noble in theory; yet nobility has yielded to today's political expediency with the result that the children of tomorrow have been "burthened," as of this writing, with a debt of $286,430,926,682. Were Jefferson elected to office in our time, one might wonder what his fiscal policies would be.

The opponents to the acquisition of Louisiana howled loudly at the democratic, Constitution-minded Jefferson, who in a single unauthorized act publicly repudiated his political beliefs. In his defense Jefferson said, "The Constitution has made no provision for our holding foreign territory, still less for incorporating foreign nations into our Union. The executive, in seizing the fugitive occurrence which so much advances the good of their country, has done an act beyond the Constitution. The legislature . . . must ratify and pay for it, and throw themselves on their country for doing for them, unauthorized, what we know they would have done for themselves had they been in a situation to do it."

Jefferson's democratic principles were not limited to Americans alone. He keenly felt the country owed an obligation to the original inhabitants of the land, toward whom he evidently felt protective and fatherly. In these paragraphs he seemed to be defending our treatment of the Indian tribes, while asking absolution for any aggressions committed against them.

forts adds the improvement of the mind and morals. We have therefore liberally furnished them with the implements of husbandry and household use; we have placed among them instructors in the arts of first necessity, and they are covered with the aegis of the law against aggressors from among ourselves.

But the endeavors to enlighten them on the fate which awaits their present course of life, to induce them to exercise their reason, follow its dictates, and change their pursuits with the change of circumstances have powerful obstacles to encounter; they are combated by the habits of their bodies, prejudices of their minds, ignorance, pride, and the influence of interested and crafty individuals among them who feel themselves something in the present order of things and fear to become nothing in any other. These persons inculcate a sanctimonious reverence for the customs of their ancestors; that whatsoever they did must be done through all time; that reason is a false guide, and to advance under its counsel in their physical, moral, or political condition is perilous innovation; that their duty is to remain as their Creator made them, ignorance being safety and knowledge full of danger; in short, my friends, among them also is seen the action and counteraction of good sense and of bigotry; they too have their antiphilosophists who find an interest in keeping things in their present state, who dread reformation, and exert all their faculties to maintain the ascendency of habit over the duty of improving our reason and obeying its mandates.

In giving these outlines I do not mean, fellow-citizens, to arrogate to myself the merit of the measures. That is due, in the first place, to the reflecting character of our citizens at large, who, by the weight of public opinion, influence and strengthen the public measures. It is due to the sound discretion with which they select from among themselves those to whom they confide the legislative duties. It is due to the zeal and wisdom of the characters thus selected, who lay the foundations of public happiness in wholesome laws, the execution of which alone remains for others, and it is due to the able and faithful auxiliaries, whose patriotism has associated them with me in the executive functions.

During this course of administration, and in order to disturb it, the artillery of the press has been levelled against us, charged with whatsoever its licentiousness could devise or dare. These abuses of an institution so important to freedom and science are deeply to be regretted, inasmuch as they tend to lessen its usefulness and to sap its safety. They might, indeed, have been corrected by the wholesome punishments reserved to and provided by the laws of the several States against falsehood and defamation, but public duties more urgent press on the time of public servants, and the offenders have therefore been left to find their punishment in the public indignation.

Nor was it uninteresting to the world that an experiment should be fairly and fully made, whether freedom of discussion, unaided by power, is not sufficient for the propagation and protection of truth —whether a government conducting itself in the true spirit of its constitution, with zeal and purity, and doing no act which it would be unwilling the whole world should witness, can be written down by falsehood and defamation. The experiment has been tried; you have witnessed the scene; our fellow-citizens looked on, cool and collected; they saw the latent source from which these outrages proceeded; they gathered around their public functionaries, and when the Constitution called them to the decision by suffrage, they

Jefferson referred here to attacks on his personal morals that appeared in the Federalist newspapers during his first term. The most vicious of these dripped from the venomous pen of a writer named J.T. Callender, an habitual drunkard who found he could make a living by writing slanderous stories about Jefferson and other political figures of the day. Washington, Hamilton, and Jefferson were the prime targets for his filth, which appeared in the Richmond Recorder, a local paper that soon enjoyed a nationwide circulation.

Despite the acute embarrassment suffered at the hands of Callender and others like him, Jefferson reaffirmed his belief that the public could be trusted to make up its own mind and come up with the right decision. This belief was vindicated when a landslide of votes returned Jefferson to office, despite the printed obscenities concerning his personal life.

pronounced their verdict, honorable to those who had served them and consolatory to the friend of man who believes that he may be trusted with the control of his own affairs.

No inference is here intended that the laws provided by the States against false and defamatory publications should not be enforced; he who has time renders a service to public morals and public tranquillity in reforming these abuses by the salutary coercions of the law; but the experiment is noted to prove that, since truth and reason have maintained their ground against false opinions in league with false facts, the press, confined to truth, needs no other legal restraint; the public judgment will correct false reasonings and opinions on a full hearing of all parties; and no other definite line can be drawn between the inestimable liberty of the press and its demoralizing licentiousness. If there be still improprieties which this rule would not restrain, its supplement must be sought in the censorship of public opinion.

Contemplating the union of sentiment now manifested so generally as auguring harmony and happiness to our future course, I offer to our country sincere congratulations. With those, too, not yet rallied to the same point the disposition to do so is gaining strength; facts are piercing through the veil drawn over them, and our doubting brethren will at length see that the mass of their fellow-citizens with whom they can not yet resolve to act as to principles and measures, think as they think and desire what they desire; that our wish as well as theirs is that the public efforts may be directed honestly to the public good, that peace be cultivated, civil and religious liberty unassailed, law and order preserved, equality of rights maintained, and that state of property, equal or unequal, which results to every man from his own industry or that of his father's. When satisfied of these views it is not in human nature that they should not approve and support them. In the meantime let us cherish them with patient affection, let us do them justice, and more than justice, in all competitions of interest, and we need not doubt that truth, reason, and their own interests will at length prevail, will gather them into the fold of their country, and will complete that entire union of opinion which gives to a nation the blessing of harmony and the benefit of all its strength.

I shall now enter on the duties to which my fellow-citizens have again called me, and shall proceed in the spirit of those principles which they have approved. I fear not that any motives of interest may lead me astray; I am sensible of no passion which could seduce me knowingly from the path of justice, but the weaknesses of human nature and the limits of my own understanding will produce errors of judgment sometimes injurious to your interests. I shall need, therefore, all the indulgence which I have heretofore experienced from my constituents; the want of it will certainly not lessen with increasing years. I shall need, too, the favor of that Being in whose hands we are, who led our fathers, as Israel of old, from their native land and planted them in a country flowing with all the necessaries and comforts of life; who has covered our infancy with His providence and our riper years with His wisdom and power, and to whose goodness I ask you to join in supplications with me that He will so enlighten the minds of your servants, guide their councils, and prosper their measures that whatsoever they do shall result in your good, and shall secure to you the peace, friendship, and approbation of all nations.

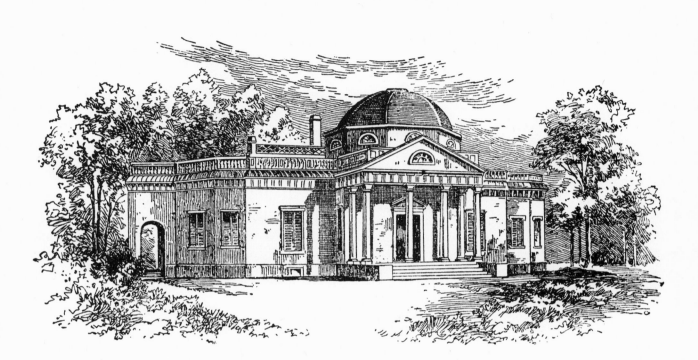

Thomas Jefferson's Monticello, Virginia, home.

THE PRESIDENT

James Madison was known as a statesman of sound judgment, unquestioned integrity, and wide knowledge. He had been called "the master-builder of the Constitution." Originally a Federalist, Madison eventually became a staunch supporter of Jefferson and a critic of Adams' administration, particularly of the Alien and Sedition Acts. Jefferson appointed Madison to the post of Secretary of State. He filled the office so ably that, when Jefferson followed Washington's precedent and refused a third term nomination, Madison was hand-picked over James Monroe by Jefferson as his successor. He was elected by a gratifying majority.

THE NATION

England was supreme on the seas; France master of the Continent. Had the two countries forgotten their differences and turned their combined strength against the United States, history might have read differently. But in their struggle for world supremacy, the two great overseas powers were too occupied to disturb the young nation at this critical time. Jefferson's second term began on a rising wave of prosperity. On June 4, 1805, the Tripolitan War ended. Early in November the Lewis and Clark Expedition, sent out by Jefferson to explore the Louisiana Territory, reached the Pacific returning to St. Louis in September, 1806. On August 3, 1807, Aaron Burr was charged with levying war against the United States. On September 1 and again on September 15 he was acquitted.

The nation's prosperity bubble burst when British orders in council and decrees by Napoleon impaired American commerce. By 1807 Jefferson was forced to retaliate with an embargo prohibiting American ships from carrying goods to foreign ports. Although this act was widely criticized, in the election of 1808 Jefferson's candidate, James Madison, was still able to poll 122 electoral votes for president to Federalist C. C. Pinckney's 47, with George Clinton receiving 113 votes for vice-president to Rufus King's 47.

THE WORLD

In April of 1805 England and Russia signed a treaty, later joined by Austria, with Prussia remaining neutral. Napoleon seized this as an excuse to abandon his invasion of England, attacked the Austrians and defeated them October 20th, the day before Nelson annihilated the combined French and Spanish fleet at Trafalgar. Napoleon entered Vienna in triumph on November 13th and on December 2nd defeated an Austro-Russian force at Austerlitz. He regrouped his forces and on October 14, 1806, in two battles crushed the Prussian army and captured Berlin. But Napoleon erred in 1808 when he forced Ferdinand VII and his father, Charles IV, to renounce their claims to the Spanish throne. Napoleon then installed his brother Joseph Bonaparte as King of Spain, causing a great outcry throughout Europe and marking the beginning of the Corsican's eventual downfall.

YOU HAVE WORKED MANY HOURS with little sleep, writing and rewriting an inaugural address in your almost feminine script until the message is condensed into only seven paragraphs. In these few words you have tried to convey your feeling that troublous times may lie ahead, despite the unmistakable excitement gripping Washington City, as inaugural day arrives. Now, sitting in your coach en route to the Capitol, clad in an Oxford cloth jacket from Hartford, merino wool breeches from New York, and black shoes and stockings, you are the first president to wear attire made in the United States. Jefferson modestly follows behind you as one of the horseback riders in the long parade, and you are agreeably surprised at the thousands of cheering people lining the route. You realize the cheers are more for the outgoing Jefferson than for your own slight, 5'4" figure. But unlike Adams you apparently feel no rancor in following a more popular predecessor, nor is there any bitterness discernible in the address you deliver shortly to the assembled members of Congress in your thin, reedy voice . . . .

James Madison

[1809–1813]

FIRST INAUGURAL ADDRESS, MARCH 4, 1809

Capitol Building, Washington, D.C.

Unwilling to depart from examples of the most revered authority, I avail myself of the occasion now presented to express the profound impression made on me by the call of my country to the station to the duties of which I am about to pledge myself by the most solemn of sanctions. So distinguished a mark of confidence, proceeding from the deliberate and tranquil suffrage of a free and virtuous nation, would under any circumstances have commanded my gratitude and devotion, as well as filled me with an awful sense of the trust to be assumed. Under the various circumstances which give peculiar solemnity to the existing period, I feel that both the honor and the responsibility allotted to me are inexpressibly enhanced.

The present situation of the world is indeed without a parallel, and that of our own country full of difficulties. The pressure of these, too, is the more severely felt because they have fallen upon us at a moment when the national prosperity being at a height not before attained, the contrast resulting from the change has been rendered the more striking. Under the benign influence of our republican institutions, and the maintenance of peace with all nations whilst so many of them were engaged in bloody and wasteful wars, the fruits of a just policy were enjoyed in an unrivaled growth of our faculties and resources. Proofs of this were seen in the improvements of agriculture, in the successful enterprises of commerce, in the progress of manufacturers and useful arts, in the increase of the public revenue and the use made of it in reducing the public debt, and in the valuable works and establishments everywhere multiplying over the face of our land.

It is a precious reflection that the transition from this prosperous condition of our country to the scene which has for some time been distressing us is not chargeable on any unwarrantable views, nor, as I trust, on any involuntary errors in the public councils. Indulging no passions which trespass on the rights or the repose of other nations, it has been the true glory of the United States to cultivate

Madison was referring to the strained relations between the United States and England, brought about primarily as a result of Jefferson's embargo. Although Jefferson had repealed the Embargo Act on March 1, 1809, just prior to leaving office, the same day he had also signed the Non-Intercourse Act, closing U.S. ports to French and English imports. The Embargo Act had in turn led to Napoleon's Bayonne decree, authorizing the seizure and confiscation of all American ships in French ports. The French reasoned that if the ships captured were English, seizure was permissible inasmuch as France and England were at war; if the ships turned out to be American, under Jefferson's embargo they were carrying goods abroad illegally and the embargo was thus enforced by the Bayonne decree.

[25]

peace by observing justice, and to entitle themselves to the respect of the nations at war by fulfilling their neutral obligations with the most scrupulous impartiality. If there be candor in the world, the truth of these assertions will not be questioned; posterity at least will do justice to them.

This unexceptionable course could not avail against the injustice and violence of the belligerent powers. In their rage against each other, or impelled by more direct motives, principles of retaliation have been introduced equally contrary to universal reason and acknowledged law. How long their arbitrary edicts will be continued in spite of the demonstrations that not even a pretext for them has been given by the United States, and of the fair and liberal attempt to induce a revocation of them, can not be anticipated. Assuring myself that under every vicissitude the determined spirit and united councils of the nation will be safeguards to its honor and its essential interests, I repair to the post assigned me with no other discouragement than what springs from my own inadequacy to its high duties. If I do not sink under the weight of this deep conviction it is because I find some support in a consciousness of the purposes and a confidence in the principles which I bring with me into this arduous service.

To cherish peace and friendly intercourse with all nations having correspondent dispositions; to maintain sincere neutrality toward belligerent nations; to prefer in all cases amicable discussion and reasonable accommodation of differences to a decision of them by an appeal to arms; to exclude foreign intrigues and foreign partialities, so degrading to all countries and so baneful to free ones; to foster a spirit of independence too just to invade the rights of others, too proud to surrender our own, too liberal to indulge unworthy prejudices ourselves and too elevated not to look down upon them in others; to hold the union of the States as the basis of their peace and happiness; to support the Constitution, which is the cement of the Union, as well in its limitations as in its authorities; to respect the rights and authorities reserved to the States and to the people as equally incorporated with and essential to the success of the general system; to avoid the slightest interference with the right of conscience or the functions of religion, so wisely exempted from civil jurisdiction; to preserve in their full energy the other salutary provisions in behalf of private and personal rights, and of the freedom of the press; to observe economy in public expenditures; to liberate the public resources by an honorable discharge of the public debts; to keep within the requisite limits a standing military force, always remembering that an armed and trained militia is the firmest bulwark of republics—that without standing armies their liberty can never be in danger, nor with large ones safe; to promote by authorized means improvements friendly to agriculture, to manufactures, and to external as well as internal commerce; to favor in like manner the advancement of science and the diffusion of information as the best aliment to true liberty; to carry on the benevolent plans which have been so meritoriously applied to the conversion of our aboriginal neighbors from the degradation and wretchedness of savage life to a participation of the improvements of which the human mind and manners are susceptible in a civilized state—as far as sentiments and intentions such as these can aid the fulfillment of my duty, they will be a resource which can not fail me.

It is my good fortune, moreover, to have the path in which I am to tread lighted by examples of illustrious services successfully

The last year of Jefferson's second term had been marked by a decided slump, caused by the drop in foreign trade as a result of the embargo on exports. Madison's first major act on assuming office would be to enforce the repeal of the Embargo Act. This action would give him, at least briefly, a tremendous popularity. But an equally tremendous humiliation lay ahead for him —and for the nation.

Comparing Jefferson's political philosophy, as set out in his first inaugural address, with Madison's, as outlined in this paragraph, reveals a striking similarity that helps explain why Jefferson selected Madison over Monroe as his immediate successor. Already the young government was developing a pattern: A strong leader elected to two terms of office would refuse a third term, but would pick a successor whose thinking most closely paralleled his own. Washington chose Adams; Jefferson chose Madison. In each case we see two dominant characters selecting successors whose policies were basically carbon copies of their predecessors'.

rendered in the most trying difficulties by those who have marched before me. Of those of my immediate predecessor it might least become me here to speak. I may, however, be pardoned for not suppressing the sympathy with which my heart is full in the rich reward he enjoys in the benedictions of a beloved country, gratefully bestowed for exalted talents zealously devoted through a long career to the advancement of its highest interest and happiness.

But the source to which I look for the aids which alone can supply my deficiencies is in the well-tried intelligence and virtue of my fellow-citizens, and in the counsels of those representing them in the other departments associated in the care of the national interests. In these my confidence will under every difficulty be best placed, next to that which we have all been encouraged to feel in the guardianship and guidance of that Almighty Being whose power regulates the destiny of nations, whose blessings have been so conspicuously dispensed to this rising Republic, and to whom we are bound to address our devout gratitude for the past, as well as our fervent supplications and best hopes for the future.

THE PRESIDENT

Madison's first term saw a wide departure in Capitol society from the homespun flavor of Jefferson's regime. Madison's gala inaugural ball set the tenor for future social functions, guided by the flamboyant Dolly Madison who dearly loved to entertain. Following a series of diplomatic frustrations Madison signed the proclamation of war against England on June 18, 1812, basing his act on these major issues: Great Britain's continued impressment of American seamen, blockading of American ports, violation of American territorial waters and coastal rights, disregard of American requests to revoke the Orders in Council. In the fall, with the country at war, Madison was renominated for president. Vice-President George Clinton had died on April 20, and Elbridge Gerry of Massachusetts was nominated as the Republican vice-presidential candidate. The Federalists and antiwar Republicans nominated DeWitt Clinton for president and Jared Ingersoll for vice-president. In the election, thanks to the backing of such war hawk Republicans as Henry Clay and John C. Calhoun, Madison received 128 electoral votes to 89 for Clinton; 131 votes to Gerry; 86 for Ingersoll. The election witnessed a brief resurgence of Federalist power that never again materialized.

THE NATION

Madison's initial surge of popularity can be laid to his endorsement of the repeal of Jefferson's embargo. Through diplomatic misunderstandings with Great Britain, however, Madison was forced to reinstate the embargo. In 1810 the third U.S. census revealed a population of 7,239,881—an increase of nearly 2,000,000 in ten years. On April 30, 1812, Louisiana was admitted as the 18th state, shortly before war with England was declared. In this year the Shawnee and other Indian tribes were organized by Tecumseh, and aided now by British arms obtained from Canada began raiding the white settlements. General William Henry Harrison, Governor of Indiana Territory, led a thousand men against a large Indian village on Tippecanoe Creek, burning the village on November 7, 1811, and stopping the raids. The Battle of Tippecanoe was hailed as a great victory, giving Harrison a stature the nation remembered throughout his lifetime.

THE WORLD

In 1810 Napoleon married Maria Luisa. Spanish colonies revolted in Venezuela, Uruguay, Paraguay, Chile, Argentina, and Mexico, with Peru following suit in 1811. King George III of England was declared insane in 1811 and the Prince of Wales became regent. In 1812 Napoleon ignored the Treaty of Tilsit and invaded Russia, forcing the retreating Russians to burn Moscow. And in the same year America declared war on England.

IN YOUR FIRST INAUGURAL ADDRESS you referred to your own "inadequacy." Now, due primarily to this same inadequacy, the nation is embroiled in an unpopular war, called by many "Mr. Madison's war." In composing your second inaugural address you take this into account, but you would be less than human if you failed to present as encouraging an analysis of present-day conditions as possible, and to make as good a case for your actions as you can. Accordingly, you phrase thoughts carefully, recasting them until you have eliminated all possible negatives while accentuating what few positives you can command. When satisfied, you proceed to your inauguration to stand before the assembled members of Congress and begin your attempt to switch your listeners' attention from your own shortcomings to those of the common enemy . . . .

James Madison

[1813–1817]

SECOND INAUGURAL ADDRESS, MARCH 4, 1813
Capitol Building, Washington, D.C.

About to add the solemnity of an oath to the obligations imposed by a second call to the station in which my country heretofore placed me, I find in the presence of this respectable assembly an opportunity of publicly repeating my profound sense of so distinguished a confidence and of the responsibility united with it. The impressions on me are strengthened by such an evidence that my faithful endeavors to discharge my arduous duties have been favorably estimated, and by a consideration of the momentous period at which the trust has been renewed. From the weight and magnitude now belonging to it I should be compelled to shrink if I had less reliance on the support of an enlightened and generous people, and felt less deeply a conviction that the war with a powerful nation, which forms so prominent a feature in our situation, is stamped with that justice which invites the smiles of Heaven on the means of conducting it to a successful termination.

May we not cherish this sentiment without presumption when we reflect on the characters by which this war is distinguished?

It was not declared on the part of the United States until it had been long made on them, in reality though not in name; until arguments and expostulations had been exhausted; until a positive declaration had been received that the wrongs provoking it would not be discontinued; nor until this last appeal could no longer be delayed without breaking down the spirit of the nation, destroying all confidence in itself and in its political institutions, and either perpetuating a state of disgraceful suffering or regaining by more costly sacrifices and more severe struggles our lost rank and respect among independent powers.

On the issue of the war are staked our national sovereignty on the high seas and the security of an important class of citizens, whose occupations give the proper value to those of every other class. Not to contend for such a stake is to surrender our equality with other powers on the element common to all and to violate the sacred title which every member of the society has to its protection.

Madison quickly took the offensive. The "justice" mentioned here invited the smiles of the war hawks rather than those of heaven. Fiery young politicians, such as Clay and Calhoun who supported Madison in the election, saw in the war a means for turning the public's deep-rooted resentment against the British to their own ends.

The picture Madison painted here was far blacker than the facts. A return to the policy of nonintercourse had wrought hardships on English commerce and shipping interests. Prime Minister Spencer Perceval was considering repeal of the orders-in-council when he was assassinated, May 11, 1812. His successor, Lord Castlereagh, announced the orders formally suspended June 23, but it was too late. Only four days previously Madison had signed his war proclamation. Was this the act of a statesman seeking to protect the nation? Or was it the calculated gamble of a politician determined at any cost to insure his reëlection in order to become the nation's second wartime president?

[29]

Blaming the war on British impressment of American seamen was calculated to inflame public opinion, and rightly so. But as the war dragged on the importance of this issue declined. No mention was made of it when the treaty was finally signed.

Note the use of the words "just," "necessary," and "noble"—none of which could truthfully be applied to Mr. Madison's War.

Now Madison launched into his diversionary attack on the common enemy. Is this the fore-runner of the "Big Lie" technique used so tellingly in modern propaganda? The chief reference here was to impressment of American seamen. Any seaman who had emigrated to America from England was considered to be a deserter from the British Navy and was treated as such rather than as a naturalized American citizen.

This is a reference to Tecumseh and the Indian tribes used by British forces in Canada to inflict defeat after defeat on American forces.

On August 24, through the efforts of Secretary of State James Monroe, Great Britain was informed that the United States would negotiate an armistice if British impressment of seamen and blockades were stopped and certain indemnities made. Lord Castlereagh rejected the offer. A month later, however, an offer to negotiate an armistice was submitted to the United States. This in turn was refused. Both attempts failed because the British were not willing to yield on impressment and the Americans were reluctant to abandon their objectives.

I need not call into view the unlawfulness of the practice by which our mariners are forced at the will of every cruising officer from their own vessels into foreign ones, nor paint the outrages inseparable from it. The proofs are in the records of each successive Administration of our Government, and the cruel sufferings of that portion of the American people have found their way to every bosom not dead to the sympathies of human nature.

As the war was just in its origin and necessary and noble in its objects, we can reflect with a proud satisfaction that in carrying it on no principle of justice or honor, no usage of civilized nations, no precept of courtesy or humanity, have been infringed. The war has been waged on our part with scrupulous regard to all these obligations, and in a spirit of liberality which was never surpassed.

How little has been the effect of this example on the conduct of the enemy!

They have retained as prisoners of war citizens of the United States not liable to be so considered under the usages of war.

They have refused to consider as prisoners of war, and threatened to punish as traitors and deserters, persons emigrating without restraint to the United States, incorporated by naturalization into our political family, and fighting under the authority of their adopted country in open and honorable war for the maintenance of its rights and safety. Such is the avowed purpose of a Government which is in the practice of naturalizing by thousands citizens of other countries, and not only of permitting but compelling them to fight its battles against their native country.

They have not, it is true, taken into their own hands the hatchet and the knife, devoted to indiscriminate massacre, but they have let loose the savages armed with these cruel instruments; have allured them into their service, and carried them to battle by their sides, eager to glut their savage thirst with the blood of the vanquished and to finish the work of torture and death on maimed and defenseless captives. And, what was never before seen, British commanders have extorted victory over the unconquerable valor of our troops by presenting to the sympathy of their chief captives awaiting massacre from their savage associates. And now we find them, in further contempt of the modes of honorable warfare, supplying the place of a conquering force by attempts to disorganize our political society, to dismember our confederated Republic. Happily, like others, these will recoil on the authors; but they mark the degenerate counsels from which they emanate, and if they did not belong to a series of unexampled inconsistencies might excite the greater wonder as proceeding from a Government which founded the very war in which it has been so long engaged on a charge against the disorganizing and insurrectional policy of its adversary.

To render the justice of the war on our part the more conspicuous, the reluctance to commence it was followed by the earliest and strongest manifestations of a disposition to arrest its progress. The sword was scarcely out of the scabbard before the enemy was apprised of the reasonable terms on which it would be resheathed. Still more precise advances were repeated, and have been received in a spirit forbidding every reliance not placed on the military resources of the nation.

These resources are amply sufficient to bring the war to an honorable issue. Our nation is in number more than half that of the British Isles. It is composed of a brave, a free, a virtuous, and an intelligent people. Our country abounds in the necessaries, the arts,

[30]

and the comforts of life. A general prosperity is visible in the public countenance. The means employed by the British cabinet to undermine it have recoiled on themselves; have given to our national faculties a more rapid development, and, draining or diverting the precious metals from British circulation and British vaults, have poured them into those of the United States. It is a propitious consideration that an unavoidable war should have found this seasonable facility for the contributions required to support it. When the public voice called for war, all knew, and still know, that without them it could not be carried on through the period which it might last, and the patriotism, the good sense, and the manly spirit of our fellow-citizens are pledges for the cheerfulness with which they will bear each his share of the common burden. To render the war short and its success sure, animated and systematic exertions alone are necessary, and the success of our arms now may long preserve our country from the necessity of another resort to them. Already have the gallant exploits of our naval heroes proved to the world our inherent capacity to maintain our rights on one element. If the reputation of our arms has been thrown under clouds on the other, presaging flashes of heroic enterprise assure us that nothing is wanting to correspondent triumphs there also but the discipline and habits which are in daily progress.

Madison's brief reference here was to the triumphs of the U.S. Navy, in particular to the exploits of the U.S.S. Constitution, *nicknamed* Old Ironsides *after two brilliant victories at sea. The first took place under Captain James Ricards Dacres, when the British 38-gun frigate* Guerriere *was sunk off Nova Scotia, on August 19, 1812; the second under Captain Henry Lambert, when the British 38-gun frigate* Java *was sunk December 29 off the Brazilian coast.*

In his final sentence, pointedly leaving the worst to the last, Madison admitted the British had outfought the Americans on land thus far. Detroit, Fort Dearborn, Fort George, and Queenston Heights were scenes of disastrous American defeat. But, bad as these had been, there were worse humiliations to come.

THE PRESIDENT

James Monroe played a leading part in the political history of America for more than half a century, which culminated in his election to the presidency in 1816. Monroe received 183 electoral votes to Federalist Rufus King's 34, with Daniel D. Tompkins being elected as vice-president.

THE NATION

Amid the stentorian clash of arms on the Continent the sounds of "Mr. Madison's war" seemed puny, but the young nation was nonetheless shaken to its still tender roots. The British blockade of American ports and harbors brought on a general price inflation due to scarcity of goods. On June 1, 1813, the British 38-gun frigate *Shannon* captured the U.S. 38-gun frigate *Chesapeake,* killing Captain James Lawrence, whose last words were said to have been, "Don't give up the ship!" In September the British were met on Lake Erie by Captain Oliver Hazard Perry in his flagship the *Lawrence,* on whose battle flag appeared Lawrence's dying words. After the battle the victorious Perry dispatched this message to General Harrison: "We have met the enemy and they are ours."

The British campaign ashore was more successful. Washington City was captured and burned on August 24 and 25, 1814, due to the poor leadership of the untrained U.S. troops. After this catastrophe Secretary of State James Monroe was made *ad interim* Secretary of War by Madison. Under Monroe's firm hand the armed forces stiffened. On September 13 and 14 Fort McHenry was bombarded by the British. The gallant American resistance inspired an onlooker, Francis Scott Key, to write the poem that became our national anthem.

Two weeks after the Peace of Ghent had been signed overseas the armies in the New World fought their last battle. Because ships were the only vehicles for carrying news America did not hear of the treaty before this time. In the last battle of the war, the Battle of New Orleans, General Andrew Jackson ("Old Hickory") won national acclaim, when his inferior force scored an astounding victory. More than 2000 enemy British were killed or wounded; only 21 Americans died or were injured.

Algiers, Tunis, and Tripoli resumed their plundering of American shipping until Captain Stephen Decatur permanently subdued the Barbary pirates, just prior to the election year of 1816. Indiana had already been admitted as the 19th state.

THE WORLD

In 1813, despite her war with the United States, England joined Prussia, Russia, and Austria in defeating Napoleon at the Battle of the Nations at Leipzig. Following the Treaty of Fontainebleau, April 13, 1814, Napoleon abdicated and retired to Elba. The House of Bourbon was restored in France under Louis XVIII. In 1815 Napoleon returned from Elba to rule for the "Hundred Days," only to be defeated by Wellington at Waterloo. He was banished to St. Helena, thus writing finis to one of the bloodiest chapters in European history.

YOU ARE DEEPLY AFFECTED by your overwhelming victory in the recent election. As you prepare your inaugural address in slanted, hard-to-read script, your feeling of enthusiasm is infused into each written passage—perhaps more so than your supporters will care to hear as your address is delivered before them. Your lanky form is clad in an elegantly cut coat and waistcoat, knee breeches, high white silk stockings, and gold-buckled slippers, a style that is to go out of favor even before you leave office . . . .

James Monroe

[1817–1821]

FIRST INAUGURAL ADDRESS, MARCH 4, 1817

Capitol Building, Washington, D.C.

I should be destitute of feeling if I was not deeply affected by the strong proof which my fellow-citizens have given me of their confidence in calling me to the high office whose functions I am about to assume. As the expression of their good opinion of my conduct in the public service, I derive from it a gratification which those who are conscious of having done all that they could to merit it can alone feel. My sensibility is increased by a just estimate of the importance of the trust and of the nature and extent of its duties, with the proper discharge of which the highest interests of a great and free people are intimately connected. Conscious of my own deficiency, I cannot enter on these duties without great anxiety for the result. From a just responsibility I will never shrink, calculating with confidence that in my best efforts to promote the public welfare my motives will always be duly appreciated and my conduct be viewed with that candor and indulgence which I have experienced in other stations.

In commencing the duties of the chief executive office it has been the practice of the distinguished men who have gone before me to explain the principles which would govern them in their respective Administrations. In following their venerated example my attention is naturally drawn to the great causes which have contributed in a principal degree to produce the present happy condition of the United States. They will best explain the nature of our duties and shed much light on the policy which ought to be pursued in future.

From the commencement of our Revolution to the present day almost forty years have elapsed, and from the establishment of this Constitution twenty-eight. Through this whole term the Government has been what may emphatically be called self-government. And what has been the effect? To whatever object we turn our attention, whether it relates to our foreign or domestic concerns, we find abundant cause to felicitate ourselves in the excellence of our institutions. During a period fraught with difficulties and marked by very extraordinary events the United States have flourished beyond example. Their citizens individually have been happy and the nation prosperous.

Under this Constitution our commerce has been wisely regulated with foreign nations and between the States; new States have been

The "happy condition" mentioned here continued throughout the entire Monroe administration, which was dubbed "the era of good feeling" by the Boston Columbian Centinel *in 1817. The name clung.*

[33]

admitted into our Union; our territory has been enlarged by fair and honorable treaty, and with great advantage to the original States; the States, respectively protected by the National Government under a mild, parental system against foreign dangers, and enjoying within their separate spheres, by a wise partition of power, a just proportion of the sovereignty, have improved their police, extended their settlements, and attained a strength and maturity which are the best proofs of wholesome laws well administered. And if we look to the condition of individuals what a proud spectacle does it exhibit! On whom has oppression fallen in any quarter of our Union? Who has been deprived of any right of person or property? Who restrained from offering his vows in the mode which he prefers to the Divine Author of his being? It is well known that all these blessings have been enjoyed in their fullest extent; and I add with peculiar satisfaction that there has been no example of a capital punishment being inflicted on anyone for the crime of high treason.

Some who might admit the competency of our Government to these beneficent duties might doubt it in trials which put to the test its strength and efficiency as a member of the great community of nations. Here too experience has afforded us the most satisfactory proof in its favor. Just as this Constitution was put into action several of the principal States of Europe had become much agitated and some of them seriously convulsed. Destructive wars ensued, which have of late only been terminated. In the course of these conflicts the United States received great injury from several of the parties. It was their interest to stand aloof from the contest, to demand justice from the party committing the injury, and to cultivate by a fair and honorable conduct the friendship of all. War became at length inevitable, and the result has shown that our Government is equal to that, the greatest of trials, under the most unfavorable circumstances. Of the virtue of the people and of the heroic exploits of the Army, the Navy, and the militia I need not speak.

Such, then, is the happy Government under which we live—a Government adequate to every purpose for which the social compact is formed; a Government elective in all its branches, under which every citizen may by his merit obtain the highest trust recognized by the Constitution; which contains within it no cause of discord, none to put at variance one portion of the community with another; a Government which protects every citizen in the full enjoyment of his rights, and is able to protect the nation against injustice from foreign powers.

Other considerations of the highest importance admonish us to cherish our Union and to cling to the Government which supports it. Fortunate as we are in our political institutions, we have not been less so in other circumstances on which our prosperity and happiness essentially depend. Situated within the temperate zone, and extending through many degrees of latitude along the Atlantic, the United States enjoy all the varieties of climate, and every production incident to that portion of the globe. Penetrating internally to the Great Lakes and beyond the sources of the great rivers which communicate through our whole interior, no country was ever happier with respect to its domain. Blessed, too, with a fertile soil, our produce has always been very abundant, leaving, even in years the least favorable, a surplus for the wants of our fellow-men in other countries. Such is our peculiar felicity that there is not a part of our Union that is not particularly interested in preserving it. The great agricultural interest of the nation prospers under its protection. Local interests are not less fostered by it. Our fellow-citizens of the North engaged in navigation find great encouragement in being made the favored carriers of the vast productions of the other portions of the United States, while the inhabitants of these are amply recompensed, in their turn, by the nursery for seamen and naval force thus formed and reared up for the support of our common rights. Our manufactures find a generous encouragement by the policy which patronizes domestic industry, and the surplus of our produce a steady and profitable market by local wants in less-favored parts at home.

Such, then, being the highly favored condition of our country, it is the interest of every citizen to maintain it. What are the dangers which menace us? If any exist they ought to be ascertained and guarded against.

In explaining my sentiments on this subject it may be asked, What raised us to the present happy state? How did we accomplish the Revolution? How remedy the defects of the first instrument of our Union, by infusing into the National Government sufficient power for national purposes, without impairing the just rights of the States or affecting those of individuals? How sustain and pass with glory through the late war? The Government has been in the hands of the people. To the people, therefore, and to the faithful and able depositaries of their trust is the credit due. Had the people of the United States been educated in different principles, had they been less intelligent, less independent, or less virtuous, can it be believed that we should have maintained the same steady and consistent career or been blessed with the same success? While, then, the constituent body retains its present sound and healthful state everything will be safe. They will choose competent and faithful representatives for every department. It is only when the people become ignorant and corrupt, when they degenerate into a populace, that they are incapable of exercising the sovereignty. Usurpation is then an easy attainment, and an usurper soon found. The people themselves become the willing instruments of their own debasement and ruin. Let us, then, look to the great cause, and endeavor to preserve it in full force. Let us by all wise and constitutional measures promote intelligence among the people as the best means of preserving our liberties.

Dangers from abroad are not less deserving of attention. Experiencing the fortune of other nations, the United States may be again involved in war, and it may in that event be the object of the adverse party to overset our Government, to break our Union, and demolish us as a nation. Our distance from Europe and the just, moderate, and pacific policy of our Government may form some security against these dangers, but they ought to be anticipated and guarded against. Many of our citizens are engaged in commerce and navigation, and all of them are in a certain degree dependent on their prosperous state. Many are engaged in the fisheries. These interests are exposed to invasion in the wars between other powers, and we should disregard the faithful admonition of experience if we did not expect it. We must support our rights or lose our character, and with it, perhaps, our liberties. A people who fail to do it can scarcely be said to hold a place among independent nations. National honor is national property of the highest value. The sentiment in the mind of every citizen is national strength. It ought therefore to be cherished.

To secure us against these dangers our coast and inland frontiers

Here Monroe planted the seed of an idea he reaped a few paragraphs later, when he revealed his adoption of many Federalist principles involving a strong central government. This was in opposition to Jefferson's policy of decentralization.

Monroe proposed to change the basic Republican policy set forth by Jefferson and followed by Madison.

The thoughts expressed in this passage became the warp and woof of the fabric from which, in later years, John Quincy Adams and Monroe were to fashion the Monroe Doctrine.

[35]

should be fortified, our Army and Navy, regulated upon just principles as to the force of each, be kept in perfect order, and our militia be placed on the best practicable footing. To put our extensive coast in such a state of defense as to secure our cities and interior from invasion will be attended with expense, but the work when finished will be permanent, and it is fair to presume that a single campaign of invasion by a naval force superior to our own, aided by a few thousand land troops, would expose us to greater expense, without taking into the estimate the loss of property and distress of our citizens, than would be sufficient for this great work. Our land and naval forces should be moderate, but adequate to the necessary purposes—the former to garrison and preserve our fortifications and to meet the first invasions of a foreign foe, and, while constituting the elements of a greater force, to preserve the science as well as all the necessary implements of war in a state to be brought into activity in the event of war; the latter, retained within the limits proper in a state of peace, might aid in maintaining the neutrality of the United States with dignity in the wars of other powers and in saving the property of their citizens from spoilation. In time of war, with the enlargement of which the great naval resources of the country render it susceptible, and which should be duly fostered in time of peace, it would contribute essentially, both as an auxiliary of defense and as a powerful engine of annoyance, to diminish the calamities of war and to bring the war to a speedy and honorable termination.

But it ought always to be held prominently in view that the safety of these States and of everything dear to a free people must depend in an eminent degree on the militia. Invasions may be made too formidable to be resisted by any land and naval force which it would comport either with the principles of our Government or the circumstances of the United States to maintain. In such cases recourse must be had to the great body of the people, and in a manner to produce the best effect. It is of the highest importance, therefore, that they be so organized and trained as to be prepared for any emergency. The arrangement should be such as to put at the command of the Government the ardent patriotism and youthful vigor of the country. If formed on equal and just principles, it can not be oppressive. It is the crisis which makes the pressure, and not the laws which provide a remedy for it. This arrangement should be formed, too, in time of peace, to be the better prepared for war. With such an organization of such a people the United States have nothing to dread from foreign invasion. At its approach an overwhelming force of gallant men might always be put in motion.

Other interests of high importance will claim attention, among which the improvement of our country by roads and canals, proceeding always with a constitutional sanction, holds a distinguished place. By thus facilitating the intercourse between the States we shall add much to the convenience and comfort of our fellow-citizens, much to the ornament of the country, and, what is of greater importance, we shall shorten distances, and, by making each part more accessible to and dependent on the other, we shall bind the Union more closely together. Nature has done so much for us by intersecting the country with so many great rivers, bays, and lakes, approaching from distant points so near to each other, that the inducement to complete the work seems to be peculiarly strong. A more interesting spectacle was perhaps never seen than is exhibited within the limits of the United States—a territory so vast and advantageously situated, containing objects so grand, so useful, so happily connected in all their parts!

Our manufacturers will likewise require the systematic and fostering care of the Government. Possessing as we do all the raw materials, the fruit of our own soil and industry, we ought not to depend in the degree we have done on supplies from other countries. While we are thus dependent the sudden event of war, unsought and unexpected, can not fail to plunge us into the most serious difficulties. It is important, too, that the capital which nourishes our manufacturers should be domestic, as its influence in that case instead of exhausting, as it may do in foreign hands, would be felt advantageously on agriculture and every other branch of industry. Equally important is it to provide at home a market for our raw materials, as by extending the competition it will enhance the price and protect the cultivator against the casualties incident to foreign markets.

Monroe seemed to be trying to appeal to almost everyone in his address—a piece of political strategy that would be emulated by virtually each successor.

With the Indian tribes it is our duty to cultivate friendly relations and to act with kindness and liberality in all our transactions. Equally proper is it to persevere in our efforts to extend to them the advantages of civilization.

Monroe's policy for the Indian tribes, toward whom Jefferson had felt so protective, was brusque. After the Creeks and Seminoles in Florida and the Delaware, Miami, Seneca, Wyandot, and Shawnee tribes under Tecumseh had fought with the British the citizens were in no mood to be lenient.

The great amount of our revenue and the flourishing state of the Treasury are a full proof of the competency of the national resources for any emergency, as they are of the willingness of our fellow-citizens to bear the burdens which the public necessities require. The vast amount of vacant lands, the value of which daily augments, forms an additional resource of great extent and duration. These resources, besides accomplishing every other necessary purpose, put it completely in the power of the United States to discharge the national debt at an early period. Peace is the best time for improvement and preparation of every kind; it is in peace that our commerce flourishes most, that taxes are most easily paid, and that the revenue is most productive.

The nation was deeper in debt than it had ever been before—yet Monroe referred to "the flourishing state of the Treasury." A Second Bank of the United States was opened in January, 1817, with a capital of $35,000,000, and its charter would remain in effect for 20 years. This would help to stabilize the nation's monetary program, until the Panic of 1819.

The Executive is charged officially in the Departments under it with the disbursement of the public money, and is responsible for the faithful application of it to the purposes for which it is raised. The Legislature is the watchful guardian over the public purse. It is its duty to see that the disbursement has been honestly made. To meet the requisite responsibility every facility should be afforded to the Executive to enable it to bring the public agents intrusted with the public money strictly and promptly to account. Nothing should be presumed against them; but if, with the requisite facilities, the public money is suffered to lie long and uselessly in their hands, they will not be the only defaulters, nor will the demoralizing effect be confined to them. It will evince a relaxation and want of tone in the Administration which will be felt by the whole community. I shall do all I can to secure economy and fidelity in this important branch of the Administration, and I doubt not that the Legislature will perform its duty with equal zeal. A thorough examination should be regularly made, and I will promote it.

It is particularly gratifying to me to enter on the discharge of these duties at a time when the United States are blessed with peace. It is a state most consistent with their prosperity and happiness. It will be my sincere desire to preserve it, so far as depends on the Executive, on just principles with all nations, claiming nothing unreasonable of any and rendering to each what is its due.

Equally gratifying is it to witness the increased harmony of opinion which pervades our Union. Discord does not belong to our system. Union is recommended as well by the free and benign

This was apparently an oblique reference to Madison, who had been accused by many Federalists of fomenting the war with England virtually singlehandedly. Actually Monroe had originally approved the idea of war as a means for increasing America's prestige abroad. But now his thinking had changed. He assured the nation he could be depended upon not to institute similar aggression, but would do all in his power to promote peace abroad and unity at home—sentiments nearly everyone wanted to hear.

principles of our Government, extending its blessings to every individual, as by the other eminent advantages attending it. The American people have encountered together great dangers and sustained severe trials with success. They constitute one great family with a common interest. Experience has enlightened us on some questions of essential importance to the country. The progress has been slow, dictated by a just reflection and a faithful regard to every interest connected with it. To promote this harmony in accord with the principles of our republican Government and in a manner to give them the most complete effect, and to advance in all other respects the best interests of our Union, will be the object of my constant and zealous exertions.

Never did a government commence under auspices so favorable, nor ever was success so complete. If we look to the history of other nations, ancient or modern, we find no example of a growth so rapid, so gigantic, of a people so prosperous and happy. In contemplating what we have still to perform, the heart of every citizen must expand with joy when he reflects how near our Government has approached to perfection; that in respect to it we have no essential improvement to make; that the great object is to preserve it in the essential principles and features which characterize it, and that that is to be done by preserving the virtue and enlightening the minds of the people; and as a security against foreign dangers to adopt such arrangements as are indispensable to the support of our independence, our rights and liberties. If we persevere in the career in which we have advanced so far and in the path already traced, we can not fail, under the favor of a gracious Providence, to attain the high destiny which seems to await us.

In the Administrations of the illustrious men who have preceded me in this high station, with some of whom I have been connected by the closest ties from early life, examples are presented which will always be found highly instructive and useful to their successors. From these I shall endeavor to derive all the advantages which they may afford. Of my immediate predecessor, under whom so important a portion of this great and successful experiment has been made, I shall be pardoned for expressing my earnest wishes that he may long enjoy in his retirement the affections of a grateful country, the best reward of exalted talents and the most faithful and meritorious service. Relying on the aid to be derived from the other departments of the Government, I enter on the trust to which I have been called by the suffrages of my fellow-citizens with my fervent prayers to the Almighty that He will be graciously pleased to continue to us that protection which He has already so conspicuously displayed in our favor.

"The Gallant Decature and his Brave Tars Capturing the Algerian Admiral" and "The Brave Tars of America Granting Peace to the Barbary States," from an English printed cotton textile, *circa* 1815.

THE PRESIDENT

When Maine was admitted to the Union during Monroe's first term there was a lengthy haggle as to whether it should enter as a slave or a free state. The slavery question was already growing more and more acute. Finally, in what has become known as the Missouri Compromise, Maine was admitted as a free state, effective March 15, 1820, with the provisions that Missouri was to follow as a slave state and slavery was to be prohibited from the Louisiana Territory above latitude 36° 30′ north. In the absence of any vital political question Monroe's candidacy for a second term was unopposed. He was accorded an electoral vote of 231 out of 235 (3 abstained and one vote was cast for John Quincy Adams). Daniel D. Tompkins was reëlected as vice-president.

THE NATION

Although Monroe's tenure in office was called the "era of good feeling," it was actually only a superficial scabbing over of basic political and economic forces that were to erupt later in the form of violent dissension on sectional and national issues: slavery, land speculation, bank failures, and the collapse of foreign trade due to high tariffs. Yet five states were admitted to the Union: Mississippi, Illinois, Alabama, Maine, and Missouri.

In 1818 General Andrew Jackson marched without official orders on Spanish-held east Florida. Although censured by such members of Congress as John Calhoun and Henry Clay, Jackson received no official punishment from President Monroe or Secretary of State John Quincy Adams because of the public's outspoken approval of "Old Hickory's" daring. The following year saw John Quincy Adams negotiate the Adams-Onís Treaty on February 22, whereby Spain permitted the United States to take full possession of Florida. Traveling from Savannah, Georgia, the *Savannah*, first paddle-wheel steamship, reached Liverpool, England, in 29 days. The United States now had something to talk about other than the brief financial panic of 1819, which had been caused by poor management of the Second Bank of the United States, speculation in real estate and commodities, and the collapse of foreign trade.

THE WORLD

The attempts of European nations to preserve peace after Napoleon's defeat were dominant factors in European politics during the decade and a half following 1815. Under Louis XVIII France enjoyed a reasonably speedy economic recovery, once it was freed of the drain on natural resources and manpower levied by Napoleon's conquests. In 1820 George IV became King of England, and the Industrial Revolution spread from England to the Continent. With no major wars to fight a period of growing prosperity enveloped not only Europe but also America.

ONCE AGAIN THE PUBLIC'S DISPLAY OF APPROVAL is interpreted by you as appreciation for your political philosophy, and is sufficient to elicit from you a message even more enthusiastic than your first inaugural address. This time you attempt to express your limitless confidence in the country's future, under your continued policies. The date of your second inauguration falls on a Sunday, so you set a precedent by postponing the ceremony until the next day, Monday, March 5, 1821. Now, reading the long address to your colleagues, you note many heads bobbing in agreement with your lengthy thoughts—or could these movements have been caused by the humid, close-packed room and the length of your address, one of the longest that will ever be read . . . ?

James Monroe

[1821–1825]

SECOND INAUGURAL ADDRESS, MARCH 5, 1821

Capitol Building, Washington, D.C.

Fellow-Citizens:

I shall not attempt to describe the grateful emotions which the new and very distinguished proof of the confidence of my fellow-citizens, evinced by my reelection to this high trust, has excited in my bosom. The approbation which it announces of my conduct in the preceding term affords me a consolation which I shall profoundly feel through life. The general accord with which it has been expressed adds to the great and never-ceasing obligations which it imposes. To merit the continuance of this good opinion, and to carry it with me into my retirement as the solace of advancing years, will be the object of my most zealous and unceasing efforts.

Having no pretensions to the high and commanding claims of my predecessors, whose names are so much more conspicuously identified with our Revolution, and who contributed so preeminently to promote its success, I consider myself rather as the instrument than the cause of the union which has prevailed in the late election. In surmounting, in favor of my humble pretensions, the difficulties which so often produce division in like occurrences, it is obvious that other powerful causes, indicating the great strength and stability of our Union, have essentially contributed to draw you together. That these powerful causes exist, and that they are permanent, is my fixed opinion; that they may produce a like accord in all questions touching, however remotely, the liberty, prosperity, and happiness of our country will always be the object of my most fervent prayers to the Supreme Author of All Good.

In a government which is founded by the people, who possess exclusively the sovereignty, it seems proper that the person who may be placed by their suffrages in this high trust should declare on commencing its duties the principles on which he intends to conduct the Administration. If the person thus elected has served the preceding term, an opportunity is afforded him to review its principal occurrences and to give such further explanation respecting them as in his judgment may be useful to his constituents. The events of one year have influence on those of another, and, in like manner, of a preceding on the succeeding Administration. The movements of a great nation are connected in all their parts. If

At the Hartford Convention (December 15, 1814 to January 5, 1815) New England Federalists had threatened secession if the war could not be brought to an end before New England shipping interests were ruined. But the Treaty of Ghent and Jackson's victory at New Orleans brought the Convention to an end, leaving Federalists an object of ridicule and virtually destroying the party. A sweeping wave of nationalism flooded the nation and swept away opposition to Monroe's policies.

errors have been committed they ought to be corrected; if the policy is sound it ought to be supported. It is by a thorough knowledge of the whole subject that our fellow-citizens are enabled to judge correctly of the past and to give a proper direction to the future.

Just before the commencement of the last term the United States had concluded a war with a very powerful nation on conditions equal and honorable to both parties. The events of that war are too recent and too deeply impressed on the memory of all to require a development from me. Our commerce had been in a great measure driven from the sea, our Atlantic and inland frontiers were invaded in almost every part; the waste of life along our coast and on some parts of our inland frontiers, to the defense of which our gallant and patriotic citizens were called, was immense, in addition to which not less than $120,000,000 were added at its end to the public debt.

As soon as the war had terminated, the nation, admonished by its events, resolved to place itself in a situation which should be better calculated to prevent the recurrence of a like evil, and, in case it should recur, to mitigate its calamities. With this view, after reducing our land force to the basis of a peace establishment, which has been further modified since, provision was made for the construction of fortifications at proper points through the whole extent of our coast and such an augmentation of our naval force as should be well adapted to both purposes. The laws making this provision were passed in 1815 and 1816, and it has been since the constant effort of the Executive to carry them into effect.

The advantage of these fortifications and of an augmented naval force in the extent contemplated, in a point of economy, has been fully illustrated by a report of the Board of Engineers and Naval Commissioners lately communicated to Congress, by which it appears that in an invasion by 20,000 men, with a correspondent naval force, in a campaign of six months only, the whole expense of the construction of the works would be defrayed by the difference in the sum necessary to maintain the force which would be adequate to our defense with the aid of those works and that which would be incurred without them. The reason of this difference is obvious. If fortifications are judiciously placed on our great inlets, as distant from our cities as circumstances will permit, they will form the only points of attack, and the enemy will be detained there by a small regular force a sufficient time to enable our militia to collect and repair to that on which the attack is made. A force adequate to the enemy, collected at that single point, with suitable preparation for such others as might be menaced, is all that would be requisite. But if there were no fortifications, then the enemy might go where he pleased, and, changing his position and sailing from place to place, our force must be called out and spread in vast numbers along the whole coast and on both sides of every bay and river as high up in each as it might be navigable for ships of war. By these fortifications, supported by our Navy, to which they would afford like support, we should present to other powers an armed front from St. Croix to the Sabine, which would protect in the event of war our whole coast and interior from invasion; and even in the wars of other powers, in which we were neutral, they would be found eminently useful, as, by keeping their public ships at a distance from our cities, peace and order in them would be preserved and the Government be protected from insult.

Monroe's terminology here should be questioned. Actually the terms of the Treaty of Ghent settled few of the issues of Mr. Madison's War. But because of Jackson's astounding success, the people quickly forgot their defeats and remembered only the final victory.

Monroe referred to the peacetime Army, fixed by Congress in 1815 at 10,000. In addition the Navy's gunboats were sold, and later the ships patrolling the Great Lakes were limited as to number and armament under the Rush-Bagot agreement between the United States and Great Britain.

Monroe's study of the recent war had convinced him of the necessity of added fortifications. But his unspoken thought may well have been to prevent another attack on the Capitol similar to the one which occurred in the War of 1812, when a Naval force under Admiral Sir George Cockburn landed, marched inland virtually unopposed, and put the torch to Washington City. The burning of the entire area was halted only by a cyclone which forced the British to seek shelter.

[42]

It need scarcely be remarked that these measures have not been resorted to in a spirit of hostility to other powers. Such a disposition does not exist toward any power. Peace and good will have been, and will hereafter be, cultivated with all, and by the most faithful regard to justice. They have been dictated by a love of peace, of economy, and an earnest desire to save the lives of our fellow-citizens from that destruction and our country from that devastation which are inseparable from war when it finds us unprepared for it. It is believed, and experience has shown, that such a preparation is the best expedient that can be resorted to to prevent war. I add with much pleasure that considerable progress has already been made in these measures of defense, and that they will be completed in a few years, considering the great extent and importance of the object, if the plan be zealously and steadily persevered in.

The conduct of the Government in what relates to foreign powers is always an object of the highest importance to the nation. Its agriculture, commerce, manufactures, fisheries, revenue, in short, its peace, may all be affected by it. Attention is therefore due to this subject.

At the period adverted to the powers of Europe, after having been engaged in long and destructive wars with each other, had concluded a peace, which happily still exists. Our peace with the power with whom we had been engaged had also been concluded. The war between Spain and the colonies in South America, which had commenced many years before, was then the only conflict that remained unsettled. This being a contest between different parts of the same community, in which other powers had not interfered, was not affected by their accommodations.

This contest was considered at an early stage by my predecessor a civil war in which the parties were entitled to equal rights in our ports. This decision, the first made by any power, being formed on great consideration of the comparative strength and resources of the parties, the length of time, and successful opposition made by the colonies, and of all other circumstances on which it ought to depend, was in strict accord with the law of nations. Congress has invariably acted on this principle, having made no change in our relations with either party. Our attitude has therefore been that of neutrality between them, which has been maintained by the Government with the strictest impartiality. No aid has been afforded to either, nor has any privilege been enjoyed by the one which has not been equally open to the other party, and every exertion has been made in its power to enforce the execution of the laws prohibiting illegal equipments with equal rigor against both.

By this equality between the parties their public vessels have been received in our ports on the same footing; they have enjoyed an equal right to purchase and export arms, munitions of war, and every other supply, the exportation of all articles whatever being permitted under laws which were passed long before the commencement of the contest; our citizens have traded equally with both, and their commerce with each has been alike protected by the Government.

Respecting the attitude which it may be proper for the United States to maintain hereafter between the parties, I have no hesitation in stating it as my opinion that the neutrality heretofore observed should still be adhered to. From the change in the Government of Spain and the negotiation now depending, invited by the Cortes and accepted by the colonies, it may be presumed, that

"The era of good feeling" was at its peak at this time during Monroe's tenure of office. But it would soon give way to an aggressive nationalism, from which would stem the "hands off the Western hemisphere" policy now known as the Monroe Doctrine.

Under the leadership of such men as Simon Bolivar, San Martín, and Bernardo O'Higgins the Latin American countries took advantage of unsettled world conditions to break away from Spain and establish independent republics. Spain, backed by France, Prussia, Austria, and Russia, attempted to quell the revolutions. But Congress, under Madison, maintained a position of neutrality —a position which Monroe stated "should still be adhered to."

their differences will be settled on the terms proposed by the colonies. Should the war be continued, the United States, regarding its occurrences, will always have it in their power to adopt such measures respecting it as their honor and interest may require.

Shortly after the general peace a band of adventurers took advantage of this conflict and of the facility which it afforded to establish a system of buccaneering in the neighboring seas, to the great annoyance of the commerce of the United States, and, as was represented, of that of other powers. Of this spirit and of its injurious bearing on the United States strong proofs were afforded by the establishment at Amelia Island, and the purposes to which it was made instrumental by this band in 1817, and by the occurrences which took place in other parts of Florida in 1818, the details of which in both instances are too well known to require to be now recited. I am satisfied had a less decisive course been adopted that the worst consequences would have resulted from it. We have seen that these checks, decisive as they were, were not sufficient to crush that piratical spirit. Many culprits brought within our limits have been condemned to suffer death, the punishment due to that atrocious crime. The decisions of upright and enlightened tribunals fall equally on all whose crimes subject them, by a fair interpretation of the law, to its censure. It belongs to the Executive not to suffer the executions under these decisions to transcend the great purpose for which punishment is necessary. The full benefit of example being secured, policy as well as humanity equally forbids that they should be carried further. I have acted on this principle, pardoning those who appear to have been led astray by ignorance of the criminality of the acts they had committed, and suffering the law to take effect on those only in whose favor no extenuating circumstances could be urged.

Great confidence is entertained that the late treaty with Spain, which has been ratified by both the parties, and the ratifications whereof have been exchanged, has placed the relations of the two countries on a basis of permanent friendship. The provision made by it for such of our citizens as have claims on Spain of the character described will, it is presumed, be very satisfactory to them, and the boundary which is established between the territories of the parties westward of the Mississippi, heretofore in dispute, has, it is thought, been settled on conditions just and advantageous to both. But to the acquisition of Florida too much importance can not be attached. It secures to the United States a territory important in itself, and whose importance is much increased by its bearing on many of the highest interests of the Union. It opens to several of the neighboring States a free passage to the ocean, through the Province ceded, by several rivers, having their sources high up within their limits. It secures us against all future annoyance from powerful Indian tribes. It gives us several excellent harbors in the Gulf of Mexico for ships of war of the largest size. It covers by its position in the Gulf the Mississippi and other great waters within our extended limits, and thereby enables the United States to afford complete protection to the vast and very valuable productions of our whole Western country, which find a market through those streams.

By a treaty with the British Government, bearing date on the 20th of October, 1818, the convention regulating the commerce between the United States and Great Britain, concluded on the 3d of July, 1815, which was about expiring, was revived and continued for the term of ten years from the time of its expiration. By that

[44]

treaty, also, the differences which had arisen under the treaty of Ghent respecting the right claimed by the United States for their citizens to take and cure fish on the coast of His Britannic Majesty's dominions in America, with other differences on important interests, were adjusted to the satisfaction of both parties. No agreement has yet been entered into respecting the commerce between the United States and the British dominions in the West Indies and on this continent. The restraints imposed on that commerce by Great Britain, and reciprocated by the United States on a principle of defense, continue still in force.

The negotiation with France for the regulation of the commercial relations between the two countries, which in the course of the last summer had been commenced at Paris, has since been transferred to this city, and will be pursued on the part of the United States in the spirit of conciliation, and with an earnest desire that it may terminate in an arrangement satisfactory to both parties.

Our relations with the Barbary Powers are preserved in the same state and by the same means that were employed when I came into this office. As early as 1801 it was found necessary to send a squadron into the Mediterranean for the protection of our commerce, and no period has intervened, a short term excepted, when it was thought advisable to withdraw it. The great interests which the United States have in the Pacific, in commerce and in the fisheries, have also made it necessary to maintain a naval force there. In disposing of this force in both instances the most effectual measures in our power have been taken, without interfering with its other duties, for the suppression of the slave trade and of piracy in the neighboring seas.

The situation of the United States in regard to their resources, the extent of their revenue, and the facility with which it is raised affords a most gratifying spectacle. The payment of nearly $67,000,000 of the public debt, with the great progress made in measures of defense and in other improvements of various kinds since the late war, are conclusive proofs of this extraordinary prosperity, especially when it is recollected that these expenditures have been defrayed without a burthen on the people, the direct tax and excise having been repealed soon after the conclusion of the late war, and the revenue applied to these great objects having been raised in a manner not to be felt. Our great resources therefore remain untouched for any purpose which may affect the vital interests of the nation. For all such purposes they are inexhaustible. They are more especially to be found in the virtue, patriotism, and intelligence of our fellow-citizens, and in the devotion with which they would yield up by any just measure of taxation all their property in support of the rights and honor of their country.

Under the present depression of prices, affecting all the productions of the country and every branch of industry, proceeding from causes explained on a former occasion, the revenue has considerably diminished, the effect of which has been to compel Congress either to abandon these great measures of defense or to resort to loans or internal taxes to supply the deficiency. On the presumption that this depression and the deficiency in the revenue arising from it would be temporary, loans were authorized for the demands of the last and present year. Anxious to relieve my fellow-citizens in 1817 from every burthen which could be dispensed with, and the state of the Treasury permitting it, I recommended the repeal of the internal taxes, knowing that such relief was then peculiarly

Stephen Decatur, hero of the conflict with Tripolitan pirates, had been shot and killed in a duel with James Barron, March 22, 1820, at Bladensburg, Maryland.

With the effects of the Panic of 1819 still apparent Monroe here attempted to explain the drop in government revenue and to justify his action in floating loans rather than resorting to a resumption of internal taxation to make up the deficit. With the Tariff of 1818 in effect on imports Monroe hoped to be able to meet the cost of government without resorting to additional sources of revenue.

necessary in consequence of the great exertions made in the late war. I made that recommendation under a pledge that should the public exigencies require a recurrence to them at any time while I remained in this trust, I would with equal promptitude perform the duty which would then be alike incumbent on me. By the experiment now making it will be seen by the next session of Congress whether the revenue shall have been so augmented as to be adequate to all these necessary purposes. Should the deficiency still continue, and especially should it be probable that it would be permanent, the course to be pursued appears to me to be obvious. I am satisfied that under certain circumstances loans may be resorted to with great advantage. I am equally well satisfied, as a general rule, that the demands of the current year, especially in time of peace, should be provided for by the revenue of that year.

I have never dreaded, nor have I ever shunned, in any situation in which I have been placed making appeals to the virtue and patriotism of my fellow-citizens, well knowing that they could never be made in vain, especially in times of great emergency or for purposes of high national importance. Independently of the exigency of the case, many considerations of great weight urge a policy having in view a provision of revenue to meet to a certain extent the demands of the nation, without relying altogether on the precarious resource of foreign commerce. I am satisfied that internal duties and excises, with corresponding imposts on foreign articles of the same kind, would, without imposing any serious burdens on the people, enhance the price of produce, promote our manufactures, and augment the revenue, at the same time that they made it more secure and permanent.

The care of the Indian tribes within our limits has long been an essential part of our system, but, unfortunately, it has not been executed in a manner to accomplish all the objects intended by it. We have treated them as independent nations, without their having any substantial pretensions to that rank. The distinction has flattered their pride, retarded their improvement, and in many instances paved the way to their destruction. The progress of our settlements westward, supported as they are by a dense population, has constantly driven them back, with almost the total sacrifice of the lands which they have been compelled to abandon. They have claims on the magnanimity and, I may add, on the justice of this nation which we must all feel. We should become their real benefactors; we should perform the office of their Great Father, the endearing title which they emphatically give to the Chief Magistrate of our Union. Their sovereignty over vast territories should cease, in lieu of which the right of soil should be secured to each individual and his posterity in competent portions; and for the territory thus ceded by each tribe some reasonable equivalent should be granted, to be vested in permanent funds for the support of civil government over them and for the education of their children, for their instruction in the arts of husbandry, and to provide sustenance for them until they could provide it for themselves. My earnest hope is that Congress will digest some plan, founded on these principles, with such improvements as their wisdom may suggest, and carry it into effect as soon as it may be practicable.

Europe is again unsettled and the prospect of war increasing. Should the flame light up in any quarter, how far it may extend it is impossible to foresee. It is our peculiar felicity to be altogether unconnected with the causes which produce this menacing aspect elsewhere. With every power we are in perfect amity, and it is our interest to remain so if it be practicable on just conditions. I see no reasonable cause to apprehend variance with any power, unless it proceed from a violation of our maritime rights. In these contests, should they occur, and to whatever extent they may be carried, we shall be neutral; but as a neutral power we have rights which it is our duty to maintain. For like injuries it will be incumbent on us to seek redress in a spirit of amity, in full confidence that, injuring none, none would knowingly injure us. For more imminent dangers we should be prepared, and it should always be recollected that such preparation adapted to the circumstances and sanctioned by the judgment and wishes of our constituents can not fail to have a good effect in averting dangers of every kind. We should recollect also that the season of peace is best adapted to these preparations.

If we turn our attention, fellow-citizens, more immediately to the internal concerns of our country, and more especially to those on which its future welfare depends, we have every reason to anticipate the happiest results. It is now rather more than forty-four years since we declared our independence, and thirty-seven since it was acknowledged. The talents and virtues which were displayed in that great struggle were a sure presage of all that has since followed. A people who were able to surmount in their infant state such great perils would be more competent as they rose into manhood to repel any which they might meet in their progress. Their physical strength would be more adequate to foreign danger, and the practice of self-government, aided by the light of experience, could not fail to produce an effect equally salutary on all those questions connected with the internal organization. These favorable anticipations have been realized.

In our whole system, national and State, we have shunned all the defects which unceasingly preyed on the vitals and destroyed the ancient Republics. In them there were distinct orders, a nobility and a people, or the people governed in one assembly. Thus, in the one instance there was a perpetual conflict between the orders in society for the ascendency, in which the victory of either terminated in the overthrow of the government and the ruin of the state; in the other, in which the people governed in a body, and whose dominions seldom exceeded the dimensions of a county in one of our States, a tumultous and disorderly movement permitted only a transitory existence. In this great nation there is but one order, that of the people, whose power, by a peculiarly happy improvement of the representative principle, is transferred from them, without impairing in the slightest degree their sovereignty, to bodies of their own creation, and to persons elected by themselves, in the full extent necessary for all the purposes of free, enlightened, and efficient government. The whole system is elective, the complete sovereignty being in the people, and every officer in every department deriving his authority from and being responsible to them for his conduct.

Our career has corresponded with this great outline. Perfection in our organization could not have been expected in the outset either in the National or State Governments or in tracing the line between their respective powers. But no serious conflict has arisen, nor any contest but such as are managed by argument and by a fair appeal to the good sense of the people, and many of the defects which experience had clearly demonstrated in both Governments have been remedied. By steadily pursuing this course in this spirit there is every reason to believe that our system will soon attain the

Monroe repeated his conviction that peacetime preparedness was essential for the nation's safety.

Monroe explained the political philosophy of the Democrat-Republicans, as they were now beginning to be called, in opposition to the principles of the Federalists, now all but a memory as a party. Jefferson had visualized a limited government in an agrarian economy, unlike the Federalists' idea of a strong central government primarily concerned with the interests of wealthy industrialists. Under Monroe the national economy grew both industrially and agriculturally: The eastern states concentrated on the manufacture of steamboats, textiles, guns, and similar articles, while Americans in the expanding western areas made use of these articles for transportation, clothing, trade goods, protection, and a means of obtaining food. Politically, too, a happy compromise seemed to have been achieved. With the Democrat-Republicans ruling Congress against virtually no opposition there was still Chief Justice Marshall and the Supreme Court to act as a check and balance against a swing too far toward a decentralized government. This was almost exactly what Madison had foreseen as necessary, when the Constitution was written under his aegis.

highest degree of perfection of which human institutions are capable, and that the movement in all its branches will exhibit such a degree of order and harmony as to command the admiration and respect of the civilized world.

Our physical attainments have not been less eminent. Twenty-five years ago the river Mississippi was shut up and our Western brethren had no outlet for their commerce. What has been the progress since that time? The river has not only become the property of the United States from its source to the ocean, with all its tributary streams (with the exception of the upper part of the Red River only), but Louisiana, with a fair and liberal boundary on the western side and the Floridas on the eastern, have been ceded to us. The United States now enjoy the complete and uninterrupted sovereignty over the whole territory from St. Croix to the Sabine. New States, settled from among ourselves in this and in other parts, have been admitted into our Union in equal participation in the national sovereignty with the original States. Our population has augmented in an astonishing degree and extended in every direction. We now, fellow-citizens, comprise within our limits the dimensions and faculties of a great power under a Government possessing all the energies of any government ever known to the Old World, with an utter incapacity to oppress the people.

Entering with these views the office which I have just solemnly sworn to execute with fidelity and to the utmost of my ability, I derive great satisfaction from a knowledge that I shall be assisted in the several Departments by the very enlightened and upright citizens from whom I have received so much aid in the preceding term. With full confidence in the continuance of that candor and generous indulgence from my fellow-citizens at large which I have heretofore experienced, and with a firm reliance on the protection of Almighty God, I shall forthwith commence the duties of the high trust to which you have called me.

With the purchase of New Orleans, as part of the Louisiana Territory, the Mississippi had been opened to trade. Fulton's steamboat had made possible upriver commerce that aided greatly in the westward surge. And with the census of 1820 showing a population of 9,638,453, Monroe's claim that the nation could now be considered a great power seemed justified.

In addition to John Quincy Adams, his Secretary of State, Monroe often consulted his unofficial advisers, Jefferson and Madison. Buttressed by these keen minds and a Cabinet of able men, Monroe could logically look forward to a successful second term. But even he could not foresee the importance of his actions in the next four years.

Webster, Clay, and Calhoun discussing the Missouri Compromise.

THE PRESIDENT

John Quincy (pronounced Quinzy) Adams was the only son of a president who was to be elected to the presidency. Adams studied law at Harvard and accompanied his father on many diplomatic missions abroad. In 1794 young Adams received his first commission in his own right, as minister to the Netherlands. In 1803 he was elected to the Senate. However, due to his refusal to vote along party lines, Adams was forced by the Federalists to resign in 1808, leaving him virtually a man without a party. In 1824 no candidate won a majority of the electoral votes. Adams was therefore elected by the House.

THE NATION

America was enjoying a period of prosperity and rapid expansion under the able statesmanship of Monroe and Adams, a working, similarly oriented team. An example is the origin of the Monroe Doctrine. In July, 1823, Secretary of State John Quincy Adams declared to the Russian minister: ". . . we should contest the right of Russia to any territorial establishment on this continent, and . . . we should assume distinctly the principle that the American continents are no longer subjects for any new European colonial establishments." Four-and-a-half months later President Monroe, in his message to the 18th Congress on December 2, 1823, set forth what has become known as the Monroe Doctrine (but which could as easily have been called the Adams-Monroe Doctrine) when he declared: ". . . the American continents, by the free and independent condition which they have assumed and maintained, are henceforth not to be considered as subjects for future colonization by any European powers." Monroe went on to clarify his doctrine further: "But with the governments who have declared their independence,

and maintain it . . . we could not view any interposition for the purpose of oppressing them or controlling in any other manner, their destiny by any European power in any other light, than as the manifestation of an unfriendly disposition toward the United States." This meant if the independent nations of the Western Hemisphere were molested, war with the United States could result. Was this the same Monroe who gave such pointed assurances of peace in his first inaugural address? Or was Adams responsible for the turnabout? In view of Adams' prior statement of the doctrine his influence would seem quite important.

The visit of the aging Lafayette and his son in the fall of 1824 climaxed Monroe's second term. When the electoral votes for the election of 1824 were counted, General Andrew Jackson had 99, John Quincy Adams 84, William H. Crawford 41, Henry Clay 37. Since no candidate had received a majority the election was thrown into the House of Representatives, where Clay switched his support to Adams, who was elected president with John C. Calhoun vice-president.

THE WORLD

The death of Napoleon at St. Helena in 1821 ended forever the threat of his escape and return to power. But other forces were at work: Peru, Guatemala, Brazil, and other Spanish-American countries declared their independence from Spain. Canning, the British Prime Minister, supported their move. In December, 1823, the United States issued the Monroe Doctrine. The same year the French army entered a weakened Spain and restored Ferdinand VII to the throne.

ADAMS' DISAPPOINTMENT IN HIS ELECTION can be readily understood if you will put yourself in his place: You are following an outstandingly successful president whose policies you helped shape as his Secretary of State. Yet, because of your independence from either political party, your efforts have not been recognized by the popular vote majority you felt was your just due. You refer to this pointedly at the conclusion of your inaugural address . . . .

John Quincy Adams

[1825–1829]

INAUGURAL ADDRESS, MARCH 4, 1825

Capitol Building, Washington, D.C.

In compliance with an usage coeval with the existence of our Federal Constitution, and sanctioned by the example of my predecessors in the career upon which I am about to enter, I appear, my fellow-citizens, in your presence and in that of Heaven to bind myself by the solemnities of religious obligation to the faithful performance of the duties alloted to me in the station to which I have been called.

In unfolding to my countrymen the principles by which I shall be governed in the fulfillment of those duties my first resort will be to that Constitution which I shall swear to the best of my ability to preserve, protect, and defend. That revered instrument enumerates the powers and prescribes the duties of the Executive Magistrate, and in its first words declares the purposes to which these and the whole action of the Government instituted by it should be invariably and sacredly devoted—to form a more perfect union, establish justice, insure domestic tranquillity, provide for the common defense, promote the general welfare, and secure the blessings of liberty to the people of this Union in their successive generations. Since the adoption of this social compact one of these generations has passed away. It is the work of our forefathers. Administered by some of the most eminent men who contributed to its formation, through a most eventful period in the annals of the world, and through all the vicissitudes of peace and war incidental to the condition of associated man, it has not disappointed the hopes and aspirations of those illustrious benefactors of their age and nation. It has promoted the lasting welfare of that country so dear to us all; it has to an extent far beyond the ordinary lot of humanity secured the freedom and happiness of this people. We now receive it as a precious inheritance from those to whom we are indebted for its establishment, doubly bound by the examples which they have left us and by the blessings which we have enjoyed as the fruits of their labors to transmit the same unimpaired to the succeeding generation.

In the compass of thirty-six years since this great national covenant was instituted a body of laws enacted under its authority and in conformity with its provisions has unfolded its powers and carried into practical operation its effective energies. Subordinate departments have distributed the executive functions in their various relations to foreign affairs, to the revenue and expenditures, and to the military force of the Union by land and sea. A coordinate department of the judiciary has expounded the Constitution and the laws,

Washington, Franklin, Hamilton were among those who had passed on, and John Adams and Thomas Jefferson had only one more year of life remaining.

settling in harmonious coincidence with the legislative will numerous weighty questions of construction which the imperfection of human language had rendered unavoidable. The year of jubilee since the first formation of our Union has just elapsed; that of the declaration of our independence is at hand. The consummation of both was effected by this Constitution.

Since that period a population of four millions has multiplied to twelve. A territory bounded by the Mississippi has been extended from sea to sea. New States have been admitted to the Union in numbers nearly equal to those of the first Confederation. Treaties of peace, amity, and commerce have been concluded with the principal dominions of the earth. The people of other nations, inhabitants of regions acquired not by conquest, but by compact, have been united with us in the participation of our rights and duties, of our burdens and blessings. The forest has fallen by the ax of our woodsmen; the soil has been made to teem by the tillage of our farmers; our commerce has whitened every ocean. The dominion of man over physical nature has been extended by the invention of our artists. Liberty and law have marched hand in hand. All the purposes of human association have been accomplished as effectively as under any other government on the globe, and at a cost little exceeding in a whole generation the expenditure of other nations in a single year.

Such is the unexaggerated picture of our condition under a Constitution founded upon the republican principle of equal rights. To admit that this picture has its shades is but to say that it is still the condition of men upon earth. From evil—physical, moral, and political—it is not our claim to be exempt. We have suffered sometimes by the visitation of Heaven through disease; often by the wrongs and injustice of other nations, even to the extremities of war; and, lastly, by dissensions among ourselves—dissensions perhaps inseparable from the enjoyment of freedom, but which have more than once appeared to threaten the dissolution of the Union, and with it the overthrow of all the enjoyments of our present lot and all our earthly hopes of the future. The causes of these dissensions have been various, founded upon differences of speculation in the theory of republican government; upon conflicting views of policy in our relations with foreign nations; upon jealousies of partial and sectional interests, aggravated by prejudices and prepossessions which strangers to each other are ever apt to entertain.

It is a source of gratification and of encouragement to me to observe that the great result of this experiment upon the theory of human rights has at the close of that generation by which it was formed been crowned with success equal to the most sanguine expectations of its founders. Union, justice, tranquillity, the common defense, the general welfare, and the blessings of liberty—all have been promoted by the Government under which we have lived. Standing at this point of time, looking back to that generation which has gone by and forward to that which is advancing, we may at once indulge in grateful exultation and in cheering hope. From the experience of the past we derive instructive lessons for the future. Of the two great political parties which have divided the opinions and feelings of our country, the candid and the just will now admit that both have contributed splendid talents, spotless integrity, ardent patriotism, and disinterested sacrifices to the formation and administration of this Government, and that both have required a liberal indulgence for a portion of human infirmity and error. The revolutionary wars of Europe, commencing pre-

[52]

cisely at the moment when the Government of the United States first went into operation under this Constitution, excited a collision of sentiments and of sympathies which kindled all the passions and imbittered the conflict of parties till the nation was involved in war and the Union was shaken to its center. This time of trial embraced a period of five and twenty years, during which the policy of the Union in its relations with Europe constituted the principal basis of our political divisions and the most arduous part of the action of our Federal Government. With the catastrophe in which the wars of the French Revolution terminated, and our own subsequent peace with Great Britain, this baneful weed of party strife was uprooted. From that time no difference of principle, connected either with the theory of government or with our intercourse with foreign nations, has existed or been called forth in force sufficient to sustain a continued combination of parties or to give more than wholesome animation to public sentiment or legislative debate. Our political creed is, without a dissenting voice that can be heard, that the will of the people is the source and the happiness of the people the end of all legitimate government upon earth; that the best security for the beneficence and the best guaranty against the abuse of power consists in the freedom, the purity, and the frequency of popular elections; that the General Government of the Union and the separate governments of the States are all sovereignties of limited powers, fellow-servants of the same masters, uncontrolled within their respective spheres, uncontrollable by encroachments upon each other; that the firmest security of peace is the preparation during peace of the defenses of war; that a rigorous economy and accountability of public expenditures should guard against the aggravation and alleviate when possible the burden of taxation; that the military should be kept in strict subordination to the civil power; that the freedom of the press and of religious opinion should be inviolate; that the policy of our country is peace and the ark of our salvation union are articles of faith upon which we are all now agreed. If there have been those who doubted whether a confederated representative democracy were a government competent to the wise and orderly management of the common concerns of a mighty nation, those doubts have been dispelled; if there have been projects of partial confederacies to be erected upon the ruins of the Union, they have been scattered to the winds; if there have been dangerous attachments to one foreign nation and antipathies against another, they have been extinguished. Ten years of peace, at home and abroad, have assuaged the animosities of political contention and blended into harmony the most discordant elements of public opinion. There still remains one effort of magnanimity, one sacrifice of prejudice and passion, to be made by the individuals throughout the nation who have heretofore followed the standards of political party. It is that of discarding every remnant of rancor against each other, of embracing as countrymen and friends, and of yielding to talents and virtue alone that confidence which in times of contention for principle was bestowed only upon those who bore the badge of party communion.

The collisions of party spirit which originate in speculative opinions or in different views of administrative policy are in their nature transitory. Those which are founded on geographical divisions, adverse interests of soil, climate, and modes of domestic life are more permanent, and therefore, perhaps, more dangerous. It is this which gives inestimable value to the character of our Government, at once federal and national. It holds out to us a perpetual

While it was true Monroe's two terms were remarkable in that opposition by the Federalists dwindled to insignificance and finally ceased altogether, the conditions of Adams' own election had already created a new "baneful weed of party strife." The supporters of Adams and Clay were labeled National Republicans, Jackson's followers were known as Democrats, both groups were subdivisions of the Democrat-Republicans.

Adams' reasoning here is evident: Why change the policies that had carried the nation to prosperity?

Once again Adams voiced his belief: The nation's welfare should be placed ahead of party considerations.

[53]

admonition to preserve alike and with equal anxiety the rights of each individual State in its own government and the rights of the whole nation in that of the Union. Whatsoever is of domestic concernment, unconnected with the other members of the Union or with foreign lands, belongs exclusively to the administration of the State governments. Whatsoever directly involves the rights and interests of the federative fraternity or of foreign powers is of the resort of this General Government. The duties of both are obvious in the general principle, though sometimes perplexed with difficulties in the detail. To respect the rights of the State governments is the inviolable duty of that of the Union; the government of every State will feel its own obligation to respect and preserve the rights of the whole. The prejudices everywhere too commonly entertained against distant strangers are worn away, and the jealousies of jarring interests are allayed by the composition and functions of the great national councils annually assembled from all quarters of the Union at this place. Here the distinguished men from every section of our country, while meeting to deliberate upon the great interests of those by whom they are deputed, learn to estimate the talents and do justice to the virtues of each other. The harmony of the nation is promoted and the whole Union is knit together by the sentiments of mutual respect, the habits of social intercourse, and the ties of personal friendship formed between the representatives of its several parts in the performance of their service at this metropolis.

Passing from this general review of the purposes and injunctions of the Federal Constitution and their results as indicating the first traces of the path of duty in the discharge of my public trust, I turn to the Administration of my immediate predecessor as the second. It has passed away in a period of profound peace, how much to the satisfaction of our country and to the honor of our country's name is known to you all. The great features of its policy, in general concurrence with the will of the Legislature, have been to cherish peace while preparing for defensive war; to yield exact justice to other nations and maintain the rights of our own; to cherish the principles of freedom and of equal rights wherever they were proclaimed; to discharge with all possible promptitude the national debt; to reduce within the narrowest limits of efficiency the military force; to improve the organization and discipline of the Army; to provide and sustain a school of military science; to extend equal protection to all the great interests of the nation; to promote the civilization of the Indian tribes, and to proceed in the great system of internal improvements within the limits of the constitutional power of the Union. Under the pledge of these promises, made by that eminent citizen at the time of his first induction to this office, in his career of eight years the internal taxes have been repealed; sixty millions of the public debt have been discharged; provision has been made for the comfort and relief of the aged and indigent among the surviving warriors of the Revolution; the regular armed force has been reduced and its constitution revised and perfected; the accountability for the expenditure of public moneys has been made more effective; the Floridas have been peaceably acquired, and our boundary has been extended to the Pacific Ocean; the independence of the southern nations of this hemisphere has been recognized, and recommended by example and by counsel to the potentates of Europe; progress has been made in the defense of the country by fortifications and the increase of the Navy, toward the effectual suppression of the African traffic in slaves, in alluring the aboriginal hunters of our land to the cultiva-

Adams, though short, chubby, and bald like his father, was such a master of oratory that his appearance was unimportant. This was particularly so when he was speaking and driving home a point in beautifully couched language, as he did here.

When summed up in a single paragraph in Adams' incisive style, the accomplishments of Monroe's two terms are clearly evident. It had indeed been "a period of profound peace."

tion of the soil and of the mind, in exploring the interior regions of the Union, and in preparing by scientific researches and surveys for the further application of our national resources to the internal improvement of our country.

In this brief outline of the promise and performance of my immediate predecessor the line of duty for his successor is clearly delineated. To pursue to their consummation those purposes of improvement in our common condition instituted or recommended by him will embrace the whole sphere of my obligations. To the topic of internal improvement, emphatically urged by him at his inauguration, I recur with peculiar satisfaction. It is that from which I am convinced that the unborn millions of our posterity who are in future ages to people this continent will derive their most fervent gratitude to the founders of the Union; that in which the beneficent action of its Government will be most deeply felt and acknowledged. The magnificence and splendor of their public works are among the imperishable glories of the ancient republics. The roads and aqueducts of Rome have been the admiration of all after ages, and have survived thousands of years after all her conquests have been swallowed up in despotism or become the spoil of barbarians. Some diversity of opinion has prevailed with regard to the powers of Congress for legislation upon objects of this nature. The most respectful deference is due to doubts originating in pure patriotism and sustained by venerated authority. But nearly twenty years have passed since the construction of the first national road was commenced. The authority for its construction was then unquestioned. To how many thousands of our countrymen has it proved a benefit? To what single individual has it ever proved an injury? Repeated, liberal, and candid discussions in the Legislature have conciliated the sentiments and approximated the opinions of enlightened minds upon the question of constitutional power. I can not but hope that by the same process of friendly, patient, and persevering deliberation all constitutional objections will ultimately be removed. The extent and limitation of the powers of the General Government in relation to this transcendently important interest will be settled and acknowledged to the common satisfaction of all, and every speculative scruple will be solved by a practical public blessing.

Fellow-citizens, you are acquainted with the peculiar circumstances of the recent election, which have resulted in affording me the opportunity of addressing you at this time. You have heard the exposition of the principles which will direct me in the fulfillment of the high and solemn trust imposed upon me in this station. Less possessed of your confidence in advance than any of my predecessors, I am deeply conscious of the prospect that I shall stand more and oftener in need of your indulgence. Intentions upright and pure, a heart devoted to the welfare of our country, and the unceasing application of all the faculties allotted to me to her service are all the pledges that I can give for the faithful performance of the arduous duties I am to undertake. To the guidance of the legislative councils, to the assistance of the executive and subordinate departments, to the friendly cooperation of the respective State governments, to the candid and liberal support of the people so far as it may be deserved by honest industry and zeal, I shall look for whatever success may attend my public service; and knowing that "except the Lord keep the city the watchman waketh but in vain," with fervent supplications for His favor, to His overruling providence I commit with humble but fearless confidence my own fate and the future destinies of my country.

Adams left no doubt he intended a continuation of Monroe's policies—especially those relating to internal improvements.

Adams evidently sensed the antagonism of Jackson's followers, for here he attempted to remove any resistance to his constructive domestic program. But his efforts were fruitless. Jackson and his supporters blocked nearly all of Adams' broadly conceived plans for new roads, a national university, and government-financed scientific and artistic projects for the betterment of the people. The unjust stigma of a sellout to Clay was carried by Adams throughout his entire four years in office.

So quickly and vociferously had Jackson and his adherents voiced their opinion of a political deal between Clay and Adams that Adams felt compelled to come to his own defense in the closing passage of his address. But his plea of "intentions upright and pure" fell on ears already deafened by the outraged cries of Jackson's Democrats. Unfortunately, Adams' "humble but fearless confidence" in his fate would never be realized, and he, like his father, would leave the presidency an embittered and frustrated man.

THE PRESIDENT

Born in a log cabin in the Waxhaws district, South Carolina, Andrew Jackson became the 7th president and the first to represent the class of citizen now known as "the common man." Jackson served as Tennessee's first representative in Congress, and later as United States Senator. He then became a justice of Tennessee's Supreme Court, retiring in 1804 to his Nashville plantation, The Hermitage, where he remained until the War of 1812 broke out. He was given command of the militia of his district, fought and defeated the Creeks in the battle of Horseshoe Bend, and on January 8, 1815, led U.S. troops to victory in the Battle of New Orleans. Sent to quell the Seminoles in 1818 he moved across the Spanish border, captured Pensacola, and in addition hanged two Englishmen—all without authority. After his defeat by Adams in 1824 Jackson was swept into the presidency four years later, by a decisive majority of both popular and electoral votes.

THE NATION

In 1825 Andrew Jackson's disgruntled followers began their four-year harassment of President John Quincy Adams. Adams and Clay were labelled "Puritan and black-leg" by John Randolph on the Senate floor. This reference to the purported deal between Adams and Clay resulting in Adams' election over Jackson followed both Adams and Clay the rest of their political lives. It even led to a duel between Clay and Randolph in which neither man was hurt.

July 4, 1826, the fiftieth anniversary of the signing of the Declaration of Independence, was to be a day of celebration. But it became a day of mourning when both John Adams and Thomas Jefferson, so long the heads of opposing parties, died within a few hours of each other.

1827 saw the first general strike in America when Philadelphia carpenters unsuccessfully sought a ten-hour day. In the case of *Martin* v. *Mott,* the U.S. Supreme Court gave the president authority to call out the militia. And the Tariff of Abominations proved to be the final ammunition Jackson's Democratic party needed to destroy Adams' hopes of a second term. Andrew Jackson rolled up 647,286 popular votes (178 electoral) to 508,064 popular votes (83 electoral) for John Quincy Adams. John C. Calhoun was reëlected vice-president.

THE WORLD

Now it was Russia's turn to step into the world spotlight. Early in 1825 Russia and Britain signed a treaty to determine the boundary between Russian and British America. Before the year was out Nicholas I succeeded Alexander I as czar and in 1826 was faced with a revolt in the Russian army. This suppressed, Nicholas declared war on Persia, and in 1828 declared war on Turkey. In the Peace of Turkamanchai, Persia ceded a piece of Armenia to Russia.

IN WRITING YOUR INAUGURAL ADDRESS your pared-down phrases are as lean as your own tough frame, a physical characteristic that earned you the nickname of Old Hickory. You waste no words in a review of what has gone before. Indeed, you would like to forget the bitterness of the election campaign, during which your opponents had branded your wife Rachel an adulteress because of confusion over her divorce. Publication of these charges helped shorten Rachel's life and she died in 1828, just three days before Christmas. And so your inauguration day finds you grief-stricken and in ill health. But you walk down the sidewalk along snow-spotted Pennsylvania Avenue to the Capitol, entering through the basement to avoid the crushing crowd outside. You appear on the Capitol steps and acknowledge the tremendous cheers of the crowd. Then, with the pages quivering in your long fingers, you begin to read your address in a thin, barely audible voice . . . .

Andrew Jackson

[1829–1833]

FIRST INAUGURAL ADDRESS, MARCH 4, 1829

Capitol Steps, Washington, D.C.

Fellow-Citizens:

About to undertake the arduous duties that I have been appointed to perform by the choice of a free people, I avail myself of this customary and solemn occasion to express the gratitude which their confidence inspires and to acknowledge the accountability which my situation enjoins. While the magnitude of their interests convinces me that no thanks can be adequate to the honor they have conferred, it admonishes me that the best return I can make is the zealous dedication of my humble abilities to their service and their good.

As the instrument of the Federal Constitution it will devolve on me for a stated period to execute the laws of the United States, to superintend their foreign and their confederate relations, to manage their revenue, to command their forces, and, by communications to the Legislature, to watch over and to promote their interests generally. And the principles of action by which I shall endeavor to accomplish this circle of duties it is now proper for me briefly to explain.

In administering the laws of Congress I shall keep steadily in view the limitations as well as the extent of the Executive power, trusting thereby to discharge the functions of my office without transcending its authority. With foreign nations it will be my study to preserve peace and to cultivate friendship on fair and honorable terms, and in the adjustment of any differences that may exist or arise to exhibit the forbearance becoming a powerful nation rather than the sensibility belonging to a gallant people.

In such measures as I may be called on to pursue in regard to the rights of the separate States I hope to be animated by a proper respect for those sovereign members of our Union, taking care not to confound the powers they have reserved to themselves with those they have granted to the Confederacy.

The management of the public revenue—that searching operation in all governments—is among the most delicate and important trusts in ours, and it will, of course, demand no inconsiderable share of my official solicitude. Under every aspect in which it can

Jackson lost no time in setting out the principles which would guide him during his tenure. His words had the sterling ring of sincerity reflecting the man of the people he was—and the people believed in him. Although Jackson's party and its basic policies had first been advocated by Jefferson, Jefferson's political coat of many colors had still failed to cover the fact that he had nevertheless remained an aristocrat in the eyes of the people whose interests he professed to serve.

Not so Old Hickory! Here was plain talk by a plain, and deeply sorrowing, man. The conservatism of Jackson's address came as a surprise to many of his vanquished opponents, who as in Jefferson's time expected a rabble-rousing speech but failed to hear it. The suspicion that Jackson's address was

be considered it would appear that advantage must result from the observance of a strict and faithful economy. This I shall aim at the more anxiously both because it will facilitate the extinguishment of the national debt, the unnecessary duration of which is incompatible with real independence, and because it will counteract that tendency to public and private profligacy which a profuse expenditure of money by the Government is but too apt to engender. Powerful auxiliaries to the attainment of this desirable end are to be found in the regulations provided by the wisdom of Congress for the specific appropriation of public money and the prompt accountability of public officers.

With regard to a proper selection of the subjects of impost with a view to revenue, it would seem to me that the spirit of equity, caution, and compromise in which the Constitution was formed requires that the great interests of agriculture, commerce, and manufactures should be equally favored, and that perhaps the only exception to this rule should consist in the peculiar encouragement of any products of either of them that may be found essential to our national independence.

Internal improvement and the diffusion of knowledge, so far as they can be promoted by the constitutional acts of the Federal Government, are of high importance.

Considering standing armies as dangerous to free governments in time of peace, I shall not seek to enlarge our present establishment, nor disregard that salutary lesson of political experience which teaches that the military should be held subordinate to the civil power. The gradual increase of our Navy, whose flag has displayed in distant climes our skill in navigation and our fame in arms; the preservation of our forts, arsenals, and dockyards, and the introduction of progressive improvements in the discipline and science of both branches of our military service are so plainly prescribed by prudence that I should be excused for omitting their mention sooner than for enlarging on their importance. But the bulwark of our defense is the national militia, which in the present state of our intelligence and population must render us invincible. As long as our Government is administered for the good of the people, and is regulated by their will; as long as it secures to us the rights of person and of property, liberty of conscience and of the press, it will be worth defending; and so long as it is worth defending a patriotic militia will cover it with an impenetrable ægis. Partial injuries and occasional mortifications we may be subjected to, but a million of armed freemen, possessed of the means of war, can never be conquered by a foreign foe. To any just system, therefore, calculated to strengthen this natural safeguard of the country I shall cheerfully lend all the aid in my power.

It will be my sincere and constant desire to observe toward the Indian tribes within our limits a just and liberal policy, and to give that humane and considerate attention to their rights and their wants which is consistent with the habits of our Government and the feelings of our people.

The recent demonstration of public sentiment inscribes on the list of Executive duties, in characters too legible to be overlooked, the task of *reform,* which will require particularly the correction of those abuses that have brought the patronage of the Federal Government into conflict with the freedom of elections, and the counteraction of those causes which have disturbed the rightful course of appointment and have placed or continued power in unfaithful or incompetent hands.

[58]

In the performance of a task thus generally delineated I shall endeavor to select men whose diligence and talents will insure in their respective stations able and faithful cooperation, depending for the advancement of the public service more on the integrity and zeal of the public officers than on their numbers.

A diffidence, perhaps too just, in my own qualifications will teach me to look with reverence to the examples of public virtue left by my illustrious predecessors, and with veneration to the lights that flow from the mind that founded and the mind that reformed our system. The same diffidence induces me to hope for instruction and aid from the coordinate branches of the Government, and for the indulgence and support of my fellow-citizens generally. And a firm reliance on the goodness of that Power whose providence mercifully protected our national infancy, and has since upheld our liberties in various vicissitudes, encourages me to offer up my ardent supplications that He will continue to make our beloved country the object of His divine care and gracious benediction.

going to replace Adams' National Republican officeholders with Democrats. This procedure has since become known as the spoils system, because of the term "to the victors belong the spoils."

The Battle of New Orleans

[59]

THE PRESIDENT

Jackson's first term was noteworthy for his veto of the bill to renew the charter of the Bank of the United States. Jackson discontinued deposits of government funds to the bank, thus hastening its demise, and leaving the nation's already precarious financial system in an even more unstable condition. Another noteworthy affair occurred between Jackson and his Cabinet and led indirectly to the election of Van Buren as vice-president in place of Calhoun. When Jackson's Secretary of War, John H. Eaton, married Margaret O'Neale Timberlake the wives of Jackson's Cabinet members refused to accept her because of stories concerning her allegedly questionable virtue. Jackson, thinking of his own dead Rachel, demanded Peggy's acceptance. Martin Van Buren, a widower and Secretary of State, befriended Mrs. Eaton, and thereby enhanced his chances of becoming president in 1836.

The Metropolitan Museum of Art, Bequest of Charles Allen Munn, 1924

THE NATION

With so much activity elsewhere the United States under Jackson was left alone to expand. The Mississippi, formerly considered the nation's perimeter, now became the jumping-off-place for new explorations into the western vastness. Jackson made a bid to purchase Texas from Mexico, but was rebuffed. Beginning in 1830 with the first covered wagon train blazing a trail to the Rockies under the guidance of Jedediah Smith and William Sublette, the trickle of settlers westward became a flood. The census of 1830 showed 12,866,020. Unrest in Europe had caused a large increase in immigrants. May 28, 1830, Jackson signed the Indian Removal Act to resettle many tribes on lands west of the Mississippi, reversing Adams' policy. But this was a palliative that only postponed the final bloody showdown.

Former President John Quincy Adams took his seat in Congress, March 4, 1831, as representative from Massachusetts. On July 4, James Monroe died at 73. He was the third former president to pass away on the anniversary of the signing of the Declaration of Independence. The National Republicans convened in December and nominated Henry Clay as their presidential candidate. In May of 1832 the Democratic party officially adopted their name at the convention in Baltimore, when Jackson was nominated for a second term. In the fall election Andrew Jackson was reëlected president with 687,502 popular votes (219 electoral) to 530,189 popular votes (49 electoral) for Henry Clay. Martin Van Buren was elected vice-president.

THE WORLD

On September 14, 1829, the Treaty of Adrianople ended the Russo-Turkish War. George IV died June 26, 1830, with William IV succeeding him as King of England. France was gripped by a revolution. Charles X abdicated and Louis Philippe became king. In September Charles of Brunswick was dethroned. November saw Poland rebel against Russia. On October 4th Belgium declared its independence. In Italy Ferdinand II became King of Naples on November 8th. And the busy year closed with the death of Simon Bolivar on December 17th. In 1831 a rising unrest gripped the young South American nations and the Russians reëntered Warsaw. The following year Turkey declared war on Egypt.

[60]

BURDENED BY YOUR SORROW OVER RACHEL'S DEATH and in bad health you had intended to serve only one term as president. But the human urge to see your actions justified proves too much to resist, and your smashing victory is deeply gratifying, a fact you acknowledge as you prepare your second inaugural address. Now, as the climax of a simple ceremony in the House of Representatives, you stand and begin your message in a voice weak with fatigue . . . .

Andrew Jackson

[1833–1837]

SECOND INAUGURAL ADDRESS, MARCH 4, 1833

Capitol Steps, Washington, D.C.

Fellow-Citizens:

The will of the American people, expressed through their unsolicited suffrages, calls me before you to pass through the solemnities preparatory to taking upon myself the duties of President of the United States for another term. For their approbation of my public conduct through a period which has not been without its difficulties, and for this renewed expression of their confidence in my good intentions, I am at a loss for terms adequate to the expression of my gratitude. It shall be displayed to the extent of my humble abilities in continued efforts so to administer the Government as to preserve their liberty and promote their happiness.

So many events have occurred within the last four years which have necessarily called forth—sometimes under circumstances the most delicate and painful—my views of the principles and policy which ought to be pursued by the General Government that I need on this occasion but allude to a few leading considerations connected with some of them.

The foreign policy adopted by our Government soon after the formation of our present Constitution, and very generally pursued by successive Administrations, has been crowned with almost complete success, and has elevated our character among the nations of the earth. To do justice to all and to submit to wrong from none has been during my Administration its governing maxim, and so happy have been its results that we are not only at peace with all the world, but have few causes of controversy, and those of minor importance, remaining unadjusted.

In the domestic policy of this Government there are two objects which especially deserve the attention of the people and their representatives, and which have been and will continue to be the subjects of my increasing solicitude. They are the preservation of the rights of the several States and the integrity of the Union.

These great objects are necessarily connected, and can only be attained by an enlightened exercise of the powers of each within its appropriate sphere in conformity with the public will constitutionally expressed. To this end it becomes the duty of all to yield a ready and patriotic submission to the laws constitutionally enacted, and thereby promote and strengthen a proper confidence in those institutions of the several States and of the United States which the people themselves have ordained for their own government.

Cob-rough Andy Jackson spoke in the vernacular of the frontier and was considered by his cultured predecessor, John Quincy Adams, as "a barbarian who could not write a sentence of grammar and hardly could spell his own name." Despite these characteristics—or perhaps because of them—Jackson's popularity with the masses was tremendous and he acknowledged this in his opening remarks.

Jackson's concern with the success of his domestic policy, the preservation of the rights of the several states, and the integrity of the Union formed the nucleus of his second inaugural address.

[61]

My experience in public concerns and the observation of a life somewhat advanced confirm the opinions long since imbibed by me, that the destruction of our State governments or the annihilation of their control over the local concerns of the people would lead directly to revolution and anarchy, and finally to despotism and military domination. In proportion, therefore, as the General Government encroaches upon the rights of the States, in the same proportion does it impair its own power and detract from its ability to fulfill the purposes of its creation. Solemnly impressed with these considerations, my countrymen will ever find me ready to exercise my constitutional powers in arresting measures which may directly or indirectly encroach upon the rights of the States or tend to consolidate all political power in the General Government. But of equal, and, indeed, of incalculable, importance is the union of these States, and the sacred duty of all to contribute to its preservation by a liberal support of the General Government in the exercise of its just powers. You have been wisely admonished to "accustom yourselves to think and speak of the Union as of the palladium of your political safety and prosperity, watching for its preservation with jealous anxiety, discountenancing whatever may suggest even a suspicion that it can in any event be abandoned, and indignantly frowning upon the first dawning of any attempt to alienate any portion of our country from the rest or to enfeeble the sacred ties which now link together the various parts." Without union our independence and liberty would never have been achieved; without union they never can be maintained. Divided into twenty-four, or even a smaller number, of separate communities, we shall see our internal trade burdened with numberless restraints and exactions; communication between distant points and sections obstructed or cut off; our sons made soldiers to deluge with blood the fields they now till in peace; the mass of our people borne down and impoverished by taxes to support armies and navies, and military leaders at the head of their victorious legions becoming our lawgivers and judges. The loss of liberty, of all good government, of peace, plenty, and happiness, must inevitably follow a dissolution of the Union. In supporting it, therefore, we support all that is dear to the freeman and the philanthropist.

The time at which I stand before you is full of interest. The eyes of all nations are fixed on our Republic. The event of the existing crisis will be decisive in the opinion of mankind of the practicability of our federal system of government. Great is the stake placed in our hands; great is the responsibility which must rest upon the people of the United States. Let us realize the importance of the attitude in which we stand before the world. Let us exercise forbearance and firmness. Let us extricate our country from the dangers which surround it and learn wisdom from the lessons they inculcate.

Deeply impressed with the truth of these observations, and under the obligation of that solemn oath which I am about to take, I shall continue to exert all my faculties to maintain the just powers of the Constitution and to transmit unimpaired to posterity the blessings of our Federal Union. At the same time, it will be my aim to inculcate by my official acts the necessity of exercising by the General Government those powers only that are clearly delegated; to encourage simplicity and economy in the expenditures of the Government; to raise no more money from the people than may be requisite for these objects, and in a manner that will best promote the interests of all classes of the community and of all portions of the Union. Constantly bearing in mind that in entering into society "individuals must give up a share of liberty to preserve the rest," it will be my desire so to discharge my duties as to foster with our brethren in all parts of the country a spirit of liberal concession and compromise, and, by reconciling our fellow-citizens to those partial sacrifices which they must unavoidably make for the preservation of a greater good, to recommend our invaluable Government and Union to the confidence and affections of the American people.

Finally, it is my most fervent prayer to that Almighty Being before whom I now stand, and who has kept us in His hands from the infancy of our Republic to the present day, that He will so overrule all my intentions and actions and inspire the hearts of my fellow-citizens that we may be preserved from dangers of all kinds and continue forever a united and happy people.

Only a few days after Jackson's inauguration South Carolina rescinded its Ordinance of Nullification and civil war was averted —or at least indefinitely postponed. With the nation rejoicing in its relief Old Hickory's popular favor reached a new peak— everywhere but in South Carolina, of course.

The Alamo

THE PRESIDENT

Martin Van Buren was the son of a Dutch farmer; the first president who had been born later than the date of the signing of the Declaration of Independence. After his admission to the bar Van Buren moved rapidly upwards through various political offices. He managed Jackson's successful 1828 campaign, and then was elected governor of New York in the same year, a post he filled for only two months. He resigned as governor to become Jackson's Secretary of State in the President's first Cabinet. Heir apparent to Jackson for eight years, Van Buren rode to victory in the election of 1836 on Old Hickory's prodigious popularity.

THE NATION

In 1833 President Jackson removed the government's deposits from the Bank of the United States and placed them in state banks, called "pet banks." As a result the Senate adopted Clay's censure resolutions against Jackson—later expunged.

In 1834, to the delight of most mining interests, the Second Coinage Act established a 16–1 ratio between silver and gold. Samuel F.B. Morse invented the telegraph. Chief Justice John Marshall died July 6, 1835. The Liberty Bell in Philadelphia cracked while tolling his death, July 8. Texas declared its independence from Mexico November 7. The Alamo was besieged and fell to Santa Anna bringing death to Davy Crockett, Jim Bowie, William Travis, and other Texans. On April 21 an army of Texans under General Sam Houston ended the brief but bloody war with a resounding victory over Santa Anna at the Battle of San Jacinto River.

James Madison died at 85, June 28, 1835.

To put a gentle curb on the rising inflation Jackson issued a Specie Circular calling for gold and silver to be accepted as payment for public land in place of paper money. But the curb became a calamity, and the nation's prosperity was trembling at the bursting point during Jackson's last days in office.

In the election of 1836 Democrat Martin Van Buren garnered a popular vote of 762,678 (170 electoral), while the other three principle candidates split 735,651 votes between them: the Anti-Masonic party's William Henry Harrison, 549,567 (73 electoral); the Anti-Jacksonian Democratic party's Hugh L. White, 145,396 (26 electoral); and the new Whig party's Daniel Webster, 41,287 (14 electoral). South Carolina gave 11 electoral votes to Willie P. Mangrum of North Carolina. The Senate was forced to choose from four vice-presidential candidates. They selected Richard M. Johnson by a vote of 33 to 16.

THE WORLD

By 1833 Britain's Reform Bill of 1832 was making itself felt in Parliament, where the nation's growing manufacturing interests began to be represented. Santa Anna became President of Mexico in 1833, and in 1834 France mourned the death of Lafayette.

NO GREATER CONTRAST to Jackson's tall, tough frame and roughhewn character could be found than in your own polished, cultured, almost effeminate personality and small, dapper figure. But you accept your new honor as eighth president with boundless optimism, which is reflected throughout the long inaugural address you prepare in your large, slanting, almost illegible scrawl, aided by your law partner, Benjamin F. Butler, and your sons, John and Abraham. On the day of your inauguration you and Jackson ride up Pennsylvania Avenue in a beautiful phaeton made from timbers taken from the frigate Constitution. *At the Capitol you stand on the historic Capitol steps in cold, wintry weather. With great dignity, in a clear, ringing voice easily heard by your twenty thousand listeners, you begin to deliver your glowing summary of the nation's expansion under democracy, including many references to a prosperity you are unaware Jackson's Specie Circular has already doomed . . . .*

Martin Van Buren

[1837–1841]

INAUGURAL ADDRESS, MARCH 4, 1837

Capitol Steps, Washington, D.C.

FELLOW-CITIZENS: The practice of all my predecessors imposes on me an obligation I cheerfully fulfill—to accompany the first and solemn act of my public trust with an avowal of the principles that will guide me in performing it and an expression of my feelings on assuming a charge so responsible and vast. In imitating their example I tread in the footsteps of illustrious men, whose superiors it is our happiness to believe are not found on the executive calendar of any country. Among them we recognize the earliest and firmest pillars of the Republic—those by whom our national independence was first declared, him who above all others contributed to establish it on the field of battle, and those whose expanded intellect and patriotism constructed, improved, and perfected the inestimable institutions under which we live. If such men in the position I now occupy felt themselves overwhelmed by a sense of gratitude for this the highest of all marks of their country's confidence, and by a consciousness of their inability adequately to discharge the duties of an office so difficult and exalted, how much more must these considerations affect one who can rely on no such claims for favor or forbearance! Unlike all who have preceded me, the Revolution that gave us existence as one people was achieved at the period of my birth; and whilst I contemplate with grateful reverence that memorable event, I feel that I belong to a later age and that I may not expect my countrymen to weigh my actions with the same kind and partial hand.

So sensibly, fellow-citizens, do these circumstances press themselves upon me that I should not dare to enter upon my path of duty did I not look for the generous aid of those who will be associated with me in the various and coordinate branches of the Government; did I not repose with unwavering reliance on the patriotism, the intelligence, and the kindness of a people who never yet deserted a public servant honestly laboring in their cause; and, above all, did I not permit myself humbly to hope for the sustaining support of an ever-watchful and beneficent Providence.

To the confidence and consolation derived from these sources it

The direct, pithy style of both his inaugural addresses was typical of Jackson, the man of action. By contrast, the style of Van Buren's address was wordy and overly dramatic.

The Whig newspapers were quick to criticize Van Buren's sometimes poorly constructed passages. One they criticized was the last sentence of his first paragraph where the "memorable event" mentioned referred to the Revolution; the Whig newspaper writers gleefully chose to believe Van Buren was referring to his birth.

Van Buren evidently tried to use his address to bring together the North and the South. He especially wanted to placate South Carolina. In the second paragraph Van Buren made his first plea for unified support.

would be ungrateful not to add those which spring from our present fortunate condition. Though not altogether exempt from embarrassments that disturb our tranquillity at home and threaten it abroad, yet in all the attributes of a great, happy, and flourishing people we stand without a parallel in the world. Abroad we enjoy the respect and, with scarcely an exception, the friendship of every nation; at home, while our Government quietly but efficiently performs the sole legitimate end of political institutions—in doing the greatest good to the greatest number—we present an aggregate of human prosperity surely not elsewhere to be found.

How imperious, then, is the obligation imposed upon every citizen, in his own sphere of action, whether limited or extended, to exert himself in perpetuating a condition of things so singularly happy! All the lessons of history and experience must be lost upon us if we are content to trust alone to the peculiar advantages we happen to possess. Position and climate and the bounteous resources that nature has scattered with so liberal a hand—even the diffused intelligence and elevated character of our people—will avail us nothing if we fail sacredly to uphold those political institutions that were wisely and deliberately formed with reference to every circumstance that could preserve or might endanger the blessings we enjoy. The thoughtful framers of our Constitution legislated for our country as they found it. Looking upon it with the eyes of statesmen and patriots, they saw all the sources of rapid and wonderful prosperity; but they saw also that various habits, opinions, and institutions peculiar to the various portions of so vast a region were deeply fixed. Distinct sovereignties were in actual existence, whose cordial union was essential to the welfare and happiness of all. Between many of them there was, at least to some extent, a real diversity of interests, liable to be exaggerated through sinister designs; they differed in size, in population, in wealth, and in actual and prospective resources and power; they varied in the character of their industry and staple productions, and [in some] existed domestic institutions which, unwisely disturbed, might endanger the harmony of the whole. Most carefully were all these circumstances weighed, and the foundations of the new Government laid upon principles of reciprocal concession and equitable compromise. The jealousies which the smaller States might entertain of the power of the rest were allayed by a rule of representation confessedly unequal at the time, and designed forever to remain so. A natural fear that the broad scope of general legislation might bear upon and unwisely control particular interests was counteracted by limits strictly drawn around the action of the Federal authority, and to the people and the States was left unimpaired their sovereign power over the innumerable subjects embraced in the internal government of a just republic, excepting such only as necessarily appertain to the concerns of the whole confederacy or its intercourse as a united community with the other nations of the world.

This provident forecast has been verified by time. Half a century, teeming with extraordinary events, and elsewhere producing astonishing results, has passed along, but on our institutions it has left no injurious mark. From a small community we have risen to a people powerful in numbers and in strength; but with our increase has gone hand in hand the progress of just principles. The privileges, civil and religious, of the humblest individual are still sacredly protected at home, and while the valor and fortitude of our people have removed far from us the slightest apprehension of foreign power,

The "human prosperity" Van Buren spoke of so glowingly would soon be only a memory. The financial panic had already begun and soon would grip the entire nation.

Another indirect reference to South Carolina and the nullificationists.

[66]

they have not yet induced us in a single instance to forget what is right. Our commerce has been extended to the remotest nations; the value and even nature of our productions have been greatly changed; a wide difference has arisen in the relative wealth and resources of every portion of our country; yet the spirit of mutual regard and of faithful adherence to existing compacts has continued to prevail in our councils and never long been absent from our conduct. We have learned by experience a fruitful lesson—that an implicit and undeviating adherence to the principles on which we set out can carry us prosperously onward through all the conflicts of circumstances and vicissitudes inseparable from the lapse of years.

The success that has thus attended our great experiment is in itself a sufficient cause for gratitude, on account of the happiness it has actually conferred and the example it has unanswerably given. But to me, my fellow-citizens, looking forward to the far-distant future with ardent prayers and confiding hopes, this retrospect presents a ground for still deeper delight. It impresses on my mind a firm belief that the perpetuity of our institutions depends upon ourselves; that if we maintain the principles on which they were established they are destined to confer their benefits on countless generations yet to come, and that America will present to every friend of mankind the cheering proof that a popular government, wisely formed, is wanting in no element of endurance or strength. Fifty years ago its rapid failure was boldly predicted. Latent and uncontrollable causes of dissolution were supposed to exist even by the wise and good, and not only did unfriendly or speculative theorists anticipate for us the fate of past republics, but the fears of many an honest patriot overbalanced his sanguine hopes. Look back on these forebodings, not hastily but reluctantly made, and see how in every instance they have completely failed.

An imperfect experience during the struggles of the Revolution was supposed to warrant the belief that the people would not bear the taxation requisite to discharge an immense public debt already incurred and to pay the necessary expenses of the Government. The cost of two wars has been paid, not only without a murmur, but with unequaled alacrity. No one is now left to doubt that every burden will be cheerfully borne that may be necessary to sustain our civil institutions or guard our honor or welfare. Indeed, all experience has shown that the willingness of the people to contribute to these ends in cases of emergency has uniformly outrun the confidence of their representatives.

In the early stages of the new Government, when all felt the imposing influence as they recognized the unequaled services of the first President, it was a common sentiment that the great weight of his character could alone bind the discordant materials of our Government together and save us from the violence of contending factions. Since his death nearly forty years are gone. Party exasperation has been often carried to its highest point; the virtue and fortitude of the people have sometimes been greatly tried; yet our system, purified and enhanced in value by all it has encountered, still preserves its spirit of free and fearless discussion, blended with unimpaired fraternal feeling.

The capacity of the people for self-government, and their willingness, from a high sense of duty and without those exhibitions of coercive power so generally employed in other countries, to submit to all needful restraints and exactions of municipal law, have also been favorably exemplified in the history of the American States.

More self-congratulatory thoughts, which the impending panic would shortly refute.

Van Buren couldn't have known how much of a prophet history would prove him. America has indeed continued to present "the cheering proof that a popular government, wisely formed, is wanting in no element of endurance or strength."

Another veiled reference to South Carolina's reluctance to pay Federal taxes. But note how adroitly Van Buren sugar-coated his thought. The "no one" mentioned could well be South Carolina's fiery John C. Calhoun. It was Van Buren's way of saying, "Come home; all is forgiven." This Calhoun soon did, for he was still ambitious to follow Van Buren as president and Van Buren, a master at handling men, in this and the following two paragraphs made it easy for Calhoun to renew his backing of Van Buren without loss of face.

[67]

Van Buren knew that the Abolitionists, who wanted to end slavery in America, felt that he had become a tool of the South because of his silence on the subject. But here he deplored mob violence and followed with a masterfully worded passage of subtle flattery, as he appealed to the "generous patriotism and sound common sense" of the great mass of fellow citizens to avoid future outbursts.

The "recent apprehensions of a similar conflict" stemmed from Jackson's message to Congress of December, 1834, in which he called for reprisals against the French government if they did not immediately pay the twenty-five million francs owed the United States as a result of raids on American commercial shipping during the Napoleonic Wars. France eventually backed down and paid up, and war was averted.

The population had risen to an estimated 15,000,000 by 1837.

Occasionally, it is true, the ardor of public sentiment, outrunning the regular progress of the judicial tribunals or seeking to reach cases not denounced as criminal by the existing law, has displayed itself in a manner calculated to give pain to the friends of free government and to encourage the hopes of those who wish for its overthrow. These occurrences, however, have been far less frequent in our country than in any other of equal population on the globe, and with the diffusion of intelligence it may well be hoped that they will constantly diminish in frequency and violence. The generous patriotism and sound common sense of the great mass of our fellow-citizens will assuredly in time produce this result; for as every assumption of illegal power not only wounds the majesty of the law, but furnishes a pretext for abridging the liberties of the people, the latter have the most direct and permanent interest in preserving the landmarks of social order and maintaining on all occasions the inviolability of those constitutional and legal provisions which they themselves have made.

In a supposed unfitness of our institutions for those hostile emergencies which no country can always avoid their friends found a fruitful source of apprehension, their enemies of hope. While they foresaw less promptness of action than in governments differently formed, they overlooked the far more important consideration that with us war could never be the result of individual or irresponsible will, but must be a measure of redress for injuries sustained, voluntarily resorted to by those who were to bear the necessary sacrifice, who would consequently feel an individual interest in the contest, and whose energy would be commensurate with the difficulties to be encountered. Actual events have proved their error; the last war, far from impairing, gave new confidence to our Government, and amid recent apprehensions of a similar conflict we saw that the energies of our country would not be wanting in ample season to vindicate its rights. We may not possess, as we should not desire to possess, the extended and ever-ready military organization of other nations; we may occasionally suffer in the outset for the want of it; but among ourselves all doubt upon this great point has ceased, while a salutary experience will prevent a contrary opinion from inviting aggression from abroad.

Certain danger was foretold from the extension of our territory, the multiplication of States, and the increase of population. Our system was supposed to be adapted only to boundaries comparatively narrow. These have been widened beyond conjecture; the members of our Confederacy are already doubled, and the numbers of our people are incredibly augmented. The alleged causes of danger have long surpassed anticipation, but none of the consequences have followed. The power and influence of the Republic have risen to a height obvious to all mankind; respect for its authority was not more apparent at its ancient than it is at its present limits; new and inexhaustible sources of general prosperity have been opened; the effects of distance have been averted by the inventive genius of our people, developed and fostered by the spirit of our institutions; and the enlarged variety and amount of interests, productions, and pursuits have strengthened the chain of mutual dependence and formed a circle of mutual benefits too apparent ever to be overlooked.

In justly balancing the powers of the Federal and State authorities difficulties nearly insurmountable arose at the outset, and subsequent collisions were deemed inevitable. Amid these it was

[68]

scarcely believed possible that a scheme of government so complex in construction could remain uninjured. From time to time embarrassments have certainly occurred; but how just is the confidence of future safety imparted by the knowledge that each in succession has been happily removed! Overlooking partial and temporary evils as inseparable from the practical operation of all human institutions, and looking only to the general result, every patriot has reason to be satisfied. While the Federal Government has successfully performed its appropriate functions in relation to foreign affairs and concerns evidently national, that of every State has remarkably improved in protecting and developing local interests and individual welfare; and if the vibrations of authority have occasionally tended too much toward one or the other, it is unquestionably certain that the ultimate operation of the entire system has been to strengthen all the existing institutions and to elevate our whole country in prosperity and renown.

The last, perhaps the greatest, of the prominent sources of discord and disaster supposed to lurk in our political condition was the institution of domestic slavery. Our forefathers were deeply impressed with the delicacy of this subject, and they treated it with a forbearance so evidently wise that in spite of every sinister foreboding it never until the present period disturbed the tranquillity of our common country. Such a result is sufficient evidence of the justice and the patriotism of their course; it is evidence not to be mistaken that an adherence to it can prevent all embarrassment from this as well as from every other anticipated cause of difficulty or danger. Have not recent events made it obvious to the slightest reflection that the least deviation from this spirit of forbearance is injurious to every interest, that of humanity included? Amidst the violence of excited passions this generous and fraternal feeling has been sometimes disregarded; and standing as I now do before my countrymen, in this high place of honor and of trust, I can not refrain from anxiously invoking my fellow-citizens never to be deaf to its dictates. Perceiving before my election the deep interest this subject was beginning to excite, I believed it a solemn duty fully to make known my sentiments in regard to it, and now, when every motive for misrepresentation has passed away, I trust that they will be candidly weighed and understood. At least they will be my standard of conduct in the path before me. I then declared that if the desire of those of my countrymen who were favorable to my election was gratified "I must go into the Presidential chair the inflexible and uncompromising opponent of every attempt on the part of Congress to abolish slavery in the District of Columbia against the wishes of the slaveholding States, and also with a determination equally decided to resist the slightest interference with it in the States where it exists." I submitted also to my fellow-citizens, with fullness and frankness, the reasons which led me to this determination. The result authorizes me to believe that they have been approved and are confided in by a majority of the people of the United States, including those whom they most immediately affect. It now only remains to add that no bill conflicting with these views can ever receive my constitutional sanction. These opinions have been adopted in the firm belief that they are in accordance with the spirit that actuated the venerated fathers of the Republic, and that succeeding experience has proved them to be humane, patriotic, expedient, honorable, and just. If the agitation of this subject was intended to reach the stability of our institutions, enough has

Another reference to the "embarrassment" caused by South Carolina. Again note Van Buren's face-saving choice of words: "... every patriot has reason to be satisfied."

Still another reference to South Carolina's reluctance to accept Federal authority.

Here Van Buren dropped subtlety in favor of a clear-cut statement as to where he stood on the question of slavery. In a pre-election speech Van Buren had flatly declared he would oppose the abolition of slavery in the District of Columbia, nor would he interfere with it "in the States where it exists." However, no mention was made of slavery in the territories.

occurred to show that it has signally failed, and that in this as in every other instance the apprehensions of the timid and the hopes of the wicked for the destruction of our Government are again destined to be disappointed. Here and there, indeed, scenes of dangerous excitement have occurred, terrifying instances of local violence have been witnessed, and a reckless disregard of the consequences of their conduct has exposed individuals to popular indignation; but neither masses of the people nor sections of the country have been swerved from their devotion to the bond of union and the principles it has made sacred. It will be ever thus. Such attempts at dangerous agitation may periodically return, but with each the object will be better understood. That predominating affection for our political system which prevails throughout our territorial limits, that calm and enlightened judgment which ultimately governs our people as one vast body, will always be at hand to resist and control every effort, foreign or domestic, which aims or would lead to overthrow our institutions.

What can be more gratifying than such a retrospect as this? We look back on obstacles avoided and dangers overcome, on expectations more than realized and prosperity perfectly secured. To the hopes of the hostile, the fears of the timid, and the doubts of the anxious actual experience has given the conclusive reply. We have seen time gradually dispel every unfavorable foreboding and our Constitution surmount every adverse circumstance dreaded at the outset as beyond control. Present excitement will at all times magnify present dangers, but true philosophy must teach us that none more threatening than the past can remain to be overcome; and we ought (for we have just reason) to entertain an abiding confidence in the stability of our institutions and an entire conviction that if administered in the true form, character, and spirit in which they were established they are abundantly adequate to preserve to us and our children the rich blessings already derived from them, to make our beloved land for a thousand generations that chosen spot where happiness springs from a perfect equality of political rights.

For myself, therefore, I desire to declare that the principle that will govern me in the high duty to which my country calls me is a strict adherence to the letter and spirit of the Constitution as it was designed by those who framed it. Looking back to it as a sacred instrument carefully and not easily framed; remembering that it was throughout a work of concession and compromise; viewing it as limited to national objects; regarding it as leaving to the people and the States all power not explicitly parted with, I shall endeavor to preserve, protect, and defend it by anxiously referring to its provision for direction in every action. To matters of domestic concernment which it has intrusted to the Federal Government and to such as relate to our intercourse with foreign nations I shall zealously devote myself; beyond those limits I shall never pass.

To enter on this occasion into a further or more minute exposition of my views on the various questions of domestic policy would be as obtrusive as it is probably unexpected. Before the suffrages of my countrymen were conferred upon me I submitted to them, with great precision, my opinions on all the most prominent of these subjects. Those opinions I shall endeavor to carry out with my utmost ability.

Our course of foreign policy has been so uniform and intelligible as to constitute a rule of Executive conduct which leaves little to my discretion, unless, indeed, I were willing to run counter to the lights of experience and the known opinions of my constituents. We sedulously cultivate the friendship of all nations as the conditions most compatible with our welfare and the principles of our Government. We decline alliances as adverse to our peace. We desire commercial relations on equal terms, being ever willing to give a fair equivalent for advantages received. We endeavor to conduct our intercourse with openness and sincerity, promptly avowing our objects and seeking to establish that mutual frankness which is as beneficial in the dealings of nations as of men. We have no disposition and we disclaim all right to meddle in disputes, whether internal or foreign, that may molest other countries, regarding them in their actual state as social communities, and preserving a strict neutrality in all their controversies. Well knowing the tried valor of our people and our exhaustless resources, we neither anticipate nor fear any designed aggression; and in the consciousness of our own just conduct we feel a security that we shall never be called upon to exert our determination never to permit an invasion of our rights without punishment or redress.

In approaching, then, in the presence of my assembled countrymen, to make the solemn promise that yet remains, and to pledge myself that I will faithfully execute the office I am about to fill, I bring with me a settled purpose to maintain the institutions of my country, which I trust will atone for the errors I commit.

In receiving from the people the sacred trust twice confided to my illustrious predecessor, and which he has discharged so faithfully and so well, I know that I can not expect to perform the arduous task with equal ability and success. But united as I have been in his counsels, a daily witness of his exclusive and unsurpassed devotion to his country's welfare, agreeing with him in sentiments which his countrymen have warmly supported, and permitted to partake largely of his confidence, I may hope that somewhat of the same cheering approbation will be found to attend upon my path. For him I but express with my own the wishes of all, that he may yet long live to enjoy the brilliant evening of his well-spent life; and for myself, conscious of but one desire, faithfully to serve my country, I throw myself without fear on its justice and its kindness. Beyond that I only look to the gracious protection of the Divine Being whose strengthening support I humbly solicit, and whom I fervently pray to look down upon us all. May it be among the dispensations of His providence to bless our beloved country with honors and with length of days. May her ways be ways of pleasantness and all her paths be peace!

On matters of foreign policy Van Buren was equally explicit, although in this statement of neutrality he seemed to leave the door open for a repudiation of the Monroe Doctrine should he be faced with a crisis.

Van Buren concluded with a sincere expression of his filial love for the aging Jackson, who had left his sickbed to attend the inauguration. With his long white hair blowing in the nippy gusts, Jackson sat among the notables flanking the incoming president during this long address.

Despite the brave optimism of Van Buren's closing words he was to enjoy his heady triumph for less than two months, before the cataclysmic Panic of 1837 convulsed the nation's economy.

THE PRESIDENT

William Henry Harrison was the son of Benjamin Harrison, one of the signers of the Declaration of Independence. He won an early reputation as an Indian fighter in Ohio with "Mad Anthony" Wayne. This later led to Harrison's appointment as governor of the Indiana Territory. In 1811 he earned the name of "Old Tippecanoe," after a costly victory over Tecumseh's brother, The Prophet. After a decisive victory in the Battle of the Thames during the War of 1812 a luster was added to Harrison's name that followed him even into semiretirement. When the Whigs disagreed on Clay as a candidate they looked for a man to oppose the aristocratic Whig candidate, Van Buren. They dusted off Harrison's hero's halo, set it aglitter again on the aging old warrior's brow; paraded him as a simple, virtuous strong man who would pull the nation out of the ever-deepening depression. A majority of the voting public bought the propaganda package—among them the pathetic figure of Harrison himself.

THE NATION

Still unaffected by foreign unrest America's amazing expansion westward continued. Arkansas became the 25th state, June 15, 1836, and Michigan followed, January 26, 1837. But Van Buren had hardly taken office when New York banks suspended specie payments, May 10, and triggered the Panic of 1837. More than 600 banks failed before the year ended.

In the face of an evasive Congress the nation's first antislavery party—the Liberty party—was organized. The Whigs, convening in December, turned away from controversial Henry Clay after an indecisive first ballot and dredged up the politically unblemished William Henry Harrison, the retired army hero of Tippecanoe. He had made a good showing in the preceding election, but had since become court clerk of Ohio's Hamilton county near his farm. In what the Whigs considered a superbly shrewd move—actually destined to backfire drastically—John Tyler, a Democrat and firm believer with Calhoun in states' rights, was nominated for the vice-presidency to draw votes from the South. The Democrats met in May, 1840, to select Van Buren but failed to agree on his running mate, as Vice-President Richard H. Johnson was felt to be unacceptable.

The Whig campaign of 1840 featured log cabins, coonskins, and barrels of hard cider. In mudslinging and hoopla the campaign topped any of those preceding it, and resulted in the victory of Harrison, who polled 1,275,016 popular votes (234 electoral) to Van Buren's 1,129,012 popular votes (60 electoral) with the hapless Liberty party's candidate, James G. Birney, the recipient of only 7,069 popular votes. John Tyler was elected vice-president.

THE WORLD

With the death of William IV on June 20, 1837, the accession of Queen Victoria ushered in a new era for Great Britain. In 1838 a French fleet set out against Mexico. The following year England sent her first large group of settlers to New Zealand and became concerned at the outbreak of war between Egypt and Turkey. Early in 1840 Queen Victoria married Prince Albert of Saxe-Coburg. In June Frederick William III of Prussia died and was succeeded by Frederick William IV.

YOU, AT SIXTY-EIGHT—the oldest president-elect in the nation's history—believe everything your campaign managers have said about you, and never suspect you have been the unwitting tool of the Whig leaders to whom you represent only a hollow figurehead. On the day of your inauguration you insist on living up to the picture of a strong man which they have sold the public. And so you make the two-hour trip to the Capitol on a white horse, with a bare head and without a saddle coat despite the raw and windy day. The huge inaugural crowd on the Capitol steps is shivering long before you finish your lengthy, platitude-packed address, which takes one hour and forty minutes to read . . . .

William Henry Harrison

[1841]

INAUGURAL ADDRESS, MARCH 4, 1841

Capitol Steps, Washington, D.C.

Called from a retirement which I had supposed was to continue for the residue of my life to fill the chief executive office of this great and free nation, I appear before you, fellow-citizens, to take the oaths which the Constitution prescribes as a necessary qualification for the performance of its duties; and in obedience to a custom coeval with our Government and what I believe to be your expectations I proceed to present to you a summary of the principles which will govern me in the discharge of the duties which I shall be called upon to perform.

It was the remark of a Roman consul in an early period of that celebrated Republic that a most striking contrast was observable in the conduct of candidates for offices of power and trust before and after obtaining them, they seldom carrying out in the latter case the pledges and promises made in the former. However much the world may have improved in many respects in the lapse of upward of two thousand years since the remark was made by the virtuous and indignant Roman, I fear that a strict examination of the annals of some of the modern elective governments would develop similar instances of violated confidence.

Although the fiat of the people has gone forth proclaiming me the Chief Magistrate of this glorious Union, nothing upon their part remaining to be done, it may be thought that a motive may exist to keep up the delusion under which they may be supposed to have acted in relation to my principles and opinions; and perhaps there may be some in this assembly who have come here either prepared to condemn those I shall now deliver, or, approving them, to doubt the sincerity with which they are now uttered. But the lapse of a few months will confirm or dispel their fears. The outline of principles to govern and measures to be adopted by an Administration not yet begun will soon be exchanged for immutable history, and I shall stand either exonerated by my countrymen or classed with the mass of those who promised that they might deceive and flattered with the intention to betray. However strong may be my present purpose to realize the expectations of a magnanimous and confiding people, I too well understand the dangerous temptations to which I shall be exposed from the magnitude of the power which

There has been no more pathetic sight at an inaugural than that of the old and infirm Harrison doing his gallant best, in the icy northwest wind sweeping around the Capitol building, to deliver his long address to the sneezing, half-frozen crowd. But the man's hopeless inadequacy for the job thrust upon him by fate—and the Whigs—was painfully apparent to those who heard the address or read it in the newspapers later on. Indeed, the incoming Secretary of State, Daniel Webster, spent many hours just before the inaugural trying to revise Harrison's flowery rhetoric. Yet it was such an impossible task that when Webster's landlady asked why he looked so weary Webster replied, "In the last twelve hours I have killed seventeen Roman proconsuls . . . dead as smelts, every one."

Stripped to essentials the address revealed that Harrison's basic policy would be to follow the leadership of Congress.

No further analysis is necessary because Harrison never lived to see any of his ideas carried out. Only one month to the day after his inauguration the pitiful old man was dead—the first president to die in office. His assassin was pneumonia, evidently brought on by the long exposure at his inaugural and by overwork, due to the avalanche of Whig office seekers who descended upon him the moment he took office.

it has been the pleasure of the people to commit to my hands not to place my chief confidence upon the aid of that Almighty Power which has hitherto protected me and enabled me to bring to favorable issues other important but still greatly inferior trusts heretofore confided to me by my country.

The broad foundation upon which our Constitution rests being the people—a breath of theirs having made, as a breath can unmake, change, or modify it—it can be assigned to none of the great divisions of government but to that of democracy. If such is its theory, those who are called upon to administer it must recognize as its leading principle the duty of shaping their measures so as to produce the greatest good to the greatest number. But with these broad admissions, if we would compare the sovereignty acknowledged to exist in the mass of our people with the power claimed by other sovereignties, even by those which have been considered most purely democratic, we shall find a most essential difference. All others lay claim to power limited only by their own will. The majority of our citizens, on the contrary, possess a sovereignty with an amount of power precisely equal to that which has been granted to them by the parties to the national compact, and nothing beyond. We admit of no government by divine right, believing that so far as power is concerned the Beneficent Creator has made no distinction amongst men; that all are upon an equality, and that the only legitimate right to govern is an express grant of power from the governed. The Constitution of the United States is the instrument containing this grant of power to the several departments composing the Government. On an examination of that instrument it will be found to contain declarations of power granted and of power withheld. The latter is also susceptible of division into power which the majority had the right to grant, but which they did not think proper to intrust to their agents, and that which they could not have granted, not being possessed by themselves. In other words, there are certain rights possessed by each individual American citizen which in his compact with the others he has never surrendered. Some of them, indeed, he is unable to surrender, being, in the language of our system, unalienable. The boasted privilege of a Roman citizen was to him a shield only against a petty provincial ruler, whilst the proud democrat of Athens would console himself under a sentence of death for a supposed violation of the national faith—which no one understood and which at times was the subject of the mockery of all—or the banishment from his home, his family, and his country with or without an alleged cause, that it was the act not of a single tyrant or hated aristocracy, but of his assembled countrymen. Far different is the power of our sovereignty. It can interfere with no one's faith, prescribe forms of worship for no one's observance, inflict no punishment but after well-ascertained guilt, the result of investigation under rules prescribed by the Constitution itself. These precious privileges, and those scarcely less important of giving expression to his thoughts and opinions, either by writing or speaking, unrestrained but by the liability for injury to others, and that of a full participation in all the advantages which flow from the Government, the acknowledged property of all, the American citizen derives from no charter granted by his fellow-man. He claims them because he is himself a man, fashioned by the same Almighty hand as the rest of his species and entitled to a full share of the blessings with which He has endowed them. Notwithstanding the limited sovereignty possessed by the people of the United States

[74]

and the restricted grant of power to the Government which they have adopted, enough has been given to accomplish all the objects for which it was created. It has been found powerful in war, and hitherto justice has been administered, an intimate union effected, domestic tranquillity preserved, and personal liberty secured to the citizen. As was to be expected, however, from the defect of language and the necessarily sententious manner in which the Constitution is written, disputes have arisen as to the amount of power which it has actually granted or was intended to grant.

This is more particularly the case in relation to that part of the instrument which treats of the legislative branch, and not only as regards the exercise of powers claimed under a general clause giving that body the authority to pass laws necessary to carry into effect the specified powers, but in relation to the latter also. It is, however, consolatory to reflect that *most* of the instances of alleged departure from the letter or spirit of the Constitution have ultimately received the sanction of a majority of the people. And the fact that many of our statesmen most distinguished for talent and patriotism have been at one time or other of their political career on both sides of each of the most warmly disputed questions forces upon us the inference that the errors, if errors there were, are attributable to the intrinsic difficulty in many instances of ascertaining the intentions of the framers of the Constitution rather than the influence of any sinister or unpatriotic motive. But the great danger to our institutions does not appear to me to be in a usurpation by the Government of power not granted by the people, but by the accumulation in one of the departments of that which was assigned to others. Limited as are the powers which have been granted, still enough have been granted to constitute a despotism if concentrated in one of the departments. This danger is greatly heightened, as it has been always observable that men are less jealous of encroachments of one department upon another than upon their own reserved rights. When the Constitution of the United States first came from the hands of the Convention which formed it, many of the sternest republicans of the day were alarmed at the extent of the power which had been granted to the Federal Government, and more particularly of that portion which had been assigned to the executive branch. There were in it features which appeared not to be in harmony with their ideas of a simple representative democracy or republic, and knowing the tendency of power to increase itself, particularly when exercised by a single individual, predictions were made that at no very remote period the Government would terminate in virtual monarchy. It would not become me to say that the fears of these patriots have been already realized; but as I sincerely believe that the tendency of measures and of men's opinions for some years past has been in that direction, it is, I conceive, strictly proper that I should take this occasion to repeat the assurances I have heretofore given of my determination to arrest the progress of that tendency if it really exists and restore the Government to its pristine health and vigor, as far as this can be effected by any legitimate exercise of the power placed in my hands.

I proceed to state in as summary a manner as I can my opinion of the sources of the evils which have been so extensively complained of and the correctives which may be applied. Some of the former are unquestionably to be found in the defects of the Constitution; others, in my judgment, are attributable to a misconstruction of some of its provisions. Of the former is the eligibility of the same individual to a second term of the Presidency. The sagacious mind of Mr. Jefferson early saw and lamented this error, and attempts have been made, hitherto without success, to apply the amendatory power of the States to its correction. As, however, one mode of correction is in the power of every President, and consequently in mine, it would be useless, and perhaps invidious, to enumerate the evils of which, in the opinion of many of our fellow-citizens, this error of the sages who framed the Constitution may have been the source and the bitter fruits which we are still to gather from it if it continues to disfigure our system. It may be observed, however, as a general remark, that republics can commit no greater error than to adopt or continue any feature in their systems of government which may be calculated to create or increase the love of power in the bosoms of those to whom necessity obliges them to commit the management of their affairs; and surely nothing is more likely to produce such a state of mind than the long continuance of an office of high trust. Nothing can be more corrupting, nothing more destructive of all those noble feelings which belong to the character of a devoted republican patriot. When this corrupting passion once takes possession of the human mind, like the love of gold it becomes insatiable. It is the never-dying worm in his bosom, grows with his growth and strengthens with the declining years of its victim. If this is true, it is the part of wisdom for a republic to limit the service of that officer at least to whom she has intrusted the management of her foreign relations, the execution of her laws, and the command of her armies and navies to a period so short as to prevent his forgetting that he is the accountable agent, not the principal; the servant, not the master. Until an amendment of the Constitution can be effected public opinion may secure the desired object. I give my aid to it by renewing the pledge heretofore given that under no circumstances will I consent to serve a second term.

But if there is danger to public liberty from the acknowledged defects of the Constitution in the want of limit to the continuance of the Executive power in the same hands, there is, I apprehend, not much less from a misconstruction of that instrument as it regards the powers actually given. I can not conceive that by a fair construction any or either of its provisions would be found to constitute the President a part of the legislative power. It can not be claimed from the power to recommend, since, although enjoined as a duty upon him, it is a privilege which he holds in common with every other citizen; and although there may be something more of confidence in the propriety of the measures recommended in the one case than in the other, in the obligations of ultimate decision there can be no difference. In the language of the Constitution, "all the legislative powers" which it grants "are vested in the Congress of the United States." It would be a solecism in language to say that any portion of these is not included in the whole.

It may be said, indeed, that the Constitution has given to the Executive the power to annul the acts of the legislative body by refusing to them his assent. So a similar power has necessarily resulted from that instrument to the judiciary, and yet the judiciary forms no part of the Legislature. There is, it is true, this difference between these grants of power: The Executive can put his negative upon the acts of the Legislature for other cause than that of want of conformity to the Constitution, whilst the judiciary can only declare void those which violate that instrument. But the decision of the judiciary is final in such a case, whereas in every instance where

The irony of this promise became all too clear when Harrison died a month later.

[76]

the veto of the Executive is applied it may be overcome by a vote of two-thirds of both Houses of Congress. The negative upon the acts of the legislative by the executive authority, and that in the hands of one individual, would seem to be an incongruity in our system. Like some others of a similar character, however, it appears to be highly expedient, and if used only with the forebearance and in the spirit which was intended by its authors it may be productive of great good and be found one of the best safeguards to the Union. At the period of the formation of the Constitution the principle does not appear to have enjoyed much favor in the State governments. It existed but in two, and in one of these there was a plural executive. If we would search for the motives which operated upon the purely patriotic and enlightened assembly which framed the Constitution for the adoption of a provision so apparently repugnant to the leading democratic principle that the majority should govern, we must reject the idea that they anticipated from it any benefit to the ordinary course of legislation. They knew too well the high degree of intelligence which existed among the people and the enlightened character of the State legislatures not to have the fullest confidence that the two bodies elected by them would be worthy representatives of such constitutents, and, of course, that they would require no aid in conceiving and maturing the measures which the circumstances of the country might require. And it is preposterous to suppose that a thought could for a moment have been entertained that the President, placed at the capital, in the center of the country, could better understand the wants and wishes of the people than their own immediate representatives, who spend a part of every year among them, living with them, often laboring with them, and bound to them by the triple tie of interest, duty, and affection. To assist or control Congress, then, in its ordinary legislation could not, I conceive, have been the motive for conferring the veto power on the President. This argument acquires additional force from the fact of its never having been thus used by the first six Presidents—and two of them were members of the Convention, one presiding over its deliberations and the other bearing a larger share in consummating the labors of that august body than any other person. But if bills were never returned to Congress by either of the Presidents above referred to upon the ground of their being inexpedient or not as well adapted as they might be to the wants of the people, the veto was applied upon that of want of conformity to the Constitution or because errors had been committed from a too hasty enactment.

There is another ground for the adoption of the veto principle, which had probably more influence in recommending it to the Convention than any other. I refer to the security which it gives to the just and equitable action of the Legislature upon all parts of the Union. It could not but have occurred to the Convention that in a country so extensive, embracing so great a variety of soil and climate, and consequently of products, and which from the same causes must ever exhibit a great difference in the amount of the population of its various sections, calling for a great diversity in the employments of the people, that the legislation of the majority might not always justly regard the rights and interests of the minority, and that acts of this character might be passed under an express grant by the words of the Constitution, and therefore not within the competency of the judiciary to declare void; that however enlightened and patriotic they might suppose from past

[77]

experience the members of Congress might be, and however largely partaking, in the general, of the liberal feelings of the people, it was impossible to expect that bodies so constituted should not sometimes be controlled by local interests and sectional feelings. It was proper, therefore, to provide some umpire from whose situation and mode of appointment more independence and freedom from such influences might be expected. Such a one was afforded by the executive department constituted by the Constitution. A person elected to that high office, having his constituents in every section, State, and subdivision of the Union, must consider himself bound by the most solemn sanctions to guard, protect, and defend the rights of all and of every portion, great or small, from the injustice and oppression of the rest. I consider the veto power, therefore, given by the Constitution to the Executive of the United States solely as a conservative power, to be used only first, to protect the Constitution from violation; secondly, the people from the effects of hasty legislation where their will has been probably disregarded or not well understood, and, thirdly, to prevent the effects of combinations violative to the rights of minorities. In reference to the second of these objects I may observe that I consider it the right and privilege of the people to decide disputed points of the Constitution arising from the general grant of power to Congress to carry into effect the powers expressly given; and I believe with Mr. Madison that "repeated recognitions under varied circumstances in acts of the legislative, executive, and judicial branches of the Government, accompanied by indications in different modes of the concurrence of the general will of the nation," as affording to the President sufficient authority for his considering such disputed points as settled.

Upward of half a century has elapsed since the adoption of the present form of government. It would be an object more highly desirable than the gratification of the curiosity of speculative statesmen if its precise situation could be ascertained, a fair exhibit made of the operations of each of its departments, of the powers which they respectively claim and exercise, of the collisions which have occurred between them or between the whole Government and those of the States or either of them. We could then compare our actual condition after fifty years' trial of our system with what it was in the commencement of its operations and ascertain whether the predictions of the patriots who opposed its adoption or the confident hopes of its advocates have been best realized. The great dread of the former seems to have been that the reserved powers of the States would be absorbed by those of the Federal Government and a consolidated power established, leaving to the States the shadow only of that independent action for which they had so zealously contended and on the preservation of which they relied as the last hope of liberty. Without denying that the result to which they looked with so much apprehension is in the way of being realized, it is obvious that they did not clearly see the mode of its accomplishment. The General Government has seized upon none of the reserved rights of the States. As far as any open warfare may have gone, the State authorities have amply maintained their rights. To a casual observer our system presents no appearance of discord between the different members which compose it. Even the addition of many new ones has produced no jarring. They move in their respective orbits in perfect harmony with the central head and with each other. But there is still an undercurrent at work by which, if not seasonably checked, the worst apprehensions of our antifederal patriots will be realized, and not only will the State authorities be overshadowed by the great increase of power in the executive department of the General Government, but the character of that Government, if not its designation, be essentially and radically changed. This state of things has been in part effected by causes inherent in the Constitution and in part by the never-failing tendency of political power to increase itself. By making the President the sole distributer of all the patronage of the Government the framers of the Constitution do not appear to have anticipated at how short a period it would become a formidable instrument to control the free operations of the State governments. Of trifling importance at first, it had early in Mr. Jefferson's Administration become so powerful as to create great alarm in the mind of that patriot from the potent influence it might exert in controlling the freedom of the elective franchise. If such could have then been the effects of its influence, how much greater must be the danger at this time, quadrupled in amount as it certainly is and more completely under the control of the Executive will than their construction of their powers allowed or the forbearing characters of all the early Presidents permitted them to make. But it is not by the extent of its patronage alone that the executive department has become dangerous, but by the use which it appears may be made of the appointing power to bring under its control the whole revenues of the country. The Constitution has declared it to be the duty of the President to see that the laws are executed, and it makes him the Commander in Chief of the Armies and Navy of the United States. If the opinion of the most approved writers upon that species of mixed government which in modern Europe is termed *monarchy* in contradistinction to *despotism* is correct, there was wanting no other addition to the powers of our Chief Magistrate to stamp a monarchical character on our Government but the control of the public finances; and to me it appears strange indeed that anyone should doubt that the entire control which the President possesses over the officers who have the custody of the public money, by the power of removal with or without cause, does, for all mischievous purposes at least, virtually subject the treasure also to his disposal. The first Roman Emperor, in his attempt to seize the sacred treasure, silenced the opposition of the officer to whose charge it had been committed by a significant allusion to his sword. By a selection of political instruments for the care of the public money a reference to their commissions by a President would be quite as effectual an argument as that of Caesar to the Roman knight. I am not insensible of the great difficulty that exists in drawing a proper plan for the safe-keeping and disbursement of the public revenues, and I know the importance which has been attached by men of great abilities and patriotism to the divorce, as it is called, of the Treasury from the banking institutions. It is not the divorce which is complained of, but the unhallowed union of the Treasury with the executive department, which has created such extensive alarm. To this danger to our republican institutions and that created by the influence given to the Executive through the instrumentality of the Federal officers I propose to apply all the remedies which may be at my command. It was certainly a great error in the framers of the Constitution not to have made the officer at the head of the Treasury Department entirely independent of the Executive. He should at least have been removable only upon the demand of the popular branch of the Legislature. I have determined never to remove a Secretary of the Treasury without communicating all the circumstances attending such removal to both Houses of Congress.

The influence of the Executive in controlling the freedom of the elective franchise through the medium of the public officers can be effectually checked by renewing the prohibition published by Mr. Jefferson forbidding their interference in elections further than giving their own votes, and their own independence secured by an assurance of perfect immunity in exercising this sacred privilege of freemen under the dictates of their own unbiased judgments. Never with my consent shall an officer of the people, compensated for his services out of their pockets, become the pliant instrument of Executive will.

There is no part of the means placed in the hands of the Executive which might be used with greater effect for unhallowed purposes than the control of the public press. The maxim which our ancestors derived from the mother country that "the freedom of the press is the great bulwark of civil and religious liberty" is one of the most precious legacies which they have left us. We have learned, too, from our own as well as the experience of other countries, that golden shackles, by whomsoever or by whatever pretense imposed, are as fatal to it as the iron bonds of despotism. The presses in the necessary employment of the Government should never be used "to clear the guilty or to varnish crime." A decent and manly examination of the acts of the Government should be not only tolerated, but encouraged.

Upon another occasion I have given my opinion at some length upon the impropriety of Executive interference in the legislation of Congress—that the article in the Constitution making it the duty of the President to communicate information and authorizing him to recommend measures was not intended to make him the source in legislation, and, in particular, that he should never be looked to for schemes of finance. It would be very strange, indeed, that the Constitution should have strictly forbidden one branch of the Legislature from interfering in the origination of such bills and that it should be considered proper that an altogether different department of the Government should be permitted to do so. Some of our best political maxims and opinions have been drawn from our parent isle. There are others, however, which can not be introduced in our system without singular incongruity and the production of much mischief, and this I conceive to be one. No matter in which of the houses of Parliament a bill may originate nor by whom introduced—a minister or a member of the opposition—by the fiction of law, or rather of constitutional principle, the sovereign is supposed to have prepared it agreeably to his will and then submitted it to Parliament for their advice and consent. Now the very reverse is the case here, not only with regard to the principle, but the forms prescribed by the Constitution. The principle certainly assigns to the only body constituted by the Constitution (the legislative body) the power to make laws, and the forms even direct that the enactment should be ascribed to them. The Senate, in relation to revenue bills, have the right to propose amendments, and so has the Executive by the power given him to return them to the House of Representatives with his objections. It is in his power also to propose amendments in the existing revenue laws, suggested by his observations upon their defective or injurious operation. But the delicate duty of devising schemes of revenue should be left where the Constitution has placed it—with the immediate representatives of the people. For similar reasons the mode of keeping the public treasure should be prescribed by them, and the further removed it may be from the control of the Executive the more wholesome the arrangement and the more in accordance with republican principle.

Connected with this subject is the character of the currency. The idea of making it exclusively metallic, however well intended, appears to me to be fraught with more fatal consequences than any other scheme having no relation to the personal rights of the citizens that has ever been devised. If any single scheme could produce the effect of arresting at once that mutation of condition by which thousands of our most indigent fellow-citizens by their industry and enterprise are raised to the possession of wealth, that is the one. If there is one measure better calculated than another to produce that state of things so much deprecated by all true republicans, by which the rich are daily adding to their hoards and the poor sinking deeper into penury, it is an exclusive metallic currency. Or if there is a process by which the character of the country for generosity and nobleness of feeling may be destroyed by the great increase and necessary toleration of usury, it is an exclusive metallic currency.

Amongst the other duties of a delicate character which the President is called upon to perform is the supervision of the government of the Territories of the United States. Those of them which are destined to become members of our great political family are compensated by their rapid progress from infancy to manhood for the partial and temporary deprivation of their political rights. It is in this District only where American citizens are to be found who under a settled policy are deprived of many important political privileges without any inspiring hope as to the future. Their only consolation under circumstances of such deprivation is that of the devoted exterior guards of a camp—that their sufferings secure tranquillity and safety within. Are there any of their countrymen, who would subject them to greater sacrifices, to any other humiliations than those essentially necessary to the security of the object for which they were thus separated from their fellow-citizens? Are their rights alone not to be guaranteed by the application of those great principles upon which all our constitutions are founded? We are told by the greatest of British orators and statesmen that at the commencement of the War of the Revolution the most stupid men in England spoke of "their American subjects." Are there, indeed, citizens of any of our States who have dreamed *of their subjects* in the District of Columbia? Such dreams can never be realized by any agency of mine. The people of the District of Columbia are not the subjects of the people of the States, but free American citizens. Being in the latter condition when the Constitution was formed, no words used in that instrument could have been intended to deprive them of that character. If there is anything in the great principle of unalienable rights so emphatically insisted upon in our Declaration of Independence, they could neither make nor the United States accept a surrender of their liberties and become the *subjects*—in other words, the slaves—of their former fellow-citizens. If this be true—and it will scarcely be denied by anyone who has a correct idea of his own rights as an American citizen—the grant to Congress of exclusive jurisdiction in the District of Columbia can be interpreted, so far as respects the aggregate people of the

United States, as meaning nothing more than to allow to Congress the controlling power necessary to afford a free and safe exercise of the functions assigned to the General Government by the Constitution. In all other respects the legislation of Congress should be adapted to their peculiar position and wants and be conformable with their deliberate opinions of their own interests.

I have spoken of the necessity of keeping the respective departments of the Government, as well as all the other authorities of our country, within their appropriate orbits. This is a matter of difficulty in some cases, as the powers which they respectively claim are often not defined by any distinct lines. Mischievous, however, in their tendencies as collisions of this kind may be, those which arise between the respective communities which for certain purposes compose one nation are much more so, for no such nation can long exist without the careful culture of those feelings of confidence and affection which are the effective bonds to union between free and confederated states. Strong as is the tie of interest, it has been often found ineffectual. Men blinded by their passions have been known to adopt measures for their country in direct opposition to all the suggestions of policy. The alternative, then, is to destroy or keep down a bad passion by creating and fostering a good one, and this seems to be the corner stone upon which our American political architects have reared the fabric of our Government. The cement which was to bind it and perpetuate its existence was the affectionate attachment between all its members. To insure the continuance of this feeling, produced at first by a community of dangers, of sufferings, and of interests, the advantages of each were made accessible to all. No participation in any good possessed by any member of our extensive Confederacy, except in domestic government, was withheld from the citizen of any other member. By a process attended with no difficulty, no delay, no expense but that of removal, the citizen of one might become the citizen of any other, and successively of the whole. The lines, too, separating powers to be exercised by the citizens of one State from those of another seem to be so distinctly drawn as to leave no room for misunderstanding. The citizens of each State unite in their persons all the privileges which that character confers and all that they may claim as citizens of the United States, but in no case can the same persons at the same time act as the citizen of two separate States, and *he is therefore positively precluded from any interference with the reserved powers of any State but that of which he is for the time being a citizen.* He may, indeed, offer to the citizens of other States his advice as to their management, and the form in which it is tendered is left to his own discretion and sense of propriety. It may be observed, however, that organized associations of citizens requiring compliance with their wishes too much resemble the *recommendations* of Athens to her allies, supported by an armed and powerful fleet. It was, indeed, to the ambition of the leading States of Greece to control the domestic concerns of the others that the destruction of that celebrated Confederacy, and subsequently of all its members, is mainly to be attributed, and it is owing to the absence of that spirit that the Helvetic Confederacy has for so many years been preserved. Never has there been seen in the institutions of the separate members of any confederacy more elements of discord. In the principles and forms of government and religion, as well as in the circumstances of the several Cantons, so marked a discrepancy was observable as to promise anything but harmony in their intercourse or permanency in their alliance, and yet for ages neither has been interrupted. Content with the positive benefits which their union produced, with the independence and safety from foreign aggression which it secured, these sagacious people respected the institutions of each other, however repugnant to their own principles and prejudices.

Our Confederacy, fellow-citizens, can only be preserved by the same forbearance. Our citizens must be content with the exercise of the powers with which the Constitution clothes them. The attempt of those of one State to control the domestic institutions of another can only result in feelings of distrust and jealousy, the certain harbingers of disunion, violence, and civil war, and the ultimate destruction of our free institutions. Our Confederacy is perfectly illustrated by the terms and principles governing a common copartnership. There is a fund of power to be exercised under the direction of the joint councils of the allied members, but that which has been reserved by the individual members is intangible by the common Government or the individual members composing it. To attempt it finds no support in the principles of our Constitution.

It should be our constant and earnest endeavor mutually to cultivate a spirit of concord and harmony among the various parts of our Confederacy. Experience has abundantly taught us that the agitation by citizens of one part of the Union of a subject not confided to the General Government, but exclusively under the guardianship of the local authorities, is productive of no other consequences than bitterness, alienation, discord, and injury to the very cause which is intended to be advanced. Of all the great interests which appertain to our country, that of union—cordial, confiding, fraternal union—is by far the most important, since it is the only true and sure guaranty of all others.

In consequence of the embarrassed state of business and the currency, some of the States may meet with difficulty in their financial concerns. However deeply we may regret anything imprudent or excessive in the engagements into which States have entered for purposes of their own, it does not become us to disparage the States' governments, nor to discourage them from making proper efforts for their own relief. On the contrary, it is our duty to encourage them to the extent of our constitutional authority to apply their best means and cheerfully to make all necessary sacrifices and submit to all necessary burdens to fulfill their engagements and maintain their credit, for the character and credit of the several States form a part of the character and credit of the whole country. The resources of the country are abundant, the enterprise and activity of our people proverbial, and we may well hope that wise legislation and prudent administration by the respective governments, each acting within its own sphere, will restore former prosperity.

Unpleasant and even dangerous as collisions may sometimes be between the constituted authorities of the citizens of our country in relation to the lines which separate their respective jurisdictions, the results can be of no vital injury to our institutions if that ardent patriotism, that devoted attachment to liberty, that spirit of moderation and forbearance for which our countrymen were once distinguished, continue to be cherished. If this continues to be the ruling passion of our souls, the weaker feeling of the mistaken enthusiast will be corrected, the Utopian dreams of the scheming politician dissipated, and the complicated intrigues of the demagogue rendered harmless. The spirit of liberty is the sovereign balm for every injury which our institutions may receive. On the contrary, no care that can be used in the construction of our Government, no division of powers, no distribution of checks in its several departments, will prove effectual to keep us a free people if this spirit is suffered to decay; and decay it will without constant nurture. To the neglect of this duty the best historians agree in attributing the ruin of all the republics with whose existence and fall their writings have made us acquainted. The same causes will ever produce the same effects, and as long as the love of power is a dominant passion of the human bosom, and as long as the understandings of men can be warped and their affections changed by operations upon their passions and prejudices, so long will the liberties of a people depend on their own constant attention to its preservation. The danger to all well-established free governments arises from the unwillingness of the people to believe in its existence or from the influence of designing men diverting their attention from the quarter whence it approaches to a source from which it can never come. This is the old trick of those who would usurp the government of their country. In the name of democracy they speak, warning the people against the influence of wealth and the danger of aristocracy. History, ancient and modern, is full of such examples. Caesar became the master of the Roman people and the senate under the pretense of supporting the democratic claims of the former against the aristocracy of the latter; Cromwell, in the character of protector of the liberties of the people, became the dictator of England, and Bolivar possessed himself of unlimited power with the title of his country's liberator. There is, on the contrary, no instance on record of an extensive and well-established republic being changed into an aristocracy. The tendencies of all such governments in their decline is to monarchy, and the antagonist principle to liberty there is the spirit of faction—a spirit which assumes the character and in times of great excitement imposes itself upon the people as the genuine spirit of freedom, and, like the false Christs whose coming was foretold by the Savior, seeks to, and were it possible would, impose upon the true and most faithful disciples of liberty. It is in periods like this that it behooves the people to be most watchful of those to whom they have intrusted power. And although there is at times much difficulty in distinguishing the false from the true spirit, a calm and dispassionate investigation will detect the counterfeit, as well by the character of its operations as the results that are produced. The true spirit of liberty, although devoted, persevering, bold, and uncompromising in principle, that secured is mild and tolerant and scrupulous as to the means it employs, whilst the spirit of party, assuming to be that of liberty, is harsh, vindictive, and intolerant, and totally reckless as to the character of the allies which it brings to the aid of its cause. When the genuine spirit of liberty animates the body of a people to a thorough examination of their affairs, it leads to the excision of every excrescence which may have fastened itself upon any of the departments of the government, and restores the system to its pristine health and beauty. But the reign of an intolerant spirit of party amongst a free people seldom fails to result in a dangerous accession to the executive power introduced and established amidst unusual professions of devotion to democracy.

The foregoing remarks relate almost exclusively to matters connected with our domestic concerns. It may be proper, however,

[84]

that I should give some indications to my fellow-citizens of my proposed course of conduct in the management of our foreign relations. I assure them, therefore, that it is my intention to use every means in my power to preserve the friendly intercourse which now so happily subsists with every foreign nation, and that although, of course, not well informed as to the state of pending negotiations with any of them, I see in the personal characters of the sovereigns, as well as in the mutual interests of our own and of the governments with which our relations are most intimate, a pleasing guaranty that the harmony so important to the interests of their subjects as well as of our citizens will not be interrupted by the advancement of any claim or pretension upon their part to which our honor would not permit us to yield. Long the defender of my country's rights in the field, I trust that my fellow-citizens will not see in my earnest desire to preserve peace with foreign powers any indication that their rights will ever be sacrificed or the honor of the nation tarnished by any admission on the part of their Chief Magistrate unworthy of their former glory. In our intercourse with our aboriginal neighbors the same liberality and justice which marked the course prescribed to me by two of my illustrious predecessors when acting under their direction in the discharge of the duties of superintendent and commissioner shall be strictly observed. I can conceive of no more sublime spectacle, none more likely to propitiate an impartial and common Creator, than a rigid adherence to the principles of justice on the part of a powerful nation in its transactions with a weaker and uncivilized people whom circumstances have placed at its disposal.

Before concluding, fellow-citizens, I must say something to you on the subject of the parties at this time existing in our country. To me it appears perfectly clear that the interest of that country requires that the violence of the spirit by which those parties are at this time governed must be greatly mitigated, if not entirely extinguished, or consequences will ensue which are appalling to be thought of.

If parties in a republic are necessary to secure a degree of vigilance sufficient to keep the public functionaries within the bounds of law and duty, at that point their usefulness ends. Beyond that they become destructive of public virtue, the parent of a spirit antagonist to that of liberty, and eventually its inevitable conqueror. We have examples of republics where the love of country and of liberty at one time were the dominant passions of the whole mass of citizens, and yet, with the continuance of the name and forms of free government, not a vestige of these qualities remaining in the bosoms of any one of its citizens. It was the beautiful remark of a distinguished English writer that "in the Roman senate Octavius had a party and Anthony a party, but the Commonwealth had none." Yet the senate continued to meet in the temple of liberty to talk of the sacredness and beauty of the Commonwealth and gaze at the statues of the elder Brutus and of the Curtii and Decii, and the people assembled in the forum, not, as in the days of Camillus and the Scipios, to cast their free votes for annual magistrates or pass upon the acts of the senate, but to receive from the hands of the leaders of the respective parties their share of the spoils and to shout for one or the other, as those collected in Gaul or Egypt and the lesser Asia would furnish the larger dividend. The spirit of liberty had fled, and, avoiding the abodes of civilized man, had sought protection in the wilds of Scythia or Scandianavia; and so under the operation of the same causes and influences it will fly from our Capitol and our forums. A calamity so awful, not only to our country, but to the world, must be deprecated by every patriot and every tendency to a state of things likely to produce it immediately checked. Such a tendency has existed—does exist. Always the friend of my countrymen, never their flatterer, it becomes my duty to say to them from this high place to which their partiality has exalted me that there exists in the land a spirit hostile to their best interests—hostile to liberty itself. It is a spirit contracted in its views, selfish in its objects. It looks to the aggrandizement of a few even to the destruction of the interests of the whole. The entire remedy is with the people. Something, however, may be effected by the means which they have placed in my hands. It is union that we want, not of a party for the sake of that party, but a union of the whole country for the sake of the whole country, for the defense of its interests and its honor against foreign aggression, for the defense of those principles for which our ancestors so gloriously contended. As far as it depends upon me it shall be accomplished. All the influence that I possess shall be exerted to prevent the formation at least of an Executive party in the halls of the legislative body. I wish for the support of no member of that body to any measure of mine that does not satisfy his judgment and his sense of duty to those from whom he holds his appointment, nor any confidence in advance from the people but that asked for by Mr. Jefferson, "to give firmness and effect to the legal administration of their affairs."

I deem the present occasion sufficiently important and solemn to justify me in expressing to my fellow-citizens a profound reverence for the Christian religion and a thorough conviction that sound morals, religious liberty, and a just sense of religious responsibility are essentially connected with all true and lasting happiness; and to that good Being who has blessed us by the gifts of civil and religious freedom, who watched over and prospered the labors of our fathers and has hitherto preserved to us institutions far exceeding in excellence those of any other people, let us unite in fervently commending every interest of our beloved country in all future time.

Fellow-citizens, being fully invested with that high office to which the partiality of my countrymen has called me, I now take an affectionate leave of you. You will bear with you to your homes the remembrance of the pledge I have this day given to discharge all the high duties of my exalted station according to the best of my ability, and I shall enter upon their performance with entire confidence in the support of a just and generous people.

Tyler is alleged to have been shooting marbles with his sons at his Williamsburg home when he received the news of President Harrison's death. He proceeded at once to the Capitol, where he was sworn in to become the 10th President of the United States and the first by succession.

John Tyler
[1841–1845]

THE PRESIDENT

John Tyler graduated from William and Mary, and after being admitted to the bar was sent to the Virginia House of Burgesses at the age of 22. Later he was elected to Congress, and in 1825 became Governor of Virginia. In 1827 Tyler was named a United States Senator. As a Senate Democrat, Tyler voted against the Tariff Bill of 1828 and against rechartering the Bank of the United States, but during Jackson's term of office aligned himself with John C. Calhoun on the question of nullification and states' rights. Outraged Jacksonian Democrats labeled him "Turncoat Tyler." He became a Whig, but with his Southern sympathies unchanged. The strategy of the Whig nomination of Tyler in 1840 for the vice-presidency backfired when Harrison died after only a month in office and Tyler stepped into the presidency.

When Tyler vetoed two of Clay's pet bills calling for the establishment of a Second Bank of the United States enraged Whigs gathered outside the White House to hiss and vilify the President. Webster and Clay tried to tell Tyler that for the good of the party he should accept their guidance and carry out Harrison's Whig policies. But Tyler stubbornly refused to become a figurehead and accepted the full responsibilities of his office. This led to a split in his Cabinet. On September 11, 1841, the entire Cabinet resigned, with the exception of Daniel Webster who remained as Secretary of State for two years in order to conclude the impending Webster-Ashburton Treaty defining the disputed boundary between Maine and Canada.

The hapless Tyler was burned in effigy and was subjected to such vituperative abuse from Whigs as to make the violent personal attacks on Van Buren seem complimentary by comparison. The Whig smear campaign became so bitter that Tyler finally said: "I appeal from the vituperations of the present day to the impartial pen of history, in confidence that neither my motives nor my acts will bear the interpretation which for sinister motives has been put upon them."

THE PRESIDENT

James Knox Polk graduated as salutatorian of his class from the University of North Carolina. He became a lawyer and served in the Tennessee legislature. He spent the next fourteen years in Congress, and became Governor of Tennessee for one term, but was twice defeated in his efforts to be reëlected. When Van Buren failed to receive the necessary two-thirds majority at the Democratic Convention of 1844 the name of the virtually unknown Polk was placed in nomination as a compromise candidate on the ninth ballot. One delegation after another deserted Van Buren in a wild scramble to get on the Polk bandwagon, which rolled to victory.

THE NATION

On March 3, 1842, Governor John Davis of Massachusetts signed the first law limiting children under twelve to a ten-hour work day. After 40 years of public service Henry Clay resigned from the Senate, May 31, 1842. On August 30 the Tariff Act was passed to restore the high protective level of 1832. April 12, 1844, the Texas Annexation Treaty was signed by the United States and Texas, providing for the admission of Texas as a territory subject to approval by Congress. On May 27, 1844, John Tyler was nominated for president at the Baltimore convention of the Tyler Democrats. However, Tyler withdrew his name in August. The Democratic National Convention also held in Baltimore in May nominated James K. Polk.

On May 24, 1844, Samuel F.B. Morse used his new telegraph to send the message, "What hath God wrought!" from Washington, D.C., to Baltimore, Maryland. He ushered in a new era in U.S. communications which eventually spread throughout the world. On June 8, 1844, the Senate voted against the Texas Annexation Treaty, angering Tyler and Calhoun, who finally pushed through a joint resolution in both houses on the last day of Tyler's administration in favor of annexation. Florida was admitted as the 27th state on March 3, 1845.

President Tyler, who had become a widower in 1842, married Julia Gardiner, June 28, 1844, thus becoming the first U.S. president to marry while in office. In this year, after eight years of unceasing effort, John Quincy Adams finally succeeded in persuading the House to lift its gag rule against introduction of abolitionist petitions.

In the 1844 election Democrat Polk polled 1,337,243 popular votes (170 electoral) and Whig Henry Clay totaled 1,299,068 popular votes (105 electoral). George M. Dallas was elected vice-president.

THE WORLD

Egypt lost Syria to Turkey in 1841, and the Great Powers of Europe guaranteed Turkish independence at the Convention of the Straits. On August 29, 1842, the Treaty of Nanking ended the opium war between Britain and China, with Hong Kong being ceded to England. 1843 saw the British conquer Sind and proclaim Natal a British colony. In September, 1844, the French war against Morocco ended with the Treaty of Tangiers.

[88]

YOU KNOW YOUR ADMINISTRATION IS FACED WITH TWO MAIN ISSUES: the problems arising from the annexation of Texas and the settlement of the dispute between Britain and the United States over the Oregon region. The campaign slogans of "Fifty-Four Forty or Fight," "All of Oregon or None" and "Texas" are still echoing in your ears as you prepare your inaugural address. You realize a definite stand on either question could mean war with England or Mexico. But you aren't called Young Hickory for nothing, and in the address you deliver in a cold, driving rain to an umbrella-shrouded crowd you spell out your policy in language almost as blunt as that which Old Hickory would have used . . . .

James K. Polk

[1845–1849]

INAUGURAL ADDRESS, MARCH 4, 1845

Capitol Steps, Washington, D.C.

Fellow-Citizens:

Without solicitation on my part, I have been chosen by the free and voluntary suffrages of my countrymen to the most honorable and most responsible office on earth. I am deeply impressed with gratitude for the confidence reposed in me. Honored with this distinguished consideration at an earlier period of life than any of my predecessors, I can not disguise the diffidence with which I am about to enter on the discharge of my official duties.

If the more aged and experienced men who have filled the office of President of the United States even in the infancy of the Republic distrusted their ability to discharge the duties of that exalted station, what ought not to be the apprehensions of one so much younger and less endowed now that our domain extends from ocean to ocean, that our people have so greatly increased in numbers, and at a time when so great diversity of opinion prevails in regard to the principles and policy which should characterize the administration of our Government? Well may the boldest fear and the wisest tremble when incurring responsibilities on which may depend our country's peace and prosperity, and in some degree the hopes and happiness of the whole human family.

In assuming responsibilities so vast I fervently invoke the aid of that Almighty Ruler of the Universe in whose hands are the destinies of nations and of men to guard this Heaven-favored land against the mischiefs which without His guidance might arise from an unwise public policy. With a firm reliance upon the wisdom of Omnipotence to sustain and direct me in the path of duty which I am appointed to pursue, I stand in the presence of this assembled multitude of my countrymen to take upon myself the solemn obligation "to the best of my ability to preserve, protect, and defend the Constitution of the United States."

A concise enumeration of the principles which will guide me in the administrative policy of the Government is not only in accordance with the examples set me by all my predecessors, but is eminently befitting the occasion.

In his opening sentences Polk referred to his surprise dark-horse nomination and also to his youth. He was the youngest president to date. Polk's lean, straight-backed body, dark hair, and aggressive manner made him seem even younger than his forty-nine years.

This could have been George Washington speaking. Polk was an ardent believer in the Constitution and took his oath of office to heart. He firmly believed in "abstaining from the exercise of doubtful or unauthorized implied powers."

Although Polk was an ardent and outspoken champion of states' rights he also was convinced that an imbalance of power in this direction could destroy the Union.

The predecessor Polk referred to was Thomas Jefferson. The two quotations are from Jefferson's memorable first inaugural address. Polk, however, changed the words "administration," and "bulwark," from the plural, as Jefferson had written them, to the singular form as they appear here.

The Constitution itself, plainly written as it is, the safeguard of our federative compact, the offspring of concession and compromise, binding together in the bonds of peace and union this great and increasing family of free and independent States, will be the chart by which I shall be directed.

It will be my first care to administer the Government in the true spirit of that instrument, and to assume no powers not expressly granted or clearly implied in its terms. The Government of the United States is one of delegated and limited powers, and it is by a strict adherence to the clearly granted powers and by abstaining from the exercise of doubtful or unauthorized implied powers that we have the only sure guaranty against the recurrence of those unfortunate collisions between the Federal and State authorities which have occasionally so much disturbed the harmony of our system and even threatened the perpetuity of our glorious Union.

"To the States, respectively, or to the people" have been reserved "the powers not delegated to the United States by the Constitution nor prohibited by it to the States." Each State is a complete sovereignty within the sphere of its reserved powers. The Government of the Union, acting within the sphere of its delegated authority, is also a complete sovereignty. While the General Government should abstain from the exercise of authority not clearly delegated to it, the States should be equally careful that in the maintenance of their rights they do not overstep the limits of powers reserved to them. One of the most distinguished of my predecessors attached deserved importance to "the support of the State governments in all their rights, as the most competent administration for our domestic concerns and the surest bulwark against antirepublican tendencies," and to the "preservation of the General Government in its whole constitutional vigor, as the sheet anchor of our peace at home and safety abroad."

To the Government of the United States has been intrusted the exclusive management of our foreign affairs. Beyond that it wields a few general enumerated powers. It does not force reform on the States. It leaves individuals, over whom it casts its protecting influence, entirely free to improve their own condition by the legitimate exercise of all their mental and physical powers. It is a common protector of each and all the States; of every man who lives upon our soil, whether of native or foreign birth; of every religious sect, in their worship of the Almighty according to the dictates of their own conscience; of every shade of opinion, and the most free inquiry; of every art, trade, and occupation consistent with the laws of the States. And we rejoice in the general happiness, prosperity, and advancement of our country, which have been the offspring of freedom, and not of power.

This most admirable and wisest system of well-regulated self-government among men ever devised by human minds has been tested by its successful operation for more than half a century, and if preserved from the usurpations of the Federal Government on the one hand and the exercise by the States of powers not reserved to them on the other, will, I fervently hope and believe, endure for ages to come and dispense the blessings of civil and religious liberty to distant generations. To effect objects so dear to every patriot I shall devote myself with anxious solicitude. It will be my desire to guard against that most fruitful source of danger to the harmonious action of our system which consists in substituting the mere discretion and caprice of the Executive or of majorities in the legislative department of the Government for powers which have been withheld from the Federal Government by the Constitution. By the theory of our Government majorities rule, but this right is not an arbitrary or unlimited one. It is a right to be exercised in subordination to the Constitution and in conformity to it. One great object of the Constitution was to restrain majorities from oppressing minorities or encroaching upon their just rights. Minorities have a right to appeal to the Constitution as a shield against such oppression.

That the blessings of liberty which our Constitution secures may be enjoyed alike by minorities and majorities, the Executive has been wisely invested with a qualified veto upon the acts of the Legislature. It is a negative power, and is conservative in its character. It arrests for the time hasty, inconsiderate, or unconstitutional legislation, invites reconsideration, and transfers questions at issue between the legislative and executive departments to the tribunal of the people. Like all other powers, it is subject to be abused. When judiciously and properly exercised, the Constitution itself may be saved from infraction and the rights of all preserved and protected.

The inestimable value of our Federal Union is felt and acknowledged by all. By this system of united and confederated States our people are permitted collectively and individually to seek their own happiness in their own way, and the consequences have been most auspicious. Since the Union was formed the number of the States has increased from thirteen to twenty-eight; two of these have taken their position as members of the Confederacy within the last week. Our population has increased from three to twenty millions. New communities and States are seeking protection under its ægis, and multitudes from the Old World are flocking to our shores to participate in its blessings. Beneath its benign sway peace and prosperity prevail. Freed from the burdens and miseries of war, our trade and intercourse have extended throughout the world. Mind, no longer tasked in devising means to accomplish or resist schemes of ambition, usurpation, or conquest, is devoting itself to man's true interests in developing his faculties and powers and the capacity of nature to minister to his enjoyments. Genius is free to announce its inventions and discoveries, and the hand is free to accomplish whatever the head conceives not incompatible with the rights of a fellow-being. All distinctions of birth or of rank have been abolished. All citizens, whether native or adopted, are placed upon terms of precise equality. All are entitled to equal rights and equal protection. No union exists between church and state, and perfect freedom of opinion is guaranteed to all sects and creeds.

These are some of the blessings secured to our happy land by our Federal Union. To perpetuate them it is our sacred duty to preserve it. Who shall assign limits to the achievements of free minds and free hands under the protection of this glorious Union? No treason to mankind since the organization of society would be equal in atrocity to that of him who would lift his hand to destroy it. He would overthrow the noblest structure of human wisdom, which protects himself and his fellow-man. He would stop the progress of free government and involve his country either in anarchy or despotism. He would extinguish the fire of liberty, which warms and animates the hearts of happy millions and invites all the nations of the earth to imitate our example. If he say that error and wrong are committed in the administration of the Government, let him remember that nothing human can be perfect, and that under

Polk was apparently misinformed. On March 3, 1845, the last day of the Tyler administration, Florida was admitted as the twenty-seventh state. But, although Polk thought the annexation of Texas on March 1, 1845, had made this our twenty-eighth state, Texas was really a territory. Not until December 29, 1845, was Texas formally admitted to the Union.

Polk, although a states' rights Democrat, refused to countenance any threat of secession. To him the preservation of the Union was paramount.

Here are the words of Old Hickory rephrased by Young Hickory Polk. By such a clear and forthright statement of policy Polk let it be known he was no political figurehead.

The "schemes and agitations" referred to are the activities of the abolitionists, who wanted to eliminate slavery even though the process brought about dissolution of the Union.

Polk clearly spelled out his stand against any plans for reviving the Second National Bank of the United States, but he failed to come up with a suitable substitute, other than a desire to enforce "strictest economy in the expenditure of the public money." This sweeping promise of economy in government served as an introduction to what Polk, judging by his italicized phrases, evidently felt was the most vital section of his speech: The need for new taxes in order to put the government on a pay-as-you-go basis, rather than alternating between periods of debt and surplus.

no other system of government revealed by Heaven or devised by man has reason been allowed so free and broad a scope to combat error. Has the sword of despots proved to be a safer or surer instrument of reform in government than enlightened reason? Does he expect to find among the ruins of this Union a happier abode for our swarming millions than they now have under it? Every lover of his country must shudder at the thought of the possibility of its dissolution, and will be ready to adopt the patriotic sentiment, "Our Federal Union—it must be preserved." To preserve it the compromises which alone enabled our fathers to form a common constitution for the government and protection of so many States and distinct communities, of such diversified habits, interests, and domestic institutions, must be sacredly and religiously observed. Any attempt to disturb or destroy these compromises, being terms of the compact of union, can lead to none other than the most ruinous and disastrous consequences.

It is a source of deep regret that in some sections of our country misguided persons have occasionally indulged in schemes and agitations whose object is the destruction of domestic institutions existing in other sections—institutions which existed at the adoption of the Constitution and were recognized and protected by it. All must see that if it were possible for them to be successful in attaining their object the dissolution of the Union and the consequent destruction of our happy form of government must speedily follow.

I am happy to believe that at every period of our existence as a nation there has existed, and continues to exist, among the great mass of our people a devotion to the Union of the States which will shield and protect it against the moral treason of any who would seriously contemplate its destruction. To secure a continuance of that devotion the compromises of the Constitution must not only be preserved, but sectional jealousies and heartburnings must be discountenanced, and all should remember that they are members of the same political family, having a common destiny. To increase the attachment of our people to the Union, our laws should be just. Any policy which shall tend to favor monopolies or the peculiar interests of sections or classes must operate to the prejudice of the interests of their fellow-citizens, and should be avoided. If the compromises of the Constitution be preserved, if sectional jealousies and heartburnings be discountenanced, if our laws be just and the Government be practically administered strictly within the limits of power prescribed to it, we may discard all apprehensions for the safety of the Union.

With these views of the nature, character, and objects of the Government and the value of the Union, I shall steadily oppose the creation of those institutions and systems which in their nature tend to pervert it from its legitimate purposes and make it the instrument of sections, classes, and individuals. We need no national banks or other extraneous institutions planted around the Government to control or strengthen it in opposition to the will of its authors. Experience has taught us how unnecessary they are as auxiliaries of the public authorities—how impotent for good and how powerful for mischief.

Ours was intended to be plain and frugal government, and I shall regard it to be my duty to recommend to Congress and, as far as the Executive is concerned, to enforce by all the means within my power the strictest economy in the expenditure of the public money which may be compatible with the public interests.

A national debt has become almost an institution of European monarchies. It is viewed in some of them as an essential prop to existing governments. Melancholy is the condition of that people whose government can be sustained only by a system which periodically transfers large amounts from the labor of the many to the coffers of the few. Such a system is incompatible with the ends for which our republican Government was instituted. Under a wise policy the debts contracted in our Revolution and during the War of 1812 have been happily extinguished. By a judicious application of the revenues not required for other necessary purposes, it is not doubted that the debt which has grown out of the circumstances of the last few years may be speedily paid off.

I congratulate my fellow-citizens on the entire restoration of the credit of the General Government of the Union and that of many of the States. Happy would it be for the indebted States if they were freed from their liabilities, many of which were incautiously contracted. Although the Government of the Union is neither in a legal nor a moral sense bound for the debts of the States, and it would be a violation of our compact of union to assume them, yet we can not but feel a deep interest in seeing all the States meet their public liabilities and pay off their just debts at the earliest practicable period. That they will do so as soon as it can be done without imposing too heavy burdens on their citizens there is no reason to doubt. The sound moral and honorable feeling of the people of the indebted States can not be questions, and we are happy to perceive a settled disposition on their part, as their ability returns after a season of unexampled pecuniary embarrassment, to pay off all just demands and to acquiesce in any reasonable measures to accomplish that object.

One of the difficulties which we have had to encounter in the practical administration of the Government consists in the adjustment of our revenue laws and the levy of the taxes necessary for the support of Government. In the general proposition that no more money shall be collected than the necessities of an economical administration shall require all parties seem to acquiesce. Nor does there seem to be any material difference of opinion as to the absence of right in the Government to tax one section of country, or one class of citizens, or one occupation, for the mere profit of another. "Justice and sound policy forbid the Federal Government to foster one branch of industry to the detriment of another, or to cherish the interests of one portion to the injury of another portion of our common country." I have heretofore declared to my fellow-citizens that "in my judgment it is the duty of the Government to extend, as far as it may be practicable to do so, by its revenue laws and all other means within its power, fair and just protection to all of the great interests of the whole Union, embracing agriculture, manufactures, the mechanic arts, commerce, and navigation." I have also declared my opinion to be "in favor of a tariff for revenue," and that "in adjusting the details of such a tariff I have sanctioned such moderate discriminating duties as would produce the amount of revenue needed and at the same time afford reasonable incidental protection to our home industry," and that I was "opposed to a tariff for protection merely, and not for revenue."

The power "to lay and collect taxes, duties, imposts, and excises" was an indispensable one to be conferred on the Federal Government, which without it would possess no means of providing for its own support. In executing this power by levying a tariff of duties

Polk had long advocated a tariff whose primary purpose was moderate revenue adequate for the needs of government, with protection a secondary factor. In this segment of his address, devoted to tariff policy, Polk dwelled at length on the reasoning which had led to his decision.

for the support of Government, the raising of *revenue* should be the *object* and *protection* the *incident*. To reverse this principle and make *protection* the *object* and *revenue* the *incident* would be to inflict manifest injustice upon all other than the protected interests. In levying duties for revenue it is doubtless proper to make such discriminations within the *revenue principle* as will afford incidental protection to our home interests. Within the revenue limit there is a discretion to discriminate; beyond that limit the rightful exercise of the power is not conceded. The incidental protection afforded to our home interests by discriminations within the revenue range it is believed will be ample. In making discriminations all our home interests should as far as practicable be equally protected. The largest portion of our people are agriculturists. Others are employed in manufactures, commerce, navigation, and the mechanic arts. They are all engaged in their respective pursuits, and their joint labors constitute the national or home industry. To tax one branch of this home industry for the benefit of another would be unjust. No one of these interests can rightfully claim an advantage over the others, or to be enriched by impoverishing the others. All are equally entitled to the fostering care and protection of the Government. In exercising a sound discretion in levying discriminating duties within the limit prescribed, care should be taken that it be done in a manner not to benefit the wealthy few at the expense of the toiling millions by taxing *lowest* the luxuries of life, or articles of superior quality and high price, which can only be consumed by the wealthy, and *highest* the necessaries of life, or articles of coarse quality and low price, which the poor and great mass of our people must consume. The burdens of government should as far as practicable be distributed justly and equally among all classes of our population. These general views, long entertained on this subject, I have deemed it proper to reiterate. It is a subject upon which conflicting interests of sections and occupations are supposed to exist, and a spirit of mutual concession and compromise in adjusting its details should be cherished by every part of our widespread country as the only means of preserving harmony and a cheerful acquiescence of all in the operation of our revenue laws. Our patriotic citizens in every part of the Union will readily submit to the payment of such taxes as shall be needed for the support of their Government, whether in peace or in war, if they are so levied as to distribute the burdens as equally as possible among them.

The Republic of Texas has made known her desire to come into our Union, to form a part of our Confederacy and enjoy with us the blessings of liberty secured and guaranteed by our Constitution. Texas was once a part of our country—was unwisely ceded away to a foreign power—is now independent, and possesses an undoubted right to dispose of a part or the whole of her territory and to merge her sovereignty as a separate and independent state in ours. I congratulate my country that by an act of the late Congress of the United States the assent of this Government has been given to the reunion, and it only remains for the two countries to agree upon the terms to consummate an object so important to both.

I regard the question of annexation as belonging exclusively to the United States and Texas. They are independent powers competent to contract, and foreign nations have no right to interfere with them or to take exceptions to their reunion. Foreign powers do not seem to appreciate the true character of our Government. Our Union is a confederation of independent States, whose policy

The middle-of-the-road tenor of Polk's remarks was strongly suggestive of Jefferson's first inaugural address. For clarity of thought, sincerity, logic, and frankness, this address of Polk's must rank with the best.

On the question of Mexico's opposition to the annexation of Texas as our twenty-eighth state Polk came out swinging. Although he knew his policy would probably lead to war Polk refused to hide behind a diplomatic smoke screen of carefully worded phrases. Instead he boldly expressed his belief that foreign nations—meaning Mexico or Britain—had "no right to interfere."

[94]

is peace with each other and all the world. To enlarge its limits is to extend the dominions of peace over additional territories and increasing millions. The world has nothing to fear from military ambition in our Government. While the Chief Magistrate and the popular branch of Congress are elected for short terms by the suffrages of those millions who must in their own persons bear all the burdens and miseries of war, our Government can not be otherwise than pacific. Foreign powers should therefore look on the annexation of Texas to the United States not as the conquest of a nation seeking to extend her dominions by arms and violence, but as the peaceful acquisition of a territory once her own, by adding another member to our confederation, with the consent of that member, thereby diminishing the chances of war and opening to them new and ever-increasing markets for their products.

To Texas the reunion is important, because the strong protecting arm of our Government would be extended over her, and the vast resources of her fertile soil and genial climate would be speedily developed, while the safety of New Orleans and of our whole southwestern frontier against hostile aggression, as well as the interests of the whole Union, would be promoted by it.

In the earlier stages of our national existence the opinion prevailed with some that our system of confederated States could not operate successfully over an extended territory, and serious objections have at different times been made to the enlargement of our boundaries. These objections were earnestly urged when we acquired Louisiana. Experience has shown that they were not well founded. The title of numerous Indian tribes to vast tracts of country has been extinguished; new States have been admitted into the Union; new Territories have been created and our jurisdiction and laws extended over them. As our population has expanded, the Union has been cemented and strengthened. As our boundaries have been enlarged and our agricultural population has been spread over a large surface, our federative system has acquired additional strength and security. It may well be doubted whether it would not be in greater danger of overthrow if our present population were confined to the comparatively narrow limits of the original thirteen States than it is now that they are sparsely settled over a more expanded territory. It is confidently believed that our system may be safely extended to the utmost bounds of our territorial limits, and that as it shall be extended the bonds of our Union, so far from being weakened, will become stronger.

None can fail to see the danger to our safety and future peace if Texas remains an independent state or becomes an ally or dependency of some foreign nation more powerful than herself. Is there one among our citizens who would not prefer perpetual peace with Texas to occasional wars, which so often occur between bordering independent nations? Is there one who would not prefer free intercourse with her to high duties on all our products and manufactures which enter her ports or cross her frontiers? Is there one who would not prefer an unrestricted communication with her citizens to the frontier obstructions which must occur if she remains out of the Union? Whatever is good or evil in the local institutions of Texas will remain her own whether annexed to the United States or not. None of the present States will be responsible for them any more than they are for the local institutions of each other. They have confederated together for certain specific objects. Upon the same principle that they would refuse to form a perpetual union

Polk showed remarkable vision and foresight in this section of his address. With the youth and vigor necessary for successful culmination of his policies of expansion, during his term the nation was destined to add Texas, New Mexico, California, and Oregon, and as he predicted the bonds of the Union became stronger instead of weaker.

with Texas because of her local institutions our forefathers would have been prevented from forming our present Union. Perceiving no valid objection to the measure and many reasons for its adoption vitally affecting the peace, the safety, and the prosperity of both countries, I shall on the broad principle which formed the basis and produced the adoption of our Constitution, and not in any narrow spirit of sectional policy, endeavor by all constitutional, honorable, and appropriate means to consummate the expressed will of the people and Government of the United States by the re-annexation of Texas to our Union at the earliest practicable period.

Nor will it become in a less degree my duty to assert and maintain by all constitutional means the right of the United States to that portion of our territory which lies beyond the Rocky Mountains. Our title to the country of the Oregon is "clear and unquestionable," and already are our people preparing to perfect that title by occupying it with their wives and children. But eighty years ago our population was confined on the west by the ridge of the Alleghanies. Within that period—within the lifetime, I might say, of some of my hearers—our people, increasing to many millions, have filled the eastern valley of the Mississippi, adventurously ascended the Missouri to its headsprings, and are already engaged in establishing the blessings of self-government in valleys of which the rivers flow to the Pacific. The world beholds the peaceful triumphs of the industry of our emigrants. To us belongs the duty of protecting them adequately wherever they may be upon our soil. The jurisdiction of our laws and the benefits of our republican institutions should be extended over them in the distant regions which they have selected for their homes. The increasing facilities of intercourse will easily bring the States, of which the formation in that part of our territory can not be long delayed, within the sphere of our federative Union. In the meantime every obligation imposed by treaty or conventional stipulations should be sacredly respected.

In the management of our foreign relations it will be my aim to observe a careful respect for the rights of other nations, while our own will be the subject of constant watchfulness. Equal and exact justice should characterize all our intercourse with foreign countries. All alliances having a tendency to jeopard the welfare and honor of our country or sacrifice any one of the national interests will be studiously avoided, and yet no opportunity will be lost to cultivate a favorable understanding with foreign governments by which our navigation and commerce may be extended and the ample products of our fertile soil, as well as the manufactures of our skillful artisans, find a ready market and remunerating prices in foreign countries.

In taking "care that the laws be faithfully executed," a strict performance of duty will be exacted from all public officers. From those officers, especially, who are charged with the collection and disbursement of the public revenue will prompt and rigid accountability be required. Any culpable failure or delay on their part to account for the moneys intrusted to them at the times and in the manner required by law will in every instance terminate the official connection of such defaulting officer with the Government.

Although in our country the Chief Magistrate must almost of necessity be chosen by a party and stand pledged to its principles and measures, yet in his official action he should not be the President of a part only, but of the whole people of the United States.

Polk's stand on the question of the nation's right to Oregon was clear and unshakable. In the territorial dispute with Great Britain, growing out of the Anglo-American joint occupancy agreement for Oregon, Polk steadfastly insisted on claiming all of Oregon south of the 49th parallel despite the threat of war with Britain.

In this passage Polk let it be known he intended to institute adequate reforms in the postal system and in any other agencies that handled public funds.

[96]

While he executes the laws with an impartial hand, shrinks from no proper responsibility, and faithfully carries out in the executive department of the Government the principles and policy of those who have chosen him, he should not be unmindful that our fellow-citizens who have differed with him in opinion are entitled to the full and free exercise of their opinions and judgments, and that the rights of all are entitled to respect and regard.

Confidently relying upon the aid and assistance of the coordinate departments of the Government in conducting our public affairs, I enter upon the discharge of the high duties which have been assigned me by the people, again humbly supplicating that Divine Being who has watched over and protected our beloved country from its infancy to the present hour to continue His gracious benedictions upon us, that we may continue to be a prosperous and happy people.

In conclusion Polk made a plea to the nation and its leaders to give him a unified backing. In executing the large and ambitious program he proposed for the next four years, he stated he intended to place the welfare of the country over the interests of the party which elected him to office, a promise he was to keep even through the campaign of 1849, which chose his successor. It was this passionate love of country over party that was to lead even Democrats to heap abuse on Polk. They wanted no man who held similarly impartial views to succeed him.

James Polk

THE PRESIDENT

General Zachary Taylor spent 40 years in the Army where he earned the nickname "Old Rough and Ready" because of his careless habits of dress and his readiness to fight. The untutored Taylor led his men to many victories in the Mexican War. Although he admitted he was almost completely unfitted for the presidency his hero's aura helped him to carry the election against better qualified men.

THE NATION

On June 8, 1845, former President Andrew Jackson died. In December of that year Texas was admitted as the 28th state. Aggressive "Young Hickory" Polk steadfastly stood by his inaugural promise to protect Texas, and on May 13, 1846, war with Mexico was declared. Under Generals Zachary Taylor and Winfield Scott the American forces swept to victory capturing Monterey, Vera Cruz, and Mexico City. The war ended February 2, 1848, with the signing of the Treaty of Guadalupe Hidalgo. The United States paid Mexico $15,000,000 in return for Texas, New Mexico, and what is now southern California. Meantime in northern California another conflict broke out: the "Bear Flag Revolt" in which California settlers tried to upset Mexican rule.

June 15, 1846, the Oregon Treaty was signed to establish the 49th parallel as the boundary between the British Northwest Territory and the Oregon Territory. On December 28 Iowa was admitted as the 29th state. July of 1847 saw Mormon emigrants settling in Utah near what was to become Salt Lake City. Then on January 24, 1848, gold was discovered at Sutter's Mill in California, precipitating the gold rush of '49. February 23, former President John Quincy Adams died. Wisconsin was admitted as the 30th state of the Union on May 29, 1848.

In the election of 1848, the first to be held on the same day throughout the country as specified in the Elections Act of 1845, Whig Zachary Taylor received 1,360,099 popular votes (163 electoral) for president. Democrat Lewis Cass received 1,220,544 popular votes (127 electoral). Martin Van Buren, nominated by the Barnburners and Free-Soilers, received only 291,263 votes. General Taylor's running mate—a quiet, personable chap named Millard Fillmore—was elected vice-president. Nothing more was expected to be heard from Fillmore by the politicians who nominated him. But once again a political shotgun was destined to backfire.

THE WORLD

Between 1845 and 1849 the simmering unrest in Europe abruptly boiled over as one established government after another collapsed in an almost universal upheaval that toppled kings and ruling classes all over the Continent. France, Austria, Prussia, Hungary, Germany, Sicily, Italy, Bavaria, Denmark, Poland, Sweden, and Ireland were among the nations to feel the scalding touch of revolution.

YOU REFUSE TO TAKE PART IN THE CAMPAIGN in any way, choosing to remain at your home in Baton Rouge, Louisiana. But when the returns are in you travel alone up the Mississippi and then overland to make a triumphal entry into Washington on Friday evening, February 23rd, the anniversary of your victory over Santa Anna at Buena Vista the previous year. Cannon roar while Roman candles and skyrockets splash a gaudy welcome across the sky. Tired by your long journey you keep to your hotel room, working on your address with the help of leading party members. On Monday, March 5th, under an overcast sky, you ride to the Capitol in an open carriage with President Polk. Before a close-pressed crowd of thirty thousand you ignore the biting east wind and occasional snow flurries and begin to read your brief address in a low, halting voice . . . .

Zachary Taylor

[1849–1850]

INAUGURAL ADDRESS, MARCH 5, 1849

Capitol Steps, Washington, D.C.

Elected by the American people to the highest office known to our laws, I appear here to take the oath prescribed by the Constitution, and, in compliance with a time-honored custom, to address those who are now assembled.

The confidence and respect shown by my countrymen in calling me to be the Chief Magistrate of a Republic holding a high rank among the nations of the earth have inspired me with feelings of the most profound gratitude; but when I reflect that the acceptance of the office which their partiality has bestowed imposes the discharge of the most arduous duties and involves the weightiest obligations, I am conscious that the position which I have been called to fill, though sufficient to satisfy the loftiest ambition, is surrounded by fearful responsibilities. Happily, however, in the performance of my new duties I shall not be without able cooperation. The legislative and judicial branches of the Government present prominent examples of distinguished civil attainments and matured experience, and it shall by my endeavor to call to my assistance in the Executive Departments individuals whose talents, integrity, and purity of character will furnish ample guaranties for the faithful and honorable performance of the trusts to be committed to their charge. With such aids and an honest purpose to do whatever is right, I hope to execute diligently, impartially, and for the best interests of the country the manifold duties devolved upon me.

In the discharge of these duties my guide will be the Constitution, which I this day swear to "preserve, protect, and defend." For the interpretation of that instrument I shall look to the decisions of the judicial tribunals established by its authority and to the practice of the Government under the earlier Presidents, who had so large a share in its formation. To the example of those illustrious patriots I shall always defer with reverence, and especially to his example who was by so many titles "the Father of his Country."

To command the Army and Navy of the United States; with the advice and consent of the Senate, to make treaties and to appoint ambassadors and other officers; to give to Congress information of the state of the Union and recommend such measures as he shall judge to be necessary; and to take care that the laws shall be faithfully executed—these are the most important functions intrusted to the President by the Constitution, and it may be expected that I shall briefly indicate the principles which will control me in their execution.

Chosen by the body of the people under the assurance that my Administration would be devoted to the welfare of the whole country, and not to the support of any particular section or merely local interest, I

These words sounded sweet indeed to Whig leaders who had nominated Taylor without knowing how he stood on any issue. In fact, as late as April 22, 1848, in a letter to his brother-in-law, Captain J.S. Allison of Louisville, Taylor had stated, "I am a Whig, but not an ultra Whig. If elected I would not be the mere president of a party. I would endeavor to act independent of Party domination. I should feel bound to administer the government untrammeled by Party schemes." Thus the Whigs snatched eagerly at what appeared to be a change in Taylor's thinking, and prepared to furnish him with all the "able coöperation" possible.

this day renew the declarations I have heretofore made and proclaim my fixed determination to maintain to the extent of my ability the Government in its original purity and to adopt as the basis of my public policy those great republican doctrines which constitute the strength of our national existence.

In reference to the Army and Navy, lately employed with so much distinction on active service, care shall be taken to insure the highest condition of efficiency, and in furtherance of that object the military and naval schools, sustained by the liberality of Congress, shall receive the special attention of the Executive.

As American freemen we can not but sympathize in all efforts to extend the blessings of civil and political liberty, but at the same time we are warned by the admonitions of history and the voice of our own beloved Washington to abstain from entangling alliances with foreign nations. In all disputes between conflicting governments it is our interest not less than our duty to remain strictly neutral, while our geographical position, the genius of our institutions and our people, the advancing spirit of civilization, and, above all, the dictates of religion direct us to the cultivation of peaceful and friendly relations with all other powers. It is to be hoped that no international question can now arise which a government confident in its own strength and resolved to protect its own just rights may not settle by wise negotiation; and it eminently becomes a government like our own, founded on the morality and intelligence of its citizens and upheld by their affections, to exhaust every resort of honorable diplomacy before appealing to arms. In the conduct of our foreign relations I shall conform to these views, as I believe them essential to the best interests and the true honor of the country.

The appointing power vested in the President imposes delicate and onerous duties. So far as it is possible to be informed, I shall make honesty, capacity, and fidelity indispensable prerequisites to the bestowal of office, and the absence of either of these qualities shall be deemed sufficient cause for removal.

It shall be my study to recommend such constitutional measures to Congress as may be necessary and proper to secure encouragement and protection to the great interests of agriculture, commerce, and manufactures, to improve our rivers and harbors, to provide for the speedy extinguishment of the public debt, to enforce a strict accountability on the part of all officers of the Government and the utmost economy in all public expenditures; but it is for the wisdom of Congress itself, in which all legislative powers are vested by the Constitution, to regulate these and other matters of domestic policy. I shall look with confidence to the enlightened patriotism of that body to adopt such measures of conciliation as may harmonize conflicting interests and tend to perpetuate that Union which should be the paramount object of our hopes and affections. In any action calculated to promote an object so near the heart of everyone who truly loves his country I will zealously unite with the coordinate branches of the Government.

In conclusion I congratulate you, my fellow-citizens, upon the high state of prosperity to which the goodness of Divine Providence has conducted our common country. Let us invoke a continuance of the same protecting care which has led us from small beginnings to the eminence we this day occupy, and let us seek to deserve that continuance by prudence and moderation in our councils, by well-directed attempts to assuage the bitterness which too often marks unavoidable differences of opinion, by the promulgation and practice of just and liberal principles, and by an enlarged patriotism, which shall acknowledge no limits but those of our own wide-spread Republic.

The untimely death of President Zachary Taylor was due to overexposure on a hot, muggy Fourth of July in 1850. The President had been present at the laying of the cornerstone of the Washington Monument and had been taken ill during the long ceremonies in the oppressive heat. He died five days later of what was diagnosed as cholera morbus, thereby opening the presidency to Vice-President Fillmore.

Millard Fillmore

[1850–1853]

THE PRESIDENT

Millard Fillmore was sworn in as the 13th President of the United States on July 10, 1850, the second to achieve that position by succession. The months Fillmore had spent as vice-president were eventful ones: former President James K. Polk had died June 15, 1849; California requested admission to the Union as a free state; the census of 1850 revealed a population of 23,191,876, an increase of six million in ten years; the Clayton-Bulwer Treaty between the United States and Great Britain established the neutrality of a proposed canal to be constructed across Central America; the gold rush to California, begun in '48 and '49, reached its peak in July of 1850, the same month Fillmore took office.

The new president typified the American success story. From a log cabin birthplace he rose to the nation's highest honor in a span of fifty years. While working as a wool carder he fell in love with the village school teacher, Abigail Powers, who helped him to learn to read and write. The town lawyer took the aspiring young student under his tutelage, and soon Fillmore was teaching school himself while studying law at every available moment. In 1826 Fillmore was married to his schoolma'am, and shortly thereafter began practicing law with such success that he was elected a member of the New York Legislature and served four terms as a member of Congress from New York. The strikingly handsome, well-groomed Fillmore established a wide reputation for honesty and adherence to Whig precepts—a sometimes difficult feat—and was nominated by the Whigs for governor of New York but was defeated. However, the Whigs made him State Controller in recognition of his unswerving loyalty to the party.

In the campaign of 1848, when the Whigs felt it essential to nominate an antislavery vice-presidential candidate to attract votes in the North, Fillmore was chosen to balance Zachary Taylor's Southern appeal. Although Taylor refused to commit himself on any issue during the campaign he was nevertheless a slaveholding Southerner. The Whigs felt this plus his Mexican War record would meld with Fillmore's virtually unblemished background to carry the election for the Whigs— as indeed it did.

In an attempt to ease the tension growing out of the slavery question the aging Henry Clay, the Great Compromiser, introduced five bills in Congress which later became known as the Compromise of 1850. Under the compromise California was admitted as a free state. New Mexico and Utah were to be admitted later as either free or slave depending on the constitution adopted in each state. There seemed to be no great outcry when these provisions became law. But when Fillmore signed the Fugitive Slave Act on September 18, 1850, as part of Clay's Compromise, radical Whigs split the party irrevocably.

Fillmore's act turned a large number of influential Whigs against him. In the election of 1852 he failed to win the nomination, and the Whigs once more chose a fighting man as their standard bearer: General Winfield Scott. And yet, strangely enough, after the convention smoke had cleared away both candidate Scott and his vice-presidential running mate, William A. Graham of North Carolina, were pledged to uphold the same Compromise that had turned so many Whigs against Fillmore.

THE PRESIDENT

Franklin Pierce was far superior in his educational background and intellectual capabilities to either of his two immediate predecessors. He graduated with honors from Bowdoin in 1824 and was admitted to the bar in 1827. In 1829 Pierce began a four-year term in the State Legislature and stepped from there to Congress in 1833. He became a Senator in 1837. Resigning in 1842, Pierce served in the Mexican War under his future political opponent, General Scott. He defeated Scott overwhelmingly at the polls in 1852, after a campaign in which neither candidate had participated actively.

THE NATION

A supershowman named P.T. Barnum introduced an unknown young girl, September 11, 1850, at Castle Garden, New York City. Her name was Jenny Lind and she was billed as the "Swedish Nightingale." Her triumphal tour through 137 cities brought thousands to her concerts, including President Fillmore and his wife. California entered the Union on September 9, 1850. The nation's interest in international sports grew considerably after the yacht *America* crossed the Atlantic, whipping fourteen English entrants in a 60-mile race around the Isle of Wight. Its crew brought back "The America's Cup," which has remained in this country's possession ever since. The Fugitive Slave Act sparked the idea for Harriet Beecher Stowe's *Uncle Tom's Cabin,* helping to crystallize Northern feeling against slavery.

In 1852 the death of Henry Clay on June 29 and Daniel Webster on October 24 deprived the Whigs of two great leaders, and helped contribute to their defeat in the election of that year. The Whigs forsook Fillmore and reverted to their previously successful formula of presenting a military hero for the presidency, backed up by a vice-presidential candidate from a different part of the country. For their candidates they nominated the vainglorious trencherman in uniform General Winfield Scott (aptly nicknamed "Old Fuss and Feathers") for president and William A. Graham of North Carolina for vice-president. But the nation rejected the two-faced Whigs and swept them out in an electoral landslide: Democrat Franklin Pierce received 1,601,274 popular votes (245 electoral), Whig Winfield Scott received 1,386,580 popular votes (42 electoral), with the Free-Soil candidate John P. Hale tallying only 155,825 votes. William R. King of Alabama was elected vice-president.

THE WORLD

At the turn of the half century the perimeter of the civilized world began to shrink with an ever-increasing rapidity. The spread of the telegraph, the laying of the first transatlantic cable between the United States and England and the use of a similar cable between Dover and Calais, the increased replacement of sail by steam—all these innovations brought the peoples of the world closer together with each passing year. England under Victoria exploited these factors to great advantage, increasing her colonial empire in all parts of the globe.

YOU ARE PROBABLY THE MOST RETICENT of all men to accept the presidency—even more so than Zachary Taylor. Besides refusing to participate in the pre-election campaign, as Taylor did, you also have a more personal and tragic reason for your lack of enthusiasm. Only two months before your inauguration on January 6, 1853, you and your wife witness the death of your third and only surviving child, Benjamin, a boy of eleven, in a train wreck. Your wife associates the tragedy with your election, and is so affected she cannot attend your inaugural even though she knows you intend to reaffirm your reputation as a superb speaker by ignoring your written address and delivering your long message entirely from memory . . . .

Franklin Pierce

[1853–1857]

INAUGURAL ADDRESS, MARCH 4, 1853

Capitol Steps, Washington, D.C.

My Countrymen:

It is a relief to feel that no heart but my own can know the personal regret and bitter sorrow which I have been borne to a position so suitable for others rather than desirable for myself.

The circumstances under which I have been called for a limited period to preside over the destinies of the Republic fill me with a profound sense of responsibility, but with nothing like shrinking apprehension. I repair to the post assigned me not as to one sought, but in obedience to the unsolicited expression of your will, answerable only for a fearless, faithful, and diligent exercise of my best powers. I ought to be, and am, truly grateful for the rare manifestation of the nation's confidence; but this, so far from lightening my obligations, only adds to their weight. You have summoned me in my weakness; you must sustain me by your strength. When looking for the fulfillment of reasonable requirements, you will not be unmindful of the great changes which have occurred, even within the last quarter of a century, and the consequent augmentation and complexity of duties imposed in the administration both of your home and foreign affairs.

Whether the elements of inherent force in the Republic have kept pace with its unparalleled progression in territory, population, and wealth has been the subject of earnest thought and discussion on both sides of the ocean. Less than sixty-four years ago the Father of his Country made "the" then "recent accession of the important State of North Carolina to the Constitution of the United States" one of the subjects of his special congratulation. At that moment, however, when the agitation consequent upon the Revolutionary struggle had hardly subsided, when we were just emerging from the weakness and embarrassments of the Confederation, there was an evident consciousness of vigor equal to the great mission so wisely and bravely fulfilled by our fathers. It was not a presumptuous assurance, but a calm faith, springing from a clear view of the sources of power in a government constituted like ours. It is no paradox to say that although comparatively weak the new-born nation was intrinsically strong. Inconsiderable in population and

Pierce's opening remark referred to the death of his son in a train wreck between Boston and Concord a month after the election. The accident so depressed Mrs. Pierce that it was two years before she shook off her melancholia and made a perfunctory appearance at the New Year's reception of 1854 in the East Room of the White House.

[103]

apparent resources, it was upheld by a broad and intelligent comprehension of rights and an all-pervading purpose to maintain them, stronger than armaments. It came from the furnace of the Revolution, tempered to the necessities of the times. The thoughts of the men of that day were as practical as their sentiments were patriotic. They wasted no portion of their energies upon idle and delusive speculations, but with a firm and fearless step advanced beyond the governmental landmarks which had hitherto circumscribed the limits of human freedom and planted their standard, where it has stood against dangers which have threatened from abroad, and internal agitation, which has at times fearfully menaced at home. They proved themselves equal to the solution of the great problem, to understand which their minds had been illuminated by the dawning lights of the Revolution. The object sought was not a thing dreamed of; it was a thing realized. They had exhibited not only the power to achieve, but, what all history affirms to be so much more unusual, the capacity to maintain. The oppressed throughout the world from that day to the present have turned their eyes hitherward, not to find those lights extinguished or to fear lest they should wane, but to be constantly cheered by their steady and increasing radiance.

In this our country has, in my judgment, thus far fulfilled its highest duty to suffering humanity. It has spoken and will continue to speak, not only by its words, but by its acts, the language of sympathy, encouragement, and hope to those who earnestly listen to tones which pronounce for the largest rational liberty. But after all, the most animating encouragement and potent appeal for freedom will be its own history—its trials and its triumphs. Preeminently, the power of our advocacy reposes in our example; but no example, be it remembered, can be powerful for lasting good, whatever apparent advantages may be gained, which is not based upon eternal principles of right and justice. Our fathers decided for themselves, both upon the hour to declare and the hour to strike. They were their own judges of the circumstances under which it became them to pledge to each other "their lives, their fortunes, and their sacred honor" for the acquisition of the priceless inheritance transmitted to us. The energy with which that great conflict was opened and, under the guidance of a manifest and beneficent Providence the uncomplaining endurance with which it was prosecuted to its consummation were only surpassed by the wisdom and patriotic spirit of concession which characterized all the counsels of the early fathers.

One of the most impressive evidences of that wisdom is to be found in the fact that the actual working of our system has dispelled a degree of solicitude which at the outset disturbed bold hearts and far-reaching intellects. The apprehension of dangers from extended territory, multiplied States, accumulated wealth, and augmented population has proved to be unfounded. The stars upon your banner have become nearly threefold their original number; your densely populated possessions skirt the shores of the two great oceans; and yet this vast increase of people and territory has not only shown itself compatible with the harmonious action of the States and Federal Government in their respective constitutional spheres, but has afforded an additional guaranty of the strength and integrity of both.

With an experience thus suggestive and cheering, the policy of my Administration will not be controlled by any timid forebodings of evil from expansion. Indeed, it is not to be disguised that our

A quotation from the last line of the Declaration of Independence.

Since the founding of the Union many statesmen had expressed doubts as to the wisdom of expanding the nation's boundaries. One such had been Zachary Taylor, who—so Polk reported in his diary—had casually stated while riding to his inauguration that California was too far away to warrant consideration as an addition to the Union.

attitude as a nation and our position on the globe render the acquisition of certain possessions not within our jurisdiction eminently important for our protection, if not in the future essential for the preservation of the rights of commerce and the peace of the world. Should they be obtained, it will be through no grasping spirit, but with a view to obvious national interest and security, and in a manner entirely consistent with the strictest observance of national faith. We have nothing in our history or position to invite aggression; we have everything to beckon us to the cultivation of relations of peace and amity with all nations. Purposes, therefore, at once just and pacific will be significantly marked in the conduct of our foreign affairs. I intend that my Administration shall leave no blot upon our fair record, and trust I may safely give the assurance that no act within the legitimate scope of my constitutional control will be tolerated on the part of any portion of our citizens which can not challenge a ready justification before the tribunal of the civilized world. An Administration would be unworthy of confidence at home or respect abroad should it cease to be influenced by the conviction that no apparent advantage can be purchased at a price so dear as that of national wrong or dishonor. It is not your privilege as a nation to speak of a distant past. The striking incidents of your history, replete with instruction and furnishing abundant grounds for hopeful confidence, are comprised in a period comparatively brief. But if your past is limited, your future is boundless. Its obligations throng the unexplored pathway of advancement, and will be limitless as duration. Hence a sound and comprehensive policy should embrace not less the distant future than the urgent present.

The great objects of our pursuit as a people are best to be attained by peace, and are entirely consistent with the tranquillity and interests of the rest of mankind. With the neighboring nations upon our continent we should cultivate kindly and fraternal relations. We can desire nothing in regard to them so much as to see them consolidate their strength and pursue the paths of prosperity and happiness. If in the course of their growth we should open new channels of trade and create additional facilities for friendly intercourse, the benefits realized will be equal and mutual. Of the complicated European systems of national polity we have heretofore been independent. From their wars, their tumults, and anxieties we have been, happily, almost entirely exempt. Whilst these are confined to the nations which gave them existence, and within their legitimate jurisdiction, they can not affect us except as they appeal to our sympathies in the cause of human freedom and universal advancement. But the vast interests of commerce are common to all mankind, and the advantages of trade and international intercourse must always present a noble field for the moral influence of a great people.

With these views firmly and honestly carried out, we have a right to expect, and shall under all circumstances require, prompt reciprocity. The rights which belong to us as a nation are not alone to be regarded, but those which pertain to every citizen in his individual capacity, at home and abroad, must be sacredly maintained. So long as he can discern every star in its place upon that ensign, without wealth to purchase for him preferment or title to secure for him place, it will be his privilege, and must be his acknowledged right, to stand unabashed even in the presence of princes, with a proud consciousness that he is himself one of a nation of sovereigns and that he can not in legitimate pursuit

Pierce evidently had the acquisition of a specific possession in mind when he made these statements. But no one can say whether he was thinking of the southern part of what is now Arizona and New Mexico, obtained later from Mexico as part of the Gadsden Purchase, or the island of Cuba, which Pierce was to attempt to annex under the disgraceful Ostend Manifesto. He later claimed to know nothing of the plan purportedly hatched by American ministers to England, Spain, and France in secret conclave at Ostend, Belgium.

A brief reference to the hands-off doctrine first spelled out by President James Monroe and his Secretary of State John Quincy Adams.

Pierce could speak from personal experience about the Army, for he first enlisted as a volunteer private when Polk declared war with Mexico. He was soon made colonel, however, and later became brigadier of volunteers. Serving under General Winfield Scott in the advance on Mexico City in 1847 Pierce was injured in the Battle of Contreras and the next day at the Battle of Churubusco, but remained in service until the war ended.

Not having sought the presidency Pierce could afford to speak out boldly against political patronage and the spoils system. When he selected his Cabinet he chose men who saw eye to eye with him on his pro-slavery policies. During his entire administration he made not a single change in his Cabinet.

wander so far from home that the agent whom he shall leave behind in the place which I now occupy will not see that no rude hand of power or tyrannical passion is laid upon him with impunity. He must realize that upon every sea and on every soil where our enterprise may rightfully seek the protection of our flag American citizenship is an inviolable panoply for the security of American rights. And in this connection it can hardly be necessary to reaffirm a principle which should now be regarded as fundamental. The rights, security, and repose of this Confederacy reject the idea of interference or colonization on this side of the ocean by any foreign power beyond present jurisdiction as utterly inadmissible.

The opportunities of observation furnished by my brief experience as a soldier confirmed in my own mind the opinion, entertained and acted upon by others from the formation of the Government, that the maintenance of large standing armies in our country would be not only dangerous, but unnecessary. They also illustrated the importance—I might well say the absolute necessity —of the military science and practical skill furnished in such an eminent degree by the institution which has made your Army what it is, under the discipline and instruction of officers not more distinguished for their solid attainments, gallantry, and devotion to the public service than for unobtrusive bearing and high moral tone. The Army as organized must be the nucleus around which in every time of need the strength of your military power, the sure bulwark of your defense—a national militia—may be readily formed into a well-disciplined and efficient organization. And the skill and self-devotion of the Navy assure you that you may take the performance of the past as a pledge for the future, and may confidently expect that the flag which has waved its untarnished folds over every sea will still float in undiminished honor. But these, like many other subjects, will be appropriately brought at a future time to the attention of the coordinate branches of the Government, to which I shall always look with profound respect and with trustful confidence that they will accord to me the aid and support which I shall so much need and which their experience and wisdom will readily suggest.

In the administration of domestic affairs you expect a devoted integrity in the public service and an observance of rigid economy in all departments, so marked as never justly to be questioned. If this reasonable expectation be not realized, I frankly confess that one of your leading hopes is doomed to disappointment, and that my efforts in a very important particular must result in a humiliating failure. Offices can be properly regarded only in the light of aids for the accomplishment of these objects, and as occupancy can confer no prerogative nor importunate desire for preferment any claim, the public interest imperatively demands that they be considered with sole reference to the duties to be performed. Good citizens may well claim the protection of good laws and the benign influence of good government, but a claim for office is what the people of a republic should never recognize. No reasonable man of any party will expect the Administration to be so regardless of its responsibility and of the obvious elements of success as to retain persons known to be under the influence of political hostility and partisan prejudice in positions which will require not only severe labor, but cordial cooperation. Having no implied engagements to ratify, no rewards to bestow, no resentments to remember, and no personal wishes to consult in selections for official station, I shall fulfill this difficult and delicate trust, admitting no motive as worthy either of my character or position which does not contemplate an efficient discharge of duty and the best interests of my country. I acknowledge my obligations to the masses of my countrymen, and to them alone. Higher objects than personal aggrandizement gave direction and energy to their exertions in the late canvass, and they shall not be disappointed. They require at my hands diligence, integrity, and capacity wherever there are duties to be performed. Without these qualities in their public servants, more stringent laws for the prevention or punishment of fraud, negligence, and peculation will be vain. With them they will be unnecessary.

But these are not the only points to which you look for vigilant watchfulness. The dangers of a concentration of all power in the general government of a confederacy so vast as ours are too obvious to be disregarded. You have a right, therefore, to expect your agents in every department to regard strictly the limits imposed upon them by the Constitution of the United States. The great scheme of our constitutional liberty rests upon a proper distribution of power between the State and Federal authorities, and experience has shown that the harmony and happiness of our people must depend upon a just discrimination between the separate rights and responsibilities of the States and your common rights and obligations under the General Government; and here, in my opinion, are the considerations which should form the true basis of future concord in regard to the questions which have most seriously disturbed public tranquillity. If the Federal Government will confine itself to the exercise of powers clearly granted by the Constitution, it can hardly happen that its action upon any question should endanger the institutions of the States or interfere with their right to manage matters strictly domestic according to the will of their own people.

Pierce spelled out his belief in states' rights and slavery in unmistakable language. If there was any doubt as to whether he might be a fence straddler it was dispelled by this forthright statement.

In expressing briefly my views upon an important subject which has recently agitated the nation to almost a fearful degree, I am moved by no other impulse than a most earnest desire for the perpetuation of that Union which has made us what we are, showering upon us blessings and conferring a power and influence which our fathers could hardly have anticipated, even with their most sanguine hopes directed to a far-off future. The sentiments I now announce were not unknown before the expression of the voice which called me here. My own position upon this subject was clear and unequivocal, upon the record of my words and my acts, and it is only recurred to at this time because silence might perhaps be misconstrued. With the Union my best and dearest earthly hopes are entwined. Without it what are we individually or collectively? What becomes of the noblest field ever opened for the advancement of our race in religion, in government, in the arts, and in all that dignifies and adorns mankind? From that radiant constellation which both illumines our own way and points out to struggling nations their course, let but a single star be lost, and, if there be not utter darkness, the luster of the whole is dimmed. Do my countrymen need any assurance that such a catastrophe is not to overtake them while I possess the power to stay it? It is with me an earnest and vital belief that as the Union has been the source, under Providence, of our prosperity to this time, so it is the surest pledge of a continuance of the blessings we have enjoyed, and which we are sacredly bound to transmit undiminished to our children. The field of calm and free discussion in our country is open, and will always be so, but never has been and never can be traversed for good in a spirit of sectionalism and uncharitableness.

[107]

Once more Pierce reiterated his belief that slavery was "recognized by the Constitution" and was therefore legal. He had formerly stated this opinion in his debates with John P. Hale.

Franklin Pierce had always favored the Compromise of 1850, with its attendant Fugitive Slave Act. He boldly stated his convictions in this section of his address to let the public know without possibility of misunderstanding exactly how he could be expected to act.

In closing Pierce cautioned the South against attempting to take advantage of his expressed proslavery leanings and trying to disrupt the Union. Pierce felt preservation of the Union more important than either slavery or the definition of states' rights.

The founders of the Republic dealt with things as they were presented to them, in a spirit of self-sacrificing patriotism, and, as time has proved, with a comprehensive wisdom which it will always be safe for us to consult. Every measure tending to strengthen the fraternal feelings of all the members of our Union has had my heartfelt approbation. To every theory of society or government, whether the offspring of feverish ambition or of morbid enthusiasm, calculated to dissolve the bonds of law and affection which unite us, I shall interpose a ready and stern resistance. I believe that involuntary servitude, as it exists in different States of this Confederacy, is recognized by the Constitution. I believe that it stands like any other admitted right, and that the States where it exists are entitled to efficient remedies to enforce the constitutional provisions. I hold that the laws of 1850, commonly called the "compromise measures," are strictly constitutional and to be unhesitatingly carried into effect. I believe that the constituted authorities of this Republic are bound to regard the rights of the South in this respect as they would view any other legal and constitutional right, and that the laws to enforce them should be respected and obeyed, not with a reluctance encouraged by abstract opinions as to their propriety in a different state of society, but cheerfully and according to the decisions of the tribunal to which their exposition belongs. Such have been, and are, my convictions, and upon them I shall act. I fervently hope that the question is at rest, and that no sectional or ambitious or fanatical excitement may again threaten the durability of our institutions or obscure the light of our prosperity.

But let not the foundation of our hope rest upon man's wisdom. It will not be sufficient that sectional prejudices find no place in the public deliberations. It will not be sufficient that the rash counsels of human passion are rejected. It must be felt that there is no national security but in the nation's humble, acknowledged dependence upon God and His overruling providence.

We have been carried in safety through a perilous crisis. Wise counsels, like those which gave us the Constitution, prevailed to uphold it. Let the period be remembered as an admonition, and not as an encouragement, in any section of the Union, to make experiments where experiments are fraught with such fearful hazard. Let it be impressed upon all hearts that, beautiful as our fabric is, no earthly power or wisdom could ever reunite its broken fragments. Standing, as I do, almost within view of the green slopes of Monticello, and, as it were, within reach of the tomb of Washington, with all the cherished memories of the past gathering around me like so many eloquent voices of exhortation from heaven, I can express no better hope for my country than that the kind Providence which smiled upon our fathers may enable their children to preserve the blessings they have inherited.

Franklin Pierce

THE PRESIDENT

James Buchanan brought a wealth of political experience to the presidency, but it was not enough to enable him to cope with the swirling maelstrom of impending civil war rapidly engulfing the nation. A veteran statesman, Buchanan began his political life as a member of the Pennsylvania state legislature in 1815–16. He went to Congress in 1821, and was appointed minister to Russia by President Jackson in 1831. Buchanan served in the Senate from 1834 to 1845, when President Polk appointed "Old Buck" his Secretary of State. President Pierce made him minister to England in 1853, a post he held until his election to the presidency.

THE NATION

The hotly disputed Kansas-Nebraska Act of May 30, 1854, repealed the Missouri Compromise and stipulated that Congress could not intervene in slavery disputes within a state. It provided, however, that such questions might be appealed to the Supreme Court, resulting in the controversial Dred Scott decision of 1857.

The fuse that set off the Civil War was lit when Kansas was thrown open to settlement in 1855 in accordance with the doctrine of popular sovereignty. Settlers from both slave and free states rushed into the area and engaged in bloody combat in their struggle to determine Kansas' status. The seesaw battle between proslavery and antislavery forces was seemingly ended in favor of the former after the intervention of President Pierce. But in protest, the free state supporters formed an army. When the fanatical John Brown led the massacre of five proslavery men in May of 1856 this action touched off guerrilla warfare between proslavery "border ruffians" and antislavery forces that surged across the territory with an estimated 200 killed and two million dollars in property loss.

The election of 1856 was held in the midst of such conflict, with Democrat James Buchanan receiving 1,838,169 popular votes (174 electoral). The Whigs, the Republicans, and the antislavery Know-Nothings combined to nominate California's John C. Frémont, who received 1,341,264 popular votes (114 electoral). The proslavery branch of the Know-Nothings, also called the American party, nominated former President Millard Fillmore, who received only 874,534 votes (8 electoral). John C. Breckinridge of Kentucky was elected vice-president.

THE WORLD

The Crimean War broke out in Europe in 1853 when Russia demanded a protectorate over all Orthodox Christians residing in Turkey. Armies allied against Russia landed in the Crimea September, 1854, and laid siege to Sebastopol, which capitulated in September, 1855. In this year tough old Nicholas I of Russia died, to be succeeded by his son, Alexander II. A brief war between Britain and Persia began November 1, 1856, and ended in the Peace of Paris, which was signed on March 4, 1857, the same day James Buchanan was inaugurated as the fifteenth president of the United States.

WHEN YOU LEARN OF YOUR VICTORY you express no particular pleasure but seem disappointed the honor is so late in coming. Now you feel you've grown too old to enjoy the presidency, and state regretfully that "all the friends I loved and wanted to reward are dead and all the enemies I hated and had marked for punishment are turned my friends." Perhaps this is the key to your quixotic character, for although you make your policies clear enough as you deliver your address still you will change them almost as soon as you have finished speaking, because of your inner desire to be all things to all people and because of the impact of the Dred Scott Supreme Court decision which is to be handed down two days after the inauguration . . . .

James Buchanan

[1857–1861]

INAUGURAL ADDRESS, MARCH 4, 1857

Capitol Steps, Washington, D.C.

Fellow-Citizens:

I appear before you this day to take the solemn oath "that I will faithfully execute the office of President of the United States and will to the best of my ability preserve, protect, and defend the Constitution of the United States."

In entering upon this great office I must humbly invoke the God of our fathers for wisdom and firmness to execute its high and responsible duties in such a manner as to restore harmony and ancient friendship among the people of the several States and to preserve our free institutions throughout many generations. Convinced that I owe my election to the inherent love for the Constitution and the Union which still animates the hearts of the American people, let me earnestly ask their powerful support in sustaining all just measures calculated to perpetuate these, the richest political blessings which Heaven has ever bestowed upon any nation. Having determined not to become a candidate for reelection, I shall have no motive to influence my conduct in administering the Government except the desire ably and faithfully to serve my country and to live in grateful memory of my countrymen.

We have recently passed through a Presidential contest in which the passions of our fellow-citizens were excited to the highest degree by questions of deep and vital importance; but when the people proclaimed their will the tempest at once subsided and all was calm.

The voice of the majority, speaking in the manner prescribed by the Constitution, was heard, and instant submission followed. Our own country could alone have exhibited so grand and striking a spectacle of the capacity of man for self-government.

What a happy conception, then, was it for Congress to apply this simple rule, that the will of the majority shall govern, to the settlement of the question of domestic slavery in the Territories! Congress is neither "to legislate slavery into any Territory or State nor to exclude it therefrom, but to leave the people thereof perfectly free to form and regulate their domestic institutions in their own way, subject only to the Constitution of the United States."

As a natural consequence, Congress has also prescribed that when

Buchanan was elected at a time when a strong personality was needed to lead the nation. But instead of taking a firm stand on the question of slavery, he tried to please both sides, apparently motivated by the desire expressed here "to live in grateful memory" of his countrymen. Even in his December 4, 1860, address to Congress Buchanan would be noncommital. His failure to take any stand would be unsatisfactory both to Southerners and Northerners. Lincoln's inauguration would see seven states already seceded from the Union, with the first shots on Fort Sumter only five weeks away.

Another example of unrealistic and wishful thinking on Buchanan's part. The "tempest," instead of subsiding, will gather strength during his four years in office, thanks to his policy of compromise and vacillation.

A quotation from the Kansas-Nebraska Act.

Another quotation from the Kansas-Nebraska Act.

the Territory of Kansas shall be admitted as a State it "shall be received into the Union with or without slavery, as their constitution may prescribe at the time of their admission."

A difference of opinion has arisen in regard to the point of time when the people of a Territory shall decide this question for themselves.

This is, happily, a matter of but little practical importance. Besides, it is a judicial question, which legitimately belongs to the Supreme Court of the United States, before whom it is now pending, and will, it is understood, be speedily and finally settled. To their decision, in common with all good citizens, I shall cheerfully submit, whatever this may be, though it has ever been my individual opinion that under the Nebraska-Kansas act the appropriate period will be when the number of actual residents in the Territory shall justify the formation of a constitution with a view to its admission as a State into the Union. But be this as it may, it is the imperative and indispensable duty of the Government of the United States to secure to every resident inhabitant the free and independent expression of his opinion by his vote. This sacred right of each individual must be preserved. That being accomplished, nothing can be fairer than to leave the people of a Territory free from all foreign interference to decide their own destiny for themselves, subject only to the Constitution of the United States.

The whole Territorial question being thus settled upon the principle of popular sovereignty—a principle as ancient as free government itself—everything of a practical nature has been decided. No other question remains for adjustment, because all agree that under the Constitution slavery in the States is beyond the reach of any human power except that of the respective States themselves wherein it exists. May we not, then, hope that the long agitation on this subject is approaching its end, and that the geographical parties to which it has given birth, so much dreaded by the Father of his Country, will speedily become extinct? Most happy will it be for the country when the public mind shall be diverted from this question to others of more pressing and practical importance. Throughout the whole progress of this agitation, which has scarcely known any intermission for more than twenty years, whilst it has been productive of no positive good to any human being it has been the prolific source of great evils to the master, to the slave, and to the whole country. It has alienated and estranged the people of the sister States from each other, and has even seriously endangered the very existence of the Union. Nor has the danger yet entirely ceased. Under our system there is a remedy for all mere political evils in the sound sense and sober judgment of the people. Time is a great corrective. Political subjects which but a few years ago excited and exasperated the public mind have passed away and are now nearly forgotten. But this question of domestic slavery is of far graver importance than any mere political question, because should the agitation continue it may eventually endanger the personal safety of a large portion of our countrymen where the institution exists. In that event no form of government, however admirable in itself and however productive of material benefits, can compensate for the loss of peace and domestic security around the family altar. Let every Union-loving man, therefore, exert his best influence to suppress this agitation, which since the recent legislation of Congress is without any legitimate object.

It is an evil omen of the times that men have undertaken to calculate the mere material value of the Union. Reasoned estimates

For a statesman of Buchanan's experience he exhibited a surprising naïveté in these remarks. The struggle in Kansas was certainly ample proof that all citizens definitely did not agree on the principle that "under the Constitution slavery in the States is beyond the reach of any human power except that of the respective States themselves wherein it exists."

[112]

have been presented of the pecuniary profits and local advantages which would result to different States and sections from its dissolution and of the comparative injuries which such an event would inflict on other States and sections. Even descending to this low and narrow view of the mighty question, all such calculations are at fault. The bare reference to a single consideration will be conclusive on this point. We at present enjoy a free trade throughout our extensive and expanding country such as the world has never witnessed. This trade is conducted on railroads and canals, on noble rivers and arms of the sea, which bind together the North and the South, the East and the West, of our Confederacy. Annihilate this trade, arrest its free progress by the geographical lines of jealous and hostile States, and you destroy the prosperity and onward march of the whole and every part and involve all in one common ruin. But such considerations, important as they are in themselves, sink into insignificance when we reflect on the terrific evils which would result from disunion to every portion of the Confederacy— to the North, not more than to the South, to the East not more than to the West. These I shall not attempt to portray, because I feel an humble confidence that the kind Providence which inspired our fathers with wisdom to frame the most perfect form of government and union ever devised by man will not suffer it to perish until it shall have been peacefully instrumental by its example in the extension of civil and religious liberty throughout the world.

Next in importance to the maintenance of the Constitution and the Union is the duty of preserving the Government free from the taint or even the suspicion of corruption. Public virtue is the vital spirit of republics, and history proves that when this has decayed and the love of money has usurped its place, although the forms of free government may remain for a season, the substance has departed forever.

Our present financial condition is without a parallel in history. No nation has ever before been embarrassed from too large a surplus in its treasury. This almost necessarily gives birth to extravagant legislation. It produces wild schemes of expenditure and begets a race of speculators and jobbers, whose ingenuity is exerted in contriving and promoting expedients to obtain public money. The purity of official agents, whether rightfully or wrongfully, is suspected, and the character of the government suffers in the estimation of the people. This is in itself a very great evil.

The natural mode of relief from this embarrassment is to appropriate the surplus in the Treasury to great national objects for which a clear warrant can be found in the Constitution. Among these I might mention the extinguishment of the public debt, a reasonable increase of the Navy, which is at present inadequate to the protection of our vast tonnage afloat, now greater than that of any other nation, as well as to the defense of our extended seacoast.

It is beyond all question the true principle that no more revenue ought to be collected from the people than the amount necessary to defray the expenses of a wise, economical, and efficient administration of the Government. To reach this point it was necessary to resort to a modification of the tariff, and this has, I trust, been accomplished in such a manner as to do as little injury as may have been practicable to our domestic manufactures, especially those necessary for the defense of the country. Any discrimination against a particular branch for the purpose of benefiting favored corporations, individuals, or interests would have been unjust to the rest of the community and inconsistent with that spirit of fairness and

More wishful thinking on the part of an old man who was trying to substitute evasion and indecision for the forthright action a man of Andrew Jackson's stature and boldness would have used. The nation, however, tiring of years of political fence straddling by members of both parties, was soon to find a new kind of leader in a self-educated rail splitter from Illinois.

Buchanan's predecessor, Franklin Pierce, left office with the nation's current financial status well in the black. The conservative Pierce had run a tidy shop, but refused a second term because of his wife's antipathy toward the presidency.

equality which ought to govern in the adjustment of a revenue tariff.

But the squandering of the public money sinks into comparative insignificance as a temptation to corruption when compared with the squandering of the public lands.

No nation in the tide of time has ever been blessed with so rich and noble an inheritance as we enjoy in the public lands. In administering this important trust, whilst it may be wise to grant portions of them for the improvement of the remainder, yet we should never forget that it is our cardinal policy to reserve these lands, as much as may be, for actual settlers, and this at moderate prices. We shall thus not only best promote the prosperity of the new States and Territories, by furnishing them a hardy and independent race of honest and industrious citizens, but shall secure homes for our children and our children's children, as well as for those exiles from foreign shores who may seek in this country to improve their condition and to enjoy the blessings of civil and religious liberty. Such emigrants have done much to promote the growth and prosperity of the country. They have proved faithful both in peace and in war. After becoming citizens they are entitled, under the Constitution and laws, to be placed on a perfect equality with native-born citizens, and in this character they should ever be kindly recognized.

The Federal Constitution is a grant from the States to Congress of certain specific powers, and the question whether this grant should be liberally or strictly construed has more or less divided political parties from the beginning. Without entering into the argument, I desire to state at the commencement of my Administration that long experience and observation have convinced me that a strict construction of the powers of the Government is the only true, as well as the only safe, theory of the Constitution. Whenever in our past history doubtful powers have been exercised by Congress, these have never failed to produce injurious and unhappy consequences. Many such instances might be adduced if this were the proper occasion. Neither is it necessary for the public service to strain the language of the Constitution, because all the great and useful powers required for a successful administration of the Government, both in peace and in war, have been granted, either in express terms or by the plainest implication.

Whilst deeply convinced of these truths, I yet consider it clear that under the war-making power Congress may appropriate money toward the construction of a military road when this is absolutely necessary for the defense of any State or Territory of the Union against foreign invasion. Under the Constitution Congress has power "to declare war," "to raise and support armies," "to provide and maintain a navy," and to call forth the militia to "repel invasions." Thus endowed, in an ample manner, with the war-making power, the corresponding duty is required that "the United States shall protect each of them [the States] against invasion." Now, how it is possible to afford this protection to California and our Pacific possessions except by means of a military road through the Territories of the United States, over which men and munitions of war may be speedily transported from the Atlantic States to meet and to repel the invader? In the event of a war with a naval power much stronger than our own we should then have no other available access to the Pacific Coast, because such a power would instantly close the route across the isthmus of Central America. It is impossible to conceive that whilst the Constitution has expressly

Buchanan's father was an Irish immigrant who became a country storekeeper near Mercersburg in Pennsylvania and was able to send his son to Dickinson College. Hence Buchanan's concern for "exiles from foreign shores."

The President-elect seemed to contradict himself in this passage. In the preceding paragraph he stated his belief in a strict interpretation of Constitutional powers. Then he immediately advanced arguments to back up his belief that the Constitution granted Congress the implied power to construct "a military road when this is absolutely necessary for the defense of any State or Territory of the Union against foreign invasion." His entire line of reasoning was based on powers he chose to believe were implied by the Constitution, in direct contrast to his preceding statement.

[114]

required Congress to defend all the States it should yet deny to them, by any fair construction, the only possible means by which one of these States can be defended. Besides, the Government, ever since its origin, has been in the constant practice of constructing military roads. It might also be wise to consider whether the love for the Union which now animates our fellow-citizens on the Pacific Coast may not be impaired by our neglect or refusal to provide for them, in their remote and isolated condition, the only means by which the power of the States on this side of the Rocky Mountains can reach them in sufficient time to "protect" them "against invasion." I forbear for the present from expressing an opinion as to the wisest and most economical mode in which the Government can lend its aid in accomplishing this great and necessary work. I believe that many of the difficulties in the way, which now appear formidable, will in a great degree vanish as soon as the nearest and best route shall have been satisfactorily ascertained.

It may be proper that on this occasion I should make some brief remarks in regard to our rights and duties as a member of the great family of nations. In our intercourse with them there are some plain principles, approved by our own experience, from which we should never depart. We ought to cultivate peace, commerce, and friendship with all nations, and this not merely as the best means of promoting our own material interests, but in a spirit of Christian benevolence toward our fellow-men, wherever their lot may be cast. Our diplomacy should be direct and frank, neither seeking to obtain more nor accepting less than is our due. We ought to cherish a sacred regard for the independence of all nations, and never attempt to interfere in the domestic concerns of any unless this shall be imperatively required by the great law of self-preservation. To avoid entangling alliances has been a maxim of our policy ever since the days of Washington, and its wisdom no one will attempt to dispute. In short, we ought to do justice in a kindly spirit to all nations and require justice from them in return.

Once more Washington was given credit for the words "entangling alliances," although credit for the phrase rightfully belonged to Jefferson.

It is our glory that whilst other nations have extended their dominions by the sword we have never acquired any territory except by fair purchase or, as in the case of Texas, by the voluntary determination of a brave, kindred, and independent people to blend their destinies with our own. Even our acquisitions from Mexico form no exception. Unwilling to take advantage of the fortune of war against a sister republic, we purchased these possessions under the treaty of peace for a sum which was considered at the time a fair equivalent. Our past history forbids that we shall in the future acquire territory unless this be sanctioned by the laws of justice and honor. Acting on this principle, no nation will have a right to interfere or to complain if in the progress of events we shall still further extend our possessions. Hitherto in all our acquisitions the people, under the protection of the American flag, have enjoyed civil and religious liberty, as well as equal and just laws, and have been contented, prosperous, and happy. Their trade with the rest of the world has rapidly increased, and thus every commercial nation has shared largely in their successful progress.

I shall now proceed to take the oath prescribed by the Constitution, whilst humbly invoking the blessing of Divine Providence on this great people.

THE PRESIDENT

At the age of 22 Abraham Lincoln clerked in a store in New Salem, Illinois. He served as captain of a company of volunteers in the Black Hawk War of 1832, and then, while studying law, worked as a postmaster from 1833 to 1836. Beginning in 1834, Lincoln spent four terms in the state legislature on the Whig side of the chamber. He was licensed as an attorney in 1836, formed a partnership with John T. Stuart in Springfield in 1837, was elected to Congress in 1846, and in 1860 captured the Republican nomination for the presidency as an unknown—a dark horse.

THE NATION

Buchanan—ridiculed in cartoons of the day as Old Buck, with an exaggerated topknot that gave him the look of an aged kewpie doll—was far too old and feeble to shoulder the crushing load of impending civil war, and snatched at the first means available to defer such action. On February 2, 1858, Buchanan recommended to Congress that Kansas be admitted as a slave state under the provisions of the Lecompton constitution. This hasty and ill-advised move resulted in a split within the Democratic party, alienated Stephen A. Douglas, and precipitated the Lincoln-Douglas debates. Minnesota and Oregon became states in 1858 and 1859 respectively.

In the fall elections the Republicans showed remarkable gains. The party was strengthened in large measure by the forthright logic of Abraham Lincoln, who now began to attract some attention outside Illinois as a man with the ability—and courage—to penetrate to the heart of a problem and state his convictions in plain, blunt words that somehow carried a razor sharpness. "A house divided against itself cannot stand," Lincoln said, applying the biblical reference to the slavery question. "I believe this government cannot endure permanently half slave and half free. I do not expect the Union to be dissolved. I do not expect the house to fall, but I do expect it will cease to be divided. It will become all one thing or all the other." There was no question as to Lincoln's stand.

After John Brown's raid on Harper's Ferry alarm spread throughout the South, helping to crystallize secession sentiment into action. The resultant split in the Democratic party made the election of the Republican candidate almost a certainty, and the outspoken Lincoln was nominated over William H. Seward after two ballots. In the 1860 election Lincoln received 1,866,452 popular votes (180 electoral—carrying 18 free states). The Democrats' Stephen A. Douglas received 1,375,157 popular votes (12 electoral—carrying only Missouri). The Southern Democrats' John C. Breckinridge garnered 847,953 popular votes (72 electoral votes—carrying 11 slave states). The Constitutional Union party, composed of what was left of the Whig and American parties, nominated John Bell of Tennessee, who received 590,631 popular votes (39 electoral votes—carrying 3 border slave states). Hannibal Hamlin was elected vice-president.

THE WORLD

In the period immediately preceding the Civil War in the United States sporadic conflicts broke out abruptly in Cuba, Turkey, Mexico, Austria, Sardinia, Venezuela, Argentina, and China, but quickly subsided as though dissipated by the war clouds over America.

BEFORE LEAVING SPRINGFIELD for the Capitol you have prepared your inaugural address and had it set in type. But you continue to make changes in your text almost to the moment you stand outside the Capitol on a specially erected wooden platform. You listen to your friend, Senator Edward D. Baker of Oregon introduce you to the restless and uneasy throng present on this sunny but nippy March day, waiting to hear for themselves what you will say about slavery. Already seven states have seceded from the Union since your election in December, and the nation has been figuratively holding its breath for this moment. Now you step forward, unroll your typeset manuscript with its many changes, adjust your spectacles, and begin to read in a high-pitched but powerful voice that carries even to the outskirts of the crowd . . . .

Abraham Lincoln

[1861–1865]

FIRST INAUGURAL ADDRESS, MARCH 4, 1861

Capitol Steps, Washington, D.C.

Fellow-Citizens of the United States:

In compliance with a custom as old as the Government itself, I appear before you to address you briefly and to take in your presence the oath prescribed by the Constitution of the United States to be taken by the President "before he enters on the execution of this office."

I do not consider it necessary at present for me to discuss those matters of administration about which there is no special anxiety or excitement.

Apprehension seems to exist among the people of the Southern States that by the accession of a Republican Administration their property and their peace and personal security are to be endangered. There has never been any reasonable cause for such apprehension. Indeed, the most ample evidence to the contrary has all the while existed and been open to their inspection. It is found in nearly all the published speeches of him who now addresses you. I do but quote from one of those speeches when I declare that—

I have no purpose, directly or indirectly, to interfere with the institution of slavery in the States where it exists. I believe I have no lawful right to do so, and I have no inclination to do so.

Those who nominated and elected me did so with full knowledge that I had made this and many similar declarations and had never recanted them; and more than this, they placed in the platform for my acceptance, and as a law to themselves and to me, the clear and emphatic resolution which I now read:

Resolved, That the maintenance inviolate of the rights of the States, and especially the right of each State to order and control its own domestic institutions according to its own judgment exclusively, is essential to that balance of power on which the perfection and endurance of our political fabric depend; and we denounce the lawless invasion by armed force of the soil of any State or Territory, no matter what pretext, as among the gravest of crimes.

I now reiterate these sentiments, and in doing so I only press upon the public attention the most conclusive evidence of which the

Lincoln began to compose his address in Springfield, where he isolated himself in an unused back room over his brother-in-law's shop near the State House. He used four references: the Constitution, Clay's speech of 1850, Jackson's nullification proclamation, and Webster's reply to Hayne. Knowing the anxiety of the proslavery Southerners, Lincoln offered them immediate reassurance, by quoting from one of his previously published speeches.

As far back as his House Divided speech Lincoln had stated his belief in nonintervention, which he here reiterated.

This was the fourth of seventeen platform planks advocated by the Republicans in 1860. The South's firing on Fort Sumter, five weeks after Lincoln took office, forced him to back up his denunciation of "lawless invasion by armed force" with an armed force wearing Union blue—and the war was on.

case is susceptible that the property, peace, and security of no section are to be in any wise endangered by the now incoming Administration. I add, too, that all the protection which, consistently with the Constitution and the laws, can be given will be cheerfully given to all the States when lawfully demanded, for whatever cause—as cheerfully to one section as to another.

There is much controversy about the delivering up of fugitives from service or labor. The clause I now read is as plainly written in the Constitution as any other of its provisions:

> No person held to service or labor in one State, under the laws thereof, escaping into another, shall, in consequence of any law or regulation therein, be discharged from such service or labor, but shall be delivered up on claim of the party to whom such service or labor may be due.

The clause quoted was from Article IV, Section 2, Clause 3 of the Constitution.

It is scarcely questioned that this provision was intended by those who made it for the reclaiming of what we call fugitive slaves; and the intention of the lawgiver is the law. All members of Congress swear their support to the whole Constitution—to this provision as much as to any other. To the proposition, then, that slaves whose cases come within the terms of this clause "shall be delivered up" their oaths are unanimous. Now, if they would make the effort in good temper, could they not with nearly equal unanimity frame and pass a law by means of which to keep good that unanimous oath?

There is some difference of opinion whether this clause should be enforced by national or by State authority, but surely that difference is not a very material one. If the slave is to be surrendered, it can be of but little consequence to him or to others by which authority it is done. And should anyone in any case be content that his oath shall go unkept on a merely unsubstantial controversy as to *how* it shall be kept?

Note the touch of ironic humor so characteristic of Lincoln.

Again: In any law upon this subject ought not all the safeguards of liberty known in civilized and humane jurisprudence to be introduced, so that a free man be not in any case surrendered as a slave? And might it not be well at the same time to provide by law for the enforcement of that clause in the Constitution which guarantees that "the citizens of each State shall be entitled to all privileges and immunities of citizens in the several States"?

I take the official oath to-day with no mental reservations and with no purpose to construe the Constitution or laws by any hypercritical rules; and while I do not choose now to specify particular acts of Congress as proper to be enforced, I do suggest that it will be much safer for all, both in official and private stations, to conform to and abide by all those acts which stand unrepealed than to violate any of them trusting to find impunity in having them held to be unconstitutional.

It is seventy-two years since the first inauguration of a President under our National Constitution. During that period fifteen different and greatly distinguished citizens have in succession administered the executive branch of the Government. They have conducted it through many perils, and generally with great success. Yet, with all this scope of precedent, I now enter upon the same task for the brief constitutional term of four years under great and peculiar difficulty. A disruption of the Federal Union, heretofore only menaced, is now formidably attempted.

I hold that in contemplation of universal law and of the Constitution the Union of these States is perpetual. Perpetuity is implied, if not expressed, in the fundamental law of all national gov-

[118]

ernments. It is safe to assert that no government proper ever had a provision in its organic law for its own termination. Continue to execute all the express provisions of our National Constitution, and the Union will endure forever, it being impossible to destroy it except by some action not provided for in the instrument itself.

Again: If the United States be not a government proper, but an association of States in the nature of contract merely, can it, as a contract, be peaceably unmade by less than all the parties who made it? One party to a contract may violate it—break it, so to speak—but does it not require all to lawfully rescind it?

Descending from these general principles, we find the proposition that in legal contemplation the Union is perpetual confirmed by the history of the Union itself. The Union is much older than the Constitution. It was formed, in fact, by the Articles of Association in 1774. It was matured and continued by the Declaration of Independence in 1776. It was further matured, and the faith of all the then thirteen States expressly plighted and engaged that it should be perpetual, by the Articles of Confederation in 1778. And finally, in 1787, one of the declared objects for ordaining and establishing the Constitution was *"to form a more perfect Union."*

But if destruction of the Union by one or by a part only of the States be lawfully possible, the Union is *less* perfect than before the Constitution, having lost the vital element of perpetuity.

It follows from these views that no State upon its own mere motion can lawfully get out of the Union; that *resolves* and *ordinances* to that effect are legally void, and that acts of violence within any State or States against the authority of the United States are insurrectionary or revolutionary, according to circumstances.

I therefore consider that in view of the Constitution and the laws the Union is unbroken, and to the extent of my ability, I shall take care, as the Constitution itself expressly enjoins upon me, that the laws of the Union be faithfully executed in all the States. Doing this I deem to be only a simple duty on my part, and I shall perform it so far as practicable unless my rightful masters, the American people, shall withhold the requisite means or in some authoritative manner direct the contrary. I trust this will not be regarded as a menace, but only as the declared purpose of the Union that it *will* constitutionally defend and maintain itself.

In doing this there needs to be no bloodshed or violence, and there shall be none unless it be forced upon the national authority. The power confided to me will be used to hold, occupy, and possess the property and places belonging to the Government and to collect the duties and imposts; but beyond what may be necessary for these objects, there will be no invasion, no using of force against or among the people anywhere. Where hostility to the United States in any interior locality shall be so great and universal as to prevent competent resident citizens from holding the Federal offices, there will be no attempt to force obnoxious strangers among the people for that object. While the strict legal right may exist in the Government to enforce the exercise of these offices, the attempt to do so would be so irritating and so nearly impracticable withal that I deem it better to forego for the time the uses of such offices.

The mails, unless repelled, will continue to be furnished in all parts of the Union. So far as possible the people everywhere shall have that sense of perfect security which is most favorable to calm thought and reflection. The course here indicated will be followed unless current events and experience shall show a modification or change to be proper, and in every case and exigency my best discretion will be exercised, according to circumstances actually existing and with a view and a hope of a peaceful solution of the national troubles and the restoration of fraternal sympathies and affections.

That there are persons in one section or another who seek to destroy the Union at all events and are glad of any pretext to do it I will neither affirm nor deny; but if there be such, I need address no word to them. To those, however, who really love the Union may I not speak?

Before entering upon so grave a matter as the destruction of our national fabric, with all its benefits, its memories, and its hopes, would it not be wise to ascertain precisely why we do it? Will you hazard so desperate a step while there is any possibility that any portion of the ills you fly from have no real existence? Will you, while the certain ills you fly to are greater than all the real ones you fly from, will you risk the commission of so fearful a mistake?

All profess to be content in the Union if all constitutional rights can be maintained. Is it true, then, that any right plainly written in the Constitution has been denied? I think not. Happily, the human mind is so constituted that no party can reach to the audacity of doing this. Think, if you can, of a single instance in which a plainly written provision of the Constitution has ever been denied. If by the mere force of numbers a majority should deprive a minority of any clearly written constitutional right, it might in a moral point of view justify revolution; certainly would if such right were a vital one. But such is not our case. All the vital rights of minorities and of individuals are so plainly assured to them by affirmations and negations, guaranties and prohibitions, in the Constitution that controversies never arise concerning them. But no organic law can ever be framed with a provision specifically applicable to every question which may occur in practical administration. No foresight can anticipate nor any document of reasonable length contain express provisions for all possible questions. Shall fugitives from labor be surrendered by national or by State authority? The Constitution does not expressly say. *May* Congress prohibit slavery in the Territories? The Constitution does not expressly say. *Must* Congress protect slavery in the Territories? The Constitution does not expressly say.

From questions of this class spring all our constitutional controversies, and we divide upon them into majorities and minorities. If the minority will not acquiesce, the majority must, or the Government must cease. There is no other alternative, for continuing the Government is acquiescence on one side or the other. If a minority in such case will secede rather than acquiesce, they make a precedent which in turn will divide and ruin them, for a minority of their own will secede from them whenever a majority refuses to be controlled by such minority. For instance, why may not any portion of a new confederacy a year or two hence arbitrarily secede again, precisely as portions of the present Union now claim to secede from it? All who cherish disunion sentiments are now being educated to the exact temper of doing this.

Is there such perfect identity of interests among the States to compose a new union as to produce harmony only and prevent renewed secession?

Plainly the central idea of secession is the essence of anarchy. A majority held in restraint by constitutional checks and limitations, and always changing easily with deliberate changes of popular opinions and sentiments, is the only true sovereign of a free people.

Southern leaders held secession to be lawful, since in their interpretation the Federal government was not a sovereign over sovereignties, but was only an agent between them. Each state, according to this doctrine of states' rights, might adhere or secede from the Union at its own sovereign pleasure. Lincoln's argument was this: No constitutional right had been violated, and an attempt by any state to leave the Union would constitute not secession but revolution.

Lincoln's penetrating argument that one secession could spawn another and another, ad infinitum, provides a shining example of his ability to think a problem through.

Lincoln used no flowery rhetoric in this terse description of the slavery schism that was dividing the country. He immediately went back to his main point: The Union must be preserved.

[120]

Whoever rejects it does of necessity fly to anarchy or to despotism. Unanimity is impossible. The rule of a minority, as a permanent arrangement, is wholly inadmissible; so that, rejecting the majority principle, anarchy or despotism in some form is all that is left.

I do not forget the position assumed by some that constitutional questions are to be decided by the Supreme Court, nor do I deny that such decisions must be binding in any case upon the parties to a suit as to the object of that suit, while they are also entitled to very high respect and consideration in all parallel cases by all other departments of the Government. And while it is obviously possible that such decision may be erroneous in any given case, still the evil effect following it, being limited to that particular case, with the chance that it may be overruled and never become a precedent for other cases, can better be borne than could the evils of a different practice. At the same time, the candid citizen must confess that if the policy of the Government upon vital questions affecting the whole people is to be irrevocably fixed by decisions of the Supreme Court, the instant they are made in ordinary litigation between parties in personal actions the people will have ceased to be their own rulers, having to that extent practically resigned their Government into the hands of that eminent tribunal. Nor is there in this view any assault upon the court or the judges. It is a duty from which they may not shrink to decide cases properly brought before them, and it is no fault of theirs if others seek to turn their decisions to political purposes.

One section of our country believes slavery is *right* and ought to be extended, while the other believes it is *wrong* and ought not to be extended. This is the only substantial dispute. The fugitive-slave clause of the Constitution and the law for the suppression of the foreign slave trade are each as well enforced, perhaps, as any law can ever be in a community where the moral sense of the people imperfectly supports the law itself. The great body of the people abide by the dry legal obligation in both cases, and a few break over in each. This, I think, can not be perfectly cured, and it would be worse in both cases *after* the separation of the sections than before. The foreign slave trade, now imperfectly suppressed, would be ultimately revived without restriction in one section, while fugitive slaves, now only partially surrendered, would not be surrendered at all by the other.

This description of an unpopular law could have been applied years later to another piece of legislation, the eighteenth amendment.

Physically speaking, we can not separate. We can not remove our respective sections from each other nor build an impassable wall between them. A husband and wife may be divorced and go out of the presence and beyond the reach of each other, but the different parts of our country can not do this. They can not but remain face to face, and intercourse, either amicable or hostile, must continue between them. Is it possible, then, to make that intercourse more advantageous or more satisfactory *after* separation than *before?* Can aliens make treaties easier than friends can make laws? Can treaties be more faithfully enforced between aliens than laws can among friends? Suppose you go to war, you can not fight always; and when, after much loss on both sides and no gain on either, you cease fighting, the identical old questions, as to terms of intercourse, are again upon you.

Again Lincoln drove home his point: Any action on the part of the Southern states was revolutionary unless authorized by a Constitutional amendment.

This country, with its institutions, belongs to the people who inhabit it. Whenever they shall grow weary of the existing Government, they can exercise their *constitutional* right of amending it or their *revolutionary* right to dismember or overthrow it. I can not be ignorant of the fact that many worthy and patriotic citizens are desirous of having the National Constitution amended. While I make no recommendation of amendments, I fully recognize the rightful authority of the people over the whole subject, to be exercised in either of the modes prescribed in the instrument itself; and I should, under existing circumstances, favor rather than oppose a fair opportunity being afforded the people to act upon it. I will venture to add that to me the convention mode seems preferable, in that it allows amendments to originate with the people themselves, instead of only permitting them to take or reject propositions originated by others, not especially chosen for the purpose, and which might not be precisely such as they would wish to either accept or refuse. I understand a proposed amendment to the Constitution—which amendment, however, I have not seen—has passed Congress, to the effect that the Federal Government shall never interfere with the domestic institutions of the States, including that of persons held to service. To avoid misconstruction of what I have said, I depart from my purpose not to speak of particular amendments so far as to say that, holding such a provision to now be implied constitutional law, I have no objection to its being made express and irrevocable.

The Chief Magistrate derives all his authority from the people, and they have conferred none upon him to fix terms for the separation of the States. The people themselves can do this if also they choose, but the Executive as such has nothing to do with it. His duty is to administer the present Government as it came to his hands and to transmit it unimpaired by him to his successor.

Why should there not be a patient confidence in the ultimate justice of the people? Is there any better or equal hope in the world? In our present differences, is either party without faith of being in the right? If the Almighty Ruler of Nations, with His eternal truth and justice, be on your side of the North, or on yours of the South, that truth and that justice will surely prevail by the judgment of this great tribunal of the American people.

By the frame of the Government under which we live this same people have wisely given their public servants but little power for mischief, and have with equal wisdom provided for the return of that little to their own hands at very short intervals. While the people retain their virtue and vigilance no Administration by any extreme of wickedness or folly can very seriously injure the Government in the short space of four years.

My countrymen, one and all, think calmly and *well* upon this whole subject. Nothing valuable can be lost by taking time. If there be an object to *hurry* any of you in hot haste to a step which you would never take *deliberately,* that object will be frustrated by taking time; but no good object can be frustrated by it. Such of you as are now dissatisfied still have the old Constitution unimpaired, and, on the sensitive point, the laws of your own framing under it; while the new Administration will have no immediate power, if it would, to change either. If it were admitted that you who are dissatisfied hold the right side in the dispute, there still is no single good reason for precipitate action. Intelligence, patriotism, Christianity, and a firm reliance on Him who has never yet forsaken this favored land are still competent to adjust in the best way all our present difficulty.

In *your* hands, my dissatisfied fellow-countrymen, and not in *mine,* is the momentous issue of civil war. The Government will not assail *you.* You can have no conflict without being yourselves the aggres-

[122]

sors. *You* have no oath registered in heaven to destroy the Government, while *I* shall have the most solemn one to "preserve, protect, and defend it."

I am loath to close. We are not enemies, but friends. We must not be enemies. Though passion may have strained it must not break our bonds of affection. The mystic chords of memory, stretching from every battlefield and patriot grave to every living heart and hearthstone all over this broad land, will yet swell the chorus of the Union, when again touched, as surely they will be, by the better angels of our nature.

Lincoln originally intended to end his address with reference to his oath to "preserve, protect and defend" the Constitution. But Secretary of State Seward suggested some final "words of affection, some of calm and cheerful confidence," and submitted a paragraph of his own. This Lincoln transformed, through the alchemy of his eloquence, into a uniquely moving plea.

THE PRESIDENT

Sherman's capture of Atlanta and Admiral Farragut's victory at Mobile took place in 1864, just in time to help sway public opinion in favor of Lincoln's reëlection. Now, with the tide of war at last running in favor of the North, Lincoln looked ahead to the aftermath, fearing perpetuation of sectional antagonism if the conquered South were dealt with too harshly. Hence the tenor of his second inaugural address, which though short as such addresses go has taken its place among the masterpieces of written or spoken composition.

THE NATION

The Civil War broke out at Charleston, South Carolina, on April 12, 1861, when Fort Sumter refused to surrender to Confederate bombardment from Fort Moultrie.

After the Union's disastrous defeats at Bull Run, Wilson's Creek, and Ball's Bluff in 1861 the Confederates were repulsed at Pea Ridge, Shiloh, Seven Pines, and Malvern Hill. The Second Battle of Bull Run ended in a Union rout which was, however, followed by a technical Union victory at Antietam. The year ended with more than 10,000 Union casualties during the Battle of Fredericksburg.

On January 1, 1863, Lincoln issued his Emancipation Proclamation, freeing all slaves in areas outside Union control. June 20, 1863, West Virginia became the 35th state to join the Union, to be followed by Nevada on October 31, 1864.

The Confederates were victorious at Chancellorsville the first week in May, 1863. But two weeks later Grant captured Vicksburg, and when Meade fought off Lee at Gettysburg the scales of war were tipped in favor of the Union. After the battles of Chickamauga, Lookout Mountain, and Missionary Ridge the Union had divided the Confederacy vertically and was ready to drive eastward to the sea.

While Sherman was slashing his devastating swath through Georgia during the summer of 1864, the nominating conventions were held in the North. In the November election the Union Party's (the name Republican was not yet in use) Abraham Lincoln received 2,213,665 popular votes (212 electoral), while the Democrat's General George McClellan received 1,802,237 popular votes (21 electoral). Andrew Johnson was elected vice-president.

THE WORLD

In the summer of 1861 both England and France proclaimed their neutrality in America's burgeoning civil war. The death of gentle Prince Albert on December 14th saddened the English-speaking world. The great Bismarck became premier of Prussia on September 23, 1862. And, with the United States embroiled in war, the French turned their attention to Mexico. Troops occupied Mexico City in June of 1863. A year later Maximilian became emperor.

LATER YOU VIEW YOUR second inaugural address thus: "I expect it to wear as well as, perhaps better than, any thing I have produced; but I believe it is not immediately popular. Men are not flattered by being shown that there has been a difference of purpose between the Almighty and them. To deny it, however, in this case, is to deny that there is a God governing the world. It is a truth which I thought needed to be told, and, as whatever of humiliation there is in it falls most directly on myself, I thought others might afford for me to tell it." But now, as you read your short address in your high voice, neither you nor your quiet audience can know some of these words and phrases are destined for immortality . . . .

Abraham Lincoln

[1865]

SECOND INAUGURAL ADDRESS, MARCH 4, 1865

Capitol Building, Washington, D.C.

Fellow-Countrymen:

At this second appearing to take the oath of the Presidential office there is less occasion for an extended address than there was at the first. Then a statement somewhat in detail of a course to be pursued seemed fitting and proper. Now, at the expiration of four years, during which public declarations have been constantly called forth on every point and phase of the great contest which still absorbs the attention and engrosses the energies of the nation, little that is new could be presented. The progress of our arms, upon which all else chiefly depends, is as well known to the public as to myself, and it is, I trust, reasonably satisfactory and encouraging to all. With high hope for the future, no prediction in regard to it is ventured.

On the occasion corresponding to this four years ago all thoughts were anxiously directed to an impending civil war. All dreaded it, all sought to avert it. While the inaugural address was being delivered from this place, devoted altogether to *saving* the Union without war, insurgent agents were in the city seeking to *destroy* it without war—seeking to dissolve the Union and divide effects by negotiation. Both parties deprecated war, but one of them would *make* war rather than let the nation survive, and the other would *accept* war rather than let it perish, and the war came.

One-eighth of the whole population were colored slaves, not distributed generally over the Union, but localized in the southern part of it. These slaves constituted a peculiar and powerful interest. All knew that this interest was somehow the cause of war. To strengthen, perpetuate, and extend this interest was the object for which the insurgents would rend the Union even by war, while the Government claimed no right to do more than to restrict the territorial enlargement of it. Neither party expected for the war the magnitude or the duration which it has already attained. Neither anticipated that the *cause* of the conflict might cease with or even before the conflict itself should cease. Each looked for an easier triumph, and a result less fundamental and astounding. Both read the same Bible and pray to the same God, and each invokes His aid

The thirteenth amendment, introduced in Congress on February 27, 1861, had finally been passed on February 1, 1865, and ratified December 18, 1865, only a month before Lincoln's second inauguration. The progress of the war had recently been far more than "reasonably satisfactory." Sherman's march to the sea November, 1865, had followed the fall of Atlanta and led to the burning of Columbia, South Carolina, on February 17. The South was beaten, and General Lee had sent out peace feelers only two days before the inauguration.

What was it that set Lincoln apart? Unpolished of manner, careless in dress, he presented a tremendous contrast to the courtly Buchanan who preceded him and to the dynamic Douglas who opposed him. But, despite these so-called shortcomings, Lincoln's humility, his deep love of people, and his unswerving belief in the Constitution and in the destiny of the United States combined to give him a kinship with the people that was to prove unshakable.

[125]

Lincoln was quoting from the King James version of the Bible. In the Revised Standard version this quotation from Matthew 18:7 reads: "Woe to the world for temptation to sin! For it is necessary that temptations come, but woe to the man by whom the temptation comes!"

A quotation from the King James version of the Bible, Psalms 19:9. In the Revised Standard version the quotation reads, "The ordinances of the Lord are true, and righteous altogether."

In this, the best-known passage of any inaugural address, Lincoln reached the pinnacle of eloquence.

against the other. It may seem strange that any men should dare to ask a just God's assistance in wringing their bread from the sweat of other men's faces, but let us judge not, that we be not judged. The prayers of both could not be answered. That of neither has been answered fully. The Almighty has His own purposes. "Woe unto the world because of offenses; for it must needs be that offenses come, but woe to that man by whom the offense cometh." If we shall suppose that American slavery is one of those offenses which, in the providence of God, must needs come, but which, having continued through His appointed time, He now wills to remove, and that He gives to both North and South this terrible war as the woe due to those by whom the offense came, shall we discern therein any departure from those divine attributes which the believers in a living God always ascribe to Him? Fondly do we hope, fervently do we pray, that this mighty scourge of war may speedily pass away. Yet, if God wills that it continue until all the wealth piled by the bondsman's two hundred and fifty years of unrequited toil shall be sunk, and until every drop of blood drawn with the lash shall be paid by another drawn with the sword, as was said three thousand years ago, so still it must be said "the judgments of the Lord are true and righteous altogether."

With malice toward none, with charity for all, with firmness in the right as God gives us to see the right, let us strive on to finish the work we are in, to bind up the nation's wounds, to care for him who shall have borne the battle and for his widow and his orphan, to do all which may achieve and cherish a just and lasting peace among ourselves and with all nations.

Andrew Johnson was awakened in his hotel room on the night of April 14, 1865, to be told that President Lincoln had been shot and was dying. Next day, shortly after Lincoln had passed away, the fifty-six-year-old vice-president was sworn in as the 17th president of the United States.

Andrew Johnson

[1865–1869]

THE PRESIDENT

Andrew Johnson was the only president who had never set foot inside a schoolroom. At ten he had been bound out by his parents to learn to be a tailor. At sixteen Johnson ran away and became a fugitive, unable to return to his native state. Three years later he married Eliza McCardle, who helped him improve his scanty education in their small village tailor shop. Johnson developed a natural talent for speaking in public, and was elected village alderman and then mayor. Next he spent six years in the Legislature, ten years in Congress, two terms as governor of Tennessee and then moved back to Washington to serve in the Senate, where he was a special advocate of the Homestead law.

When the Civil War began, Johnson's Tennessee home was taken over by the Confederacy because Johnson, although a Southerner and a Democrat, refused to sanction secession. In the election of 1864 Johnson was chosen as a candidate by the National Union party to attract the votes of the War Democrats and Southern Unionists.

Lincoln's policy of reconstruction in the South had met with rising opposition in Congress where power-hungry radicals clamored for revenge.

With the death of Lincoln these men felt Johnson—a poor white whose home had been taken over by the South—would listen to their furious demands for vengeance. Johnson's rejection of these vengeful policies touched off a concerted campaign to undermine the President. Faced with a two-thirds majority in both House and Senate, Johnson saw his vetoes overriden again and again—with disastrous results in a South pillaged by carpetbaggers. These men moved in and took control of the defeated states under an authority granted them by the first three Reconstruction Acts, all passed over Johnson's vetoes in 1867. Congress also passed the Tenure of Office Act, which in essence provided that the president could not remove those officials appointed or approved by the Senate without the consent of that body.

When Johnson attempted to remove his Secretary of War, Edwin M. Stanton, radicals in Congress tried to impeach the President. In the ensuing trial by the Senate court of impeachment that began on March 13, 1868, the President's opponents failed by only one vote to secure the necessary two-thirds majority needed for conviction; Johnson was acquitted.

THE PRESIDENT

Ulysses Simpson Grant graduated from the U.S. Military Academy in 1843, in time to serve under Zachary Taylor and Winfield Scott in the war with Mexico. In 1854 Grant resigned from the army and for six years drifted from one occupation to another, a failure at all of them. But the outbreak of civil war thrust Grant back into his uniform. He wore it until he had earned the nation's praise and won its highest honors, culminating in the presidency.

THE NATION

While the South was struggling with reconstruction great progress was being made in the North in industry, commerce, and education. Many new universities had been chartered, including the University of Minnesota (1851), University of Illinois (1867), West Virginia University (1867), the University of California (1868), the University of Nebraska (1869), and Johns Hopkins University (1876). New inventions poured forth, soon to become the basis of new industries: the typewriter, the refrigerator car, the pullman car, ready-made cigarettes, the railroad car air brake, the elevator. The still unknown Thomas A. Edison patented his first invention for an electric voting machine.

Susan B. Anthony became president of the National Woman Suffrage Association, baseball was growing more and more popular, the B.P.O.E. (Benevolent Protective Order of Elks)

was organized in New York City. The literary world acknowledged such giants as Mark Twain, Walt Whitman, Louisa M. Alcott, Bret Harte, William Dean Howells, and Horatio Alger.

Western settlements expanded despite growing Indian resistance. Desperadoes discovered railroad trains could be robbed almost as easily as stagecoaches—and they promised far greater rewards. Abilene, Kansas, became the cattle-shipping focal point, as Chicago's packing houses demanded more and more beef for eastern markets. Nebraska became a state on March 1, 1867.

In the November, 1868, election, the Republican party's nominee General Ulysses S. Grant barely defeated the Democrats' Horatio Seymour. Grant polled 3,012,833 popular votes (214 electoral) to Seymour's 2,703,249 popular votes (80 electoral). Schuyler Colfax of Indiana was elected vice-president.

THE WORLD

With peace restored to the United States a series of armed conflicts broke out elsewhere between 1865 and 1869: Paraguay invaded Brazil and Argentina; the Fenians rioted in Ireland; Haiti suffered a military insurrection; Spain bombarded cities in Chile and Peru; Prussia, with Italy as an ally, declared war on Austria; the Greeks in Crete rose in revolt against Turkey; Maximilian was overthrown in Mexico and executed; civil war raged in Japan between supporters of the Mikado and the Shoguns, with the Mikado ultimately victorious.

YOU HATE WAR AND DETEST POLITICS, yet you have become the savior of the union and have been elected to the presidency by a grateful nation. But, despite the fame and glory, you are still the shy, gullible country boy who had difficulty holding a job as a clerk in your father's leather store in Galena, Illinois. Small wonder, then, that professional politicians and eastern financiers see you as an easy mark for their manipulations. But none of this enters your mind as you prepare your address. An embittered President Johnson has refused to attend your inauguration and so you ride alone in your carriage to the Capitol, acknowledging the cheers of the throngs lining Pennsylvania Avenue. When you at last stand on the Capitol steps and begin in a low voice to deliver your short, sincere address life seems good to you, but this feeling of well-being is to be short-lived . . . .

Ulysses S. Grant

[1869–1873]

FIRST INAUGURAL ADDRESS, MARCH 4, 1869

Capitol Steps, Washington, D.C.

Citizens of the United States:

Your suffrages having elected me to the office of President of the United States, I have, in conformity to the Constitution of our country, taken the oath of office prescribed therein. I have taken this oath without mental reservation and with the determination to do to the best of my ability all that is required of me. The responsibilities of the position I feel, but accept them without fear. The office has come to me unsought; I commence its duties untrammeled. I bring to it a conscious desire and determination to fill it to the best of my ability to the satisfaction of the people.

On all leading questions agitating the public mind I will always express my views to Congress and urge them according to my judgment, and when I think it advisable will exercise the constitutional privilege of interposing a veto to defeat measures which I oppose; but all laws will be faithfully executed, whether they meet my approval or not.

I shall on all subjects have a policy to recommend, but none to enforce against the will of the people. Laws are to govern all alike —those opposed as well as those who favor them. I know no method to secure the repeal of bad or obnoxious laws so effective as their stringent execution.

The country having just emerged from a great rebellion, many questions will come before it for settlement in the next four years which preceding Administrations have never had to deal with. In meeting these it is desirable that they should be approached calmly, without prejudice, hate, or sectional pride, remembering that the greatest good to the greatest number is the object to be attained.

This requires security of persons, property, and free religious and political opinion in every part of our common country, without regard to local prejudice. All laws to secure these ends will receive my best efforts for their enforcement.

A great debt has been contracted in securing to us and our posterity the Union. The payment of this, principal and interest, as

The "great debt" facing Grant's administration was $400,000,000. But, despite his obvious sincerity in making the promises of his address Grant would succeed in reducing the debt by only $80,000,000 during his two terms.

[129]

well as the return to a specie basis as soon as it can be accomplished without material detriment to the debtor class or to the country at large, must be provided for. To protect the national honor, every dollar of Government indebtedness should be paid in gold, unless otherwise expressly stipulated in the contract. Let it be understood that no repudiator of one farthing of our public debt will be trusted in public place, and it will go far toward strengthening a credit which ought to be the best in the world, and will ultimately enable us to replace the debt with bonds bearing less interest than we now pay. To this should be added a faithful collection of the revenue, a strict accountability to the Treasury for every dollar collected, and the greatest practicable retrenchment in expenditure in every department of Government.

When we compare the paying capacity of the country now, with the ten States in poverty from the effects of war, but soon to emerge, I trust, into greater prosperity than ever before, with its paying capacity twenty-five years ago, and calculate what it probably will be twenty-five years hence, who can doubt the feasibility of paying every dollar then with more ease than we now pay for useless luxuries? Why, it looks as though Providence had bestowed upon us a strong box in the precious metals locked up in the sterile mountains of the far West, and which we are now forging the key to unlock, to meet the very contingency that is now upon us.

Ultimately it may be necessary to insure the facilities to reach these riches, and it may be necessary also that the General Government should give its aid to secure this access; but that should only be when a dollar of obligation to pay secures precisely the same sort of dollar to use now, and not before. Whilst the question of specie payments is in abeyance the prudent business man is careful about contracting debts payable in the distant future. The nation should follow the same rule. A prostrate commerce is to be rebuilt and all industries encouraged.

The young men of the country—those who from their age must be its rulers twenty-five years hence—have a peculiar interest in maintaining the national honor. A moment's reflection as to what will be our commanding influence among the nations of the earth in their day, if they are only true to themselves, should inspire them with national pride. All divisions—geographical, political, and religious—can join in this common sentiment. How the public debt is to be paid or specie payments resumed is not so important as that a plan should be adopted and acquiesced in. A united determination to do is worth more than divided counsels upon the method of doing. Legislation upon this subject may not be necessary now, nor even advisable, but it will be when the civil law is more fully restored in all parts of the country and trade resumes its wonted channels.

It will be my endeavor to execute all laws in good faith, to collect all revenues assessed, and to have them properly accounted for and economically disbursed. I will to the best of my ability appoint to office those only who will carry out this design.

In regard to foreign policy, I would deal with nations as equitable law requires individuals to deal with each other, and I would protect the law-abiding citizen, whether of native or foreign birth, wherever his rights are jeopardized or the flag of our country floats. I would respect the rights of all nations, demanding equal respect for our own. If others depart from this rule in their dealings with us, we may be compelled to follow their precedent.

[130]

The proper treatment of the original occupants of this land—the Indians—is one deserving of careful study. I will favor any course toward them which tends to their civilization and ultimate citizenship.

The question of suffrage is one which is likely to agitate the public so long as a portion of the citizens of the nation are excluded from its privileges in any State. It seems to me very desirable that this question should be settled now, and I entertain the hope and express the desire that it may be by the ratification of the fifteenth article of amendment of the Constitution.

In conclusion I ask patient forbearance one toward another throughout the land, and a determined effort on the part of every citizen to do his share toward cementing a happy union; and I ask the prayers of the nation to Almighty God in behalf of this consummation.

Grant would see his wish fulfilled. The fifteenth amendment had been passed February 27, 1869, and would be ratified March 30, 1870.

THE PRESIDENT

With few exceptions Grant surrounded himself with incompetent and unscrupulous politicians who used his friendship to further their own ends. As a consequence Grant's two administrations were notorious for scandals such as the Star Route frauds, the Whiskey Ring, the Belknap scandal, and the gold corner.

THE NATION

In Grant's first term the nation had grown to 39,818,449 and was beginning to feel the first feeble stirrings of new ideas and ideologies that would eventually exert profound influences on the American way of life.

The Prohibition party was organized in September, 1869. December 10 of the same year Wyoming Territory granted the first woman suffrage in the United States. Labor unions began to spread throughout growing American industries. In May, 1869, a golden spike was driven at Promontory Point, Utah, commemorating the completion of the first transcontinental railroad.

One by one the seceded Southern states were readmitted to the Union. The fifteenth amendment was ratified March 30, 1870, providing that no state shall deny or abridge the right of any citizen to vote because of race, color, or previous condition of servitude. March 3, 1871, the Indian Appropriation Act was passed, nullifying all previous treaties and making all Indians wards of the government. The disastrous Chicago fire began October 8, 1871, and destroyed about 17,450 buildings.

In the election of 1872 the Republicans renominated Grant, who defeated the Democratic party's Horace Greeley by a satisfying margin. Grant received 3,597,132 popular votes (286 electoral), while Greeley polled 2,834,125 popular votes (66 electoral). Henry Wilson was elected vice-president.

THE WORLD

On July 19, 1870, France began a disastrous war with Germany. January, 1871, Paris echoed to the triumphant tramp of victorious German troops under the leadership of Chancellor Bismarck, who proclaimed the formation of the German Empire. In the ensuing treaty Alsace and part of Lorraine, including Metz, were ceded to Germany and reparations of $1,000,000,000 were levied against the hapless French. Victor Emmanuel II united Italy and took over Rome, ending the temporal power of the Roman Catholic Church.

YOUR REËLECTION HAS PLEASED YOU IMMENSELY, as you consider it a vindication of your administration, even though you have been the center of many controversies brought on largely by the men around you. In preparing your second inaugural address you set forth in your typically blunt language a summary of the past four years and your outline of what you hope to accomplish in the second term, delivering your message in five above zero weather . . . .

Ulysses S. Grant

[1873–1877]

SECOND INAUGURAL ADDRESS, MARCH 4, 1873

Capitol Steps, Washington, D.C.

Fellow-Citizens:

Under Providence I have been called a second time to act as Executive over this great nation. It has been my endeavor in the past to maintain all the laws, and, so far as lay in my power, to act for the best interests of the whole people. My best efforts will be given in the same direction in the future, aided, I trust, by my four years' experience in the office.

When my first term of the office of Chief Executive began, the country had not recovered from the effects of a great internal revolution, and three of the former States of the Union had not been restored to their Federal relations.

It seemed to me wise that no new questions should be raised so long as that condition of affairs existed. Therefore the past four years, so far as I could control events, have been consumed in the effort to restore harmony, public credit, commerce, and all the arts of peace and progress. It is my firm conviction that the civilized world is tending toward republicanism, or government by the people through their chosen representatives, and that our own great Republic is destined to be the guiding star to all others.

Under our Republic we support an army less than that of any European power of any standing and a navy less than that of either of at least five of them. There could be no extension of territory on the continent which would call for an increase of this force, but rather might such extension enable us to diminish it.

The theory of government changes with general progress. Now that the telegraph is made available for communicating thought, together with rapid transit by steam, all parts of a continent are made contiguous for all purposes of government, and communication between the extreme limits of the country made easier than it was throughout the old thirteen States at the beginning of our national existence.

The effects of the late civil strife have been to free the slave and make him a citizen. Yet he is not possessed of the civil rights which citizenship should carry with it. This is wrong, and should be corrected. To this correction I stand committed, so far as Executive influence can avail.

Grant was apparently in error as there were four Southern states readmitted to the Union after he took office: Virginia, January 26, 1870; Mississippi, February 23, 1870; Texas, March 30, 1870; Georgia, July 15, 1870.

[133]

Social equality is not a subject to be legislated upon, nor shall I ask that anything be done to advance the social status of the colored man, except to give him a fair chance to develop what there is good in him, give him access to the schools, and when he travels let him feel assured that his conduct will regulate the treatment and fare he will receive.

The States lately at war with the General Government are now happily rehabilitated, and no Executive control is exercised in any one of them that would not be exercised in any other State under like circumstances.

In the first year of the past Administration the proposition came up for the admission of Santo Domingo as a Territory of the Union. It was not a question of my seeking, but was a proposition from the people of Santo Domingo, and which I entertained. I believe now, as I did then, that it was for the best interest of this country, for the people of Santo Domingo, and all concerned that the proposition should be received favorably. It was, however, rejected constitutionally, and therefore the subject was never brought up again by me.

In future, while I hold my present office, the subject of acquisition of territory must have the support of the people before I will recommend any proposition looking to such acquisition. I say here, however, that I do not share in the apprehension held by many as to the danger of governments becoming weakened and destroyed by reason of their extension of territory. Commerce, education, and rapid transit of thought and matter by telegraph and steam have changed all this. Rather do I believe that our Great Maker is preparing the world, in His own good time, to become one nation, speaking one language, and when armies and navies will be no longer required.

My efforts in the future will be directed to the restoration of good feeling between the different sections of our common country; to the restoration of our currency to a fixed value as compared with the world's standard of values—gold—and, if possible, to a par with it; to the construction of cheap routes of transit throughout the land, to the end that the products of all may find a market and leave a living remuneration to the producer; to the maintenance of friendly relations with all our neighbors and with distant nations; to the reestablishment of our commerce and share in the carrying trade upon the ocean; to the encouragement of such manufacturing industries as can be economically pursued in this country, to the end that the exports of home products and industries may pay for our imports—the only sure method of returning to and permanently maintaining a specie basis; to the elevation of labor; and, by a human course, to bring the aborigines of the country under the benign influences of education and civilization. It is either this or war of extermination. Wars of extermination, engaged in by people pursuing commerce and all industrial pursuits, are expensive even against the weakest people, and are demoralizing and wicked. Our superiority of strength and advantages of civilization should make us lenient toward the Indian. The wrong inflicted upon him should be taken into account and the balance placed to his credit. The moral view of the question should be considered and the question asked, Can not the Indian be made a useful and productive member of society by proper teaching and treatment? If the effort is made in good faith, we will stand better before the civilized nations of the earth and in our own consciences for having made it.

[134]

All these things are not to be accomplished by one individual, but they will receive my support and such recommendations to Congress as will in my judgment best serve to carry them into effect. I beg your support and encouragement.

It has been, and is, my earnest desire to correct abuses that have grown up in the civil service of the country. To secure this reformation rules regulating methods of appointment and promotions were established and have been tried. My efforts for such reformation shall be continued to the best of my judgment. The spirit of the rules adopted will be maintained.

I acknowledged before this assemblage, representing, as it does, every section of our country, the obligation I am under to my countrymen for the great honor they have conferred on me by returning me to the highest office within their gift, and the further obligation resting on me to render to them the best services within my power. This I promise, looking forward with the greatest anxiety to the day when I shall be released from responsibilities that at times are almost overwhelming, and from which I have scarcely had a respite since the eventful firing upon Fort Sumter, in April, 1861, to the present day. My services were then tendered and accepted under the first call for troops growing out of that event.

I did not ask for place or position, and was entirely without influence or the acquaintance of persons of influence, but was resolved to perform my part in a struggle threatening the very existence of the nation. I performed a conscientious duty, without asking promotion or command, and without a revengeful feeling toward any section or individual.

Notwithstanding this, throughout the war, and from my candidacy for my present office in 1868 to the close of the last Presidential campaign, I have been the subject of abuse and slander scarcely ever equaled in political history, which to-day I feel that I can afford to disregard in view of your verdict, which I gratefully accept as my vindication.

In his closing paragraphs Grant expressed deep need for the vindication of his services during his first four years in office. Unfortunately his second term would see more scandals come to light, blame for which would be heaped on Grant and the Republicans.

The presentation of the freedom of the city of London to Ulysses S. Grant, who is signing the record of the Guildhall Library.

THE PRESIDENT

Rutherford Birchard Hayes attended Harvard Law School for a year and a half. He won the rank of brevet major general in the Civil War and was so admired by his fellow Ohioans that they sent him to Congress after the war. This fighting Puritan later served three terms as governor of Ohio. In 1876, when the Republicans cast about for a candidate whose reputation was unassailable, Hayes, Ohio's favorite son, captured the nomination.

THE NATION

Grant's second term included the Coinage Act which demonetized silver, the "Salary Grab" Act which doubled President Grant's salary, and the failure of the large banking firm of Jay Cooke which triggered the Panic of 1873–4. The Whiskey Ring, a conspiracy to defraud the government of its tax on whiskey, was led by a Grant appointee, John McDonald, and involved the President's private secretary, General O.E. Babcock.

Colorado became a state on August 1, 1876.

The presidential election of 1876 culminated in a long battle over the counting of disputed electoral votes. The Democratic party's Samuel J. Tilden had apparently beaten Republican Rutherford B. Hayes by 250,000 popular votes. But the Republicans refused to accept the electoral vote count in Florida, Oregon, Louisiana, and South Carolina. When an Electoral Commission was set up pressure from Republicans and some Southern Democrats induced the tie-breaking fifteenth man on the commission to credit the disputed votes to Hayes, who was declared elected on March 2, 1877, with an electoral vote count of 185 to Tilden's 184. William A. Wheeler was elected vice-president.

THE WORLD

The newly formed Third French Republic elected its second president in 1873, and the country slowly recovered from the devastating effects of the Franco-Prussian War. In the dual monarchy of Austria-Hungary, Francis Joseph I was beginning his reign. Elsewhere on the Continent and in England the effects of improved communications and the use of steamships and railroads combined with better manufacturing methods to bring a new standard of living to the masses.

"THE CASE OF THE STOLEN ELECTION" might have been the title for the behind-the-scenes manipulations that result in your victory over Samuel J. Tilden. You, however, have nothing whatever to do with the decision. In fact, when you and Mrs. Hayes take the train for Washington and the inauguration ceremonies you still do not know whether you or Tilden will deliver the inaugural address. When your train stops briefly at Harrisburg, Pennsylvania, you get the news that the Electoral Commission has decided in your favor. March 4th falls on a Sunday, so President Grant invites you and your wife to the White House for dinner on Saturday night, March 3rd. Chief Justice Waite is also present. Before going into dinner the Chief Justice, the President, Secretary of State Hamilton Fish, and you quietly slip into the Red Room where you are quickly sworn in by Waite, thus preventing the nation from being without a Chief Executive on Sunday, the date President Grant's term legally expires. On Monday you appear with Grant on the Capitol steps where a huge throng has gathered to hear your address . . . .

Rutherford B. Hayes

[1877–1881]

INAUGURAL ADDRESS, MARCH 5, 1877

Capitol Steps, Washington, D.C.

Fellow-Citizens:

We have assembled to repeat the public ceremonial, begun by Washington, observed by all my predecessors, and now a time-honored custom, which marks the commencement of a new term of the Presidential office. Called to the duties of this great trust, I proceed, in compliance with usage, to announce some of the leading principles, on the subjects that now chiefly engage the public attention, by which it is my desire to be guided in the discharge of those duties. I shall not undertake to lay down irrevocably principles or measures of administration, but rather to speak of the motives which should animate us, and to suggest certain important ends to be attained in accordance with our institutions and essential to the welfare of our country.

At the outset of the discussions which preceded the recent Presidential election it seemed to me fitting that I should fully make known my sentiments in regard to several of the important questions which then appeared to demand the consideration of the country. Following the example, and in part adopting the language, of one of my predecessors, I wish now, when every motive for misrepresentation has passed away, to repeat what was said before the election, trusting that my countrymen will candidly weigh and understand it, and that they will feel assured that the sentiments declared in accepting the nomination for the Presidency will be the standard of my conduct in the path before me, charged, as I now am, with the grave and difficult task of carrying them out in the practical administration of the Government so far as depends, under the Constitution and laws, on the Chief Executive of the nation.

The permanent pacification of the country upon such principles and by such measures as will secure the complete protection of all its citizens in the free enjoyment of all their constitutional rights is

Hayes referred to Lincoln's first inaugural address, in which the Great Emancipator began by quoting from his preëlection speeches, to prove that once elected he still intended to adhere to his platform.

now the one subject in our public affairs which all thoughtful and patriotic citizens regard as of supreme importance.

Many of the calamitous effects of the tremendous revolution which has passed over the Southern States still remain. The immeasurable benefits which will surely follow, sooner or later, the hearty and generous acceptance of the legitimate results of that revolution have not yet been realized. Difficult and embarrassing questions meet us at the threshold of this subject. The people of those States are still impoverished, and the inestimable blessing of wise, honest, and peaceful local self-government is not fully enjoyed. Whatever difference of opinion may exist as to the cause of this condition of things, the fact is clear that in the progress of events the time has come when such government is the imperative necessity required by all the varied interests, public and private, of those States. But it must not be forgotten that only a local government which recognizes and maintains inviolate the rights of all is a true self-government.

With respect to the two distinct races whose peculiar relations to each other have brought upon us the deplorable complications and perplexities which exist in those States, it must be a government which guards the interests of both races carefully and equally. It must be a government which submits loyally and heartily to the Constitution and the laws—the laws of the nation and the laws of the States themselves—accepting and obeying faithfully the whole Constitution as it is.

Resting upon this sure and substantial foundation, the superstructure of beneficient local governments can be built up, and not otherwise. In furtherance of such obedience to the letter and the spirit of the Constitution, and in behalf of all that its attainment implies, all so-called party interests lose their apparent importance, and party lines may well be permitted to fade into insignificance. The question we have to consider for the immediate welfare of those States of the Union is the question of government or no government; of social order and all the peaceful industries and the happiness that belongs to it, or a return to barbarism. It is a question in which every citizen of the nation is deeply interested, and with respect to which we ought not to be, in a partisan sense, either Republicans or Democrats, but fellow-citizens and fellow-men, to whom the interests of a common country and a common humanity are dear.

The sweeping revolution of the entire labor system of a large portion of our country and the advance of 4,000,000 people from a condition of servitude to that of citizenship, upon an equal footing with their former masters, could not occur without presenting problems of the gravest moment, to be dealt with by the emancipated race, by their former masters, and by the General Government, the author of the act of emancipation. That it was a wise, just, and providential act, fraught with good for all concerned, is not generally conceded throughout the country. That a moral obligation rests upon the National Government to employ its constitutional power and influence to establish the rights of the people it has emancipated, and to protect them in the enjoyment of those rights when they are infringed or assailed, is also generally admitted.

The evils which afflict the Southern States can only be removed or remedied by the united and harmonious efforts of both races, actuated by motives of mutual sympathy and regard; and while in duty bound and fully determined to protect the rights of all by every constitutional means at the disposal of my Administration, I am sincerely anxious to use every legitimate influence in favor of honest and efficient local *self*-government as the true resource of those States for the promotion of the contentment and prosperity of their citizens. In the effort I shall make to accomplish this purpose I ask the cordial cooperation of all who cherish an interest in the welfare of the country, trusting that party ties and the prejudice of race will be freely surrendered in behalf of the great purpose to be accomplished. In the important work of restoring the South it is not the political situation alone that merits attention. The material development of that section of the country has been arrested by the social and political revolution through which it has passed, and now needs and deserves the considerate care of the National Government within the just limits prescribed by the Constitution and wise public economy.

But at the basis of all prosperity, for that as well as for every other part of the country, lies the improvement of the intellectual and moral condition of the people. Universal suffrage should rest upon universal education. To this end, liberal and permanent provision should be made for the support of free schools by the State governments, and, if need be, supplemented by legitimate aid from national authority.

Let me assure my countrymen of the Southern States that it is my earnest desire to regard and promote their truest interest—the interests of the white and of the colored people both and equally —and to put forth my best efforts in behalf of a civil policy which will forever wipe out in our political affairs the color line and the distinction between North and South, to the end that we may have not merely a united North or a united South, but a united country.

I ask the attention of the public to the paramount necessity of reform in our civil service—a reform not merely as to certain abuses and practices of so-called official patronage which have come to have the sanction of usage in the several Departments of our Government, but a change in the system of appointment itself; a reform that shall be thorough, radical, and complete; a return to the principles and practices of the founders of the Government. They neither expected nor desired from public officers any partisan service. They meant that public officers should owe their whole service to the Government and to the people. They meant that the officer should be secure in his tenure as long as his personal character remained untarnished and the performance of his duties satisfactory. They held that appointments to office were not to be made nor expected merely as rewards for partisan services, nor merely on the nomination of members of Congress, as being entitled in any respect to the control of such appointments.

The fact that both the great political parties of the country, in declaring their principles prior to the election, gave a prominent place to the subject of reform of our civil service, recognizing and strongly urging its necessity, in terms almost identical in their specific import with those I have here employed, must be accepted as a conclusive argument in behalf of these measures. It must be regarded as the expression of the united voice and will of the whole country upon this subject, and both political parties are virtually pledged to give it their unreserved support.

The President of the United States of necessity owes his election to office to the suffrage and zealous labors of a political party, the members of which cherish with ardor and regard as of essential

In Hayes the South found a champion, who although a Republican brought to the White House an all-encompassing understanding and sympathy that transcended the barriers of party politics in a manner reminiscent of Lincoln. Hayes had no easy task in ending military reconstruction in the South, for the Democrats had control of the House in 1876 and of both House and Senate in 1878.

More of Lincoln's philosophy. Unfortunately, however, the sentiments expressed here are not yet realized, nearly a century later.

Hayes had high hopes for civil service reform, but the Republicans lacked sufficient power in Congress to insure the complete success of his efforts. Hayes persisted, and as a result he alienated powerful interests whose patronage would be curtailed if the reform was carried out as thoroughly as Hayes insisted.

[139]

Although Hayes failed to see this amendment accomplished, he staunchly refused to consider running for a second term. In his acceptance of the nomination he stated that he would not run for another term, and he did not change this position.

Hayes's optimism would soon be borne out in a period of farm prosperity, which would begin in 1879 and continue until 1884 when agricultural prices would go into a twelve-year decline due to overproduction and an influx of foreign-grown commodities.

The Specie Resumption Act passed in 1875 stipulated specie payments must be resumed by January 1, 1879, with greenbacks in circulation reduced to $300,000,000. But the nation's gold reserves had risen to $200,000,000 by 1879. For this reason no greenbacks were retired from circulation. Instead all paper currency outstanding was declared to possess the face value of gold.

The subject receiving most of Hayes's attention was the way in which he had been declared president. This controversial matter was of great importance to the President-elect, and he did what he could to explain how the unprecedented situation had arisen and had been settled. In counting the electoral votes there had been some whose validity had been questioned. If counted by the members of the Republican-dominated Senate the Hayes electoral votes would have been accepted and Hayes elected. If counted by the members of the predominently Democratic House of Representatives Tilden would have been elected.

importance the principles of their party organization; but he should strive to be always mindful of the fact that he serves his party best who serves the country best.

In furtherance of the reform we seek, and in other important respects a change of great importance, I recommend an amendment to the Constitution prescribing a term of six years for the Presidential office and forbidding a reelection.

With respect to the financial condition of the country, I shall not attempt an extended history of the embarrassment and prostration which we have suffered during the past three years. The depression in all our varied commercial and manufacturing interests throughout the country, which began in September, 1873, still continues. It is very gratifying, however, to be able to say that there are indications all around us of a coming change to prosperous times.

Upon the currency question, intimately connected, as it is, with this topic, I may be permitted to repeat here the statement made in my letter of acceptance, that in my judgment the feeling of uncertainty inseparable from an irredeemable paper currency, with its fluctuation of values, is one of the greatest obstacles to a return to prosperous times. The only safe paper currency is one which rests upon a coin basis and is at all times and promptly convertible into coin.

I adhere to the views heretofore expressed by me in favor of Congressional legislation in behalf of an early resumption of specie payments, and I am satisfied not only that this is wise, but that the interests, as well as the public sentiment, of the country imperatively demand it.

Passing from these remarks upon the condition of our own country to consider our relations with other lands, we are reminded by the international complications abroad, threatening the peace of Europe, that our traditional rule of noninterference in the affairs of foreign nations has proved of great value in past times and ought to be strictly observed.

The policy inaugurated by my honored predecessor, President Grant, of submitting to arbitration grave questions in dispute between ourselves and foreign powers points to a new, and incomparably the best, instrumentality for the preservation of peace, and will, as I believe, become a beneficent example of the course to be pursued in similar emergencies by other nations.

If, unhappily, questions of difference should at any time during the period of my Administration arise between the United States and any foreign government, it will certainly be my disposition and my hope to aid in their settlement in the same peaceful and honorable way, thus securing to our country the great blessings of peace and mutual good offices with all the nations of the world.

Fellow-citizens, we have reached the close of a political contest marked by the excitement which usually attends the contests between great political parties whose members espouse and advocate with earnest faith their respective creeds. The circumstances were, perhaps, in no respect extraordinary save in the closeness and the consequent uncertainty of the result.

For the first time in the history of the country it has been deemed best, in view of the peculiar circumstances of the case, that the objections and questions in dispute with reference to the counting of the electoral votes should be referred to the decision of a tribunal appointed for this purpose.

That tribunal—established by law for this sole purpose; its members, all of them, men of long-established reputation for integrity and intelligence, and, with the exception of those who are also members of the supreme judiciary, chosen equally from both political parties; its deliberations enlightened by the research and the arguments of able counsel—was entitled to the fullest confidence of the American people. Its decisions have been patiently waited for, and accepted as legally conclusive by the general judgment of the public. For the present, opinion will widely vary as to the wisdom of the several conclusions announced by that tribunal. This is to be anticipated in every instance where matters of dispute are made the subject of arbitration under the forms of law. Human judgment is never unerring, and is rarely regarded as otherwise than wrong by the unsuccessful party in the contest.

The fact that two great political parties have in this way settled a dispute in regard to which good men differ as to the facts and the law no less than as to the proper course to be pursued in solving the question in controversy is an occasion for general rejoicing.

Upon one point there is entire unanimity in public sentiment—that conflicting claims to the Presidency must be amicably and peaceably adjusted, and that when so adjusted the general acquiescence of the nation ought surely to follow.

It has been reserved for a government of the people, where the right of suffrage is universal, to give to the world the first example in history of a great nation, in the midst of the struggle of opposing parties for power, hushing its party tumults to yield the issue of the contest to adjustment according to the forms of law.

Looking for the guidance of that Divine Hand by which the destinies of nations and individuals are shaped, I call upon you, Senators, Representatives, judges, fellow-citizens, here and everywhere, to unite with me in an earnest effort to secure to our country the blessings, not only of material prosperity, but of justice, peace, and union—a union depending not upon the constraint of force, but upon the loving devotion of a free people; "and that all things may be so ordered and settled upon the best and surest foundations that peace and happiness, truth and justice, religion and piety, may be established among us for all generations."

The Constitution gave no clue, simply stating: "The President of the Senate shall, in the presence of the Senate and the House of Representatives, open all certificates and the votes shall then be counted." Congress attempted to solve the dilemma by appointing an Electoral Commission. Five members of the House, five of the Senate, and five justices of the Supreme Court were selected, fourteen of whom were split evenly along party lines. The fifteenth was to have been an independent—Justice David Davis. But when h e was elected to the Senate, Davis was replaced by Justice Bradley, a Republican, who although he originally favored Tilden was influenced by powerful Republican interests to switch to Hayes.

No amount of explanation by Hayes could cover up the reason for Justice Bradley's switch, and the Democratic outcry was loud and prolonged despite Hayes's plea for "general acquiescence."

THE PRESIDENT

James Abram Garfield was a brilliant and knowledgeable lawyer, who had served in the Ohio Legislature prior to the Civil War. He distinguished himself at the Battle of Shiloh in the war and in 1862 became a brigadier general. At Chickamauga he was made a major general for his gallantry. Garfield was a member of the Electoral Commission in 1876 and voted for Hayes, following the Republican party line. In 1880 he was senator-elect when picked as a presidential candidate, a compromise between Grant and Blaine.

THE NATION

The West was in its heyday. Dodge City, Kansas, became the center for cattle shipments to eastern markets. Ruthless extermination of the buffalo for meat, hides, tallow, and bones had virtually been completed by the beginning of the 1880's. In the Southwest the Apache tribes were on the warpath, as were the Nez Perce Indians in Idaho, the Utes in Colorado, and the plains tribes, whose chiefs were making a last desperate attempt to capitalize on the death of the feared General George A. Custer in 1876. But the Indian war cry, like the sound of thundering hooves in a buffalo stampede, was soon destined to be only a memory.

The Bland-Allison Act of 1878, passed over President Hayes's veto, provided for the free and limited coinage of silver at a 16-1 ratio.

1879 saw the formation of the Edison Electric Light Company, the first of its kind in America. The spread of Edison's invention, coupled with the introduction and wide use of the telephone, served greatly to aid in the development of large metropolitan areas. The state of New York was recorded to have a population of more than 5,000,000 in the census of 1880, which revealed a total population of 50,155,783.

In the Republican convention of 1880 Hayes had declared himself ineligible for reëlection. A deadlock developed between Grant and James A. Blaine. The "Stalwarts" were Grant supporters; the "Half-Breeds" backed Blaine. But after 36 ballots a dark horse named James A. Garfield from Ohio was backed by the Half-Breeds. A Stalwart supporter named Chester A. Arthur was selected as Garfield's running mate.

The Democrats nominated Winfield Scott Hancock and William H. English, but went down to defeat in an election that gave Garfield a plurality of only 9,464 out of 9,218,251 popular votes cast. The Republican party's James A. Garfield polled 4,454,416 popular votes (214 electoral). The Democratic party's Hancock received 4,444,952 popular votes (155 electoral). The Greenback Labor party's James B. Weaver polled 308,578 and the Prohibition party's Neal Dow received 10,305. Chester A. Arthur was elected vice-president.

THE WORLD

Russia declared war on Turkey, April 24, 1877. The peace treaty was signed in March of the following year, just prior to the congress held in Berlin which attempted to settle boundary questions in Continental Europe. Montenegro, Serbia, and Rumania were made independent, and Bulgaria became a self-governing state under the nominal suzerainty of Turkey.

[142]

LOOKING BACK OVER YOUR LIFE, as you prepare your inaugural address, you realize you are the living epitome of the "rags-to-riches" American success story. For you were born in a log cabin and in true Horatio Alger style have worked and fought your way to success in your profession, and now to national prominence as the twentieth president. You begin the address by reviewing the country's progress over the past century, and then express your faith in the future of the union, if both North and South will learn to forget the past and look only to the future. And your faith in the people seems justified when, as you and retiring President Hayes are riding up Pennsylvania Avenue to the Capitol, a group of ex-Confederate soldiers wave the American flag and cheer you heartily. But alas, not all Americans accept defeat so gracefully. For an unsuccessful office seeker will send you to your death less than a year from the moment you face the small group of 15,000 on the Capitol steps, who braved the cold to hear your optimistic message . . . .

James A. Garfield

[1881]

INAUGURAL ADDRESS, MARCH 4, 1881

Capitol Steps, Washington, D.C.

Fellow-Citizens:

We stand to-day upon an eminence which overlooks a hundred years of national life—a century crowded with perils, but crowned with the triumphs of liberty and law. Before continuing the onward march let us pause on this height for a moment to strengthen our faith and renew our hope by a glance at the pathway along which our people have traveled.

It is now three days more than a hundred years since the adoption of the first written constitution of the United States—the Articles of Confederation and Perpetual Union. The new Republic was then beset with danger on every hand. It had not conquered a place in the family of nations. The decisive battle of the war for independence, whose centennial anniversary will soon be gratefully celebrated at Yorktown, had not yet been fought. The colonists were struggling not only against the armies of a great nation, but against the settled opinions of mankind; for the world did not then believe that the supreme authority of government could be safely intrusted to the guardianship of the people themselves.

We can not overestimate the fervent love of liberty, the intelligent courage, and the sum of common sense with which our fathers made the great experiment of self-government. When they found, after a short trial, that the confederacy of States, was too weak to meet the necessities of a vigorous and expanding republic, they boldly set it aside, and in its stead established a National Union, founded directly upon the will of the people, endowed with full power of self-preservation and ample authority for the accomplishment of its great object.

Under this Constitution the boundaries of freedom have been enlarged, the foundations of order and peace have been strengthened, and the growth of our people in all the better elements of national life has indicated the wisdom of the founders and given new hope to their descendants. Under this Constitution our people long ago made themselves safe against danger from without and

Maryland had refused to ratify the Articles of Confederation from November, 1777, until February 27, 1781. Congress then chose March 1 as the final ratification date, and on March 2, 1781, adopted a new official title: "The United States in Congress Assembled."

secured for their mariners and flag equality of rights on all the seas. Under this Constitution twenty-five States have been added to the Union, with constitutions and laws, framed and enforced by their own citizens, to secure the manifold blessings of local self-government.

The jurisdiction of this Constitution now covers an area fifty times greater than that of the original thirteen States and a population twenty times greater than that of 1780.

The supreme trial of the Constitution came at last under the tremendous pressure of civil war. We ourselves are witnesses that the Union emerged from the blood and fire of that conflict purified and made stronger for all the beneficent purposes of good government.

And now, at the close of this first century of growth, with the inspirations of its history in their hearts, our people have lately reviewed the condition of the nation, passed judgment upon the conduct and opinions of political parties, and have registered their will concerning the future administration of the Government. To interpret and to execute that will in accordance with the Constitution is the paramount duty of the Executive.

Even from this brief review it is manifest that the nation is resolutely facing to the front, resolved to employ its best energies in developing the great possibilities of the future. Sacredly preserving whatever has been gained to liberty and good government during the century, our people are determined to leave behind them all those bitter controversies concerning things which have been irrevocably settled, and the further discussion of which can only stir up strife and delay the onward march.

The supremacy of the nation and its laws should be no longer a subject of debate. That discussion, which for half a century threatened the existence of the Union, was closed at last in the high court of war by a decree from which there is no appeal—that the Constitution and the laws made in pursuance thereof are and shall continue to be the supreme law of the land, binding alike upon the States and the people. This decree does not disturb the autonomy of the States nor interfere with any of their necessary rights of local self-government, but it does fix and establish the permanent supremacy of the Union.

The will of the nation, speaking with the voice of battle and through the amended Constitution, has fulfilled the great promise of 1776 by proclaiming "liberty throughout the land to all the inhabitants thereof."

The elevation of the negro race from slavery to the full rights of citizenship is the most important political change we have known since the adoption of the Constitution of 1787. No thoughtful man can fail to appreciate its beneficent effect upon our institutions and people. It has freed us from the perpetual danger of war and dissolution. It has added immensely to the moral and industrial forces of our people. It has liberated the master as well as the slave from a relation which wronged and enfeebled both. It has surrendered to their own guardianship the manhood of more than 5,000,000 people, and has opened to each one of them a career of freedom and usefulness. It has given new inspiration to the power of self-help in both races by making labor more honorable to the one and more necessary to the other. The influence of this force will grow greater and bear richer fruit with the coming years.

No doubt this great change has caused serious disturbance to our Southern communities. This is to be deplored, though it was perhaps unavoidable. But those who resisted the change should remember

The colonial population of 1781 was estimated to be approximately 2,800,000, and the census of 1880 revealed a population of 50,155,783.

Garfield's thought here was nobly conceived, but many people, rather than leave behind the "bitter controversies," seemed determined to keep alive the old animosities.

Apparently a reference to the Constitution's thirteenth, fourteenth, and fifteenth amendments.

The Constitution was adopted September 17, 1787, and became effective on June 21, 1788, with ratification by the ninth state, New Hampshire. But the Constitution was not declared effective until the first session of Congress was held on March 4, 1789.

that under our institutions there was no middle ground for the negro race between slavery and equal citizenship. There can be no permanent disfranchised peasantry in the United States. Freedom can never yield its fullness of blessings so long as the law or its administration places the smallest obstacle in the pathway of any virtuous citizen.

The emancipated race has already made remarkable progress. With unquestioning devotion to the Union, with a patience and gentleness not born of fear, they have "followed the light as God gave them to see the light." They are rapidly laying the material foundations of self-support, widening their circle of intelligence, and beginning to enjoy the blessings that gather around the homes of the industrious poor. They deserve the generous encouragement of all good men. So far as my authority can lawfully extend, they shall enjoy the full and equal protection of the Constitution and the laws.

The free enjoyment of equal suffrage is still in question, and a frank statement of the issue may aid its solution. It is alleged that in many communities negro citizens are practically denied the freedom of the ballot. In so far as the truth of this allegation is admitted, it is answered that in many places honest local government is impossible if the mass of uneducated negroes are allowed to vote. These are grave allegations. So far as the latter is true, it is the only palliation that can be offered for opposing the freedom of the ballot. Bad local government is certainly a great evil, which ought to be prevented; but to violate the freedom and sanctities of the suffrage is more than an evil. It is a crime which, if persisted in, will destroy the Government itself. Suicide is not a remedy. If in other lands it be high treason to compass the death of the king, it shall be counted no less a crime here to strangle our sovereign power and stifle its voice.

It has been said that unsettled questions have no pity for the repose of nations. It should be said with the utmost emphasis that this question of the suffrage will never give repose or safety to the States or to the nation until each, within its own jurisdiction, makes and keeps the ballot free and pure by the strong sanctions of the law.

But the danger which arises from ignorance in the voter can not be denied. It covers a field far wider than that of negro suffrage and the present condition of the race. It is a danger that lurks and hides in the sources of fountains of power in every state. We have no standard by which to measure the disaster that may be brought upon us by ignorance and vice in the citizens when joined to corruption and fraud in the suffrage.

The voters of the Union, who make and unmake constitutions, and upon whose will hang the destinies of our governments, can transmit their supreme authority to no successors save the coming generation of voters, who are the sole heirs of sovereign power. If that generation comes to its inheritance blinded by ignorance and corrupted by vice, the fall of the Republic will be certain and remediless.

The census has already sounded the alarm in the appalling figures which mark how dangerously high the tide of illiteracy has risen among our voters and their children.

To the South this question is of supreme importance. But the responsibility for the existence of slavery did not rest upon the South alone. The nation itself is responsible for the extension of the suffrage, and is under special obligations to aid in removing the illiteracy which it has added to the voting population. For the North and South alike there is but one remedy. All the constitutional power of the nation and of the States and all the volunteer forces of the people should be surrendered to meet this danger by the savory influence of universal education.

It is the high privilege and sacred duty of those now living to educate their successors and fit them, by intelligence and virtue, for the inheritance which awaits them.

In this beneficent work sections and races should be forgotten and partisanship should be unknown. Let our people find a new meaning in the divine oracle which declares that "a little child shall lead them," for our own little children will soon control the destinies of the Republic.

My countrymen, we do not now differ in our judgment concerning the controversies of past generations, and fifty years hence our children will not be divided in their opinions concerning our controversies. They will surely bless their fathers and their fathers' God that the Union was preserved, that slavery was overthrown, and that both races were made equal before the law. We may hasten or we may retard, but we can not prevent, the final reconciliation. Is it not possible for us now to make a truce with time by anticipating and accepting its inevitable verdict?

Enterprises of the highest importance to our moral and material well-being unite us and offer ample employment of our best powers. Let all our people, leaving behind them the battlefields of dead issues, move forward and in their strength of liberty and the restored Union win the grander victories of peace.

The prosperity which now prevails is without parallel in our history. Fruitful seasons have done much to secure it, but they have not done all. The preservation of the public credit and the resumption of specie payments, so successfully attained by the Administration of my predecessors, have enabled our people to secure the blessings which the seasons brought.

By the experience of commercial nations in all ages it has been found that gold and silver afford the only safe foundation for a monetary system. Confusion has recently been created by variations in the relative value of the two metals, but I confidently believe that arrangements can be made between the leading commercial nations which will secure the general use of both metals. Congress should provide that the compulsory coinage of silver now required by law may not disturb our monetary system by driving either metal out of circulation. If possible, such an adjustment should be made that the purchasing power of every coined dollar will be exactly equal to its debt-paying power in all the markets of the world.

The chief duty of the National Government in connection with the currency of the country is to coin money and declare its value. Grave doubts have been entertained whether Congress is authorized by the Constitution to make any form of paper money legal tender. The present issue of United States notes has been sustained by the necessities of war; but such paper should depend for its value and currency upon its convenience in use and its prompt redemption in coin at the will of the holder, and not upon its compulsory circulation. These notes are not money, but promises to pay money. If the holders demand it, the promise should be kept.

The refunding of the national debt at a lower rate of interest should be accomplished without compelling the withdrawal of the

[146]

national-bank notes, and thus disturbing the business of the country.

I venture to refer to the position I have occupied on financial questions during a long service in Congress, and to say that time and experience have strengthened the opinions I have so often expressed on these subjects.

The finances of the Government shall suffer no detriment which it may be possible for my Administration to prevent.

The interests of agriculture deserve more attention from the Government than they have yet received. The farms of the United States afford homes and employment for more than one-half our people, and furnish much the largest part of all our exports. As the Government lights our coasts for the protection of mariners and the benefit of commerce, so it should give to the tillers of the soil the best lights of practical science and experience.

Our manufacturers are rapidly making us industrially independent, and are opening to capital and labor new and profitable fields of employment. Their steady and healthy growth should still be matured. Our facilities for transportation should be promoted by the continued improvement of our harbors and great interior waterways and by the increase of our tonnage on the ocean.

The development of the world's commerce has led to an urgent demand for shortening the great sea voyage around Cape Horn by constructing ship canals or railways across the isthmus which unites the continents. Various plans to this end have been suggested and will need consideration, but none of them has been sufficiently matured to warrant the United States in extending pecuniary aid. The subject, however, is one which will immediately engage the attention of the Government with a view to a thorough protection to American interests. We will urge no narrow policy nor seek peculiar or exclusive privileges in any commercial route; but, in the language of my predecessor, I believe it to be the right "and duty of the United States to assert and maintain such supervision and authority over any interoceanic canal across the isthmus that connects North and South America as will protect our national interest."

The Constitution guarantees absolute religious freedom. Congress is prohibited from making any law respecting an establishment of religion or prohibiting the free exercise thereof. The Territories of the United States are subject to the direct legislative authority of Congress, and hence the General Government is responsible for any violation of the Constitution in any of them. It is therefore a reproach to the Government that in the most populous of the Territories the constitutional guaranty is not enjoyed by the people and the authority of Congress is set at naught. The Mormon Church not only offends the moral sense of manhood by sanctioning polygamy, but prevents the administration of justice through ordinary instrumentalities of law.

In my judgment it is the duty of Congress, while respecting to the uttermost the conscientious convictions and religious scruples of every citizen, to prohibit within its jurisdiction all criminal practices, especially of that class which destroy the family relations and endanger social order. Nor can any ecclesiastical organization be safely permitted to usurp in the smallest degree the functions and powers of the National Government.

The civil service can never be placed on a satisfactory basis until it is regulated by law. For the good of the service itself, for the protection of those who are intrusted with the appointing power against the waste of time and obstruction to the public business caused by the inordinate pressure for place, and for the protection of incumbents against intrigue and wrong, I shall at the proper time ask Congress to fix the tenure of the minor offices of the several Executive Departments and prescribe the grounds upon which removals shall be made during the terms for which incumbents have been appointed.

Finally, acting always within the authority and limitations of the Constitution, invading neither the rights of the States nor the reserved rights of the people, it will be the purpose of my Administration to maintain the authority of the nation in all places within its jurisdiction; to enforce obedience to all the laws of the Union in the interests of the people; to demand rigid economy in all the expenditures of the Government, and to require the honest and faithful service of all executive officers, remembering that the offices were created, not for the benefit of incumbents or their supporters, but for the service of the Government.

And now, fellow-citizens, I am about to assume the great trust which you have committed to my hands. I appeal to you for that earnest and thoughtful support which makes this Government in fact, as it is in law, a government of the people.

I shall greatly rely upon the wisdom and patriotism of Congress and of those who may share with me the responsibilities and duties of administration, and, above all, upon our efforts to promote the welfare of this great people and their Government I reverently invoke the support and blessings of Almighty God.

President Garfield died of an assassin's bullet after a lingering illness, and Chester Alan Arthur was sworn in at his home on Lexington Avenue in New York City at 1:30 A.M., September 20, 1881. The oath of office was formally administered in Washington two days later.

Chester A. Arthur

[1881–1885]

THE PRESIDENT

When Arthur became president the entire nation was amazed to see the former machine politician place his country above old friendships. He began to rebuild the United States Navy, backed the Pendleton Civil Service Act, vetoed an outrageous pork barrel rivers and harbors bill (which was passed over his veto), and vigorously prosecuted the star route mail frauds, earning the admiration of the nation.

He was a tall man with an elegant manner and a love for fashionable clothes and fine food. When he moved into the White House he brought in the best decorator of his time: Louis Comfort Tiffany. When Tiffany had finished, the White House had been virtually transformed.

During his term of office Chester A. Arthur entertained often in the newly refurbished executive mansion, a habit his enemies used to his disadvantage. Although Arthur won the plaudits of the country at large by his political about-face he lost the support of the Republican party machine, and with it all chance of reëlection.

THE PRESIDENT

Stephen Grover Cleveland (he disliked his first name and dropped it in his youth) studied law in Buffalo, New York, and was admitted to the bar in 1859. Like Arthur, Cleveland was a preacher's son. Cleveland bulled his way up from obscurity to become the Democratic mayor of Buffalo in 1881. His honesty, ability, and dependability set him apart from the machine politicians of the day, and he was elected governor of New York in 1882. Called "Grover the Good" —by his backers, at least—Cleveland locked horns with Blaine in what was unquestionably the dirtiest campaign up to this date. The Cleveland camp alleged Blaine had taken a large bribe from a railroad. Blaine men claimed Cleveland was the father of an illegitimate child. The voters chose Cleveland.

THE NATION

The postwar growth of the nation continued. There was a tremendous influx of men, women, and children from nearly every country of the globe. The country's businessmen were perfecting principles of mass production. Each year saw new improvements on basic inventions—the telephone, the electric light, the steamboat, the steam engine, the telegraph—that were to become the backbone of American industry. The steel mills were running full blast, and the young oil industry, led by a financial wizard named John D. Rockefeller, was growing rapidly.

P.T. Barnum made news in 1881 by combining his "Greatest Show on Earth" with Bailey's rival circus and "Barnum and Bailey" became a familiar name to generations of Americans, young and old. Women's interests were catered to by new magazines, like the *Ladies' Home Journal*. Sports were becoming popular in the early 1880's. The first skyscraper—a ten-story building for the Home Insurance Company—was built in Chicago. In the east the opening of the Brooklyn Bridge May 24, 1883, after 13 years of construction was cause for a great celebration.

The election year of 1884 brought six nominating conventions, with four presidential candidates finally listed on the ballot. When the votes were counted, the Democratic party's Grover Cleveland polled 4,874,986 popular votes (219 electoral), Republican James G. Blaine received 4,851,981 popular votes (182 electoral), the Greenback party's General Benjamin F. Butler received 175,370, and the Prohibition party's John P. St. John tallied 150,369. Thomas A. Hendricks was elected vice-president.

THE WORLD

On March 13, 1881, Alexander II, Czar of Russia, was assassinated in St. Petersburg by Nihilists. In the field of medicine much progress was made by tireless researchers such as Professor Robert Koch. On March 24, 1882, Koch announced in Berlin the discovery of the tuberculosis germ. That same year saw another in the seemingly endless alliances formed, when Germany, Italy, and Austria banded together in a Triple Alliance that was to last until 1914 when World War I broke out.

AS YOU PREPARE YOUR INAUGURAL ADDRESS the no-holds-barred tactics of the recent campaign are still fresh in your mind, and you touch on this briefly in an attempt to justify the mudslinging of both major parties. Inauguration day dawns with a biting March snap in the air, but there is no snow falling to spoil your ride to the Capitol with outgoing President Arthur beside you in the carriage. Later, as you move out onto the platform erected on the steps of the Capitol, the huge crowd cheers you thunderously and you are gratified that apparently the public has not let the published scandal about you influence its opinion of your ability. After you have been sworn in you hold up one hand, the huge crowd quiets down, and you begin to deliver your address entirely from memory in a high penetrating voice . . . .

Grover Cleveland

[1885–1889]

FIRST INAUGURAL ADDRESS, MARCH 4, 1885

Capitol Steps, Washington, D.C.

Fellow-Citizens:

In the presence of this vast assemblage of my countrymen I am about to supplement and seal by the oath which I shall take the manifestation of the will of a great and free people. In the exercise of their power and right of self-government they have committed to one of their fellow-citizens a supreme and sacred trust, and he here consecrates himself to their service.

This impressive ceremony adds little to the solemn sense of responsibility with which I contemplate the duty I owe to all the people of the land. Nothing can relieve men from anxiety lest by any act of mine their interests may suffer, and nothing is needed to strengthen my resolution to engage every faculty and effort in the promotion of their welfare.

Amid the din of party strife the people's choice was made, but its attendant circumstances have demonstrated anew the strength and safety of a government by the people. In each succeeding year it more clearly appears that our democratic principle needs no apology, and that in its fearless and faithful application is to be found the surest guaranty of good government.

But the best results in the operation of a government wherein every citizen has a share largely depend upon a proper limitation of purely partisan zeal and effort and a correct appreciation of the time when the heat of the partisan should be merged in the patriotism of the citizen.

To-day the executive branch of the Government is transferred to new keeping. But this is still the Government of all the people, and it should be none the less an object of their affectionate solicitude. At this hour the animosities of political strife, the bitterness of partisan defeat, and the exultation of partisan triumph should be supplanted by an ungrudging acquiescence in the popular will and a sober, conscientious concern for the general weal. Moreover, if from this hour we cheerfully and honestly abandon all sectional prejudice and distrust, and determine, with manly confidence in one another, to work out harmoniously the achievements of our national destiny, we shall deserve to realize all the benefits which our happy form of government can bestow.

On this auspicious occasion we may well renew the pledge of our devotion to the Constitution, which, launched by the founders of the Republic and consecrated by their prayers and patriotic devotion, has for almost a century borne the hopes and the aspirations of a great people through prosperity and peace and through the shock of foreign conflicts and the perils of domestic strife and vicissitudes.

By the Father of his Country our Constitution was commended for adoption as "the result of a spirit of amity and mutual concession." In that same spirit it should be administered, in order to promote the last-

Cleveland meant every word of his first paragraph. He became a man consecrated to the presidency, working nearly every night until long after midnight, painstakingly reading every piece of proposed legislation submitted to him. He lived up to the Democratic party's platform, which included reform, rigid economy, reduction of taxation, and a lower tariff levied for revenue only. Cleveland favored an American continental policy; believed in honest money of gold, silver, and easily convertible currency; equal justice for all; free education; prevention of monopoly; unrestricted labor; and retention of public lands for settlers.

ing welfare of the country and to secure the full measure of its priceless benefits to us and to those who will succeed to the blessings of our national life. The large variety of diverse and competing interests subject to Federal control, persistently seeking the recognition of their claims, need give us no fear that "the greatest good to the greatest number" will fail to be accomplished if in the halls of national legislation that spirit of amity and mutual concession shall prevail in which the Constitution had its birth. If this involves the surrender or postponement of private interests and the abandonment of local advantages, compensation will be found in the assurance that the common interest is subserved and the general welfare advanced.

In the discharge of my official duty I shall endeavor to be guided by a just and unstrained construction of the Constitution, a careful observance of the distinction between the powers granted to the Federal Government and those reserved to the States or to the people, and by a cautious appreciation of those functions which by the Constitution and laws have been especially assigned to the executive branch of the Government.

But he who takes the oath to-day to preserve, protect, and defend the Constitution of the United States only assumes the solemn obligation which every patriotic citizen—on the farm, in the workshop, in the busy marts of trade, and everywhere—should share with him. The Constitution which prescribes his oath, my countrymen, is yours; the Government you have chosen him to administer for a time is yours; the suffrage which executes the will of freemen is yours; the laws and the entire scheme of our civil rule, from the town meeting to the State capitals and the national capital, is yours. Your every voter, as surely as your Chief Magistrate, under the same high sanction, though in a different sphere, exercises a public trust. Nor is this all. Every citizen owes to the country a vigilant watch and close scrutiny of its public servants and a fair and reasonable estimate of their fidelity and usefulness. Thus is the people's will impressed upon the whole framework of our civil polity—municipal, State, and Federal; and this is the price of our liberty and the inspiration of our faith in the Republic.

It is the duty of those serving the people in public place to closely limit public expenditures to the actual needs of the Government economically administered, because this bounds the right of the Government to exact tribute from the earnings of labor or the property of the citizen, and because public extravagance begets extravagance among the people. We should never be ashamed of the simplicity and prudential economies which are best suited to the operation of a republican form of government and most compatible with the mission of the American people. Those who are selected for a limited time to manage public affairs are still of the people, and may do much by their example to encourage, consistently with the dignity of their official functions, that plain way of life which among their fellow-citizens aids integrity and promotes thrift and prosperity.

The genius of our institutions, the needs of our people in their home life, and the attention which is demanded for the settlement and development of the resources of our vast territory dictate the scrupulous avoidance of any departure from that foreign policy commended by the history, the traditions, and the prosperity of our Republic. It is the policy of independence, favored by our position and defended by our known love of justice and by our power. It is the policy of peace suitable to our interests. It is the policy of neutrality, rejecting any share in foreign broils and ambitions upon other continents and repelling their intrusion here. It is the policy of Monroe and of Washington and of Jefferson—"Peace, commerce, and honest friendship with all nations; entangling alliance with none."

A due regard for the interests and prosperity of all the people demands that our finances shall be established upon such a sound and sensible basis as shall secure the safety and confidence of business interests and make the wage of labor sure and steady, and that our system of revenue shall be so adjusted as to relieve the people of unnecessary taxation, having a due regard to the interests of capital invested and workingmen employed in American industries, and preventing the accumulation of a surplus in the Treasury to tempt extravagance and waste.

Care for the property of the nation and for the needs of future settlers requires that the public domain should be protected from purloining schemes and unlawful occupation.

The conscience of the people demands that the Indians within our boundaries shall be fairly and honestly treated as wards of the Government and their education and civilization promoted with a view to their ultimate citizenship, and that polygamy in the Territories, destructive of the family relation and offensive to the moral sense of the civilized world, shall be repressed.

The laws should be rigidly enforced which prohibit the immigration of a servile class to compete with American labor, with no intention of acquiring citizenship, and bringing with them and retaining habits and customs repugnant to our civilization.

The people demand reform in the administration of the Government and the application of business principles to public affairs. As a means to this end, civil-service reform should be in good faith enforced. Our citizens have the right to protection from the incompetency of public employees who hold their places solely as the reward of partisan service, and from the corrupting influence of those who promise and the vicious methods of those who expect such rewards; and those who worthily seek public employment have the right to insist that merit and competency shall be recognized instead of party subserviency or the surrender of honest political belief.

In the administration of a government pledged to do equal and exact justice to all men there should be no pretext for anxiety touching the protection of the freedmen in their rights or their security in the enjoyment of their privileges under the Constitution and its amendments. All discussion as to their fitness for the place accorded to them as American citizens is idle and unprofitable except as it suggests the necessity for their improvement. The fact that they are citizens entitles them to all the rights due to that relation and charges them with all its duties, obligations, and responsibilities.

These topics and the constant and ever-varying wants of an active and enterprising population may well receive the attention and the patriotic endeavor of all who make and execute the Federal law. Our duties are practical and call for industrious application, an intelligent perception of the claims of public office, and, above all, a firm determination, by united action, to secure to all the people of the land the full benefits of the best form of government ever vouchsafed to man. And let us not trust to human effort alone, but humbly acknowledging the power and goodness of Almighty God, who presides over the destiny of nations, and who has at all times been revealed in our country's history, let us invoke His aid and His blessing upon our labors.

The reference to "polygamy in the Territories" referred to the Mormon religion, which permitted a man to have more than one wife.

The "servile class" was the Chinese people, who had been immigrating to the West Coast in large groups until 1882. Then, during President Arthur's administration, the Chinese Exclusion Act was passed, which suspended the immigration of Chinese skilled and unskilled laborers for ten years. The Act was regularly renewed until 1920, when specific quotas were set up.

THE PRESIDENT

Benjamin Harrison was the grandson of William Henry Harrison, the nation's 9th president. A graduate of Miami University, Harrison was admitted to the bar in 1853. He served in the 70th Indiana Volunteer Infantry in the Civil War and was breveted a brigadier-general. He sat in the U.S. Senate from 1881 to 1887, where his opposition to President Cleveland's pension vetoes attracted the attention of veterans disgruntled with the President's deaf ear to their appeals for Federal aid. But what was more important, Harrison's belief in a high protective tariff fitted in with wealthy manufacturing interests. These interests backed him with a huge campaign fund which helped immeasurably to win the election.

THE NATION

A new name caught the attention of many Americans: Theodore Roosevelt. As an aggressive champion of civil service reform both before and after Harrison's election Roosevelt earned the public's confidence and trust, but developed powerful enemies.

In 1886 the Apache Geronimo surrendered to General George Crook. In May of the same year a bomb was exploded among anarchist labor leaders in Haymarket Square, Chicago. On October 28, 1886, the copper-sheathed Statue of Liberty was dedicated. During Cleveland's administration Secretary of the Navy Whitney actively pushed for the construction of the new steel Navy to replace wood-hulled vessels.

To eliminate future electoral vote wrangles, such as had occurred in the election of 1876, Congress passed the Electoral Count Act on February 3, 1887. Next day the Interstate Commerce Act to regulate the operation of the railroads was passed. President Cleveland was kept busy vetoing a continual stream of special pension bills to benefit veterans of the Civil War. On March 5, 1887, the Tenure of Office Act, which had indirectly resulted in the impeachment of President Andrew Johnson, was at last repealed under pressure instigated by Cleveland.

In the election of 1888 votes were split among five parties. Republican Benjamin Harrison polled fewer popular votes than the Democrat Cleveland. But Harrison carried New York and Indiana, thus winning the election with 5,439,853 popular votes (233 electoral) to Cleveland's 5,540,309 (168 electoral). The Prohibition party's Clinton B. Fisk received 249,506 votes, the Union Labor party's Olson J. Streeter polled 146,935, while the United Labor party's Robert H. Cowdrey received 2,818. Levi P. Morton became vice-president.

THE WORLD

Great Britain was at her zenith as a world power. Her influence dominated millions of the world's population. Throughout the Continent the Industrial Revolution was itself to undergo a revolution, as electricity began to come into use, although coal and steam were at the time still the chief sources of power. As the world approached the last decade of the nineteenth century preparations were being made for a world's fair to be held in Paris.

[154]

IN PREPARING YOUR INAUGURAL ADDRESS you apparently use your grandfather's as a model. As he did, you begin with a long look at the past—although you peer no farther back than the origin of the union one hundred years ago, fortunately eschewing the history of ancient Athens and Rome of which Grandfather had obviously been so enamoured. Your inauguration day boasts typical March weather—heavy rains and strong winds—but still permits a tremendous audience to gather on the Capitol steps to hear you read your address . . . .

Benjamin Harrison

[1889–1893]

INAUGURAL ADDRESS, MARCH 4, 1889

Capitol Steps, Washington, D.C.

Fellow-citizens:

There is no constitutional or legal requirement that the President shall take the oath of office in the presence of the people, but there is so manifest an appropriateness in the public induction to office of the chief executive officer of the nation that from the beginning of the Government the people, to whose service the official oath consecrates the officer, have been called to witness the solemn ceremonial. The oath taken in the presence of the people becomes a mutual covenant. The officer covenants to serve the whole body of the people by a faithful execution of the laws, so that they may be the unfailing defense and security of those who respect and observe them, and that neither wealth, station, nor the power of combinations shall be able to evade their just penalties or to wrest them from a beneficent public purpose to serve the ends of cruelty or selfishness.

My promise is spoken; yours unspoken, but not the less real and solemn. The people of every State have here their representatives. Surely I do not misinterpret the spirit of the occasion when I assume that the whole body of the people covenant with me and with each other to-day to support and defend the Constitution and the Union of the States, to yield willing obedience to all the laws and each to every other citizen his equal civil and political rights. Entering thus solemnly into covenant with each other, we may reverently invoke and confidently expect the favor and help of Almighty God—that He will to give me wisdom, strength, and fidelity, and to our people a spirit of fraternity and a love of righteousness and peace.

This occasion derives peculiar interest from the fact that the Presidential term which begins this day is the twenty-sixth under our Constitution. The first inauguration of President Washington took place in New York, where Congress was then sitting, on the 30th day of April, 1789, having been deferred by reason of delays

These were noble sentiments, but the meek, pliable Harrison never had the courage to break with his wealthy backers and place the country's welfare above the private interests to whom he owed his victory.

[155]

attending the organization of the Congress and the canvass of the electoral vote. Our people have already worthily observed the centennials of the Declaration of Independence, of the battle of Yorktown, and of the adoption of the Constitution, and will shortly celebrate in New York the institution of the second great department of our constitutional scheme of government. When the centennial of the institution of the judicial department, by the organization of the Supreme Court, shall have been suitably observed, as I trust it will be, our nation will have fully entered its second century.

I will not attempt to note the marvelous and in great part happy contrasts between our country as it steps over the threshold into its second century of organized existence under the Constitution and that weak but wisely ordered young nation that looked undauntedly down the first century, when all its years stretched out before it.

Our people will not fail at this time to recall the incidents which accompanied the institution of government under the Constitution, or to find inspiration and guidance in the teachings and example of Washington and his great associates, and hope and courage in the contrast which thirty-eight populous and prosperous States offer to the thirteen States, weak in everything except courage and the love of liberty, that then fringed our Atlantic seaboard.

The Territory of Dakota has now a population greater than any of the original States (except Virginia) and greater than the aggregate of five of the smaller States in 1790. The center of population when our national capital was located was east of Baltimore, and it was argued by many well-informed persons that it would move eastward rather than westward; yet in 1880 it was found to be near Cincinnati, and the new census about to be taken will show another stride to the westward. That which was the body has come to be only the rich fringe of the nation's robe. But our growth has not been limited to territory, population and aggregate wealth, marvelous as it has been in each of those directions. The masses of our people are better fed, clothed, and housed than their fathers were. The facilities for popular education have been vastly enlarged and more generally diffused.

The virtues of courage and patriotism have given recent proof of their continued presence and increasing power in the hearts and over the lives of our people. The influences of religion have been multiplied and strengthened. The sweet offices of charity have greatly increased. The virtue of temperance is held in higher estimation. We have not attained an ideal condition. Not all of our people are happy and prosperous; not all of them are virtuous and law-abiding. But on the whole the opportunities offered to the individual to secure the comforts of life are better than are found elsewhere and largely better than they were here one hundred years ago.

The surrender of a large measure of sovereignty to the General Government, effected by the adoption of the Constitution, was not accomplished until the suggestions of reason were strongly reenforced by the more imperative voice of experience. The divergent interests of peace speedily demanded a "more perfect union." The merchant, the shipmaster, and the manufacturer discovered and disclosed to our statesmen and to the people that commercial emancipation must be added to the political freedom which had been so bravely won. The commercial policy of the mother country had not relaxed any of its hard and oppressive features. To hold in

The census of 1890 revealed a population of 62,947,714, with the center of population located 20 miles east of Columbus, Indiana.

[156]

check the development of our commercial marine, to prevent or retard the establishment and growth of manufactures in the States, and so to secure the American market for their shops and the carrying trade for their ships, was the policy of European statesmen, and was pursued with the most selfish vigor.

Petitions poured in upon Congress urging the imposition of discriminating duties that should encourage the production of needed things at home. The patriotism of the people, which no longer found a field of exercise in war, was energetically directed to the duty of equipping the young Republic for the defense of its independence by making its people self-dependent. Societies for the promotion of home manufactures and for encouraging the use of domestics in the dress of the people were organized in many of the States. The revival at the end of the century of the same patriotic interest in the preservation and development of domestic industries and the defense of our working people against injurious foreign competition is an incident worthy of attention. It is not a departure but a return that we have witnessed. The protective policy had then its opponents. The argument was made, as now, that its benefits inured to particular classes or sections.

If the question became in any sense or at any time sectional, it was only because slavery existed in some of the States. But for this there was no reason why the cotton-producing States should not have led or walked abreast with the New England States in the production of cotton fabrics. There was this reason only why the States that divide with Pennsylvania the mineral treasures of the great southeastern and central mountain ranges should have been so tardy in bringing to the smelting furnace and to the mill the coal and iron from their near opposing hillsides. Mill fires were lighted at the funeral pile of slavery. The emancipation proclamation was heard in the depths of the earth as well as in the sky; men were made free, and material things became our better servants.

The sectional element has happily been eliminated from the tariff discussion. We have no longer States that are necessarily only planting States. None are excluded from achieving that diversification of pursuits among the people which brings wealth and contentment. The cotton plantation will not be less valuable when the product is spun in the country town by operatives whose necessities call for diversified crops and create a home demand for garden and agricultural products. Every new mine, furnace, and factory is an extension of the productive capacity of the State more real and valuable than added territory.

Shall the prejudices and paralysis of slavery continue to hang upon the skirts of progress? How long will those who rejoice that slavery no longer exists cherish or tolerate the incapacities it put upon their communities? I look hopefully to the continuance of our protective system and to the consequent development of manufacturing and mining enterprises in the States hitherto wholly given to agriculture as a potent influence in the perfect unification of our people. The men who have invested their capital in these enterprises, the farmers who have felt the benefit of their neighborhood, and the men who work in shop or field will not fail to find and to defend a community of interest.

Is it not quite possible that the farmers and the promoters of the great mining and manufacturing enterprises which have recently been established in the South may yet find that the free ballot of the workingman, without distinction of race, is needed for their

Here Harrison began to explain his belief in a high protective tariff. This policy was the real reason for heavy campaign contributions made by manufacturers, who stood to gain most by such a policy.

Despite Harrison's argument—that a high protective tariff would benefit all interests alike, whether North or South—benefits derived from his tariff policy would go mainly to industrialists in the North and East rather than to plantation owners of the South or to cattle or mining interests of the West.

[157]

defense as well as for his own? I do not doubt that if those men in the South who now accept the tariff views of Clay and the constitutional expositions of Webster would courageously avow and defend their real convictions they would not find it difficult, by friendly instruction and cooperation, to make the black man their efficient and safe ally, not only in establishing correct principles in our national administration, but in preserving for their local communities the benefits of social order and economical and honest government. At least until the good offices of kindness and education have been fairly tried the contrary conclusion can not be plausibly urged.

I have altogether rejected the suggestion of a special Executive policy for any section of our country. It is the duty of the Executive to administer and enforce in the methods and by the instrumentalities pointed out and provided by the Constitution all the laws enacted by Congress. These laws are general and their administration should be uniform and equal. As a citizen may not elect what laws he will obey, neither may the Executive elect which he will enforce. The duty to obey and to execute embraces the Constitution in its entirety and the whole code of laws enacted under it. The evil example of permitting individuals, corporations, or communities to nullify the laws because they cross some selfish or local interest or prejudices is full of danger, not only to the nation at large, but much more to those who use this pernicious expedient to escape their just obligations or to obtain an unjust advantage over others. They will presently themselves be compelled to appeal to the law for protection, and those who would use the law as a defense must not deny that use of it to others.

If our great corporations would more scrupulously observe their legal limitations and duties, they would have less cause to complain of the unlawful limitations of their rights or of violent interference with their operations. The community that by concert, open or secret, among its citizens denies to a portion of its members their plain rights under the law has severed the only safe bond of social order and prosperity. The evil works from a bad center both ways. It demoralizes those who practice it and destroys the faith of those who suffer by it in the efficiency of the law as a safe protector. The man in whose breast that faith has been darkened is naturally the subject of dangerous and uncanny suggestions. Those who use unlawful methods, if moved by no higher motive than the selfishness that prompted them, may well stop and inquire what is to be the end of this.

An unlawful expedient can not become a permanent condition of government. If the educated and influential classes in a community either practice or connive at the systematic violation of laws that seem to them to cross their convenience, what can they expect when the lesson that convenience or a supposed class interest is a sufficient cause for lawlessness has been well learned by the ignorant classes? A community where law is the rule of conduct and where courts, not mobs, execute its penalties is the only attractive field for business investments and honest labor.

Our naturalization laws should be so amended as to make the inquiry into the character and good disposition of persons applying for citizenship more careful and searching. Our existing laws have been in their administration an unimpressive and often an unintelligible form. We accept the man as a citizen without any knowledge of his fitness, and he assumes the duties of citizenship without any knowledge as to what they are. The privileges of American citizen-

This suggestion of Harrison's was eventually carried out in 1913, when an Immigration Act was passed over President Woodrow Wilson's veto. The act excluded most Asiatic laborers, but admitted Japanese.

[158]

ship are so great and its duties so grave that we may well insist upon a good knowledge of every person applying for citizenship and a good knowledge by him of our institutions. We should not cease to be hospitable to immigration, but we should cease to be careless as to the character of it. There are men of all races, even the best, whose coming is necessarily a burden upon our public revenues or a threat to social order. These should be identified and excluded.

We have happily maintained a policy of avoiding all interference with European affairs. We have been only interested spectators of their contentions in diplomacy and in war, ready to use our friendly offices to promote peace, but never obtruding our advice and never attempting unfairly to coin the distresses of other powers into commercial advantage to ourselves. We have a just right to expect that our European policy will be the American policy of European courts.

A restatement of the Monroe Doctrine, particularly applied to the Central American countries of Panama and Nicaragua, where a canal was already being considered.

It is so manifestly incompatible with those precautions for our peace and safety which all the great powers habitually observe and enforce in matters affecting them that a shorter waterway between our eastern and western seaboards should be dominated by any European Government that we may confidently expect that such a purpose will not be entertained by any friendly power.

We shall in the future, as in the past, use every endeavor to maintain and enlarge our friendly relations with all the great powers, but they will not expect us to look kindly upon any project that would leave us subject to the dangers of a hostile observation or environment. We have not sought to dominate or to absorb any of our weaker neighbors, but rather to aid and encourage them to establish free and stable governments resting upon the consent of their own people. We have a clear right to expect, therefore, that no European Government will seek to establish colonial dependencies upon the territory of these independent American States. That which a sense of justice restrains us from seeking they may be reasonably expected willingly to forego.

It must not be assumed, however, that our interests are so exclusively American that our entire inattention to any events that may transpire elsewhere can be taken for granted. Our citizens domiciled for purposes of trade in all countries and in many of the islands of the sea demand and will have our adequate care in their personal and commercial rights. The necessities of our Navy require convenient coaling stations and dock and harbor privileges. These and other trading privileges we will feel free to obtain only by means that do not in any degree partake of coercion, however feeble the government from which we ask such concessions. But having fairly obtained them by methods and for purposes entirely consistent with the most friendly disposition toward all other powers, our consent will be necessary to any modification or impairment of the concession.

We shall neither fail to respect the flag of any friendly nation or the just rights of its citizens, nor to exact the like treatment for our own. Calmness, justice, and consideration should characterize our diplomacy. The offices of an intelligent diplomacy or of friendly arbitration in proper cases should be adequate to the peaceful adjustment of all international difficulties. By such methods we will make our contribution to the world's peace, which no nation values more highly, and avoid the opprobrium which must fall upon the nation that ruthlessly breaks it.

The duty devolved by law upon the President to nominate and, by and with the advice and consent of the Senate, to appoint all public officers whose appointment is not otherwise provided for in the Constitution or by act of Congress has become very burdensome and its wise and efficient discharge full of difficulty. The civil list is so large that a personal knowledge of any large number of the applicants is impossible. The President must rely upon the representations of others, and these are often made inconsiderately and without any just sense of responsibility. I have a right, I think, to insist that those who volunteer or are invited to get advice as to appointments shall exercise consideration and fidelity. A high sense of duty and an ambition to improve the service should characterize all public officers.

There are many ways in which the convenience and comfort of those who have business with our public offices may be promoted by a thoughtful and obliging officer, and I shall expect those whom I may appoint to justify their selection by a conspicuous efficiency in the discharge of their duties. Honorable party service will certainly not be esteemed by me a disqualification for public office, but it will in no case be allowed to serve as a shield of official negligence, incompetency, or delinquency. It is entirely creditable to seek public office by proper methods and with proper motives, and all applicants will be treated with consideration; but I shall need, and the heads of Departments will need, time for inquiry and deliberation. Persistent importunity will not, therefore, be the best support of an application for office. Heads of Departments, bureaus, and all other public officers having any duty connected therewith will be expected to enforce the civil-service law fully and without evasion. Beyond this obvious duty I hope to do something more to advance the reform of the civil service. The ideal, or even my own ideal, I shall probably not attain. Retrospect will be a safer basis of judgment than promises. We shall not, however, I am sure, be able to put our civil service upon a nonpartisan basis until we have secured an incumbency that fair-minded men of the opposition will approve for impartiality and integrity. As the number of such in the civil list is increased removals from office will diminish.

While a Treasury surplus is not the greatest evil, it is a serious evil. Our revenue should be ample to meet the ordinary annual demands upon our Treasury, with a sufficient margin for those extraordinary but scarcely less imperative demands which arise now and then. Expenditure should always be made with economy and only upon public necessity. Wastefulness, profligacy, or favoritism in public expenditures is criminal. But there is nothing in the condition of our country or of our people to suggest that anything presently necessary to the public prosperity, security, or honor should be unduly postponed.

It will be the duty of Congress wisely to forecast and estimate these extraordinary demands, and, having added them to our ordinary expenditures, to so adjust our revenue laws that no considerable annual surplus will remain. We will fortunately be able to apply to the redemption of the public debt any small and unforeseen excess of revenue. This is better than to reduce our income below our necessary expenditures, with the resulting choice between another change of our revenue laws and an increase of the public debt. It is quite possible, I am sure, to effect the necessary reduction in our revenues without breaking down our protective tariff or seriously injuring any domestic industry.

The construction of a sufficient number of modern war ships and of their necessary armament should progress as rapidly as is consistent with care and perfection in plans and workmanship. The spirit, courage, and skill of our naval officers and seamen have many times in our history given to weak ships and inefficient guns a rating greatly beyond that of the naval list. That they will again do so upon occasion I do not doubt; but they ought not, by premeditation or neglect, to be left to the risks and exigencies of an unequal combat. We should encourage the establishment of American steamship lines. The exchanges of commerce demand stated, reliable, and rapid means of communication, and until these are provided the development of our trade with the States lying south of us is impossible.

Our pension laws should give more adequate and discriminating relief to the Union soldiers and sailors and to their widows and orphans. Such occasions as this should remind us that we owe everything to their valor and sacrifice.

It is a subject of congratulation that there is a near prospect of the admission into the Union of the Dakotas and Montana and Washington Territories. This act of justice has been unreasonably delayed in the case of some of them. The people who have settled these Territories are intelligent, enterprising, and patriotic, and the accession of these new States will add strength to the nation. It is due to the settlers in the Territories who have availed themselves of the invitations of our land laws to make homes upon the public domain that their titles should be speedily adjusted and their honest entries confirmed by patent.

It is very gratifying to observe the general interest now being manifested in the reform of our election laws. Those who have been for years calling attention to the pressing necessity of throwing about the ballot box and about the elector further safeguards, in order that our elections might not only be free and pure, but might clearly appear to be so, will welcome the accession of any who did no so soon discover the need of reform. The National Congress has not as yet taken control of elections in that case over which the Constitution gives it jurisdiction, but has accepted and adopted the election laws of the several States, provided penalties for their violation and a method of supervision. Only the inefficiency of the State laws or an unfair partisan administration of them could suggest a departure from this policy.

Election laws would be enacted after the turn of the century. The primary system would be made mandatory in 1903, the preferential ballot system would be put into effect in 1909, and the state-wide presidential preference primary system would become effective in 1912.

It was clearly, however, in the contemplation of the framers of the Constitution that such an exigency might arise, and provision was wisely made for it. The freedom of the ballot is a condition of our national life, and no power vested in Congress or in the Executive to secure or perpetuate it should remain unused upon occasion. The people of all the Congressional districts have an equal interest that the election in each shall truly express the views and wishes of a majority of the qualified electors residing within it. The results of such elections are not local, and the insistence of electors residing in other districts that they shall be pure and free does not savor at all of impertinence.

If in any of the States the public security is thought to be threatened by ignorance among the electors, the obvious remedy is education. The sympathy and help of our people will not be withheld from any community struggling with special embarrassments or difficulties connected with the suffrage if the remedies proposed proceed upon lawful lines and are promoted by just and honorable methods. How shall those who practice election frauds recover that respect for the sanctity of the ballot which is the first condition and obligation of good citizenship? The man who has come to regard the ballot box as a juggler's hat has renounced his allegiance.

Let us exalt patriotism and moderate our party contentions. Let those who would die for the flag on the field of battle give a better proof of their patriotism and a higher glory to their country by promoting fraternity and justice. A party success that is achieved by unfair methods or by practices that partake of revolution is hurtful and evanescent even from a party standpoint. We should hold our differing opinions in mutual respect, and, having submitted them to the arbitrament of the ballot, should accept an adverse judgment with the same respect that we would have demanded of our opponents if the decision had been in our favor.

No other people have a government more worthy of their respect and love or a land so magnificent in extent, so pleasant to look upon, and so full of generous suggestion to enterprise and labor. God has placed upon our head a diadem and has laid at our feet power and wealth beyond definition or calculation. But we must not forget that we take these gifts upon the condition that justice and mercy shall hold the reins of power and that the upward avenues of hope shall be free to all the people.

I do not mistrust the future. Dangers have been in frequent ambush along our path, but we have uncovered and vanquished them all. Passion has swept some of our communities, but only to give us a new demonstration that the great body of our people are stable, patriotic, and law-abiding. No political party can long pursue advantage at the expense of public honor or by rude and indecent methods without protest and fatal disaffection in its own body. The peaceful agencies of commerce are more fully revealing the necessary unity of all our communities, and the increasing intercourse of our people in promoting mutual respect. We shall find unalloyed pleasure in the revelation which our next census will make of the swift development of the great resources of some of the States. Each State will bring its generous contribution to the great aggregate of the nation's increase. And when the harvests from the fields, the cattle from the hills, and the ores of the earth shall have been weighed, counted, and valued, we will turn from them all to crown with the highest honor the State that has most promoted education, virtue, justice, and patriotism among its people.

The October 28, 1886, invitation to the inauguration of the Statue of Liberty.

THE PRESIDENT

When Cleveland was called upon to run for the presidency again he made tariff reform the chief issue of the campaign. In his letter accepting the nomination he wrote, "Tariff reform is still our purpose. Though we oppose the theory that tariff laws may be passed having for their object the granting of discriminating and unfair governmental aid to private ventures, we wage no exterminating war against any American interests." Thus the McKinley Act became the main issue of the election campaign, and the farmers, many of whom disliked the act, switched their votes to Cleveland.

THE NATION

At noon of April 22, 1889, Oklahoma was opened to settlers. On May 31 the dam above Johnstown, Pennsylvania, broke and buried the town under 30 feet of water, killing an estimated 3,000 persons. Four new states joined the Union in November of 1889, bringing the total to 42: November 2, North and South Dakota; November 8, Montana; November 11, Washington.

The census of 1890 disclosed a population of 62,947,714, swollen by immigrants who continued to pour into the growing nation. The Sherman Anti-Trust Act was passed on July 2, 1890. The following day Idaho became the 43rd state to join the Union. Wyoming was admitted July 11, 1890. The Sherman Silver Purchase Act was passed on July 14, requiring the purchase of 4,500,000 ounces of silver per month and repealing the Bland-Allison Act. True to his inaugural promise President Harrison signed the McKinley Tariff Act, which set tariff levels higher than ever before. Harrison was influenced by the manufacturing interests who had contributed to Harrison's huge campaign fund.

The peerless John L. Sullivan was nearing the end of his career. The first Army-Navy football game was played, with Navy victorious 24–0; baseball was growing in popularity; and basketball had just been invented by a Y.M.C.A. physical education instructor, Dr. James A. Naismith. There were other firsts in 1891: the International 6-day bike race, the correspondence school, an American patent for a motion-picture camera, sun photography with the new spectro-heliograph invention.

In the election year of 1892 the Democratic party's Grover Cleveland was nominated for the third time, and made it two victories out of three by defeating Republican Harrison. Election returns showed 5,556,918 popular votes for Cleveland (277 electoral), to 5,176,108 popular votes for Harrison (145 electoral). The People's party with James B. Weaver as standard bearer polled a respectable 1,041,028 popular votes (22 electoral), Prohibitionist John Bidwell received 264,133, and the Socialist Labor party's Simon Wing polled 21,164. Adlai E. Stevenson was elected vice-president.

THE WORLD

In 1889 France became the focal point of the world's interest when the Paris Exposition was opened on May 6th. The 984-foot Eiffel Tower, at that time the world's tallest steel structure, was featured. Various industries in England were suffering from prolonged strikes which caused widespread suffering and readjustment. In Germany the great Bismarck resigned his chancellorship in 1890 after a long and history-making career. 1891 witnessed the start of the Trans-Siberian railroad in Russia and a renewal of the Triple Alliance between Austria, Germany, and Italy. Anarchist demonstrations broke out in Europe; famine and plague brought death to thousands of peasants.

COMPARED TO THE COLORLESS, PLIANT HARRISON to many voters you seem as sturdy as the Rock of Gibraltar. In a widespread reaction against Harrison's meek subservience to powerful interests you seem to be a wise, dependable, and fearless leader who will pull the nation back from the crumbling edge of another of the cyclical depressions of the era. Sensing this, you devote the bulk of your inaugural address to the financial state of the nation. And when you stand to deliver your message to an audience salted by sporadic flurries of sleet your optimism warms the emotions of present listeners and later those of the nation, but your words are powerless to hold back the inexorable world-wide freezing of economic activity . . . .

Grover Cleveland

[1893–1897]

SECOND INAUGURAL ADDRESS, MARCH 4, 1893

Capitol Steps, Washington, D.C.

My fellow citizens:

In obedience to the mandate of my countrymen I am about to dedicate myself to their service under the sanction of a solemn oath. Deeply moved by the expression of confidence and personal attachment which has called me to this service, I am sure my gratitude can make no better return than the pledge I now give before God and these witnesses of unreserved and complete devotion to the interests and welfare of those who have honored me.

I deem it fitting on this occasion, while indicating the opinions I hold concerning public questions of present importance, to also briefly refer to the existence of certain conditions and tendencies among our people which seem to menace the integrity and usefulness of their Government.

While every American citizen must contemplate with the utmost pride and enthusiasm the growth and expansion of our country, the sufficiency of our institutions to stand against the rudest shocks of violence, the wonderful thrift and enterprise of our people, and the demonstrated superiority of our free government, it behooves us to constantly watch for every symptom of insidious infirmity that threatens our national vigor.

The strong man who in the confidence of sturdy health courts the sternest activities of life and rejoices in the hardihood of constant labor may still have lurking near his vitals the unheeded disease that dooms him to sudden collapse.

It can not be doubted that our stupendous achievements as a people and our country's robust strength have given rise to heedlessness of those laws governing our national health which we can no more evade than human life can escape the laws of God and nature.

Manifestly nothing is more vital to our supremacy as a nation and to the beneficent purposes of our Government than a sound and stable currency. Its exposure to degradation should at once arouse to activity the most enlightened statesmanship, and the danger of depreciation in the purchasing power of the wages paid

One such "symptom of insidious infirmity" was the Sherman Silver Purchase Act. Cleveland would have to exert all pressure possible to repeal it.

to toil should furnish the strongest incentive to prompt and conservative precaution.

In dealing with our present embarrassing situation as related to this subject we will be wise if we temper our confidence and faith in our national strength and resources with the frank concession that even these will not permit us to defy with impunity the inexorable laws of finance and trade. At the same time, in our efforts to adjust differences of opinion we should be free from intolerance or passion, and our judgments should be unmoved by alluring phrases and unvexed by selfish interests.

I am confident that such an approach to the subject will result in prudent and effective remedial legislation. In the meantime, so far as the executive branch of the Government can intervene, none of the powers with which it is invested will be withheld when their exercise is deemed necessary to maintain our national credit or avert financial disaster.

Closely related to the exaggerated confidence in our country's greatness which tends to a disregard of the rules of national safety, another danger confronts us not less serious. I refer to the prevalence of a popular disposition to expect from the operation of the Government especial and direct individual advantages.

The verdict of our voters which condemned the injustice of maintaining protection for protection's sake enjoins upon the people's servants the duty of exposing and destroying the brood of kindred evils which are the unwholesome progeny of paternalism. This is the bane of republican institutions and the constant peril of our government by the people. It degrades to the purposes of wily craft the plan of rule our fathers established and bequeathed to us as an object of our love and veneration. It perverts the patriotic sentiments of our countrymen and tempts them to pitiful calculation of the sordid gain to be derived from their Government's maintenance. It undermines the self-reliance of our people and substitutes in its place dependence upon governmental favoritism. It stifles the spirit of true Americanism and stupefies every ennobling trait of American citizenship.

The lessons of paternalism ought to be unlearned and the better lesson taught that while the people should patriotically and cheerfully support their Government its functions do not include the support of the people.

The acceptance of this principle leads to a refusal of bounties and subsidies, which burden the labor and thrift of a portion of our citizens to aid ill-advised or languishing enterprises in which they have no concern. It leads also to a challenge of wild and reckless pension expenditure, which overleaps the bounds of grateful recognition of patriotic service and prostitutes to vicious uses the people's prompt and generous impulse to aid those disabled in their country's defense.

Every thoughtful American must realize the importance of checking at its beginning any tendency in public or private station to regard frugality and economy as virtues which we may safely outgrow. The toleration of this idea results in the waste of the people's money by their chosen servants and encourages prodigality and extravagence in the home life of our countrymen.

Under our scheme of government the waste of public money is a crime against the citizen, and the contempt of our people for economy and frugality in their personal affairs deplorably saps the strength and sturdiness of our national character.

It is a plain dictate of honesty and good government that public expenditures should be limited by public necessity, and that this should be measured by the rules of strict economy; and it is equally clear that frugality among the people is the best guaranty of a contented and strong support of free institutions.

One mode of the misappropriation of public funds is avoided when appointments to office, instead of being the rewards of partisan activity, are awarded to those whose efficiency promises a fair return of work for the compensation paid to them. To secure the fitness and competency of appointees to office and remove from political action the demoralizing madness for spoils, civil-service reform has found a place in our public policy and laws. The benefits already gained through this instrumentality and the further usefulness it promises entitle it to the hearty support and encouragement of all who desire to see our public service well performed or who hope for the elevation of political sentiment and the purification of political methods.

The existence of immense aggregations of kindred enterprises and combinations of business interests formed for the purpose of limiting production and fixing prices is inconsistent with the fair field which ought to be open to every independent activity. Legitimate strife in business should not be superseded by an enforced concession to the demands of combinations that have the power to destroy, nor should the people to be served lose the benefit of cheapness which usually results from wholesome competition. These aggregations and combinations frequently constitute conspiracies against the interests of the people, and in all their phases they are unnatural and opposed to our American sense of fairness. To the extent that they can be reached and restrained by Federal power the General Government should relieve our citizens from their interference and exactions.

Loyalty to the principles upon which our Government rests positively demands that the equality before the law which it guarantees to every citizen should be justly and in good faith conceded in all parts of the land. The enjoyment of this right follows the badge of citizenship wherever found, and, unimpaired by race or color, it appeals for recognition to American manliness and fairness.

Our relations with the Indians located within our border impose upon us responsibilities we can not escape. Humanity and consistency require us to treat them with forbearance and in our dealings with them to honestly and considerately regard their rights and interests. Every effort should be made to lead them, through the paths of civilization and education, to self-supporting and independent citizenship. In the meantime, as the nation's wards, they should be promptly defended against the cupidity of designing men and shielded from every influence or temptation that retards their advancement.

The people of the United States have decreed that on this day the control of their Government in its legislative and executive branches shall be given to a political party pledged in the most positive terms to the accomplishment of tariff reform. They have thus determined in favor of a more just and equitable system of Federal taxation. The agents they have chosen to carry out their purposes are bound by their promises not less than by the command of their masters to devote themselves unremittingly to this service.

While there should be no surrender of principle, our task must

Despite these platitudes concerning the nation's benevolent attitude toward them the Indians continued to be fair prey for "the cupidity of designing men." The Cherokee Strip, which had been "purchased" from the Cherokees in 1891, was to be opened to another land rush involving more than 100,000 settlers.

be undertaken wisely and without heedless vindictiveness. Our mission is not punishment, but the rectification of wrong. If in lifting burdens from the daily life of our people we reduce inordinate and unequal advantages too long enjoyed, this is but a necessary incident of our return to right and justice. If we exact from unwilling minds acquiescence in the theory of an honest distribution of the fund of the governmental beneficence treasured up for all, we but insist upon a principle which underlies our free institutions. When we tear aside the delusions and misconceptions which have blinded our countrymen to their condition under vicious tariff laws, we but show them how far they have been led away from the paths of contentment and prosperity. When we proclaim that the necessity for revenue to support the Government furnishes the only justification for taxing the people, we announce a truth so plain that its denial would seem to indicate the extent to which judgment may be influenced by familiarity with perversions of the taxing power. And when we seek to reinstate the self-confidence and business enterprise of our citizens by discrediting an abject dependence upon governmental favor, we strive to stimulate those elements of American character which support the hope of American achievement.

Anxiety for the redemption of the pledges which my party has made and solicitude for the complete justification of the trust the people have reposed in us constrain me to remind those with whom I am to cooperate that we can succeed in doing the work which has been especially set before us only by the most sincere, harmonious, and disinterested effort. Even if insuperable obstacles and opposition prevent the consummation of our task, we shall hardly be excused; and if failure can be traced to our fault or neglect we may be sure the people will hold us to a swift and exacting accountability.

The oath I now take to preserve, protect, and defend the Constitution of the United States not only impressively defines the great responsibility I assume, but suggests obedience to constitutional commands as the rule by which my official conduct must be guided. I shall to the best of my ability and within my sphere of duty preserve the Constitution by loyally protecting every grant of Federal power it contains, by defending all its restraints when attacked by impatience and restlessness, and by enforcing its limitations and reservations in favor of the States and the people.

Fully impressed with the gravity of the duties that confront me and mindful of my weakness, I should be appalled if it were my lot to bear unaided the responsibilities which await me. I am, however, saved from discouragement when I remember that I shall have the support and the counsel and cooperation of wise and patriotic men who will stand at my side in Cabinet places or will represent the people in their legislative halls.

I find also much comfort in remembering that my countrymen are just and generous and in the assurance that they will not condemn those who by sincere devotion to their service deserve their forbearance and approval.

Above all, I know there is a Supreme Being who rules the affairs of men and whose goodness and mercy have always followed the American people, and I know He will not turn from us now if we humbly and reverently seek His powerful aid.

The "insuperable obstacles" would appear all too soon in the form of another depression, and true to Cleveland's prophecy the people would hold the Democrats to "swift and exacting accountability." The depression would have been worse if the public had not been kept in ignorance of Cleveland's precarious health. Shortly after his inauguration he had to submit to an operation to remove a cancerous growth from the roof of his mouth. The operation was performed at night on a yacht steaming up the East River. So successful was the surgery and so closely was the secret guarded that the public did not know of it until long after Cleveland had left the presidency.

Johnstown, Pennsylvania, in 1889 at the height of the flood.

THE PRESIDENT

William McKinley was the last veteran of the Civil War to be elected president; the third president to be assassinated. He was admitted to the bar in 1867, and served as a Republican congressman from 1877 to 1891, with the exception of the 1883–85 term. His sponsorship of the McKinley Tariff led to his defeat in the 1890 election, but he was promptly made governor of Ohio in 1891 and again in 1893. He was victorious in his campaign for the presidency in 1896. His platform advocated a high protective tariff and a sound currency based on the gold standard.

THE NATION

The Chicago World's Fair attracted worldwide attention from May through October of 1893, with nearly every country represented.

Democratic domination in the Senate and House of Representatives lasted only until the 1894 mid-term election. The public's loss of confidence in Cleveland's administration was due to the Panic of 1893, when the U.S. gold reserve dropped below the $100,000,000 level, sending stocks crashing in May and June and deepening the depression which had been slowly engulfing the nation. In November the Sherman Silver Purchase Act was finally repealed after a 90-day struggle which split the Democratic party and helped restore the Republicans to power. In April of 1894 "Coxey's Army" of unemployed men marched on Washington to appeal to Cleveland for relief. Utah entered the Union on January 4, 1896.

The split in the Democratic party brought to national prominence William Jennings Bryan and Richard P. Bland, who were leaders of the free silver bloc in the House of Representatives. The campaign of 1896 was based largely on the issue of gold vs. free silver, with Bryan advocating free silver and the Republican candidate, William McKinley, gold.

In the election Republican William McKinley polled 7,104,779 popular votes (271 electoral). Democrat William Jennings Bryan received 6,502,925 popular votes (176 electoral). Some 300,000 votes were split among the other four candidates: Prohibitionist Joshua Levering, 132,007; National Democrat John M. Palmer, 133,148; Socialist Charles H. Matchett, 36,274; Nationalist Charles E. Bentley, 13,969. Garrett A. Hobart was elected vice-president.

THE WORLD

In 1893 strikes were still tying up British industry. Anarchists were active in nearly every country on the Continent. The following year Gladstone resigned as British Prime Minister and was succeeded by Lord Rosebery. In 1894 Japan declared war on China. On November 1, 1894, Czar Alexander III died, to be succeeded by Nicholas II. In December Captain Alfred Dreyfus received a life sentence on Devil's Island for allegedly selling military secrets to another nation. Japan continued its string of victories in the war with China and destroyed the Chinese fleet, opening the way to peace negotiations. The French, rivals of the British on Madagascar, sent an expedition against the capital in September, 1895, and on January 16, 1896, proclaimed possession. On August 6th the island was declared a French colony.

YOU REMAIN QUIETLY AT HOME in Canton, Ohio, and make your carefully worded campaign speeches on your front porch, while William Jennings Bryan, "The boy orator of the Platte," charges about the country attacking moneyed interests and trusts, while espousing free silver. When the smoke clears, your conservative appeal has carried more weight with the voters than the flamboyant fist-waving of the silver-tongued Bryan—you are decisively victorious. This same spirit of quiet determination is also apparent in your long inaugural address, on which you spend many hours working to achieve the proper tone of firmness mixed with conciliation, particularly concerning the threat of war with Spain. Your inauguration day is bright with sunshine that helps dispel the chill of March in the air. As you stand to begin your address you can look down into the faces of your wife, your son, and your mother, sitting directly in front of the flag-draped speaker's platform, eagerly awaiting what you are about to say in company with the huge crowd . . . .

William McKinley

[1897–1901]

FIRST INAUGURAL ADDRESS, MARCH 4, 1897

Capitol Steps, Washington, D.C.

Fellow-Citizens:

In obedience to the will of the people, and in their presence, by the authority vested in me by this oath, I assume the arduous and responsible duties of President of the United States, relying upon the support of my countrymen and invoking the guidance of Almighty God. Our faith teaches that there is no safer reliance than upon the God of our fathers, who has so singularly favored the American people in every national trial, and who will not forsake us so long as we obey His commandments and walk humbly in His footsteps.

The responsibilities of the high trust to which I have been called —always of grave importance—are augmented by the prevailing business conditions, entailing idleness upon willing labor and loss to useful enterprises. The country is suffering from industrial disturbances from which speedy relief must be had. Our financial system needs some revision; our money is all good now, but its value must not further be threatened. It should all be put upon an enduring basis, not subject to easy attack, nor its stability to doubt or dispute. Our currency should continue under the supervision of the Government. The several forms of our paper money offer, in my judgment, a constant embarrassment to the Government and a safe balance in the Treasury. Therefore I believe it necessary to devise a system which, without diminishing the circulating medium or offering a premium for its contraction, will present a remedy for those arrangements which, temporary in their nature, might well in the years of our prosperity have been displaced by wiser provisions. With adequate revenue secured, but not until then, we can enter upon such changes in our fiscal laws as will, while insuring safety and volume to our money, no longer impose upon the Government the necessity of maintaining so large a gold reserve, with its attendant and inevitable temptations to

One of McKinley's campaign strategies had been the repeated promise stressing prosperity and full dinner pails for the unemployed. With the backing of wealthy industrialist Mark Hanna, who shrewdly masterminded McKinley's front-porch campaign, millions of copies of McKinley's campaign promises and catchwords were circulated throughout the nation in a mass advertising appeal that brought out Republican voters as never before.

speculation. Most of our financial laws are the outgrowth of experience and trial, and should not be amended without investigation and demonstration of the wisdom of the proposed changes. We must be both "sure we are right" and "make haste slowly." If, therefore, Congress, in its wisdom, shall deem it expedient to create a commission to take under early consideration the revision of our coinage, banking and currency laws, and give them that exhaustive, careful and dispassionate examination that their importance demands, I shall cordially concur in such action. If such power is vested in the President, it is my purpose to appoint a commission of prominent, well-informed citizens of different parties, who will command public confidence, both on account of their ability and special fitness for the work. Business experience and public training may thus be combined, and the patriotic zeal of the friends of the country be so directed that such a report will be made as to receive the support of all parties, and our finances cease to be the subject of mere partisan contention. The experiment is, at all events, worth a trial, and, in my opinion, it can but prove beneficial to the entire country.

The question of international bimetallism will have early and earnest attention. It will be my constant endeavor to secure it by co-operation with the other great commercial powers of the world. Until that condition is realized when the parity between our gold and silver money springs from and is supported by the relative value of the two metals, the value of the silver already coined and of that which may hereafter be coined, must be kept constantly at par with gold by every resource at our command. The credit of the Government, the integrity of its currency, and the inviolability of its obligations must be preserved. This was the commanding verdict of the people, and it will not be unheeded.

Economy is demanded in every branch of the Government at all times, but especially in periods, like the present, of depression in business and distress among the people. The severest economy must be observed in all public expenditures, and extravagance stopped wherever it is found, and prevented wherever in the future it may be developed. If the revenues are to remain as now, the only relief that can come must be from decreased expenditures. But the present must not become the permanent condition of the Government. It has been our uniform practice to retire, not increase our outstanding obligations, and this policy must again be resumed and vigorously enforced. Our revenues should always be large enough to meet with ease and promptness not only our current needs and the principal and interest of the public debt, but to make proper and liberal provision for that most deserving body of public creditors, the soldiers and sailors and the widows and orphans who are the pensioners of the United States.

The Government should not be permitted to run behind or increase its debt in times like the present. Suitably to provide against this is the mandate of duty—the certain and easy remedy for most of our financial difficulties. A deficiency is inevitable so long as the expenditures of the Government exceed its receipts. It can only be met by loans or an increased revenue. While a large annual surplus of revenue may invite waste and extravagance, inadequate revenue creates distrust and undermines public and private credit. Neither should be encouraged. Between more loans and more revenue there ought to be but one opinion. We should have more revenue, and that without delay, hindrance, or postponement. A surplus in the Treasury created by loans is not a permanent or safe

Fortunately for McKinley the Klondike gold rush of 1896 began to replenish the nation's depleted gold reserves. By 1898 the gold standard would once more be stabilized.

Despite McKinley's brave words on economy the public debt increased from $1,808,770,-043.40 in 1897 to a high of $2,092,686,-024.42 in 1899.

[172]

reliance. It will suffice while it lasts, but it can not last long while the outlays of the Government are greater than its receipts, as has been the case during the past two years. Nor must it be forgotten that however much such loans may temporarily relieve the situation, the Government is still indebted for the amount of the surplus thus accrued, which it must ultimately pay, while its ability to pay is not strengthened, but weakened by a continued deficit. Loans are imperative in great emergencies to preserve the Government or its credit, but a failure to supply needed revenue in time of peace for the maintenance of either has no justification.

The best way for the Government to maintain its credit is to pay as it goes—not by resorting to loans, but by keeping out of debt—through an adequate income secured by a system of taxation, external or internal, or both. It is the settled policy of the Government, pursued from the beginning and practised by all parties and Administrations, to raise the bulk of our revenue from taxes upon foreign productions entering the United States for sale and consumption, and avoiding, for the most part, every form of direct taxation, except in time of war. The country is clearly opposed to any needless additions to the subject of internal taxation, and is committed by its latest popular utterance to the system of tariff taxation. There can be no misunderstanding, either, about the principle upon which this tariff taxation shall be levied. Nothing has ever been made plainer at a general election than that the controlling principle in the raising of revenue from duties on imports is zealous care for American interests and American labor. The people have declared that such legislation should be had as will give ample protection and encouragement to the industries and the development of our country. It is, therefore, earnestly hoped and expected that Congress will, at the earliest practicable moment, enact revenue legislation that shall be fair, reasonable, conservative, and just, and which, while supplying sufficient revenue for public purposes, will still be signally beneficial and helpful to every section and every enterprise of the people. To this policy we are all, of whatever party, firmly bound by the voice of the people—a power vastly more potential than the expression of any political platform. The paramount duty of Congress is to stop deficiencies by the restoration of that protective legislation which has always been the firmest prop of the Treasury. The passage of such a law or laws would strengthen the credit of the Government both at home and abroad, and go far toward stopping the drain upon the gold reserve held for the redemption of our currency, which has been heavy and well-nigh constant for several years.

In the revision of the tariff especial attention should be given to the re-enactment and extension of the reciprocity principle of the law of 1890, under which so great a stimulus was given to our foreign trade in new and advantageous markets for our surplus agricultural and manufactured products. The brief trial given this legislation amply justifies a further experiment and additional discretionary power in the making of commercial treaties, the end in view always to be the opening up of new markets for the products of our country, by granting concessions to the products of other lands that we need and cannot produce ourselves, and which do not involve any loss of labor to our own people, but tend to increase their employment.

The depression of the past four years has fallen with especial severity upon the great body of toilers of the country, and upon none more than the holders of small farms. Agriculture has lan-

The Republican-dominated Congress was quick to respond to McKinley's high tariff appeal. They enacted the Dingley Tariff Act, July 7, 1897, which was much higher than any previous tariff to date.

McKinley referred to his own McKinley Tariff Act, which authorized a policy of reciprocal tariff arrangements.

guished and labor suffered. The revival of manufacturing will be a relief to both. No portion of our population is more devoted to the institution of free government nor more loyal in their support, while none bears more cheerfully or fully its proper share in the maintenance of the Government or is better entitled to its wise and liberal care and protection. Legislation helpful to producers is beneficial to all. The depressed condition of industry on the farm and in the mine and factory has lessened the ability of the people to meet the demands upon them, and they rightfully expect that not only a system of revenue shall be established that will secure the largest income with the least burden, but that every means will be taken to decrease, rather than increase, our public expenditures. Business conditions are not the most promising. It will take time to restore the prosperity of former years. If we cannot promptly attain it, we can resolutely turn our faces in that direction and aid its return by friendly legislation. However troublesome the situation may appear, Congress will not, I am sure, be found lacking in disposition or ability to relieve it as far as legislation can do so. The restoration of confidence and the revival of business, which men of all parties so much desire, depend more largely upon the prompt, energetic, and intelligent action of Congress than upon any other single agency affecting the situation.

It is inspiring, too, to remember that no great emergency in the one hundred and eight years of our eventful national life has ever arisen that has not been met with wisdom and courage by the American people, with fidelity to their best interests and highest destiny, and to the honor of the American name. These years of glorious history have exalted mankind and advanced the cause of freedom throughout the world, and immeasurably strengthened the precious free institutions which we enjoy. The people love and will sustain these institutions. The great essential to our happiness and prosperity is that we adhere to the principles upon which the Government was established and insist upon their faithful observance. Equality of rights must prevail, and our laws be always and everywhere respected and obeyed. We may have failed in the discharge of our full duty as citizens of the great Republic, but it is consoling and encouraging to realize that free speech, a free press, free thought, free schools, the free and unmolested right of religious liberty and worship, and free and fair elections are dearer and more universally enjoyed to-day than ever before. These guaranties must be sacredly preserved and wisely strengthened. The constituted authorities must be cheerfully and vigorously upheld. Lynchings must not be tolerated in a great and civilized country like the United States; courts, not mobs, must execute the penalties of the law. The preservation of public order, the right of discussion, the integrity of courts, and the orderly administration of justice must continue forever the rock of safety upon which our Government securely rests.

One of the lessons taught by the late election, which all can rejoice in, is that the citizens of the United States are both law-respecting and law-abiding people, not easily swerved from the path of patriotism and honor. This is in entire accord with the genius of our institutions, and but emphasizes the advantages of inculcating even a greater love for law and order in the future. Immunity should be granted to none who violate the laws, whether individuals, corporations, or communities; and as the Constitution imposes upon the President the duty of both its own execution, and of the statutes enacted in pursuance of its provisions, I shall endeavor carefully to carry them into effect. The declaration of the party now restored to power has been in the past that of "opposition to all combinations of capital organized in trusts, or otherwise, to control arbitrarily the condition of trade among our citizens," and it has supported "such legislation as will prevent the execution of all schemes to oppress the people by undue charges on their supplies, or by unjust rates for the transportation of their products to the market." This purpose will be steadily pursued, both by the enforcement of the laws now in existence and the recommendation and support of such new statutes as may be necessary to carry it into effect.

Our naturalization and immigration laws should be further improved to the constant promotion of a safer, a better, and a higher citizenship. A grave peril to the Republic would be a citizenship too ignorant to understand or too vicious to appreciate the great value and beneficence of our institutions and laws, and against all who come here to make war upon them our gates must be promptly and tightly closed. Nor must we be unmindful of the need of improvement among our own citizens, but with the zeal of our forefathers encourage the spread of knowledge and free education. Illiteracy must be banished from the land if we shall attain that high destiny as the foremost of the enlightened nations of the world which, under Providence, we ought to achieve.

Reforms in the civil service must go on; but the changes should be real and genuine, not perfunctory, or prompted by a zeal in behalf of any party simply because it happens to be in power. As a member of Congress I voted and spoke in favor of the present law, and I shall attempt its enforcement in the spirit in which it was enacted. The purpose in view was to secure the most efficient service of the best men who would accept appointment under the Government, retaining faithful and devoted public servants in office, but shielding none, under the authority of any rule or custom, who are inefficient, incompetent, or unworthy. The best interests of the country demand this, and the people heartily approve the law wherever and whenever it has been thus administrated.

Congress should give prompt attention to the restoration of our American merchant marine, once the pride of the seas in all the great ocean highways of commerce. To my mind, few more important subjects so imperatively demand its intelligent consideration. The United States has progressed with marvelous rapidity in every field of enterprise and endeavor until we have become foremost in nearly all the great lines of inland trade, commerce, and industry. Yet, while this is true, our American merchant marine has been steadily declining until it is now lower, both in the percentage of tonnage and the number of vessels employed, than it was prior to the Civil War. Commendable progress has been made of late years in the upbuilding of the American Navy, but we must supplement these efforts by providing as a proper consort for it a merchant marine amply sufficient for our own carrying trade to foreign countries. The question is one that appeals both to our business necessities and the patriotic aspirations of a great people.

It has been the policy of the United States since the foundation of the Government to cultivate relations of peace and amity with all the nations of the world; and this accords with my conception of our duty now. We have cherished the policy of non-interference with the affairs of foreign governments wisely inaugurated by Washington, keeping ourselves free from entanglement, either as

Quotations from the Republican party platform of 1896.

Congress had created the Bureau of Immigration on August 18, 1894, as a step toward stricter immigration control. President Cleveland, however, had vetoed an immigration bill calling for a literacy test.

An improvement in the civil service had been accomplished under Cleveland, when rural free postal delivery was established October 1, 1896.

By authority of an act of Congress, March 3, 1883, the Navy had been authorized to embark on a program of limited expansion. The first ships to be built had been three steel-hulled cruisers, which though steam powered still carried sails. Through the efforts of Admiral Alfred T. Mahan the importance of a first-rate Naval force was made clear to Congress and the American people.

[175]

True to his nonaggression policy, outlined in this segment of his address, McKinley would exhaust every possible means of avoiding the rapidly growing threat of war with Spain over Cuba. But when the battleship Maine *was blown up in Havana harbor and 260 Americans were killed, McKinley would finally be compelled to yield to the battle cry that swept the nation: "Remember the* Maine!"

McKinley's purpose in calling a special session of Congress was to point out that in the last three years and eight months of Cleveland's administration the government had incurred a deficit of $186,661,880.44. Consequently McKinley would demand in his first message to Congress, March 10, 1897, that before other business be transacted, "ample revenues must be supplied not only for the ordinary expenses of the government, but for the prompt payment of liberal pensions and the liquidation of the principal and interest of the public debt."

allies or foes, content to leave undisturbed with them the settlement of their own domestic concerns. It will be our aim to pursue a firm and dignified foreign policy, which shall be just, impartial, ever watchful of our national honor, and always insisting upon the enforcement of the lawful rights of American citizens everywhere. Our diplomacy should seek nothing more and accept nothing less than is due us. We want no wars of conquest; we must avoid the temptation of territorial aggression. War should never be entered upon until every agency of peace has failed; peace is preferable to war in almost every contingency. Arbitration is the true method of settlement of international as well as local or individual differences. It was recognized as the best means of adjustment of differences between employers and employees by the Forty-ninth Congress, in 1886, and its application was extended to our diplomatic relations by the unanimous concurrence of the Senate and House of the Fifty-first Congress in 1890. The latter resolution was accepted as the basis of negotiations with us by the British House of Commons in 1893, and upon our invitation a treaty of arbitration between the United States and Great Britain was signed at Washington and transmitted to the Senate for its ratification in January last. Since this treaty is clearly the result of our own initiative; since it has been recognized as the leading feature of our foreign policy throughout our entire national history—the adjustment of difficulties by judicial methods rather than force of arms—and since it presents to the world the glorious example of reason and peace, not passion and war, controlling the relations between two of the greatest nations in the world, an example certain to be followed by others, I respectfully urge the early action of the Senate thereon, not merely as a matter of policy, but as a duty to mankind. The importance and moral influence of the ratification of such a treaty can hardly be overestimated in the cause of advancing civilization. It may well engage the best thought of the statesmen and people of every country, and I cannot but consider it fortunate that it was reserved to the United States to have the leadership in so grand a work.

It has been the uniform practice of each President to avoid, as far as possible, the convening of Congress in extraordinary session. It is an example which, under ordinary circumstances and in the absence of a public necessity, is to be commended. But a failure to convene the representatives of the people in Congress in extra session when it involves neglect of a public duty places the responsibility of such neglect upon the Executive himself. The condition of the public Treasury, as has been indicated, demands the immediate consideration of Congress. It alone has the power to provide revenues for the Government. Not to convene it under such circumstances I can view in no other sense than the neglect of a plain duty. I do not sympathize with the sentiment that Congress in session is dangerous to our general business interests. Its members are the agents of the people, and their presence at the seat of Government in the execution of the sovereign will should not operate as an injury, but a benefit. There could be no better time to put the Government upon a sound financial and economic basis than now. The people have only recently voted that this should be done, and nothing is more binding upon the agents of their will than the obligation of immediate action. It has always seemed to me that the postponement of the meeting of Congress until more than a year after it has been chosen deprived Congress too often of the inspiration of the popular will and the country of the cor-

[176]

responding benefits. It is evident, therefore, that to postpone action in the presence of so great a necessity would be unwise on the part of the Executive because unjust to the interests of the people. Our action now will be freer from mere partisan consideration than if the question of tariff revision was postponed until the regular session of Congress. We are nearly two years from a Congressional election, and politics cannot so greatly distract us as if such contest was immediately pending. We can approach the problem calmly and patriotically, without fearing its effect upon an early election.

Our fellow-citizens who may disagree with us upon the character of this legislation prefer to have the question settled now, even against their preconceived views, and perhaps settled so reasonably, as I trust and believe it will be, as to insure great permanence, than to have further uncertainty menacing the vast and varied business interests of the United States. Again, whatever action Congress may take will be given a fair opportunity for trial before the people are called to pass judgment upon it, and this I consider a great essential to the rightful and lasting settlement of the question. In view of these considerations, I shall deem it my duty as President to convene Congress in extraordinary session on Monday, the 15th day of March, 1897.

In conclusion, I congratulate the country upon the fraternal spirit of the people and the manifestations of good will everywhere so apparent. The recent election not only most fortunately demonstrated the obliteration of sectional or geographical lines, but to some extent also the prejudices which for years have distracted our councils and marred our true greatness as a nation. The triumph of the people, whose verdict is carried into effect today, is not the triumph of one section, nor wholly of one party, but of all sections and all the people. The North and the South no longer divide on the old lines, but upon principles and policies; and in this fact surely every lover of the country can find cause for true felicitation. Let us rejoice in and cultivate this spirit; it is ennobling and will be both a gain and a blessing to our beloved country. It will be my constant aim to do nothing, and permit nothing to be done, that will arrest or disturb this growing sentiment of unity and co-operation, this revival of esteem and affiliation which now animates so many thousands in both the old antagonistic sections, but I shall cheerfully do everything possible to promote and increase it.

Let me again repeat the words of the oath administered by the Chief Justice which, in their respective spheres, so far as applicable, I would have all my countrymen observe: "I will faithfully execute the office of President of the United States, and will, to the best of my ability, preserve, protect, and defend the Constitution of the United States." This is the obligation I have reverently taken before the Lord Most High. To keep it will be my single purpose, my constant prayer; and I shall confidently rely upon the forbearance and assistance of all the people in the discharge of my solemn responsibilities.

With the question of gold versus free silver finally settled prosperity was soon to be restored, and the next decade would become one of the most prosperous in the nation's history.

THE PRESIDENT

The peace-loving McKinley was pushed into war with Spain. Once committed, however, he threw the full force of the Army and Navy into the three scenes of action—Cuba, Guam, and the Philippines—with the result that victory was achieved in less than a year—the shortest war in American history. The Filipinos, however, resented American rule as much as they had Spain's. Under their leader, Aguinaldo, a long guerrilla warfare began that dragged on for another two-and-a-half years. Despite this unpopular suppression of the Filipino insurgents McKinley was at the peak of his career in 1900. With the colorful, well-liked Theodore Roosevelt as vice-presidential candidate McKinley easily won the presidency.

THE NATION

At the turn of the century the United States still deferred to England as the world's mightiest sea power. Yet with the blowing up of the U.S. battleship *Maine* in Havana harbor, "Remember the Maine!" became the nation's rallying cry. President McKinley sent a war message to Congress, which sided with the Cubans, who were trying to throw off the yoke of Spanish rule, and demanded Spain's withdrawal from the island. With war under way Congress also voted the necessary funds for a naval building program that would continue until the U.S. Navy had usurped England's top spot. Under Commodore George Dewey afloat and Colonel Leonard Wood with brash Lieutenant Colonel Theodore Roosevelt ashore a quick victory was won. On December 10, 1898, the treaty ending the Spanish-American War was signed in Paris. Spain gave up control of Cuba and ceded Puerto Rico and Guam to the U.S. We agreed to pay Spain twenty million dollars for the Philippines. The Philippine transaction, however, led to three years of guerrilla warfare against the Americans by insurgent Filipinos, who considered they had been grievously wronged.

In 1900 the census revealed 75,994,575—an increase of 13,000,000. Republican William McKinley won the election of 1900 by nearly a million popular votes. The totals were: McKinley, 7,207,923 popular votes (292 electoral); Democrat William Jennings Bryan, 6,358,133 popular votes (155 electoral); Social Democrat Eugene V. Debs, 87,814; Populist Wharton Barker, 50,373; Prohibitionist John C. Woolley, 208,914.

New York's governor Theodore Roosevelt was elected vice-president.

THE WORLD

May 18, 1899, witnessed the opening at The Hague of the International Peace Conference between twenty-six nations. When the conference closed on July 29th its chief accomplishment was the establishment of a permanent court of arbitration. In the same year Great Britain began a long and costly campaign to subjugate the Boers. July 29, 1900, Italy's King Humbert was assassinated by an anarchist from Paterson, New Jersey, and Victor Emmanuel III succeeded to the throne. In England Queen Victoria died, January 22, 1901, after a reign spanning sixty-four years. Edward VII succeeded to the throne.

IN PREPARING THE SECOND INAUGURAL ADDRESS you feel justifiably proud of the nation's progress made during your first term in office. Consequently you devote the bulk of your address to a comparison of conditions as they were four years ago, as they are today, and as you anticipate them to be in the future which stretches ahead so invitingly—the future which will prove so disastrous to you personally. The day of your inauguration is dull and drizzly. As you stand between the white columns of the temporary inaugural portico on the Capitol steps you can look out over a sea of bowler hats, sprouting the mushroom shapes of occasional umbrellas. Now the crowd is quiet, waiting for you to begin. You lean forward, rest the fingertips of your right hand on the flag-covered railing, and begin to read the address you hold in your left hand . . . .

William McKinley

[1901]

SECOND INAUGURAL ADDRESS, MARCH 4, 1901

Capitol Steps, Washington, D.C.

My fellow-Citizens:

When we assembled here on the 4th of March, 1897, there was great anxiety with regard to our currency and credit. None exists now. Then our Treasury receipts were inadequate to meet the current obligations of the Government. Now they are sufficient for all public needs, and we have a surplus instead of a deficit. Then I felt constrained to convene the Congress in extraordinary session to devise revenues to pay the ordinary expenses of the Government. Now I have the satisfaction to announce that the Congress just closed has reduced taxation in the sum of $41,000,000. Then there was deep solicitude because of the long depression in our manufacturing, mining, agricultural, and mercantile industries and the consequent distress of our laboring population. Now every avenue of production is crowded with activity, labor is well employed, and American products find good markets at home and abroad.

Our diversified productions, however, are increasing in such unprecedent volume as to admonish us of the necessity of still further enlarging our foreign markets by broader commercial relations. For this purpose reciprocal trade arrangements with other nations should in liberal spirit be carefully cultivated and promoted.

The national verdict of 1896 has for the most part been executed. Whatever remains unfulfilled is a continuing obligation resting with undiminished force upon the Executive and the Congress. But fortunate as our condition is, its permanence can only be assured by sound business methods and strict economy in national administration and legislation. We should not permit our great prosperity to lead us to reckless ventures in business or profligacy in public expenditures. While the Congress determines the objects and the sum of appropriations, the officials of the executive departments are responsible for honest and faithful disbursement, and it should be their constant care to avoid waste and extravagance.

Honesty, capacity, and industry are nowhere more indispensable than in public employment. These should be fundamental requisites to original appointment and the surest guaranties against removal.

The currency had been stabilized by the influx of gold from Klondike and South African mining activities. On March 14, 1900, an act making gold the single standard of currency had been passed by Congress. This had added further stability to the nation's currency and permanently ended the free silver controversy, although die-hard William Jennings Bryan would continue his harangues on the subject for another decade.

McKinley's desire to add new markets was behind his sudden switch to an imperialist policy to annex the Philippines. In this respect McKinley's actions were reminiscent of James Madison's in instigating the War of 1812. McKinley refused to wait for Congressional approval before dispatching troops to the Philippines. The islands were to be taken over, so McKinley announced, under his policy of "benevolent assimilation." Had this policy been instigated by a nation other than our own it would promptly have been labeled for what it was: naked aggression.

[179]

Four years ago we stood on the brink of war without the people knowing it and without any preparation or effort at preparation for the impending peril. I did all that in honor could be done to avert the war, but without avail. It became inevitable; and the Congress at its first regular session, without party division, provided money in anticipation of the crisis and in preparation to meet it. It came. The result was signally favorable to American arms and in the highest degree honorable to the Government. It imposed upon us obligations from which we cannot escape and from which it would be dishonorable to seek escape. We are now at peace with the world, and it is my fervent prayer that if differences arise between us and other powers they may be settled by peaceful arbitration and that hereafter we may be spared the horrors of war.

Intrusted by the people for a second time with the office of President, I enter upon its administration appreciating the great responsibilities which attach to this renewed honor and commission, promising unreserved devotion on my part to their faithful discharge and reverently invoking for my guidance the direction and favor of Almighty God. I should shrink from the duties this day assumed if I did not feel that in their performance I should have the co-operation of the wise and patriotic men of all parties. It encourages me for the great task which I now undertake to believe that those who voluntarily committed to me the trust imposed upon the Chief Executive of the Republic will give to me generous support in my duties to "preserve, protect, and defend the Constitution of the United States" and to "care that the laws be faithfully executed." The national purpose is indicated through a national election. It is the constitutional method of ascertaining the public will. When once it is registered it is a law to us all, and faithful observance should follow its decrees.

Strong hearts and helpful hands are needed, and, fortunately, we have them in every part of our beloved country. We are reunited. Sectionalism has disappeared. Division on public questions can no longer be traced by the war maps of 1861. These old differences less and less disturb the judgment. Existing problems demand the thought and quicken the conscience of the country, and the responsibility for their presence, as well as for their righteous settlement, rests upon us all—no more upon me than upon you. There are some national questions in the solution of which patriotism should exclude partisanship. Magnifying their difficulties will not take them off our hands nor facilitate their adjustment. Distrust of the capacity, integrity, and high purposes of the American people will not be an inspiring theme for future political contests. Dark pictures and gloomy forebodings are worse than useless. These only becloud, they do not help to point the way of safety and honor. "Hope maketh not ashamed." The prophets of evil were not the builders of the Republic, nor in its crises since have they saved or served it. The faith of the fathers was a mighty force in its creation, and the faith of their descendants has wrought its progress and furnished its defenders. They are obstructionists who despair, and who would destroy confidence in the ability of our people to solve wisely and for civilization the mighty problems resting upon them. The American people, intrenched in freedom at home, take their love for it with them wherever they go, and they reject as mistaken and unworthy the doctrine that we lose our own liberties by securing the enduring foundations of liberty to others. Our institutions will not deteriorate by extension, and our sense of justice will not abate under tropic suns in distant seas. As heretofore, so hereafter will the nation demonstrate its fitness to administer any new estate which events devolve upon it, and in the fear of God will "take occasion by the hand and make the bounds of freedom wider yet." If there are those among us who would make our way more difficult, we must not be disheartened, but the more earnestly dedicate ourselves to the task upon which we have rightly entered. The path of progress is seldom smooth. New things are often found hard to do. Our fathers found them so. We find them so. They are inconvenient. They cost us something. But are we not made better for the effort and sacrifice, and are not those we serve lifted up and blessed?

We will be consoled, too, with the fact that opposition has confronted every onward movement of the Republic from its opening hour until now, but without success. The Republic has marched on and on, and its step has exalted freedom and humanity. We are undergoing the same ordeal as did our predecessors nearly a century ago. We are following the course they blazed. They triumphed. Will their successors falter and plead organic impotency in the nation? Surely after 125 years of achievement for mankind we will not now surrender our equality with other powers on matters fundamental and essential to nationality. With no such purpose was the nation created. In no such spirit has it developed its full and independent sovereignty. We adhere to the principle of equality among ourselves, and by no act of ours will we assign to ourselves a subordinate rank in the family of nations.

My fellow-citizens, the public events of the past four years have gone into history. They are too near to justify recital. Some of them were unforeseen; many of them momentous and far-reaching in their consequences to ourselves and our relations with the rest of the world. The part which the United States bore so honorably in the thrilling scenes in China, while new to American life, has been in harmony with its true spirit and best traditions, and in dealing with the results its policy will be that of moderation and fairness.

We face at this moment a most important question—that of the future relations of the United States and Cuba. With our near neighbors we must remain close friends. The declaration of the purposes of this Government in the resolution of April 20, 1898, must be made good. Ever since the evacuation of the island by the army of Spain the Executive, with all practicable speed, has been assisting its people in the successive steps necessary to the establishment of a free and independent government prepared to assume and perform the obligations of international law which now rest upon the United States under the treaty of Paris. The convention elected by the people to frame a constitution is approaching the completion of its labors. The transfer of American control to the new government is of such great importance, involving an obligation resulting from our intervention and the treaty of peace, that I am glad to be advised by the recent act of Congress of the policy which the legislative branch of the Government deems essential to the best interests of Cuba and the United States. The principles which led to our intervention require that the fundamental law upon which the new government rests should be adapted to secure a government capable of performing the duties and discharging the functions of a separate nation, of observing its international obligations of protecting life and property, insuring order, safety, and liberty, and conforming to the established and historical policy of the United States in its relation to Cuba.

The peace which we are pledged to leave to the Cuban people

The reference here was to America's part in China's Boxer Rebellion of 1900. The Boxers were members of a Chinese secret society, which rebelled against foreign residents in China. When Boxer revolutionists besieged Americans and other foreigners in Peking an international force composed of fighting men from five nations, including the United States, was dispatched to the scene, and drove off the attackers on August 14, 1900.

In McKinley's first inaugural address he summed up his administration's foreign policy with these words: "We want no wars of conquest; we must avoid the temptation of territorial aggression." Four years later no mention was made of these assertions. Instead McKinley attempted to defend his discarded policy by discussing at length the alleged advantages of the American policy of "benevolent assimilation" for the Filipinos. In 1899 McKinley revealed to a number of Methodist clergymen that ". . . there was nothing left for us to do but take them, all, and to educate the Filipinos and civilize and Christianize them, and by God's grace do the very best we can for them. . . ."

must carry with it the guaranties of permanence. We became sponsors for the pacification of the island, and we remain accountable to the Cubans, no less than to our own country and people, for the reconstruction of Cuba as a free commonwealth on abiding foundations of right, justice, liberty, and assured order. Our enfranchisement of the people will not be completed until free Cuba shall "be a reality, not a name; a perfect entity, not a hasty experiment bearing within itself the elements of failure."

While the treaty of peace with Spain was ratified on the 6th of February, 1899, and ratifications were exchanged nearly two years ago, the Congress has indicated no form of government for the Philippine Islands. It has, however, provided an army to enable the Executive to suppress insurrection, restore peace, give security to the inhabitants, and establish the authority of the United States throughout the archipelago. It has authorized the organization of native troops as auxiliary to the regular force. It has been advised from time to time of the acts of the military and naval officers in the islands, of my action in appointing civil commissions, of the instructions with which they were charged, of their duties and powers, of their recommendations, and of their several acts under executive commission, together with the very complete general information they have submitted. These reports fully set forth the conditions, past and present, in the islands, and the instructions clearly show the principles which will guide the Executive until the Congress shall, as it is required to do by the treaty, determine "the civil rights and political status of the native inhabitants." The Congress having added the sanction of its authority to the powers already possessed and exercised by the Executive under the Constitution, thereby leaving with the Executive the responsibility for the government of the Philippines, I shall continue the efforts already begun until order shall be restored throughout the islands, and as fast as conditions permit will establish local governments, in the formation of which the full co-operation of the people has been already invited, and when established will encourage the people to administer them. The settled purpose, long ago proclaimed, to afford the inhabitants of the islands self-government as fast as they were ready for it will be pursued with earnestness and fidelity. Already something has been accomplished in this direction. The Government's representatives, civil and military, are doing faithful and noble work in their mission of emancipation and merit the approval and support of their countrymen. The most liberal terms of amnesty have already been communicated to the insurgents, and the way is still open for those who have raised their arms against the Government for honorable submission to its authority. Our countrymen should not be deceived. We are not waging war against the inhabitants of the Philippine Islands. A portion of them are making war against the United States. By far the greater part of the inhabitants recognize American sovereignty and welcome it as a guaranty of order and of security for life, property, liberty, freedom of conscience, and the pursuit of happiness. To them full protection will be given. They shall not be abandoned. We will not leave the destiny of the loyal millions in the islands to the disloyal thousands who are in rebellion against the United States. Order under civil institutions will come as soon as those who now break the peace shall keep it. Force will not be needed or used when those who make war against us shall make it no more. May it end without further bloodshed, and there be ushered in the reign of peace to be made permanent by a government of liberty under law!

On September 13, 1901, Vice-President Theodore Roosevelt was hunting and mountain climbing in the Adirondacks. A guide brought him the news that President McKinley was dying after apparently starting to recover from an assassin's bullets that had wounded him September 6. Roosevelt hurried to Buffalo, where he arrived at the home of John G. Milburn after McKinley's death. On September 14, 1901, Theodore Roosevelt was administered the oath of office by Judge Elihu Root and became the 26th president of the United States.

Theodore Roosevelt

[1901–1905]

THE PRESIDENT

Roosevelt left an indelible impression as one of the greatest presidents in the nation's history. Afflicted during childhood with asthma and poor health, Roosevelt systematically built up his body until he attained a vigor that carried him through the great pressures of his adult life. Early in his career he fought corruption in New York politics when he was elected to the New York State Assembly in 1882. He had recently graduated from Harvard and had done postgraduate work at Columbia Law School. Through the ensuing years Roosevelt mixed ranching in the west with sporadic political ventures in the east. He became Assistant Secretary of the Navy during McKinley's first term.

With the advent of the Spanish-American War Roosevelt organized the First U.S. Volunteer Cavalry (called the Rough Riders) and distinguished himself by leading a charge up Kettle Hill at San Juan. Returning home a colonel by brevet, Roosevelt again turned his astonishing vigor to politics, becoming governor of New York in 1898. In this office he grappled with proponents of the spoils system, usually coming off victorious. Against his will he was drafted for the vice-presidential nomination in the election of 1900. Roosevelt was so convinced that the vice-presidency meant the end of the line for his political career that when the post was offered to him before the convention he wrote: "I will not accept under any circumstances and that is all there is about it."

However, Bryan's chances looked bright, and Republican committeemen convinced the stub-born Roosevelt he owed it to his party to accept the nomination. Reluctantly he agreed and shrugged off his decision with a fatalistic remark which certainly was not characteristic of the man in later life: "I do not expect to go any further in politics." But once again fate surprised Roosevelt and the politicans who had prevailed upon him to accept the vice-presidential nomination.

When Roosevelt succeeded McKinley he pledged himself to carry out the policies established by his predecessor. But Roosevelt was a fighter with a deep love of his country. When, as president, he saw how the eastern money magnates had been setting up sprawling interlocking directorates, trusts, and mergers under McKinley's administration Roosevelt boldly struck out on his own against such monopolies. As a result he lost the support of the interests who had persuaded him to become vice-president, but he gained a tremendous personal following among the people. An indefatigable letter writer, an energetic public speaker, rancher, soldier, author of numerous books, big game hunter, mountain climber, and world traveler, Roosevelt was the youngest man to occupy the White House and perhaps the most popular since Old Hickory.

There can be little doubt that the death of McKinley was a blessing in tragic disguise. For had not a man of Roosevelt's fearless volatility been catapulted into the presidency, the monopoly-minded men he fought so vigorously would never have allowed him to be nominated in the next election campaign. Roosevelt would indeed have failed "to go any further in politics."

[183]

THE PRESIDENT

Roosevelt's pledge to carry out McKinley's policies had to be repudiated when the new president discovered how lax McKinley's enforcement of the Sherman Anti-Trust Act had been. Roosevelt's first move was his decision on February 18, 1902, to prosecute one of J.P. Morgan's corporate holdings: the Northern Securities Company. This was followed in July by intervention in a coal strike at Shenandoah, Pennsylvania, and the setting up of a commission to settle the strike. On February 14 Roosevelt signed into law a bill creating the Department of Commerce and Labor, which became the ninth Cabinet office.

THE NATION

1900 saw the creation of the Socialist party, the U.S. Army Dental Corps, and the Army Nurse Corps. On March 30, 1901, Emilio Aguinaldo, Filipino insurgent leader, was captured by Brigadier General Frederick Funston.

In Washington, two months after President McKinley's death, the second Hay-Pauncefote Treaty was signed, November 18, 1901. This treaty gave the United States a free hand to build, control, and, by implication, to fortify a canal across the Isthmus of Panama.

In June and July of 1902 Congress passed three acts that would prove increasingly important through later years: the Reclamation Act, giving the president authority to set aside public lands as Forest Reserves, National Parks, National Forests, and others; the Isthmian Canal Act, authorizing the construction of a canal across the isthmus of either Panama or Nicaragua; the Philippine Government Act, authorizing the president to appoint a governing commission for the territory. The negotiation of the Hay-Bunau-Varilla Treaty, November 18, 1903, gave the United States authority over a 10-mile-wide strip of land across the Panamanian isthmus. President Roosevelt proceeded to appoint a seven-man Panama Canal Commission with authority to construct the canal.

1903 also saw the opening of the Pacific cable, making round-the-world messages possible in less than 15 minutes. Automobiles were becoming more common on the dirt roads of the era. And at Kitty Hawk, North Carolina, Orville and Wilbur Wright successfully flew their heavier-than-air machine on December 17.

In the presidential election of 1904, despite his trust-busting activities, the Republicans had no choice but to nominate Theodore Roosevelt because of his phenomenal personal popularity. Roosevelt polled 7,623,486 popular votes (336 electoral) to Democrat Alton B. Parker's 5,077,911 popular votes (140 electoral). Socialist Eugene V. Debs polled 402,283, Prohibitionist Silas C. Swallow polled 258,536, Thomas E. Watson of the People's party polled 117,183, and Charles H. Corregan of the Socialist Labor party polled 31,239. Charles W. Fairbanks was elected vice-president.

THE WORLD

On March 26, 1902, the great developer of South Africa, Cecil Rhodes, died and left much of his wealth for the Rhodes Scholarships at Oxford. In the Transvaal the Boers still fought on against the British until May 31, 1902, when terms of surrender were finally signed. June 28, 1902, the Triple Alliance between Austria-Hungary, Germany, and Italy was once again renewed. The coronation of Edward VII was held at Westminster Abbey on August 9th. Early in 1904 the Russo-Japanese War broke out.

ON THE NIGHT BEFORE YOUR INAUGURATION you receive a remarkable gift from Secretary of State John Hay: a ring engraved with your initials and those of Abraham Lincoln, and containing a lock of Lincoln's hair snipped off as he lay on his deathbed. In Hay's accompanying note he asks you to wear the ring because of your knowledge and appreciation of Lincoln, with whom Hay had been on intimate terms—having served as his private secretary when a young man. And so, while you are standing on the flower-bedecked inaugural platform on the Capitol steps, unnoticed by the cheering crowd, Hay's ring gleams on the hand you rest on the presidential flag draped over the white railing before you. And somehow you feel the ring gives you a spiritual kinship with the martyred Lincoln that colors your voice as the sea of people surrounding you finally quiets and you begin to speak . . . .

Theodore Roosevelt

[1905–1909]

INAUGURAL ADDRESS, MARCH 4, 1905

Capitol Steps, Washington, D.C.

My fellow-citizens, no people on earth have more cause to be thankful than ours, and this is said reverently, in no spirit of boastfulness in our own strength, but with gratitude to the Giver of Good who has blessed us with the conditions which have enabled us to achieve so large a measure of well-being and of happiness. To us as a people it has been granted to lay the foundations of our national life in a new continent. We are the heirs of the ages, and yet we have had to pay few of the penalties which in old countries are exacted by the dead hand of a bygone civilization. We have not been obliged to fight for our existence against any alien race; and yet our life has called for the vigor and effort without which the manlier and hardier virtues wither away. Under such conditions it would be our own fault if we failed; and the success which we have had in the past, the success which we confidently believe the future will bring, should cause in us no feeling of vainglory, but rather a deep and abiding realization of all which life has offered us; a full acknowledgment of the responsibility which is ours; and a fixed determination to show that under a free government a mighty people can thrive best, alike as regards the things of the body and the things of the soul.

Much has been given us, and much will rightfully be expected from us. We have duties to others and duties to ourselves; and we can shirk neither. We have become a great nation, forced by the fact of its greatness into relations with the other nations of the earth, and we must behave as beseems a people with such responsibilities. Toward all other nations, large and small, our attitude must be one of cordial and sincere friendship. We must show not only in our words, but in our deeds, that we are earnestly desirous of securing their good will by acting toward them in a spirit of just and gen-

Roosevelt was quick to enunciate his belief in the Monroe Doctrine, which to him meant "speak softly and carry a big stick." When Congress assembled after McKinley's death Roosevelt spelled out his policies in his first message to Congress, delivered December 3, 1901. In this address he stated the need for an Army and Navy second to none, in order to back up the "hands-off-the-Western-hemisphere" policy we had laid down. Now, as Roosevelt entered his second term, he reiterated much of what he had said nearly four years before.

This last provision, the famous Teller amendment, had been added to the original resolutions after it came to the Senate from the Foreign Relations Committee. It was adopted without a dissenting vote.

erous recognition of all their rights. But justice and generosity in a nation, as in an individual, count most when shown not by the weak but by the strong. While ever careful to refrain from wrongdoing others, we must be no less insistent that we are not wronged ourselves. We wish peace, but we wish the peace of justice, the peace of righteousness. We wish it because we think it is right and not because we are afraid. No weak nation that acts manfully and justly should ever have cause to fear us, and no strong power should ever be able to single us out as a subject for insolent aggression.

Our relations with the other powers of the world are important; but still more important are our relations among ourselves. Such growth in wealth, in population, and in power as this nation has seen during the century and a quarter of its national life is inevitably accompanied by a like growth in the problems which are ever before every nation that rises to greatness. Power invariably means both responsibility and danger. Our forefathers faced certain perils which we have outgrown. We now face other perils, the very existence of which it was impossible that they should foresee. Modern life is both complex and intense, and the tremendous changes wrought by the extraordinary industrial development of the last half century are felt in every fiber of our social and political being. Never before have men tried so vast and formidable an experiment as that of administering the affairs of a continent under the forms of a Democratic republic. The conditions which have told for our marvelous material well-being, which have developed to a very high degree our energy, self-reliance, and individual initiative, have also brought the care and anxiety inseparable from the accumulation of great wealth in industrial centers. Upon the success of our experiment much depends, not only as regards our own welfare, but as regards the welfare of mankind. If we fail, the cause of free self-government throughout the world will rock to its foundations, and therefore our responsibility is heavy, to ourselves, to the world as it is to-day, and to the generations yet unborn. There is no good reason why we should fear the future, but there is every reason why we should face it seriously, neither hiding from ourselves the gravity of the problems before us nor fearing to approach these problems with the unbending, unflinching purpose to solve them aright.

Yet, after all, though the problems are new, though the tasks set before us differ from the tasks set before our fathers who founded and preserved this Republic, the spirit in which these tasks must be undertaken and these problems faced, if our duty is to be well done, remains essentially unchanged. We know that self-government is difficult. We know that no people needs such high traits of character as that people which seeks to govern its affairs aright through the freely expressed will of the freemen who compose it. But we have faith that we shall not prove false to the memories of the men of the mighty past. They did their work, they left us the splendid heritage we now enjoy. We in our turn have an assured confidence that we shall be able to leave this heritage unwasted and enlarged to our children and our children's children. To do so we must show, not merely in great crises, but in the everyday affairs of life, the qualities of practical intelligence, of courage, of hardihood, and endurance, and above all the power of devotion to a lofty ideal, which made great the men who founded this Republic in the days of Washington, which made great the men who preserved this Republic in the days of Abraham Lincoln.

In Roosevelt's first message to Congress he also sounded the keynote of what would become an unceasing attack on corporate interests. These interests had seized exorbitant power under McKinley's administration, due to his refusal to enforce the Sherman Anti-Trust Act. Roosevelt said, "Artificial bodies, such as corporations and joint stock or other associations . . . should be subject to proper governmental supervision." And later, "The nation should . . . assume power of supervision and regulation over all corporations doing an interstate business."

Now, nearly four years later, Roosevelt once again referred to his conviction that the "accumulation of great wealth in industrial centers" had brought about serious problems, which if unsolved might adversely affect "the cause of free self-government throughout the world."

President Theodore Roosevelt delivering his inaugural address on March 4, 1905.

THE PRESIDENT

William Howard Taft brought a background of wide judicial experience to the White House, but otherwise his political naïveté made him a poor choice as Theodore Roosevelt's personally selected successor. A graduate of Cincinnati Law School, Taft had moved his ponderous bulk slowly but inexorably up the judicial ladder: assistant prosecuting attorney in 1881, assistant county solicitor in 1885, judge of Superior Court of Ohio in 1887, Harrison's Solicitor-General of the United States in 1890, U.S. Circuit Judge for the Sixth Judicial Circuit in 1892, McKinley's Commissioner and Civil Governor of the Philippines in 1900, Roosevelt's Secretary of War in 1904, and finally President in 1909—at the age of fifty-one. The trust-busting Roosevelt picked Taft because of his success in the Philippines, where he had established limited self-government and brought about needed reforms. With this background Roosevelt felt Taft was the strong man he wanted to see as his successor. But the Philippines were not the United States —as both Roosevelt and Taft would soon discover.

THE NATION

The earth-shaking event of 1906, speaking literally, was the violent earthquake of April 18–19, which destroyed the city of San Francisco, leaving half-a-million persons homeless.

Stimulated by such muckraking books as Upton Sinclair's *The Jungle*—a novel revealing unsanitary conditions in the meat-packing industry—the nation's first comprehensive Pure Food and Drug Act was passed June 30, 1906. In October, 1907, a brief currency panic caused many banks throughout the nation to close, until stability had been restored through the intervention of J. Pierpont Morgan and his associates. On November 16 of this uneasy year Oklahoma was admitted to the Union as the 46th state.

In the November, 1908, election Roosevelt's hand-picked successor, Republican William Howard Taft, polled 7,678,908 popular votes (321 electoral), while Democrat William Jennings Bryan received 6,409,104 popular votes (162 electoral). Socialist Eugene V. Debs polled 420,793 votes, Prohibitionist Eugene Chaffin received 253,840 votes, the Independence Party's Thomas L. Hisgen polled 82,872 votes, the People's party candidate Thomas E. Watson polled 29,100 votes, and the Socialist Labor party candidate August Gillhaus polled 14,021 votes. James S. Sherman was elected vice-president.

THE WORLD

In the Russo-Japanese War an armistice suggestion made by President Roosevelt led to a peace treaty signed September 5th and ratified October 14, 1905. 1906 was marked by a devastating earthquake in Formosa that killed thousands. The second Peace Conference at The Hague began June 15, 1907. In the same year the premier of Persia was assassinated, as were King Carlos and the Crown Prince of Portugal in 1908. Elsewhere, relations between Continental powers began the final deterioration that would lead to the outbreak of World War I.

YOU ARE WELL AWARE THE REPUBLICANS would have preferred one other than yourself in the White House, and left to yourself you would have refused the presidential nomination. But because of your wife's affirmative reaction to Roosevelt's suggestion that you become his successor you agree to accept the honor even though still unsure of yourself. You spend a great deal of time on your inaugural address and submit it somewhat uneasily to Roosevelt, whose reassuring comment is typically enthusiastic: "I think your inaugural is simply fine!" After you take the oath of office on the open platform on the Capitol steps the near-zero weather and wind-driven snow force the balance of the ceremony to be held in the House of Representatives. Now, as you stand before the assembly, you draw your six-foot, three hundred-pound figure to its full height, and begin to read your long address which has been prepared with all the detailed precision of a legal brief....

William Howard Taft

[1909–1913]

INAUGURAL ADDRESS, MARCH 4, 1909

House of Representatives, Washington, D.C.

My Fellow Citizens:

Anyone who has taken the oath I have just taken must feel a heavy weight of responsibility. If not, he has no conception of the powers and duties of the office upon which he is about to enter, or he is lacking in a proper sense of the obligation which the oath imposes.

The office of an inaugural address is to give a summary outline of the main policies of the new administration, so far as they can be anticipated. I have had the honor to be one of the advisers of my distinguished predecessor, and, as such, to hold up his hands in the reforms he has initiated. I should be untrue to myself, to my promises, and to the declarations of the party platform upon which I was elected to office, if I did not make the maintenance and enforcement of those reforms a most important feature of my administration. They were directed to the suppression of the lawlessness and abuses of power of the great combinations of capital invested in railroads and in industrial enterprises carrying on interstate commerce. The steps which my predecessor took and the legislation passed on his recommendation have accomplished much, have caused a general halt in the vicious policies which created popular alarm, and have brought about in the business affected a much higher regard for existing law.

To render the reforms lasting, however, and to secure at the same time freedom from alarm on the part of those pursuing proper and progressive business methods, further legislative and executive action are needed. Relief of the railroads from certain restrictions of the antitrust law have been urged by my predecessor and will be urged by me. On the other hand, the administration is pledged to legislation looking to a proper federal supervision and restriction to prevent excessive issues of bonds and stocks by companies owning and operating interstate-commerce railroads.

Then, too, a reorganization of the Department of Justice, of the Bureau of Corporations in the Department of Commerce and Labor, and of the Interstate Commerce Commission, looking to effective cooperation of these agencies, is needed to secure a more rapid and certain enforcement of the laws affecting interstate railroads and industrial combinations.

The Republican platform of 1908 promised a downward revision of the Dingley Tariff Law, Federal incorporation of interstate commerce corporations, establishment of postal savings banks, settlement of certain questions concerning income tax, regulation of railroad stock and bond issues by the Interstate Commerce Commission, legalizing of rate agreements after approval by the Commission, more efficient execution of the interstate commerce and antitrust laws, issuance of mail subsidies to Pacific and South American lines, statutory reform in issuance of injunctions, and the continuance of Theodore Roosevelt's policies regarding conservation of national resources.

I hope to be able to submit at the first regular session of the incoming Congress, in December next, definite suggestions in respect to the needed amendments to the antitrust and the interstate commerce law and the changes required in the executive departments concerned in their enforcement.

It is believed that with the changes to be recommended American business can be assured of that measure of stability and certainty in respect to those things that may be done and those that are prohibited which is essential to the life and growth of all business. Such a plan must include the right of the people to avail themselves of those methods of combining capital and effort deemed necessary to reach the highest degree of economic efficiency, at the same time differentiating between combinations based upon legitimate economic reasons and those formed with the intent of creating monopolies and artificially controlling prices.

The work of formulating into practical shape such changes is creative work of the highest order, and requires all the deliberation possible in the interval. I believe that the amendments to be proposed are just as necessary in the protection of legitimate business as in the clinching of the reforms which properly bear the name of my predecessor.

A matter of most pressing importance is the revision of the tariff. In accordance with the promises of the platform upon which I was elected, I shall call Congress into extra session to meet on the 15th day of March, in order that consideration may be at once given to a bill revising the Dingley Act. This should secure an adequate revenue and adjust the duties in such a manner as to afford to labor and to all industries in this country, whether of the farm, mine or factory, protection by tariff equal to the difference between the cost of production abroad and the cost of production here, and have a provision which shall put into force, upon executive determination of certain facts, a higher or maximum tariff against those countries whose trade policy toward us equitably requires such discrimination. It is thought that there has been such a change in conditions since the enactment of the Dingley Act, drafted on a similarly protective principle, that the measure of the tariff above stated will permit the reduction of rates in certain schedules and will require the advancement of few, if any.

The proposal to revise the tariff made in such an authoritative way as to lead the business community to count upon it necessarily halts all those branches of business directly affected; and as these are most important, it disturbs the whole business of the country. It is imperatively necessary, therefore, that a tariff bill be drawn in good faith in accordance with promises made before the election by the party in power, and as promptly passed as due consideration will permit. It is not that the tariff is more important in the long run than the perfecting of the reforms in respect to antitrust legislation and interstate commerce regulation, but the need for action when the revision of the tariff has been determined upon is more immediate to avoid embarrassment of business. To secure the needed speed in the passage of the tariff bill, it would seem wise to attempt no other legislation at the extra session. I venture this as a suggestion only, for the course to be taken by Congress, upon the call of the Executive, is wholly within its discretion.

In the making of a tariff bill the prime motive is taxation and the securing thereby of a revenue. Due largely to the business depression which followed the financial panic of 1907, the revenue from customs and other sources has decreased to such an extent

Taft's first move would be to call the special session mentioned here and push through his proposed revision of the Dingley Tariff Law as promised.

Taft would live up to his promises by signing the Payne-Aldrich Tariff Act, August 5, 1909. In doing so he would incur much criticism of the drastically protective act, which he, however, would publicly call the finest tariff legislation to be enacted by the Republican party.

that the expenditures for the current fiscal year will exceed the receipts by $100,000,000. It is imperative that such a deficit shall not continue, and the framers of the tariff bill must, of course, have in mind the total revenues likely to be produced by it and so arrange the duties as to secure an adequate income. Should it be impossible to do so by import duties, new kinds of taxation must be adopted, and among these I recommend a graduated inheritance tax as correct in principle and as certain and easy of collection.

Taft's idea of a graduated inheritance tax has been carried out and expanded.

The obligation on the part of those responsible for the expenditures made to carry on the Government, to be as economical as possible, and to make the burden of taxation as light as possible, is plain, and should be affirmed in every declaration of government policy. This is especially true when we are face to face with a heavy deficit. But when the desire to win the popular approval leads to the cutting off of expenditures really needed to make the Government effective and to enable it to accomplish its proper objects, the result is as much to be condemned as the waste of government funds in unnecessary expenditure. The scope of a modern government in what it can and ought to accomplish for its people has been widened far beyond the principles laid down by the old "laissez faire" school of political writers, and this widening has met popular approval.

In the Department of Agriculture the use of scientific experiments on a large scale and the spread of information derived from them for the improvement of general agriculture must go on.

The importance of supervising business of great railways and industrial combinations and the necessary investigation and prosecution of unlawful business methods are another necessary tax upon Government which did not exist half a century ago.

Supervision of the railroads and large corporate empires as well as conservation of our national resources had always been subjects of prime importance to Theodore Roosevelt. Taft here pledged himself to carry on the ideals set by his predecessor. Through the efforts of Roosevelt and Taft nearly 150,000,000 acres of land were set aside as national preserves.

The putting into force of laws which shall secure the conservation of our resources, so far as they may be within the jurisdiction of the Federal Government, including the most important work of saving and restoring our forests and the great improvement of waterways, are all proper government functions which must involve large expenditure if properly performed. While some of them, like the reclamation of arid lands, are made to pay for themselves, others are of such an indirect benefit that this cannot be expected of them. A permanent improvement, like the Panama Canal, should be treated as a distinct enterprise, and should be paid for by the proceeds of bonds, the issue of which will distribute its cost between the present and future generations in accordance with the benefits derived. It may well be submitted to the serious consideration of Congress whether the deepening and control of the channel of a great river system, like that of the Ohio or of the Mississippi, when definite and practical plans for the enterprise have been approved and determined upon, should not be provided for in the same way.

Then, too, there are expenditures of Government absolutely necessary if our country is to maintain its proper place among the nations of the world, and is to exercise its proper influence in defense of its own trade interests in the maintenance of traditional American policy against the colonization of European monarchies in this hemisphere, and in the promotion of peace and international morality. I refer to the cost of maintaining a proper army, a proper navy, and suitable fortifications upon the mainland of the United States and in its dependencies.

A strong Army and Navy was another Roosevelt policy to which Taft paid lip service. He would be able to do little for the armed forces during his administration, however, because of Congress' reluctance to provide necessary funds.

We should have an army so organized and so officered as to be capable in time of emergency, in cooperation with the national militia and under the provisions of a proper national volunteer law, rapidly to expand into a force sufficient to resist all probable invasion from abroad and to furnish a respectable expeditionary force if necessary in the maintenance of our traditional American policy which bears the name of President Monroe.

Our fortifications are yet in a state of only partial completeness, and the number of men to man them is insufficient. In a few years however, the usual annual appropriations for our coast defenses, both on the mainland and in the dependencies, will make them sufficient to resist all direct attack, and by that time we may hope that the men to man them will be provided as a necessary adjunct. The distance of our shores from Europe and Asia of course reduces the necessity for maintaining under arms a great army, but it does not take away the requirement of mere prudence—that we should have an army sufficiently large and so constituted as to form a nucleus out of which a suitable force can quickly grow.

What has been said of the army may be affirmed in even a more emphatic way of the navy. A modern navy can not be improvised. It must be built and in existence when the emergency arises which calls for its use and operation. My distinguished predecessor has in many speeches and messages set out with great force and striking language the necessity for maintaining a strong navy commensurate with the coast line, the governmental resources, and the foreign trade of our Nation; and I wish to reiterate all the reasons which he has presented in favor of the policy of maintaining a strong navy as the best conservator of our peace with other nations, and the best means of securing respect for the assertion of our rights, the defense of our interests, and the exercise of our influence in international matters.

Our international policy is always to promote peace. We shall enter into any war with a full consciousness of the awful consequences that it always entails, whether successful or not, and we, of course, shall make every effort consistent with national honor and the highest national interest to avoid a resort to arms. We favor every instrumentality, like that of the Hague Tribunal and arbitration treaties made with a view to its use in all international controversies, in order to maintain peace and to avoid war. But we should be blind to existing conditions and should allow ourselves to become foolish idealists if we did not realize that, with all the nations of the world armed and prepared for war, we must be ourselves in a similar condition, in order to prevent other nations from taking advantage of us and of our inability to defend our interests and assert our rights with a strong hand.

In the international controversies that are likely to arise in the Orient growing out of the question of the open door and other issues the United States can maintain her interests intact and can secure respect for her just demands. She will not be able to do so, however, if it is understood that she never intends to back up her assertion of right and her defense of her interest by anything but mere verbal protest and diplomatic note. For these reasons the expenses of the army and navy and of coast defenses should always be considered as something which the Government must pay for, and they should not be cut off through mere consideration of economy. Our Government is able to afford a suitable army and a suitable navy. It may maintain them without the slightest danger to the Republic or the cause of free institutions, and fear of additional taxation ought not to change a proper policy in this regard.

The policy of the United States in the Spanish war and since has given it a position of influence among the nations that it never had before, and should be constantly exerted to securing to its bona fide

Under Roosevelt's aegis a fleet of 28 warships, painted white, had been sent on a voyage around the world as a demonstration of American Naval strength. The voyage began December 16, 1907, and ended February 23, 1909. While overseas nations were impressed by our seagoing strength, many Congressmen objected to the expense and made it difficult for the Navy to obtain additional funds for further expansion of the fleet.

This mention of the "open door" in the Orient referred to the policy established in 1899 by McKinley's Secretary of State John Hay. On September 6, 1899, Hay requested each of the great powers to agree to and respect the "open door" in China. Equal treatment was to be given all business enterprises in their sphere of influence, and Chinese tariff rates were to remain in force.

citizens, whether native or naturalized, respect for them as such in foreign countries. We should make every effort to prevent humiliating and degrading prohibition against any of our citizens wishing temporarily to sojourn in foreign countries because of race or religion.

The admission of Asiatic immigrants who cannot be amalgamated with our population has been made the subject either of prohibitory clauses in our treaties and statutes or of strict administrative regulation secured by diplomatic negotiation. I sincerely hope that we may continue to minimize the evils likely to arise from such immigration without unnecessary friction and by mutual concessions between self-respecting governments. Meantime we must take every precaution to prevent, or failing that, to punish outbursts of race feeling among our people against foreigners of whatever nationality who have by our grant a treaty right to pursue lawful business here and to be protected against lawless assault or injury.

This leads me to point out a serious defect in the present federal jurisdiction, which ought to be remedied at once. Having assured to other countries by treaty the protection of our laws for such of their subjects or citizens as we permit to come within our jurisdiction, we now leave to a state or a city, not under the control of the Federal Government, the duty of performing our international obligations in this respect. By proper legislation we may, and ought to, place in the hands of the Federal Executive the means of enforcing the treaty rights of such aliens in the courts of the Federal Government. It puts our Government in a pusillanimous position to make definite engagements to protect aliens and then to excuse the failure to perform those engagements by an explanation that the duty to keep them is in States or cities, not within our control. If we would promise we must put ourselves in a position to perform our promise. We cannot permit the possible failure of justice, due to local prejudice in any State or municipal government, to expose us to the risk of a war which might be avoided if federal jurisdiction was asserted by suitable legislation by Congress and carried out by proper proceedings instituted by the Executive in the courts of the National Government.

One of the reforms to be carried out during the incoming administration is a change of our monetary and banking laws, so as to secure greater elasticity in the forms of currency available for trade and to prevent the limitations of law from operating to increase the embarrassment of a financial panic. The monetary commission, lately appointed, is giving full consideration to existing conditions and to all proposed remedies, and will doubtless suggest one that will meet the requirements of business and of public interest.

We may hope that the report will embody neither the narrow view of those who believe that the sole purpose of the new system should be to secure a large return on banking capital or of those who would have greater expansion of currency with little regard to provisions for its immediate redemption or ultimate security. There is no subject of economic discussion so intricate and so likely to evoke differing views and dogmatic statements as this one. The commission, in studying the general influence of currency on business and of business on currency, have wisely extended their investigations in European banking and monetary methods. The information that they have derived from such experts as they have found abroad will undoubtedly be found helpful in the solution of the difficult problem they have in hand.

The incoming Congress should promptly fulfill the promise of the Republican platform and pass a proper postal savings bank bill.

Taft referred to the tremendous flood of immigrants pouring into the United States from virtually every country of the earth. In 1907 nearly 1,300,000 aliens had entered during the fiscal year. In 1908 a great protest had been voiced on the Pacific coast because of Japanese immigrants who were keeping labor's wages low. This antagonism would culminate in the controversial Webb Alien Land Holding Bill of 1913, which would in effect prevent the Japanese from owning land in California. The state law so incensed Japan and the Japanese in America that prompt diplomatic action by President Wilson was necessary to avoid a break with Japan.

The failure of the Currency Act of 1900 to stabilize the nation's currency had created the need for additional controls. Taft recognized this need, but it would be nearly five years before President Wilson would push through the passage of the Owens-Glass Act, establishing the Federal Reserve System and assuring the nation of a controlled decentralized banking system and a stabilized, yet flexible, currency.

It will not be unwise or excessive paternalism. The promise to repay by the Government will furnish an inducement to savings deposits which private enterprise can not supply and at such a low rate of interest as not to withdraw custom from existing banks. It will substantially increase the funds available for investment as capital in useful enterprises. It will furnish absolute security which makes the proposed scheme of government guaranty of deposits so alluring, without its pernicious results.

I sincerely hope that the incoming Congress will be alive, as it should be, to the importance of our foreign trade and of encouraging it in every way feasible. The possibility of increasing this trade in the Orient, in the Philippines, and in South America are known to everyone who has given the matter attention. The direct effect of free trade between this country and the Philippines will be marked upon our sales of cottons, agricultural machinery, and other manufactures. The necessity of the establishment of direct lines of steamers between North and South America has been brought to the attention of Congress by my predecessor and by Mr. Root before and after his noteworthy visit to that continent, and I sincerely hope that Congress may be induced to see the wisdom of a tentative effort to establish such lines by the use of mail subsidies.

The importance of the part which the Departments of Agriculture and of Commerce and Labor may play in ridding the markets of Europe of prohibitions and discriminations against the importation of our products is fully understood, and it is hoped that the use of the maximum and minimum feature of our tariff law to be soon passed will be effective to remove many of those restrictions.

The Panama Canal will have a most important bearing upon the trade between the eastern and far western sections of our country, and will greatly increase the facilities for transportation between the eastern and the western seaboard, and may possibly revolutionize the transcontinental rates with respect to bulky merchandise. It will also have a most beneficial effect to increase the trade between the eastern seaboard of the United States and the western coast of South America, and, indeed, with some of the important ports on the east coast of South America reached by rail from the west coast.

The work on the canal is making most satisfactory progress. The type of the canal as a lock canal was fixed by Congress after a full consideration of the conflicting reports of the majority and minority of the consulting board, and after the recommendation of the War Department and the Executive upon those reports. Recent suggestion that something had occurred on the Isthmus to make the lock type of the canal less feasible than it was supposed to be when the reports were made and the policy determined on led to a visit to the Isthmus of a board of competent engineers to examine the Gatun dam and locks, which are the key of the lock type. The report of that board shows nothing has occurred in the nature of newly revealed evidence which should change the views once formed in the original discussion. The construction will go on under a most effective organization controlled by Colonel Goethals and his fellow army engineers associated with him, and will certainly be completed early in the next administration, if not before.

Some type of canal must be constructed. The lock type has been selected. We are in favor of having it built as promptly as possible. We must not now, therefore, keep up a fire in the rear of the agents whom we have authorized to do our work on the Isthmus. We must hold up their hands, and speaking for the incoming administration I wish to say that I propose to devote all the energy possible and under my control to pushing of this work on the plans which have been adopted, and to stand behind the men who are doing faithful, hard work to bring about the early completion of this, the greatest constructive enterprise of modern times.

The governments of our dependencies in Porto Rico and the Philippines are progressing as favorably as could be desired. The prosperity of Porto Rico continues unabated. The business conditions in the Philippines are not all that we could wish them to be, but with the passage of the new tariff bill permitting free trade between the United States and the archipelago, with such limitations on sugar and tobacco as shall prevent injury to domestic interests in those products, we can count on an improvement in business conditions in the Philippines and the development of a mutually profitable trade between this country and the islands. Meantime our Government in each dependency is upholding the traditions of civil liberty and increasing popular control which might be expected under American auspices. The work which we are doing there redounds to our credit as a nation.

I look forward with hope to increasing the already good feeling between the South and the other sections of the country. My chief purpose is not to effect a change in the electoral vote of the Southern States. That is a secondary consideration. What I look forward to is an increase in the tolerance of political views of all kinds and their advocacy throughout the South, and the existence of a respectable political opposition in every State; even more than this, to an increased feeling on the part of all the people in the South that this Government is their Government, and that its officers in their states are their officers.

The consideration of this question can not, however, be complete and full without reference to the negro race, its progress and its present condition. The thirteenth amendment secured them freedom; the fourteenth amendment due process of law, protection of property, and the pursuit of happiness; and the fifteenth amendment attempted to secure the negro against any deprivation of the privilege to vote because he was a negro. The thirteenth and fourteenth amendments have been generally enforced and have secured the objects for which they are intended. While the fifteenth amendment has not been generally observed in the past, it ought to be observed, and the tendency of Southern legislation today is toward the enactment of electoral qualifications which shall square with that amendment. Of course, the mere adoption of a constitutional law is only one step in the right direction. It must be fairly and justly enforced as well. In time both will come. Hence it is clear to all that the domination of an ignorant, irresponsible element can be prevented by constitutional laws which shall exclude from voting both negroes and whites not having education or other qualifications thought to be necessary for a proper electorate. The danger of the control of an ignorant electorate has therefore passed. With this change, the interest which many of the Southern white citizens take in the welfare of the negroes has increased. The colored men must base their hope on the results of their own industry, self-restraint, thrift, and business success, as well as upon the aid and comfort and sympathy which they may receive from their white neighbors of the South.

There was a time when Northerners who sympathized with the negro in his necessary struggle for better conditions sought to give him the suffrage as a protection to enforce its exercise against the prevailing sentiment of the South. The movement proved to be a

Note Taft's spelling of Porto Rico, the accepted spelling of the day. Now, however, Puerto Rico is correct. Taft's years in the Philippines as commissioner and governor had given him a close kinship with the Filipinos, to whom he referred as "my little brown brothers."

Although not mentioned by name, this long passage in Taft's address was obviously directed at localized operations of the Ku Klux Klan and similar organizations in the South. Their chief purpose was to keep Negroes away from the polls, in order to perpetuate control of local governments by ex-Confederate soldiers and other sympathizers of the Confederacy. Section I of the fifteenth amendment stated, "The right of the citizens of the United States to vote shall not be denied or abridged by the United States or by any State on account of race, color, or previous condition of servitude." Thus the vote had been guaranteed to Negroes, provided they wished to exercise their right to vote. But no one could make them go to the polls against their will. And the threat of white-sheeted, cross-burning Klansmen and members of similar groups was still strong enough to keep a large percentage of Negroes at home on election day.

The Knights of the White Camellia, strongest in the Gulf states, was a Southern organization similar to the Ku Klux Klan. Founded in 1867, the Knights were reputed to have an even larger membership than the Klan. Thomas Dixon's novel The Clansman, published in 1905, furnished the basis for D. W. Griffith's epic motion picture The Birth of a Nation.

[195]

failure. What remains is the fifteenth amendment to the Constitution and the right to have statutes of States specifying qualifications for electors subjected to the test of compliance with that amendment. This is a great protection to the negro. It never will be repealed, and it never ought to be repealed. If it had not passed, it might be difficult now to adopt it; but with it in our fundamental law, the policy of Southern legislation must and will tend to obey it, and so long as the statutes of the States meet the test of this amendment and are not otherwise in conflict with the Constitution and laws of the United States, it is not the disposition or within the province of the Federal Government to interfere with the regulation by Southern States of their domestic affairs. There is in the South a stronger feeling than ever among the intelligent well-to-do, and influential element in favor of the industrial education of the negro and the encouragement of the race to make themselves useful members of the community. The progress which the negro has made in the last fifty years, from slavery, when its statistics are reviewed, is marvelous, and it furnishes every reason to hope that in the next twenty-five years a still greater improvement in his condition as a productive member of society, on the farm, and in the shop, and in other occupations may come.

The negroes are now Americans. Their ancestors came here years ago against their will, and this is their only country and their only flag. They have shown themselves anxious to live for it and to die for it. Encountering the race feeling against them, subjected at time to cruel injustice growing out of it, they may well have our profound sympathy and aid in the struggle they are making. We are charged with the sacred duty of making their path as smooth and easy as we can. Any recognition of their distinguished men, any appointment to office from among their number, is properly taken as an encouragement and an appreciation of their progress, and this just policy should be pursued when suitable occasion offers.

But it may well admit of doubt whether, in the case of any race, an appointment of one of their number to a local office in a community in which the race feeling is so widespread and acute as to interfere with the ease and facility and which the local government business can be done by the appointee is of sufficient benefit by way of encouragement to the race to outweigh the recurrence and increase of race feeling which such an appointment is likely to engender. Therefore the Executive, in recognizing the negro race by appointments, must exercise a careful discretion not thereby to do it more harm than good. On the other hand, we must be careful not to encourage the mere pretense of race feeling manufactured in the interest of individual political ambition.

Personally, I have not the slightest race prejudice or feeling, and recognition of its existence only awakens in my heart a deeper sympathy for those who have to bear it or suffer from it, and I question the wisdom of a policy which is likely to increase it. Meantime, if nothing is done to prevent it, a better feeling between the negroes and the whites in the South will continue to grow, and more and more of the white people will come to realize that the future of the South is to be much benefited by the industrial and intellectual progress of the negro. The exercise of political franchises by those of this race who are intelligent and well to do will be acquiesced in, and the right to vote will be withheld only from the ignorant and irresponsible of both races.

There is one other matter to which I shall refer. It was made the subject of great controversy during the election and calls for at least a passing reference now. My distinguished predecessor has given much attention to the cause of labor, with whose struggle for better things he has shown the sincerest sympathy. At his instance Congress has passed the bill fixing the liability of interstate carriers to their employees for injury sustained in the course of employment, abolishing the rule of fellow-servant and the common-law rule as to contributory negligence, and substituting therefor the so-called rule of "comparative negligence." It has also passed a law fixing the compensation of government employees for injuries sustained in the employ of the Government through the negligence of the superior. It has also passed a model child-labor law for the District of Columbia. In previous administrations an arbitration law for interstate commerce railroads and their employees, and laws for the application of safety devices to save the lives and limbs of employees of interstate railroads had been passed. Additional legislation of this kind was passed by the outgoing Congress.

I wish to say that insofar as I can I hope to promote the enactment of further legislation of this character. I am strongly convinced that the Government should make itself as responsible to employees injured in its employ as an interstate-railway corporation is made responsible by federal law to its employees; and I shall be glad, whenever any additional reasonable safety device can be invented to reduce the loss of life and limb among railway employees, to urge Congress to require its adoption by interstate railways.

Another labor question has arisen which has awakened the most excited discussion. That is in respect to the power of the federal courts to issue injunctions in industrial disputes. As to that, my convictions are fixed. Take away from the courts, if it could be taken away, the power to issue injunctions in labor disputes, and it would create a privileged class among the laborers and save the lawless among their number from a most needful remedy available to all men for the protection of their business against lawless invasion. The proposition that business is not a property or pecuniary right which can be protected by equitable injunction is utterly without foundation in precedent or reason. The proposition is usually linked with one to make the secondary boycott lawful. Such a proposition is at variance with the American instinct, and will find no support, in my judgment, when submitted to the American people. The secondary boycott is an instrument of tyranny, and ought not to be made legitimate.

The issue of a temporary restraining order without notice has in several instances been abused by its inconsiderate exercise, and to remedy this the platform upon which I was elected recommends the formulation in a statute of the conditions under which such a temporary restraining order ought to issue. A statute can and ought to be framed to embody the best modern practice, and can bring the subject so closely to the attention of the court as to make abuses of the process unlikely in the future. The American people, if I understand them, insist that the authority of the courts shall be sustained, and are opposed to any change in the procedure by which the powers of a court may be weakened and the fearless and effective administration of justice be interfered with.

Having thus reviewed the questions likely to recur during my administration, and having expressed in a summary way the position which I expect to take in recommendations to Congress and in my conduct as an Executive, I invoke the considerate sympathy and support of my fellow-citizens and the aid of the Almighty God in the discharge of my responsible duties.

In 1904 a National Child Labor Committee had been formed to investigate child labor conditions and lobby for adequate protective legislation. These efforts resulted in a bill passed by Congress, May 28, 1908, which regulated child labor in the District of Columbia. The bill also served as a guide for the rest of the nation.

Taft's interest in protecting railroad employees and regulating railroad operations would lead to the passage of the Mann-Elkins Act, June 18, 1910, and to the establishment of the Employers' Liability and Workmen's Compensation Commission, June 25, 1910.

Taft's concern over the thorny question of using injunctions in labor disputes would be expressed again in his first and second annual messages to Congress. But it would require passage of the Clayton Antitrust Act of 1914 under Wilson's administration to bring about a change. Under this bill unions would be exempted from the operation of the antitrust laws. The law also forbade the use of injunctions in labor disputes, except to avoid "irreparable" damage to property.

[197]

THE PRESIDENT

Wilson, along with Thomas Jefferson and Theodore Roosevelt, was one of the most literate and articulate of the presidents. The son of a Presbyterian minister, Thomas Woodrow Wilson dropped his first name in his youth. He was a graduate of Princeton but gave up his law practice while working toward a Ph.D. A teacher of political economy and history at Bryn Mawr and Wesleyan, he stepped up to a professorship of jurisprudence and political economy at Princeton in 1890, becoming president of the university from 1902–10. Wilson was elected governor of New Jersey in 1910; was later nominated as the Democratic presidential candidate, and carried his party to victory.

THE NATION

On April 6, 1909, Robert E. Peary reached the North Pole.

The census of 1910 revealed a population of 91,972,266. President Taft appointed the Governor of New York, Charles Evans Hughes, to the Supreme Court on April 25. This same year saw the passage of the Mann-Elkins Act, which widened the jurisdiction of the Interstate Commerce Commission.

January 6, 1912, New Mexico became the 47th state to join the Union, with Arizona the 48th on February 14. On April 14 the ocean liner *Titanic* struck an iceberg at 10:30 P.M. The next morning she sank, at 2:20 A.M. The death toll was a tragic 1,503 passengers and crew lost. John D. Rockefeller's Standard Oil Company was ordered dissolved by a May 15 decision of the Supreme Court. This was followed on May 29 by an order from the Court dissolving the America Tobacco Company, which had violated the Sherman Anti-Trust Act.

Theodore Roosevelt broke with Taft in the election year of 1912 and formed his own progressive or Bull Moose branch of the Republican party. The resultant split in Republican votes made the Democratic candidate's election a possibility, where before it was considered a distinct improbability.

In the November, 1912, election Democrat Woodrow Wilson polled 6,293,454 popular votes (435 electoral). Progressive (Bull Moose) Theodore Roosevelt received 4,119,538 popular votes (88 electoral). Republican William H. Taft received 3,484,980 popular votes (8 electoral). Socialist Eugene V. Debs polled 900,672, while Prohibitionist Eugene W. Chaffin received 206,275 votes. Thomas R. Marshall was elected vice-president.

THE WORLD

The British Empire observed a period of mourning after the death of King Edward VII, May 6, 1910. Westminster Abbey was the scene of the coronation of King George V and Queen Mary, June 11, 1911. On December 14th the Norwegian explorer Roald Amundsen reached the South Pole. Early in 1912 Italy and Turkey began to belabor each other, and on April 18, 1912, Italian warships shelled Turkish forts at the entrance to the Dardanelles. On October 8, 1912, Montenegro declared war against Turkey, to be followed by Bulgaria, Serbia, and Greece; and fighting began in the Balkans. In December an armistice was agreed on, but the peace conference held in London failed to come to terms and war was resumed February 3, 1913. Had the conference been successful World War I might well have been averted.

STANDING ON THE CAPITOL'S TEMPORARY PLATFORM you look out over the upturned sea of faces before you and note a large roped-off area directly below the platform. Quickly you send an order to the soldiers holding back the vast throng gathered here on a clear, cold though windy day. "Remove the ropes and let the people in," you direct, and wait until the crowd has closed in to the base of the platform before you begin to deliver your address . . . .

Woodrow Wilson

[1913–1917]

FIRST INAUGURAL ADDRESS, MARCH 4, 1913

Capitol Steps, Washington, D.C.

There has been a change of government. It began two years ago, when the House of Representatives became Democratic by a decisive majority. It has now been completed. The State about to assemble will also be Democratic. The offices of President and Vice-President have been put into the hands of Democrats. What does the change mean? That is the question that is uppermost in our minds to-day. That is the question I am going to try to answer, in order, if I may, to interpret the occasion.

It means much more than the mere success of a party. The success of a party means little except when the Nation is using that party for a large and definite purpose. No one can mistake the purpose for which the Nation now seeks to use the Democratic Party. It seeks to use it to interpret a change in its own plans and point of view. Some old things with which we had grown familiar, and which had begun to creep into the very habit of our thought and of our lives, have altered their aspect as we have latterly looked critically upon them, with fresh, awakened eyes; have dropped their disguises and shown themselves alien and sinister. Some new things, as we look frankly upon them, willing to comprehend their real character, have come to assume the aspect of things long believed in and familiar, stuff of our own convictions. We have been refreshed by a new insight into our own life.

We see that in many things that life is very great. It is incomparably great in its material aspects, in its body of wealth, in the diversity and sweep of its energy, in the industries which have been conceived and built up by the genius of individual men and the limitless enterprise of groups of men. It is great, also, very great, in its moral force. Nowhere else in the world have noble men and women exhibited in more striking forms the beauty and the energy of sympathy and helpfulness and counsel in their efforts to rectify wrong, alleviate suffering, and set the weak in the way of strength and hope. We have built up, moreover, a great system of government, which has stood through a long age as in many respects a model for those who seek to set liberty upon foundations that will endure against fortuitous change, against storm and accident. Our life contains every great thing, and contains it in rich abundance.

It is interesting to compare Taft's literary style with that of Wilson's. The former's precise, dogmatic documentation revealed his conservative judge's background. Although Wilson had practiced law, his eloquent rhetoric was more characteristic of a college professor gifted with a brilliant, facile mind than of a lawyer.

[199]

This was evidently a reference to the plundering of our national resources. Destruction had gone on virtually unchecked until Roosevelt had launched his vigorous program of conservation, which was carried on by Taft and would be further implemented by Wilson.

Throughout his early political career Wilson possessed the rare faculty of being able to sense what most people wanted and of putting these thoughts into words. Disturbed by conflict between the genial, too-pliant Taft and the tough, overly aggressive Roosevelt, the nation had heeded Wilson's plea for a liberal program of wide legislative reform, under the catch phrase the "New Freedom." In this segment of his address Wilson promised to restore the high standards under which the nation had been conceived. In the latter part of the address he mentioned briefly some of the more pertinent items on his schedule of intended reforms. He was able to put into operation a remarkable number of these, a majority of which are still in force.

Some of the legislation which would be enacted during Wilson's tenure of office was: ratification of the seventeenth amendment, providing for popular election of United States Senators; the Underwood-Simmons Tariff Act, reducing duties on nearly a thousand items; the Glass-Owens bill, which established the Federal Reserve System; the Clayton Antitrust Act, which exempted unions from the provisions of the antitrust laws; the Smith-Lever Act, which provided Federal funds for state agricultural colleges; the Federal Trade Commission, which was created to prevent monopolies; the Federal Farm Loan Act, which set up a land bank system for loans to farmers; the Keating-Owen Act, which kept children under fourteen from working in factories; the Adamson Bill, which provided an eight-hour day for the majority of railroad employees; the

But the evil has come with the good, and much fine gold has been corroded. With riches has come inexcusable waste. We have squandered a great part of what we might have used, and have not stopped to conserve the exceeding bounty of nature, without which our genius for enterprise would have been worthless and impotent, scorning to be careful, shamefully prodigal as well as admirably efficient. We have been proud of our industrial achievements, but we have not hitherto stopped thoughtfully enough to count the human cost, the cost of lives snuffed out, of energies overtaxed and broken, the fearful physical and spiritual cost to the men and women and children upon whom the dead weight and burden of it all has fallen pitilessly the years through. The groans and agony of it all had not yet reached our ears, the solemn, moving undertone of our life, coming up out of the mines and factories and out of every home where the struggle had its intimate and familiar seat. With the great Government went many deep secret things which we too long delayed to look into and scrutinize with candid, fearless eyes. The great Government we loved has too often been made use of for private and selfish purposes, and those who used it had forgotten the people.

At last a vision has been vouchsafed us of our life as a whole. We see the bad with the good, the debased and decadent with the sound and vital. With this vision we approach new affairs. Our duty is to cleanse, to reconsider, to restore, to correct the evil without impairing the good, to purify and humanize every process of our common life without weakening or sentimentalizing it. There has been something crude and heartless and unfeeling in our haste to succeed and be great. Our thought has been "Let every man look out for himself, let every generation look out for itself," while we reared giant machinery which made it impossible that any but those who stood at the levers of control should have a chance to look out for themselves. We had not forgotten our morals. We remembered well enough that we had set up a policy which was meant to serve the humblest as well as the most powerful, with an eye single to the standards of justice and fair play, and remembered it with pride. But we were very heedless and in a hurry to be great.

We have come now to the sober second thought. The scales of heedlessness have fallen from our eyes. We have made up our minds to square every process of our national life again with the standards we so proudly set up at the beginning and have always carried at our hearts. Our work is a work of restoration.

We have itemized with some degree of particularity the things that ought to be altered and here are some of the chief items: A tariff which cuts us off from our proper part in the commerce of the world, violates the just principles of taxation, and makes the Government a facile instrument in the hand of private interests; a banking and currency system based upon the necessity of the Government to sell its bonds fifty years ago and perfectly adapted to concentrating cash and restricting credits; an industrial system which, take it on all its sides, financial as well as administrative, holds capital in leading strings, restricts the liberties and limits the opportunities of labor, and exploits without renewing or conserving the natural resources of the country; a body of agricultural activities never yet given the efficiency of great business undertakings or served as it should be through the instrumentality of science taken directly to the farm, or afforded the facilities of credit best suited to its practical needs; watercourses undeveloped, waste places un-

[200]

reclaimed, forests untended, fast disappearing without plan or prospect of renewal, unregarded waste heaps at every mine. We have studied as perhaps no other nation has the most effective means of production, but we have not studied cost or economy as we should either as organizers of industry, as statesmen, or as individuals.

Nor have we studied and perfected the means by which government may be put at the service of humanity, in safeguarding the health of the Nation, the health of its men and its women and its children, as well as their rights in the struggle for existence. This is no sentimental duty. The firm basis of government is justice, not pity. These are matters of justice. There can be no equality or opportunity, the first essential of justice in the body politic, if men and women and children be not shielded in their lives, their very vitality, from the consequences of great industrial and social processes which they can not alter, control, or singly cope with. Society must see to it that it does not itself crush or weaken or damage its own constituent parts. The first duty of law is to keep sound the society it serves. Sanitary laws, pure food laws, and laws determining conditions of labor which individuals are powerless to determine for themselves are intimate parts of the very business of justice and legal efficiency.

These are some of the things we ought to do, and not leave the others undone, the old-fashioned, never-to-be-neglected, fundamental safeguarding of property and of individual right. This is the high enterprise of the new day: To lift everything that concerns our life as a Nation to the light that shines from the hearthfire of every man's conscience and vision of the right. It is inconceivable that we should do this as partisans; it is inconceivable we should do it in ignorance of the facts as they are or in blind haste. We shall restore, not destroy. We shall deal with our economic system as it is and as it may be modified, not as it might be if we had a clean sheet of paper to write upon; and step by step we shall make it what it should be, in the spirit of those who question their own wisdom and seek counsel and knowledge, not shallow self-satisfaction or the excitement of excursions whether they can not tell. Justice, and only justice, shall always be our motto.

And yet it will be no cool process of mere science. The Nation has been deeply stirred, stirred by a solemn passion, stirred by the knowledge of wrong, of ideals lost, of government too often debauched and made an instrument of evil. The feelings with which we face this new age of right and opportunity sweep across our heartstrings like some air out of God's own presence, where justice and mercy are reconciled and the judge and the brother are one. We know our task to be no mere task of politics but a task which shall search us through and through, whether we be able to understand our time and the need of our people, whether we be indeed their spokesmen and interpreters, whether we have the pure heart to comprehend and the rectified will to choose our high course of action.

This is not a day of triumph; it is a day of dedication. Here muster, not the forces of party, but the forces of humanity. Men's hearts wait upon us; men's lives hang in the balance; men's hopes call upon us to say what we will do. Who shall live up to the great trust? Who dares fail to try? I summon all honest men, all patriotic, all forward-looking men, to my side. God helping me, I will not fail them, if they will but counsel and sustain me!

Federal Board for Vocational Education, which stimulated development of agricultural and trade schools; and the eighteenth amendment, which prohibited the manufacture and sale of intoxicating liquor in the United States.

This was Wilson the idealist speaking. It was the same selfless dedication to the good of his country that was to lead Wilson to make a fatal error in assuming that politicians of both parties would, as he did, place love of country ahead of selfish interests. When Congress refused to support Wilson's dream of a League of Nations, it contributed greatly to his death.

THE PRESIDENT

Wilson began his first term with high hopes for the reform program he called the New Freedom. His aim was the restoration of individual competition by the curtailment of monopolistic practices on the part of business leaders. But three factors arose to deter him from a vigorous prosecution of these policies: a business slump in 1914, the outbreak of the war in Europe, and the revolution in Mexico. Wilson ordered Pershing to invade Mexico, thus displeasing Senator Henry Cabot Lodge. The order was one of the factors that created a rift between the two men, which worsened steadily and would eventually play a tremendous part in America's future. Although Wilson was horrified at Germany's invasion of Belgium his instincts were to remain neutral. Despite bitter attacks by Theodore Roosevelt and other interventionists the nation still believed in neutrality.

THE NATION

May 31, 1913, the seventeenth amendment was ratified, providing for popular election of U.S. Senators. While the world's attention was drawn to the struggle in Europe, Francisco Villa crossed the United States-Mexico border and raided Columbus, New Mexico, and Glen Springs, Texas. General John J. Pershing was dispatched to the area with orders to invade Mexico. The National Defense Act was passed June 3, 1916. A Council of National Defense was formed, August 31, and the United States Shipping Board was created on September 17, 1916, to enlarge the Merchant Marine.

In the election of 1916 the Democrats eked out a narrow victory. Wilson polled 9,129,606 popular votes (277 electoral). Republican Charles Evans Hughes received 8,538,221 popular votes (254 electoral). Socialist Allen L. Benson polled 585,113 votes, Prohibitionist Frank Hanly received 220,506, and Socialist Laborite Arthur E. Reimer polled 13,403. Thomas R. Marshall was reëlected vice-president.

THE WORLD

The assassination of Archduke Francis Ferdinand of Austria, June 28, 1914, by the Serbian Gavrilo Princip in Sarajevo, Bosnia, triggered World War I. In the next thirty days Austria declared war on Serbia. Russia supported Serbia. France was Russia's ally. Germany mobilized to back Austria, her ally under the Triple Alliance. In August of 1914 Germany declared war against Russia and France. When Germany entered Belgium in violation of a British treaty Britain declared war on Germany. Japan declared war on Germany and Austria declared war on Japan, with Turkey and Bulgaria throwing in with the Central Powers. Following the trend of public opinion, on August 4, 1914, President Wilson proclaimed America's neutrality. But the sinking of the liner *Lusitania,* May 7, 1915, with a loss of 124 American lives began to swing the pendulum of public opinion from neutrality to belligerence. Henry Ford organized a "peace ship" and sailed for Europe on December 4, 1915. It proved to be a futile trip.

YOU ARE A PEACE-LOVING MAN who shrinks from even the mention of blood; and you have done all in your power to keep the country out of war without compromising her honor. But since the election in November when the slogan "Vote for Wilson, he kept us out of war" kept you in the White House, the situation with Germany has steadily worsened, with Germany's declaration of unrestricted warfare closely followed on February 3, 1917, by your severance of diplomatic relations with the German aggressors. Now, a month later, you realize war with Germany is apparently inevitable. So you couch your inaugural address in terms of sufficient flexibility to accommodate the impending declaration of war you feel must soon follow this day. You stand in velvet-collared chesterfield and silk hat and read your short message from the temporary stand on the humanity-packed steps of the Capitol . . . .

Woodrow Wilson

[1917–1921]

SECOND INAUGURAL ADDRESS, MARCH 5, 1917

Capitol Steps, Washington, D.C.

My Fellow Citizens:

The four years which have elapsed since last I stood in this place have been crowded with counsel and action of the most vital interest and consequence. Perhaps no equal period in our history has been so fruitful of important reforms in our economic and industrial life or so full of significant changes in the spirit and purpose of our political action. We have sought very thoughtfully to set our house in order, correct the grosser errors and abuses of our industrial life, liberate and quicken the processes of our national genius and energy, and lift our politics to a broader view of the people's essential interests.

It is a record of singular variety and singular distinction. But I shall not attempt to review it. It speaks for itself and will be of increasing influence as the years go by. This is not the time for retrospect. It is time rather to speak our thoughts and purposes concerning the present and the immediate future.

Although we have centered counsel and action with such unusual concentration and success upon the great problems of domestic legislation to which we addressed ourselves four years ago, other matters have more and more forced themselves upon our attention—matters lying outside our own life as a nation and over which we had no control, but which, despite our wish to keep free of them, have drawn us more and more irresistibly into their own current and influence.

It has been impossible to avoid them. They have affected the life of the whole world. They have shaken men everywhere with a passion and an apprehension they never knew before. It has been hard to preserve calm counsel while the thought of our own people swayed this way and that under their influence. We are a composite and cosmopolitan people. We are of the blood of all the nations that are at war. The currents of our thoughts as well as the currents of our trade run quick at all seasons back and forth between us and them. The war inevitably set its mark from the first

[203]

On January 31, 1917, Germany had announced resumption of unrestricted submarine warfare. On February 3, 1917, the
American liner Housatonic had been sunk.
On February 26 Wilson asked Congress
for authority to arm American merchant
ships. His proposed bill was filibustered to
death in the Senate.

Wilson, however, was not to be denied.
Secretary of State Robert Lansing informed
the President that he already had the authority he asked for, and on March 12 Wilson would announce that all merchant ships
would be armed. In retrospect it seems plain
that Wilson had this action in mind, when
he wrote his second inaugural address. In
this passage he referred to the possibility of
"a more active assertion of our rights" and
"a more immediate association with the
great struggle itself."

Here Wilson revealed that in his own mind
at least the nation was already at war. For
Germany had violated in varying degrees
all seven of "the principles of a liberated
mankind," those principles Wilson had
arbitrarily designated as worthy of the nation's protection, by going to war if necessary. Had the nation given Wilson this
mandate? On the contrary, he had been
reëlected largely because of his "he kept us
out of war" platform. The people's unspoken assumption had been that Wilson
would continue to do so.

alike upon our minds, our industries, our commerce, our politics
and our social action. To be indifferent to it, or independent of it,
was out of the question.

And yet all the while we have been conscious that we were not
part of it. In that consciousness, despite many divisions, we have
drawn closer together. We have been deeply wronged upon the
seas, but we have not wished to wrong or injure in return; have
retained throughout the consciousness of standing in some sort
apart, intent upon an interest that transcended the immediate
issues of the war itself.

As some of the injuries done us have become intolerable we have
still been clear that we wished nothing for ourselves that we were
not ready to demand for all mankind—fair dealing, justice, the
freedom to live and to be at ease against organized wrong.

It is in this spirit and with this thought that we have grown more
and more aware, more and more certain that the part we wished
to play was the part of those who mean to vindicate and fortify
peace. We have been obliged to arm ourselves to make good our
claim to a certain minimum of right and of freedom of action. We
stand firm in armed neutrality since it seems that in no other way
we can demonstrate what it is we insist upon and cannot forget.
We may even be drawn on, by circumstances, not by our own purpose or desire, to a more active assertion of our rights as we see
them and a more immediate association with the great struggle
itself. But nothing will alter our thought or our purpose. They are
too clear to be obscured. They are too deeply rooted in the principles of our national life to be altered. We desire neither conquest
nor advantage. We wish nothing that can be had only at the cost
of another people. We always professed unselfish purpose and we
covet the opportunity to prove our professions are sincere.

There are many things still to be done at home, to clarify our
own politics and add new vitality to the industrial processes of our
own life, and we shall do them as time and opportunity serve, but
we realize that the greatest things that remain to be done must
be done with the whole world for stage and in co-operation with
the wide and universal forces of mankind, and we are making our
spirits ready for those things.

We are provincials no longer. The tragic events of the thirty
months of vital turmoil through which we have just passed have
made us citizens of the world. There can be no turning back. Our
own fortunes as a nation are involved whether we would have it
so or not.

And yet we are not the less Americans on that account. We shall
be the more American if we but remain true to the principles in
which we have been bred. They are not the principles of a province
or of a single continent. We have known and boasted all along that
they were the principles of a liberated mankind. These, therefore,
are the things we shall stand for, whether in war or in peace:

That all nations are equally interested in the peace of the world
and in the political stability of free peoples, and equally responsible for their maintenance; that the essential principle of peace is
the actual equality of nations in all matters of right or privilege;
that peace cannot securely or justly rest upon an armed balance of
power; that governments derive all their just powers from the consent of the governed and that no other powers should be supported
by the common thought, purpose or power of the family of nations;
that the seas should be equally free and safe for the use of all peoples,
under rules set up by common agreement and consent, and that,

so far as practicable, they should be accessible to all upon equal terms; that national armaments shall be limited to the necessities of national order and domestic safety; that the community of interest and of power upon which peace must henceforth depend imposes upon each nation the duty of seeing to it that all influences proceeding from its own citizens meant to encourage or assist revolution in other states should be sternly and effectually suppressed and prevented.

I need not argue these principles to you, my fellow countrymen; they are your own, part and parcel of your own thinking and your own motives in affairs. They spring up native amongst us. Upon this as a platform of purpose and of action we can stand together. And it is imperative that we should stand together. We are being forged into a new unity amidst the fires that now blaze throughout the world. In their ardent heat we shall, in God's Providence, let us hope, be purged of faction and division, purified of the errant humors of party and of private interest, and shall stand forth in the days to come with a new dignity of national pride and spirit. Let each man see to it that the dedication is in his own heart, the high purpose of the nation in his own mind, ruler of his own will and desire.

I stand here and have taken the high and solemn oath to which you have been audience because the people of the United States have chosen me for this august delegation of power and have by their gracious judgment named me their leader in affairs.

I know now what the task means. I realize to the full the responsibility which it involves. I pray God I may be given the wisdom and the prudence to do my duty in the true spirit of this great people. I am their servant and can succeed only as they sustain and guide me by their confidence and their counsel. The thing I shall count upon, the thing without which neither counsel nor action will avail, is the unity of America—an America united in feeling, in purpose and in its vision of duty, of opportunity and of service.

We are to beware of all men who would turn the tasks and the necessities of the nation to their own private profit or use them for the building up of private power.

United alike in the conception of our duty and in the high resolve to perform it in the face of all men, let us dedicate ourselves to the great task to which we must now set our hand. For myself I beg your tolerance, your countenance and your united aid.

The shadows that now lie dark upon our path will soon be dispelled, and we shall walk with the light all about us if we be but true to ourselves—to ourselves as we have wished to be known in the counsels of the world and in the thought of all those who love liberty and justice and the right exalted.

In the three weeks following Wilson's inauguration five American ships would be sunk by German submarines. Thus it was that only a month after he delivered his inaugural message, obviously designed to soften the blow of a declaration of war, Wilson would stand before a hurriedly convened Congress to deliver a war message that would lead to a joint Congressional resolution proclaiming the existence of a state of war with Germany.

THE PRESIDENT

Warren Gamaliel Harding was the first newspaper publisher to be elected to the presidency. He stepped into the political arena in 1898 as state senator, moved up to the lieutenant governorship of Ohio in 1904, but suffered a defeat in the 1910 election for governor. As U.S. Senator from Ohio, Harding won the presidential nomination in 1920. Handsome Harding, with his small-town background, his opposition to the League of Nations, and his support of woman's suffrage, the eighteenth amendment, and the Volstead Act, easily rolled over the Democratic team of James M. Cox and Franklin D. Roosevelt.

THE NATION

Once Wilson's election had been assured, the "he kept us out of war" campaign slogan was quietly discarded and every propaganda weapon available was used on the malleable mind of the masses. Posters depicting Belgian children with hands chopped off at their wrists by the bloodthirsty, spike-helmeted Huns quickly replaced the pacifistic billboards of the election. Isolationists suddenly learned the nettle sting of a new word, slacker. By October American troops were in the trenches on the Western front. Throughout the first ten months of 1918 victory followed victory. The abdication, November 9, 1918, of Kaiser Wilhelm II as German emperor and king of Prussia was the prelude to the signing of the armistice two days later, but the final treaty was never ratified by the United States. Wilson attempted to win public support for the treaty, but the public failed to respond, and on his return to Washington, Woodrow Wilson suffered a stroke resulting in permanent paralysis of his left side.

January 29, 1919, the eighteenth amendment to the Constitution was ratified and prohibition became effective. The census of 1920 revealed a population of 105,710,620. In the election that year the Republican candidate, Warren G. Harding, took a leaf from President McKinley's successful "front porch campaign" of 1896. With the help of the slogan "back to normalcy"—the latter a coined word not then found in any dictionary —Harding and the Republicans were swept to victory in a landslide. Harding polled 16,152,200 popular votes (404 electoral). Democrat James M. Cox received 9,147,353 popular votes (127 electoral). Socialist Eugene V. Debs polled 919,799, Prohibitionist Aaron S. Watkins received 189,408, Socialist-Laborite W.W. Cox polled 31,715, and Farmer-Laborite Parley P. Christensen polled 265,411. Calvin Coolidge was elected vice-president.

THE WORLD

The Central Powers were sure of victory in the spring of 1917. Submarine warfare was at its peak. Russia was torn by revolution and civil war after the abdication of the czar on March 15th. Italy had been hard hit, and the Allies were fighting a desperate defensive battle all along the Western Front until June, when American troops landed in France and helped turn back the enemy. In November Bolsheviks under Lenin seized control of Russia, and on March 3rd of the following year a peace treaty was signed in Brest-Litovsk between the Central Powers and Russia. The Allies, bolstered by American troops and supplies, forced the Germans eventually to abandon the Hindenburg line. The armistice was signed November 11, 1918. Despite lack of American support the League of Nations came into being January 20, 1920.

A GENIAL, TOBACCO CHEWING MAN and a lover of poker, golf, and baseball, you seem to be a typical "Main Streeter" to the average American, and the nation responds to your "front porch" campaign pleas for a return to "normalcy." On inauguration day a partially paralyzed Wilson rides with you to the Capitol, where between the administration of the oath of office and your address you wave greetings to the cheering crowd. Then you poise your glasses on your bold nose, compress your lips, and begin to read your address slowly and distinctly, carefully spacing each word in order to prevent slurring them over the strange new amplifying system being used for the first time at an inaugural . . . .

Warren G. Harding

[1921–1923]

INAUGURAL ADDRESS, MARCH 4, 1921

Capitol Steps, Washington, D. C.

My Countrymen:

When one surveys the world about him after the great storm, noting the marks of destruction and yet rejoicing in the ruggedness of the things which withstood it, if he is an American he breathes the clarified atmosphere with a strange mingling of regret and new hope. We have seen a world passion spend its fury, but we contemplate our Republic unshaken, and hold our civilization secure. Liberty—liberty within the law—and civilization are inseparable, and though both were threatened we find them now secure; and there comes to Americans the profound assurance that our representative government is the highest expression and surest guaranty of both.

Standing in this presence, mindful of the solemnity of this occasion, feeling the emotions which no one may know until he senses the great weight of responsibility for himself, I must utter my belief in the divine inspiration of the founding fathers. Surely there must have been God's intent in the making of this new-world Republic. Ours is an organic law which had but one ambiguity, and we saw that effaced in a baptism of sacrifice and blood, with union maintained, the Nation supreme, and its concord inspiring. We have seen the world rivet its hopeful gaze on the great truths on which the founders wrought. We have seen civil, human, and religious liberty verified and glorified. In the beginning the Old World scoffed at our experiment; today our foundations of political and social belief stand unshaken, a precious inheritance to ourselves, an inspiring example of freedom and civilization to all mankind. Let us express renewed and strengthened devotion, in grateful reverence for the immortal beginning, and utter our confidence in the supreme fulfillment.

The recorded progress of our Republic, materially and spiritually, in itself proves the wisdom of the inherited policy of non-involvement in Old World affairs. Confident of our ability to work out our own destiny, and jealously guarding our right to do so, we seek no part in directing the destinies of the Old World. We do not mean to be entangled. We will accept no responsibility except as our own conscience and judgment, in each instance, may determine.

The "ambiguity" to which Harding referred was the question, "Should slavery be permitted under the Constitution?" It had taken the Civil War's "baptism of sacrifice and blood" to provide an answer.

Newspaper reports of Harding's address commented on the loud applause elicited by this reference to Wilson's idea for a League of Nations. To the Senators who agreed with Henry Cabot Lodge participation in the League was unthinkable without additional reservations to protect American interests. But Wilson had refused to compromise. Had he better understood the reluctance of the people and many Congressmen in particular to enter into any commitment with a foreign power Wilson might have attempted to sway public opinion before going to Paris or might have been more flexible after his return.

[207]

Our eyes never will be blind to a developing menace, our ears never deaf to the call of civilization. We recognize the new order in the world, with the closer contacts which progress has wrought. We sense the call of the human heart for fellowship, fraternity, and co-operation. We crave friendship and harbor no hate. But America, our America, the America builded on the foundation laid by the inspired fathers, can be a party to no permanent military alliance. It can enter into no political commitments, nor assume any economic obligations which will subject our decisions to any other than our own authority.

I am sure our own people will not misunderstand, nor will the world misconstrue. We have no thought to impede the paths to closer relationship. We wish to promote understanding. We want to do our part in making offensive warfare so hateful that Governments and peoples who resort to it must prove the righteousness of their cause or stand as outlaws before the bar of civilization.

We are ready to associate ourselves with the nations of the world, great and small, for conference, for counsel; to seek the expressed views of world opinion; to recommend a way to approximate disarmament and relieve the crushing burdens of military and naval establishments. We elect to participate in suggesting plans for mediation, conciliation, and arbitration, and would gladly join in that expressed conscience of progress, which seeks to clarify and write the laws of international relationship, and establish a world court for the disposition of such justiciable questions as nations are agreed to submit thereto. In expressing aspirations, in seeking practical plans, in translating humanity's new concept of righteousness and justice and its hatred of war into recommended action we are ready most heartily to unite, but every commitment must be made in the exercise of our national sovereignty. Since freedom impelled, and independence inspired, and nationality exalted, a world super-government is contrary to everything we cherish and can have no sanction by our Republic. This is not selfishness, it is sanctity. It is not aloofness, it is security. It is not suspicion of others, it is patriotic adherence to the things which made us what we are.

Today, better than ever before, we know the aspirations of human-kind, and share them. We have come to a new realization of our place in the world and a new appraisal of our Nation by the world. The unselfishness of these United States is a thing proven; our devotion to peace for ourselves and for the world is well established; our concern for preserved civilization has had its impassioned and heroic expression. There was no American failure to resist the attempted reversion of civilization; there will be no failure today or tomorrow.

The success of our popular government rests wholly upon the correct interpretation of the deliberate, intelligent, dependable popular will of America. In a deliberate questioning of a suggested change of national policy, where internationality was to supersede nationality, we turned to a referendum, to the American people. There was ample discussion, and there is a public mandate in manifest understanding.

America is ready to encourage, eager to initiate, anxious to participate in any seemly program likely to lessen the probability of war, and promote that brotherhood of mankind which must be God's highest conception of human relationship. Because we cherish ideals of justice and peace, because we appraise international comity and helpful relationship no less highly than any people of the world, we aspire to a high place in the moral leadership of civilization, and we hold a maintained America, the proven Republic, the unshaken temple of representative democracy, to be not only an inspiration and example, but the highest agency of strengthening good will and promoting accord on both continents.

Mankind needs a world-wide benediction of understanding. It is needed among individuals, among peoples, among governments, and it will inaugurate an era of good feeling to mark the birth of a new order. In such understanding men will strive confidently for the promotion of their better relationships and nations will promote the comities so essential to peace.

We must understand that ties of trade bind nations in closest intimacy, and none may receive except as he gives. We have not strengthened ours in accordance with our resources or our genius, notably on our own continent, where a galaxy of Republics reflects the glory of new-world democracy, but in the new order of finance and trade we mean to promote enlarged activities and seek expanded confidence.

Perhaps we can make no more helpful contribution by example than prove a Republic's capacity to emerge from the wreckage of war. While the world's embittered travail did not leave us devastated lands nor desolated cities, left no gaping wounds, no breast with hate, it did involve us in the delirium of expenditure, in expanded currency and credits, in unbalanced industry, in unspeakable waste, and disturbed relationships. While it uncovered our portion of hateful selfishness at home, it also revealed the heart of America as sound and fearless, and beating in confidence unfailing.

Amid it all we have riveted the gaze of all civilization to the unselfishness and the righteousness of representative democracy, where our freedom never has made offensive warfare, never has sought territorial aggrandizement through force, never has turned to the arbitrament of arms until reason has been exhausted. When the Governments of the earth shall have established a freedom like our own and shall have sanctioned the pursuit of peace as we have practiced it, I believe the last sorrow and the final sacrifice of international warfare will have been written.

Let me speak to the maimed and wounded soldiers who are present today, and through them convey to their comrades the gratitude of the Republic for their sacrifices in its defense. A generous country will never forget the services you rendered, and you may hope for a policy under Government that will relieve any maimed successors from taking your places on another such occasion as this.

Our supreme task is the resumption of our onward, normal way. Reconstruction, readjustment, restoration—all these must follow. I would like to hasten them. If it will lighten the spirit and add to the resolution with which we take up the task, let me repeat for our Nation, we shall give no people just cause to make war upon us; we hold no national prejudices; we entertain no spirit of revenge; we do not hate; we do not covet; we dream of no conquest, nor boast of armed prowess.

If, despite this attitude, war is again forced upon us, I earnestly hope a way may be found which will unify our individual and collective strength and consecrate all America, materially and spiritually, body and soul, to national defense. I can vision the ideal republic, where every man and woman is called under the flag for assignment to duty for whatever service, military or civic, the individual is best fitted; where we may call to universal service every plant, agency, or facility, all in the sublime sacrifice for country,

A scrupulous adherence to historical fact justifies questioning Harding's unqualified statement here. What else but "offensive warfare" was Andrew Jackson's unauthorized attack on the Spaniards in Florida or "Mr. Madison's war" or the Spanish-American conflict and Theodore Roosevelt's subsequent actions as the "silent partner" of the Panamanian insurrectionists who threw off the yoke of Colombian rule?

[209]

Newspaper reports of the address commented on the wave of applause from Harding's audience, as he proclaimed his antipathy toward "war profits." But Harding, in his relationships with the Cabinet and other officials of his administration, was to prove even more gullible than President Grant. For the Harding administration would spawn scandals that would make the odor of Grant's regime sweet by comparison.

The war had cost America approximately $21,850,000,000, not including loans to the Allies of $10,350,000,000.

Once more Harding's listeners broke into his address and cheered his reference to the need for elimination of war taxation.

The war had made necessary many controls on business and industry. New organizations had been created during the emergency: the War Industries Board, headed by Bernard M. Baruch; the Food and Fuel Control Act, administered by Herbert Hoover; the National War Labor Board, which arbitrated labor disputes; the War Finance Corporation, which had helped finance production; the Liberty Loan Act of 1917, which had enabled five loans to be floated to the public; and the War Trade Board, which had controlled international trade. Even railroads had been placed under Federal controls.

and not one penny of war profit shall inure to the benefit of private individual, corporation, or combination, but all above the normal shall flow into the defense chest of the Nation. There is something inherently wrong, something out of accord with the ideals of representative democracy, when one portion of our citizenship turns its activities to private gain amid defensive war while another is fighting, sacrificing, or dying for national preservation.

Out of such universal service will come a new unity of spirit and purpose, a new confidence and consecration, which would make our defense impregnable, our triumph assured. Then we should have little or no disorganization of our economic, industrial, and commercial systems at home, no staggering war debts, no swollen fortunes to flout the sacrifices of our soldiers, no excuse for sedition, no pitiable slackerism, no outrage of treason. Envy and jealousy would have no soil for their menacing development, and revolution would be without the passion which engenders it.

A regret for the mistakes of yesterday must not, however, blind us to the tasks of today. War never left such an aftermath. There has been staggering loss of life and measureless wastage of materials. Nations are still groping for return to stable ways. Discouraging indebtedness confronts us like all the war-torn nations, and these obligations must be provided for. No civilization can survive repudiation.

We can reduce the abnormal expenditures, and we will. We can strike at war taxation, and we must. We must face the grim necessity, with full knowledge that the task is to be solved, and we must proceed with a full realization that no statute enacted by man can repeal the inexorable laws of nature. Our most dangerous tendency is to expect too much of government, and at the same time do for it too little.

We contemplate the immediate task of putting our public household in order. We need a rigid and yet sane economy, combined with fiscal justice, and it must be attended by individual prudence and thrift, which are so essential to this trying hour and reassuring for the future.

The business world reflects the disturbance of war's reaction. Herein flows the lifeblood of material existence. The economic mechanism is intricate and its parts interdependent, and has suffered the shocks and jars incident to abnormal demands, credit inflations, and price upheavals. The normal balances have been impaired, the channels of distribution have been clogged, the relations of labor and management have been strained. We must seek the readjustment with care and courage. Our people must give and take. Prices must reflect the receding fever of war activities. Perhaps we never shall know the old levels of wages again, because war invariably readjusts compensations, and the necessaries of life will show their inseparable relationship, but we must strive for normalcy to reach stability. All the penalties will not be light, nor evenly distributed. There is no way of making them so. There is no instant step from disorder to order. We must face a condition of grim reality, charge off our losses and start afresh. It is the oldest lesson of civilization. I would like government to do all it can to mitigate; then, in understanding, in mutuality of interest, in concern for the common good, our tasks will be solved. No altered system will work a miracle. Any wild experiment will only add to the confusion. Our best assurance lies in efficient administration of our proven system.

The forward course of the business cycle is unmistakable. Peo-

[210]

ples are turning from destruction to production. Industry has sensed the changed order and our own people are turning to resume their normal, onward way. The call is for productive America to go on. I know that Congress and the Administration will favor every wise Government policy to aid the resumption and encourage continued progress.

I speak for administrative efficiency, for lightened tax burdens, for sound commercial practices, for adequate credit facilities, for sympathetic concern for all agricultural problems, for the omission of unnecessary interference of Government with business, for an end to Government's experiment in business, and for more efficient business in Government administration. With all of this must attend a mindfulness of the human side of all activities, so that social, industrial, and economic justice will be squared with the purposes of a righteous people.

With the nation-wide induction of womanhood into our political life, we may count upon her intuitions, her refinements, her intelligence, and her influence to exalt the social order. We count upon her exercise of the full privileges and the performance of the duties of citizenship to speed the attainment of the highest state.

The nineteenth amendment was declared Constitutional by the Supreme Court on February 27, 1922.

I wish for an America no less alert in guarding against dangers from within than it is watchful against enemies from without. Our fundamental law recognizes no class, no group, no section; there must be none in legislation or administration. The supreme inspiration is the common weal. Humanity hungers for international peace, and we crave it with all mankind. My most reverent prayer for America is for industrial peace, with its rewards, widely and generally distributed, amid the inspirations of equal opportunity. No one justly may deny the equality of opportunity which made us what we are. We have mistaken unpreparedness to embrace it to be a challenge of the reality, and due concern for making all citizens fit for participation will give added strength of citizenship and magnify our achievement.

If revolution insists upon overturning established order, let other peoples make the tragic experiment. There is no place for it in America. When World War threatened civilization we pledged our resources and our lives to its preservation, and when revolution threatens we unfurl the flag of law and order and renew our consecration. Ours is a constitutional freedom where the popular will is the law supreme and minorities are sacredly protected. Our revisions, reformations, and evolutions reflect a deliberate judgment and an orderly progress, and we mean to cure our ills, but never destroy or permit destruction by force.

Harding's reference to the threat of revolution, which caused America to "unfurl the flag of law and order," may have been made because American troops had joined British and French forces in 1918 to protect Allied property in Murmansk, Archangel, and other north Russian towns against attacks by Bolshevik troops.

I had rather submit our industrial controversies to the conference table in advance than to a settlement table after conflict and suffering. The earth is thirsting for the cup of good will, understanding is its fountain source. I would like to acclaim an era of good feeling amid dependable prosperity and all the blessings which attend.

It has been proved again and again that we cannot, while throwing our markets open to the world, maintain American standards of living and opportunity, and hold our industrial eminence in such unequal competition. There is a luring fallacy in the theory of banished barriers of trade, but preserved American standards require our higher production costs to be reflected in our tariffs on imports. Today, as never before, when peoples are seeking trade restoration and expansion, we must adjust our tariffs to the new order. We seek participation in the world's exchanges, because therein lies our way to widened influence and the triumphs of peace.

[211]

Harding's hope for a richer, stronger economy was to be dampened by a short but virulent postwar depression in the latter part of 1921. However, an adjustment was to be made quickly. Recovery brought on an eight-year era of prosperity, now known as the Roaring Twenties.

Harding, a Republican, set forth a series of ideals he was destined never to see fulfilled. It would take another dozen years after Harding's unexpected death in 1923 for a Democratic successor, Franklin D. Roosevelt, to give these and other remedies for social and economic disorders intensive testing.

We know full well we cannot sell where we do not buy, and we cannot sell successfully where we do not carry. Opportunity is calling not alone for the restoration, but for a new era in production, transportation and trade. We shall answer it best by meeting the demand of a surpassing home market, by promoting self-reliance in production, and by bidding enterprise, genius, and efficiency to carry our cargoes in American bottoms to the marts of the world.

We would not have an America living within and for herself alone, but we would have her self-reliant, independent, and ever nobler, stronger, and richer. Believing in our higher standards, reared through constitutional liberty and maintained opportunity, we invite the world to the same heights. But pride in things wrought is no reflex of a completed task. Common welfare is the goal of our national endeavor. Wealth is not inimical to welfare; it ought to be its friendliest agency. There never can be equality of rewards or possessions so long as the human plan contains varied talents and differing degrees of industry and thrift, but ours ought to be a country free from the great blotches of distressed poverty. We ought to find a way to guard against the perils and penalties of unemployment. We want an America of homes, illumined with hope and happiness, where mothers, freed from the necessity for long hours of toil beyond their own doors, may preside as befits the hearthstone of American citizenship. We want the cradle of American childhood rocked under conditions so wholesome and so hopeful that no blight may touch it in its development, and we want to provide that no selfish interest, no material necessity, no lack of opportunity shall prevent the gaining of that education so essential to best citizenship.

There is no short cut to the making of these ideals into glad realities. The world has witnessed again and again the futility and the mischief of ill-considered remedies for social and economic disorders. But we are mindful today as never before of the friction of modern industrialism, and we must learn its causes and reduce its evil consequences by sober and tested methods. Where genius has made for great possibilities, justice and happiness must be reflected in a greater common welfare.

Service is the supreme commitment of life. I would rejoice to acclaim the era of the Golden Rule and crown it with the autocracy of service. I pledge an administration wherein all the agencies of Government are called to serve, and ever promote an understanding of Government purely as an expression of the popular will.

One cannot stand in this presence and be unmindful of the tremendous responsibility. The world upheaval has added heavily to our tasks. But with the realization comes the surge of high resolve, and there is reassurance in belief in the God-given destiny of our Republic. If I felt that there is to be sole responsibility in the Executive for the America of tomorrow I should shrink from the burden. But here are a hundred millions, with common concern and shared responsibility, answerable to God and country. The Republic summons them to their duty, and I invite co-operation.

I accept my part with single-mindedness of purpose and humility of spirit, and implore the favor and guidance of God in His Heaven. With these I am unafraid, and confidently face the future.

I have taken the solemn oath of office on that passage of Holy Writ wherein it is asked: "What doth the Lord require of thee but to do justly, and to love mercy, and to walk humbly with thy God?" This I plight to God and country.

Once again the nation was without a president for a few hours. News of President Harding's death in San Francisco was transmitted across the nation to the rural community of Plymouth, Vermont, where Vice-President Coolidge was staying. Awakened at two-thirty on the morning of August 3 Coolidge was then sworn in by his father, Colonel John Coolidge, a notary public and justice of the peace. The formal oath of office was administered to Coolidge in Washington, August 17, 1923, by Justice A.A. Hoehling of the Supreme Court of the District of Columbia.

Calvin Coolidge
[1923–1925]

THE PRESIDENT

John Calvin Coolidge, like two other presidents before him, dropped his first name early in life. Coolidge was admitted to the bar in 1897. Two years later his taciturnity, hard work, and rocklike integrity helped him to be elected to the city council of Northampton, Massachusetts, and from there he moved up the political ladder rapidly: city solicitor, 1900–01; clerk of the courts, 1904; member of the Massachusetts House of Representatives, 1907–08; mayor of Northampton, 1910–11; state senator, 1912–15; president of the Senate, 1914–15; and lieutenant governor, 1916–18.

Coolidge was elected governor of Massachusetts in 1919 and won notoriety that year by his firm stand on the Boston police strike, during which he wired Samuel Gompers, head of the American Federation of Labor: "There is no right to strike against the public safety by anybody, anywhere, at any time."

The coolness of Coolidge's actions in dealing with the Boston police strike assured his reëlection as governor in 1920 and placed his name before the Republican national convention of that year. He received 34 votes for the presidential nomination. But when the deadlock over General Wood and Frank O. Lowden, Governor of Illinois, had been broken in favor of Harding, Coolidge received 674¼ votes for the vice-presidential nomination.

THE PRESIDENT

While Coolidge was busy assuming his myriad responsibilities as Chief Executive, he was plagued by the revelation of widespread corruption, which the genial, easygoing Harding had unknowingly allowed to flourish. The most notorious of these was the Teapot Dome scandal, involving secret leasing of naval oil reserves to Harry F. Sinclair and Edward L. Doheny through the efforts of Secretary of the Interior Albert B. Fall, who had accepted "loans" from Sinclair and Doheny during negotiations for the leases. Despite this stigma on the Republican record the staunch integrity and quiet conservatism of Coolidge assured his renomination in 1924, and his subsequent victory at the polls.

THE NATION

One of the outstanding achievements of the Harding-Coolidge administration was the Washington Conference of 1921. The five powers met in Washington, D.C.—the United States, Great Britain, Japan, France, and Italy—and agreed to a limitation of battleship tonnage in the ratio of 5:5:3:1.67:1.67, in the order shown. In other fields the nation was reacting to wartime austerity and entering an era of hip flasks, knee-length skirts, speak-easies, national radio hookups, silent movies, jazz, the Charleston, raccoon coats, dance marathons, flivvers, flappers, and flagpole sitters.

In August of 1921 a handsome young politician named Franklin Delano Roosevelt, who had gone down to defeat as the vice-presidential candidate the preceding year, was stricken with infantile paralysis and dropped out of pub-

lic sight. And an even younger army officer named Dwight David Eisenhower was about to receive routine change of duty orders sending him to an obscure post in the Panama Canal Zone for two years.

The 1924 election was a triumph for Coolidge. He received a landslide of 15,725,016 popular votes (382 electoral), while Democrat John W. Davis polled only 8,386,503 popular votes (136 electoral). The Progressive party's Robert M. La Follette polled a respectable 4,822,856 popular votes (13 electoral). Prohibitionist H. P. Faris received 57,520 votes, Socialist-Laborite F. T. Johns polled 36,428 votes, and the communistic Workers' party candidate, William Z. Foster, polled 36,386 votes. Charles G. Dawes was elected vice-president.

THE WORLD

While the war-ravaged nations of Europe were slowly digging out from under the rubble of their ruins disturbing forces were beginning to seethe during the uneasy peace. In Russia the civil war between the Whites and the Reds (led by Lenin, Trotsky, and Stalin) raged until early 1921 when the Bolsheviks, already known as the Russian Communist Party, emerged in control. But Lenin's efforts led to his death in 1924. After the ensuing struggle among his followers Stalin emerged in control. In Germany a daring ex-corporal named Adolf Hitler joined a beer house group which he reshaped into the National Socialist German Worker's Party in 1920.

In Italy another disgruntled war veteran named Benito Mussolini organized the Fascist party in November, 1921. The following year King Victor Emmanuel III requested Mussolini to set up a strong cabinet to combat the postwar unemployment and depression. This was all Mussolini needed to transform the monarchy gradually into a dictatorship. In Japan the rise to power of the military would ultimately result in the attack on Pearl Harbor.

FOR A TACITURN MAN your inaugural address is noteworthy for its length. Rain clouds blot out the sun on the morning of your inauguration, but toward noon the sharp winds break up the dark clouds to let the sun through sporadically, as you stand before a battery of six radio microphones and begin to deliver your message in your typically quiet, unhurried way . . . .

Calvin Coolidge

[1925–1929]

INAUGURAL ADDRESS, MARCH 4, 1925

Capitol Steps, Washington, D.C.

My Countrymen:

No one can contemplate current conditions without finding much that is satisfying and still more that is encouraging. Our own country is leading the world in the general readjustment to the results of the great conflict. Many of its burdens will bear heavily upon us for years, and the secondary and indirect effects we must expect to experience for some time. But we are beginning to comprehend more definitely what course should be pursued, what remedies ought to be applied, what actions should be taken for our deliverance, and are clearly manifesting a determined will faithfully and conscientiously to adopt these methods of relief. Already we have sufficiently rearranged our domestic affairs so that confidence has returned, business has revived, and we appear to be entering an era of prosperity which is gradually reaching into every part of the Nation. Realizing that we can not live unto ourselves alone, we have contributed of our resources and our counsel to the relief of the suffering and the settlement of the disputes among the European nations. Because of what America is and what America has done, a firmer courage, a higher hope, inspires the heart of all humanity.

These results have not occurred by mere chance. They have been secured by a constant and enlightened effort marked by many sacrifices and extending over many generations. We can not continue these brilliant successes in the future, unless we continue to learn from the past. It is necessary to keep the former experiences of our country both at home and abroad continually before us, if we are to have any science of government. If we wish to erect new structures, we must have a definite knowledge of the old foundations. We must realize that human nature is about the most constant thing in the universe and that the essentials of human relationship do not change. We must frequently take our bearings from these fixed stars of our political firmament if we expect to hold a true course. If we examine carefully what we have done, we can determine the more accurately what we can do.

We stand at the opening of the one hundred and fiftieth year since our national consciousness first asserted itself by unmistakable action with an array of force. The old sentiment of detached and dependent colonies disappeared in the new sentiment of a united and independent Nation. Men began to discard the narrow con-

Coolidge was a good prophet. The country was indeed entering an era of prosperity which gradually reached into every part of the nation—and when the prosperity bubble burst, the resultant shock was felt not only throughout the nation, but the whole world as well.

Other presidents had made oblique references to the Monroe Doctrine's dual principles: No intervention and no colonization by European powers would be permitted in the Western hemisphere. But Coolidge was the first to mention the doctrine by name in an inaugural address.

Coolidge was no man to decry the use of slogans. He owed his victory at the polls in part to the Republican party's banal but nonetheless effective slogans: "Keep Cool with Coolidge" and "Keep Cool and Keep Coolidge."

Another inaugural first for Coolidge was this reference to submarines and airplanes, which had become important during World War I.

A reference to the Washington Conference and the 5:5:3:1.67:1.67 limitation on battleship tonnage agreed to by the United States, Great Britain, Japan, France, and Italy.

fines of a local charter for the broader opportunities of a national constitution. Under the eternal urge of freedom we became an independent Nation. A little less than 50 years later that freedom and independence were reasserted in the face of all the world, and guarded, supported, and secured by the Monroe doctrine. The narrow fringe of States along the Atlantic seaboard advanced its frontiers across the hills and plains of an intervening continent until it passed down the golden slope to the Pacific. We made freedom a birthright. We extended our domain over distant islands in order to safeguard our own interests and accepted the consequent obligation to bestow justice and liberty upon less favored peoples. In the defense of our own ideals and in the general cause of liberty we entered the Great War. When victory had been fully secured, we withdrew to our own shores unrecompensed save in the consciousness of duty done.

Throughout all these experiences we have enlarged our freedom, we have strengthened our independence. We have been, and propose to be, more and more American. We believe that we can best serve our own country and most successfully discharge our obligations to humanity by continuing to be openly and candidly, intensely and scrupulously, American. If we have any heritage, it has been that. If we have any destiny, we have found it in that direction.

But if we wish to continue to be distinctively American, we must continue to make that term comprehensive enough to embrace the legitimate desires of a civilized and enlightened people determined in all their relations to pursue a conscientious and religious life. We can not permit ourselves to be narrowed and dwarfed by slogans and phrases. It is not the adjective, but the substantive, which is of real importance. It is not the name of the action, but the result of the action, which is the chief concern. It will be well not to be too much disturbed by the thought of either isolation or entanglement of pacifists and militarists. The physical configuration of the earth has separated us from all of the Old World, but the common brotherhood of man, the highest law of all our being, has united us by inseparable bonds with all humanity. Our country represents nothing but peaceful intentions toward all the earth, but it ought not to fail to maintain such a military force as comports with the dignity and security of a great people. It ought to be a balanced force, intensely modern, capable of defense by sea and land, beneath the surface and in the air. But it should be so conducted that all the world may see in it, not a menace, but an instrument of security and peace.

This Nation believes thoroughly in an honorable peace under which the rights of its citizens are to be everywhere protected. It has never found that the necessary enjoyment of such a peace could be maintained only by a great and threatening array of arms. In common with other nations, it is now more determined than ever to promote peace through friendliness and good will, through mutual understandings and mutual forbearance. We have never practiced the policy of competitive armaments. We have recently committed ourselves by covenants with the other great nations to a limitation of our sea power. As one result of this, our Navy ranks larger, in comparison, than it ever did before. Removing the burden of expense and jealousy, which must always accrue from a keen rivalry, is one of the most effective methods of diminishing that unreasonable hysteria and misunderstanding which are the most potent means of fomenting war. This policy represents a new de-

[216]

parture in the world. It is a thought, an ideal, which has led to an entirely new line of action. It will not be easy to maintain. Some never moved from their old position, some are constantly slipping back to the old ways of thought and the old action of seizing a musket and relying on force. America has taken the lead in this new direction, and that lead America must continue to hold. If we expect others to rely on our fairness and justice we must show that we rely on their fairness and justice.

If we are to judge by past experience, there is much to be hoped for in international relations from frequent conferences and consultations. We have before us the beneficial results of the Washington conference and the various consultations recently held upon European affairs, some of which were in response to our suggestions and in some of which we were active participants. Even the failures can not but be accounted useful and an immeasurable advance over threatened or actual warfare. I am strongly in favor of a continuation of this policy, whenever conditions are such that there is even a promise that practical and favorable results might be secured.

In conformity with the principle that a display of reason rather than a threat of force should be the determining factor in the intercourse among nations, we have long advocated the peaceful settlement of disputes by methods of arbitration and have negotiated many treaties to secure that result. The same considerations should lead to our adherence to the Permanent Court of International Justice. Where great principles are involved, where great movements are under way which promise much for the welfare of humanity by reason of the very fact that many other nations have given such movements their actual support, we ought not to withhold our own sanction because of any small and inessential difference, but only upon the ground of the most important and compelling fundamental reasons. We can not barter away our independence or our sovereignty, but we ought to engage in no refinements of logic, no sophistries, and no subterfuges, to argue away the undoubted duty of this country by reason of the might of its numbers, the power of its resources, and its position of leadership in the world, actively and comprehensively to signify its approval and to bear its full share of the responsibility of a candid and disinterested attempt at the establishment of a tribunal for the administration of evenhanded justice between nation and nation. The weight of our enormous influence must be cast upon the side of a reign not of force but of law and trial, not by battle but by reason.

We have never any wish to interfere in the political conditions of any other countries. Especially are we determined not to become implicated in the political controversies of the Old World. With a great deal of hesitation, we have responded to appeals for help to maintain order, protect life and property, and establish responsible government in some of the small countries of the Western Hemisphere. Our private citizens have advanced large sums of money to assist in the necessary financing and relief of the Old World. We have not failed, nor shall we fail to respond, whenever necessary to mitigate human suffering and assist in the rehabilitation of distressed nations. These, too, are requirements which must be met by reason of our vast powers and the place we hold in the world.

Some of the best thought of mankind has long been seeking for a formula for permanent peace. Undoubtedly the clarification of the principles of international law would be helpful, and the efforts of scholars to prepare such a work for adoption by the various

The "various consultations" Coolidge mentioned were: the Second Central American Conference which met at Washington on December 4, 1922, to draw up a treaty of neutrality between Nicaragua and Honduras and set up a Central American court of justice for use by all Central American republics; the World War Foreign Debt Commission which attempted to recover, with indifferent success, the war loans and reparations due the United States; and increasing American participation in League of Nations conferences.

Both Harding and Coolidge had favored participation in the League of Nations and the Permanent Court of International Justice, which eventually became known as the World Court. For a variety of reasons, however, the United States would never join this body.

nations should have our sympathy and support. Much may be hoped for from the earnest studies of those who advocate the outlawing of aggressive war. But all these plans and preparations, these treaties and covenants, will not of themselves be adequate. One of the greatest dangers to peace lies in the economic pressure to which people find themselves subjected. One of the most practical things to be done in the world is to seek arrangements under which such pressure may be removed, so that opportunity may be renewed and hope may be revived. There must be some assurance that effort and endeavor will be followed by success and prosperity. In the making and financing of such adjustments there is not only an opportunity, but a real duty, for America to respond with her counsel and her resources. Conditions must be provided under which people can make a living and work out of their difficulties. But there is another element, more important than all, without which there can not be the slightest hope of a permanent peace. That element lies in the heart of humanity. Unless the desire for peace be cherished there, unless this fundamental and only natural source of brotherly love be cultivated to its highest degree, all artificial efforts will be in vain. Peace will come when there is realization that only under a reign of law, based on righteousness and supported by the religious conviction of the brotherhood of man, can there be any hope of a complete and satisfying life. Parchment will fail, the sword will fail, it is only the spiritual nature of man that can be triumphant.

It seems altogether probable that we can contribute most to these important objects by maintaining our position of political detachment and independence. We are not identified with any Old World interest. This position should be made more and more clear in our relations with all foreign countries. We are at peace with all of them. Our program is never to oppress, but always to assist. But while we do justice to others, we must require that justice be done to us. With us a treaty of peace means peace, and a treaty of amity means amity. We have made great contributions to the settlement of contentious differences in both Europe and Asia. But there is a very definite point beyond which we can not go. We can only help those who help themselves. Mindful of these limitations, the one great duty that stands out requires us to use our enormous powers to trim the balance of the world.

While we can look with a great deal of pleasure upon what we have done abroad, we must remember that our continued success in that direction depends upon what we do at home. Since its very outset, it has been found necessary to conduct our Government by means of political parties. That system would not have survived from generation to generation if it had not been fundamentally sound and provided the best instrumentalities for the most complete expression of the popular will. It is not necessary to claim that it has always worked perfectly. It is enough to know that nothing better has been devised. No one would deny that there should be full and free expression and an opportunity for independence of action within the party. There is no salvation in a narrow and bigoted partisanship. But if there is to be responsible party government, the party label must be something more than a mere device for securing office. Unless those who are elected under the same party designation are willing to assume sufficient responsibility and exhibit sufficient loyalty and coherence, so that they can cooperate with each other in the support of the broad general principles of the party

Coolidge was never noted for his eloquence, but this passage dealing with peace could well rank with the most profound observations of any of his peers.

Still another inaugural first for Coolidge. Here, in a sentence, he put into words the opening wedge against Washington's and Jefferson's long-standing policy of no entangling alliances with foreign powers. For the unspoken corollary to Coolidge's pledge "to use our enormous powers to trim the balance of the world" could only mean eventual entanglements the world over. We are so committed today.

[218]

platform, the election is merely a mockery, no decision is made at the polls, and there is no representation of the popular will. Common honesty and good faith with the people who support a party at the polls require that party, when it enters office, to assume the control of that portion of the Government to which it has been elected. Any other course is bad faith and a violation of the party pledges.

When the country has bestowed its confidence upon a party by making it a majority in the Congress, it has a right to expect such unity of action as will make the party majority an effective instrument of government. This administration has come into power with a very clear and definite mandate from the people. The expression of the popular will in favor of maintaining our constitutional guarantees was overwhelming and decisive. There was a manifestation of such faith in the integrity of the courts that we can consider that issue rejected for some time to come. Likewise, the policy of public ownership of railroads and certain electric utilities met with unmistakable defeat. The people declared that they wanted their rights to have not a political but a judicial determination, and their independence and freedom continued and supported by having the ownership and control of their property, not in the Government, but in their own hands. As they always do when they have a fair chance, the people demonstrated that they are sound and are determined to have a sound government.

When we turn from what was rejected to inquire what was accepted, the policy that stands out with the greatest clearness is that of economy in public expenditure with reduction and reform of taxation. The principle involved in this effort is that of conservation. The resources of this country are almost beyond computation. No mind can comprehend them. But the cost of our combined governments is likewise almost beyond definition. Not only those who are now making their tax returns, but those who meet the enhanced cost of existence in their monthly bills, know by hard experience what this great burden is and what it does. No matter what others may want, these people want a drastic economy. They are opposed to waste. They know that extravagance lengthens the hours and diminishes the rewards of their labor. I favor the policy of economy, not because I wish to save money, but because I wish to save people. The men and women of this country who toil are the ones who bear the cost of the Government. Every dollar that we carelessly waste means that their life will be so much the more meager. Every dollar that we prudently save means that their life will be so much the more abundant. Economy is idealism in its most practical form.

If extravagance were not reflected in taxation, and through taxation both directly and indirectly injuriously affecting the people, it would not be of so much consequence. The wisest and soundest method of solving our tax problem is through economy. Fortunately, of all the great nations this country is best in a position to adopt that simple remedy. We do not any longer need war-time revenues. The collection of any taxes which are not absolutely required, which do not beyond reasonable doubt contribute to the public welfare, is only a species of legalized larceny. Under this Republic the rewards of industry belong to those who earn them. The only constitutional tax is the tax which ministers to public necessity. The property of the country belongs to the people of the country. Their title is absolute. They do not support any privileged class; they do not need to maintain great military forces; they ought not to be

The Democratic platform favored the items ticked off by Coolidge. Using his huge margin of popular votes as a yardstick Coolidge felt he had a clear mandate in the widespread rejection of the Democratic platform and acceptance of the Republican campaign planks, the most important of which was economy—or so Coolidge thought. Consequently he pared and cut government expenditures until income exceeded expenditures. To his surprise he found his frugality was ignored by the masses and cursed by the classes who stood to benefit by larger Federal spending. For the prosperity boom and the big bull market of the late twenties made thrift and living within one's income go out of style. As a consequence, Republicans saw many Democrats seated in Congress in the 1926 mid-term election.

True to his promise outlined here Coolidge would push through the Revenue Act of 1926. This bill reduced personal income taxes and curtailed or abolished many surtaxes and nuisance taxes.

The "restrictive immigration" mentioned here referred to the Immigration Act of May 19, 1921. The Act introduced a quota system, which limited immigration in any year to 3% of the total of each nationality already in the United States as disclosed by the 1910 census.

burdened with a great array to public employees. They are not required to make any contribution to Government expenditures except that which they voluntarily assess upon themselves through the action of their own representatives. Whenever taxes become burdensome a remedy can be applied by the people; but if they do not act for themselves, no one can be very successful in acting for them.

The time is arriving when we can have further tax reduction, when, unless we wish to hamper the people in their right to earn a living, we must have tax reform. The method of raising revenue ought not to impede the transaction of business; it ought to encourage it. I am opposed to extremely high rates, because they produce little or no revenue, because they are bad for the country, and, finally, because they are wrong. We can not finance the country, we can not improve social conditions, through any system of injustice, even if we attempt to inflict it upon the rich. Those who suffer the most harm will be the poor. This country believes in prosperity. It is absurd to suppose that it is envious of those who are already prosperous. The wise and correct course to follow in taxation and all other economic legislation is not to destroy those who have already secured success but to create conditions under which every one will have a better chance to be successful. The verdict of the country has been given on this question. That verdict stands. We shall do well to heed it.

These questions involve moral issues. We need not concern ourselves much about the rights of property if we will faithfully observe the rights of persons. Under our institutions their rights are supreme. It is not property but the right to hold property, both great and small, which our Constitution guarantees. All owners of property are charged with a service. These rights and duties have been revealed, through the conscience of society, to have a divine sanction. The very stability of our society rests upon production and conservation. For individuals or for governments to waste and squander their resources is to deny these rights and disregard these obligations. The result of economic dissipation to a nation is always moral decay.

These policies of better international understandings, greater economy, and lower taxes have contributed largely to peaceful and prosperous industrial relations. Under the helpful influences of restrictive immigration and a protective tariff, employment is plentiful, the rate of pay is high, and wage earners are in a state of contentment seldom before seen. Our transportation systems have been gradually recovering and have been able to meet all the requirements of the service. Agriculture has been very slow in reviving, but the price of cereals at last indicates that the day of its deliverance is at hand.

We are not without our problems, but our most important problem is not to secure new advantages but to maintain those which we already possess. Our system of government made up of three separate and independent departments, our divided sovereignty composed of Nation and State, the matchless wisdom that is enshrined in our Constitution, all these need constant effort and tireless vigilance for their protection and support.

In a republic the first rule for the guidance of the citizen is obedience to law. Under a despotism the law may be imposed upon the subject. He has no voice in its making, no influence in its administration, it does not represent him. Under a free government the citizen makes his own laws, chooses his own administrators, which do represent him. Those who want their rights respected under the Constitution and the law ought to set the example themselves of observing the Constitution and the law. While there may be those of high intelligence who violate the law at times, the barbarian and the defective always violate it. Those who disregard the rules of society are not exhibiting a superior intelligence, are not promoting freedom and independence, are not following the path of civilization, but are displaying the traits of ignorance, of servitude, of savagery, and treading the way that leads back to the jungle.

The essence of a republic is representative government. Our Congress represents the people and the States. In all legislative affairs it is the natural collaborator with the President. In spite of all the criticism which often falls to its lot, I do not hesitate to say that there is no more independent and effective legislative body in the world. It is, and should be, jealous of its prerogative. I welcome its cooperation, and expect to share with it not only the responsibility, but the credit, for our common effort to secure beneficial legislation.

These are some of the principles which America represents. We have not by any means put them fully into practice, but we have strongly signified our belief in them. The encouraging feature of our country is not that it has reached its destination, but that it has overwhelmingly expressed its determination to proceed in the right direction. It is true that we could, with profit, be less sectional and more national in our thought. It would be well if we could replace much that is only a false and ignorant prejudice with a true and enlightened pride of race. But the last election showed that appeals to class and nationality had little effect. We were all found loyal to a common citizenship. The fundamental precept of liberty is toleration. We can not permit any inquisition either within or without the law or apply any religious test to the holding of office. The mind of America must be forever free.

It is in such contemplations, my fellow countrymen, which are not exhaustive but only representative, that I find ample warrant for satisfaction and encouragement. We should not let the much that is to do obscure the much which has been done. The past and present show faith and hope and courage fully justified. Here stands our country, an example of tranquillity at home, a patron of tranquillity abroad. Here stands its Government, aware of its might but obedient to its conscience. Here it will continue to stand, seeking peace and prosperity, solicitous for the welfare of the wage earner, promoting enterprise, developing waterways and natural resources, attentive to the intuitive counsel of womanhood, encouraging education, desiring the advancement of religion, supporting the cause of justice and honor among the nations. America seeks no earthly empire built on blood and force. No ambition, no temptation, lures her to thought of foreign dominions. The legions which she sends forth are armed, not with the sword, but with the cross. The higher state to which she seeks the allegiance of all mankind is not of human, but of divine origin. She cherishes no purpose save to merit the favor of Almighty God.

In bringing up the question of prejudice Coolidge had in mind the tremendously expanded efforts of the Ku Klux Klan, which had been revived from virtual extinction to a membership of between four and five million in the twenties. The Klan's growth was due to fear of foreign entanglements such as participation in the League of Nations and aversion to bolshevism—or communism, as it was beginning to be called.

This brief reference to "the intuitive counsel of womanhood" was Coolidge's way of paying lip service to the American woman's right to vote, guaranteed by the nineteenth amendment. The influence of women in politics was at first a matter of amusement and even ridicule to male voters. But in later elections more and more attention would be paid to influencing feminine voters, when politicians realized woman's suffrage was here to stay.

THE PRESIDENT

Herbert Clark Hoover's early years as a mining engineer were spent in Europe, Asia, Africa, and Australia, as well as in this country. Placed in charge of distributing food to the victims of China's Boxer Rebellion in 1900, Hoover was called on again during and after World War I to serve on various committees engaged in relief work. He was named Secretary of Commerce by Harding and continued to serve under Coolidge until his election to the presidency in 1928.

THE NATION

On April 14, 1927, Bert Acosta and Clarence Chamberlin set a nonstop endurance flight record of 51 hours and 11 minutes. May 1, America's Pan-American Goodwill flyers returned to Bolling Field from a 20,470-mile journey around South America. May 20, Charles A. Lindbergh landed at Le Bourget Field, Paris, in his "Spirit of St. Louis," after flying solo from New York—a distance of 3,610 miles—in 33 hours, 29 minutes, 30 seconds. June 4 and 5, Clarence Chamberlin and Charles A. Levine flew nonstop from New York to Germany.

The business picture was briefly sketched by Secretary of Commerce Herbert Hoover on New Year's Day of 1927 when he said: "No one will deny that 1926 has shown the highest total production and consumption of industrial commodities of any year in the history of the United States. The United States will enter the New Year with the whole nation better fed, better housed, and better clothed than any other nation." Optimistic statements such as these coupled with an outstanding record made Hoover the Republican party's choice in the election of 1928, after Coolidge shrugged off the nomination with his now-famous handwritten note: "I do not choose to run for President in nineteen hundred and twenty-eight."

In the election of 1928 Republican Hoover polled 21,391,381 popular votes (444 electoral). Democrat Alfred E. Smith received 15,016,443 popular votes (87 electoral). Totals for other parties were: Socialist Norman Thomas, 267,835; the Workers party candidate, William Z. Foster, 21,181; Socialist Laborite Verne L. Reynolds, 21,603; Prohibitionist William F. Varney, 20,106; and Farmer-Laborite Frank E. Webb, 6,390. Charles V. Curtis was elected vice-president.

THE WORLD

In October of 1925 representatives of Great Britain, France, Germany, Italy, Belgium, Poland, and Czechoslovakia met in Locarno and agreed to European peace treaties. By these Locarno pacts Germany was sanctioned admission to the League of Nations. Wireless telephone communications were established between New York and London. In October, 1926, Queen Marie was given a royal welcome on her visit to America. 1927 was noted for its aviation "firsts," which focused the world's attention on the United States.

IN PREPARING YOUR INAUGURAL ADDRESS you feel yourself to be in your own words "somewhat hampered by the fact that I was succeeding a President of my own party, a man for whom I had the warmest personal feeling, for whose integrity I had the highest respect, and to whom I was indebted for many kindnesses." You realize you cannot in good taste say anything indicating certain differences between you and former President Coolidge, so you confine yourself to paying tribute to your predecessor wherever you can honestly do so. You ignore the steady rain that soaks you to the skin, as you stand bareheaded on the speaker's platform in front of the Capitol and begin to deliver your long and tactfully phrased address . . . .

Herbert Hoover

[1929–1933]

INAUGURAL ADDRESS, MARCH 4, 1929

Capitol Steps, Washington, D.C.

My Countrymen:

This occasion is not alone the administration of the most sacred oath which can be assumed by an American citizen. It is a dedication and consecration under God to the highest office in service of our people. I assume this trust in the humility of knowledge that only through the guidance of Almighty Providence can I hope to discharge its ever-increasing burdens.

It is in keeping with tradition throughout our history that I should express simply and directly the opinions which I hold concerning some of the matters of present importance.

Our Progress

If we survey the situation of our Nation both at home and abroad, we find many satisfactions; we find some causes for concern. We have emerged from the losses of the Great War and the reconstruction following it with increased virility and strength. From this strength we have contributed to the recovery and progress of the world. What America has done has given renewed hope and courage to all who have faith in government by the people. In the large view, we have reached a higher degree of comfort and security than ever existed before in the history of the world. Through liberation from widespread poverty we have reached a higher degree of individual freedom than ever before. The devotion to and concern for our institutions are deep and sincere. We are steadily building a new race—a new civilization great in its own attainments. The influence and high purposes of our Nation are respected among the peoples of the world. We aspire to distinction in the world, but to a distinction based upon confidence in our sense of justice as well as our accomplishments within our own borders and in our own lives. For wise guidance in this great period of recovery the Nation is deeply indebted to Calvin Coolidge.

But all this majestic advance should not obscure the constant dangers from which self-government must be safeguarded. The strong man must at all times be alert to the attack of insidious disease.

The Failure of Our System of Criminal Justice

The most malign of all these dangers to-day is disregard and disobedience of law. Crime is increasing. Confidence in rigid and

Hoover's optimism was typical of the general feeling throughout the nation. The bull market of 1929 was entering its final, frenzied state. But the end would come on Black Thursday, October 24, 1929, when 16,410,030 shares would be traded as the bottom dropped out of the market, and the nation was plunged into the seemingly bottomless pit of depression.

Whether or not Coolidge deserved this recognition is debatable. Due to his strict economy the budget had been balanced, payments had been made on the nation's war debt, and business and industry had enjoyed an unprecedented expansion. But along with these benefits had come evils. And Hoover carefully pinpointed the sore spots in the economy, outlining proposed remedies in the remainder of his address.

Hoover's first act in the reform of law enforcement would be to appoint William D. Mitchell of Minnesota attorney general, and work with him to raise the standards of judges and prosecuting officers. Under the careful scrutiny of both Hoover and Mitchell only the best-qualified men received appointments, among them Charles E. Hughes, who was nominated for Chief Justice of the Supreme Court.

The Federal Bureau of Investigation was authorized by the Department of Justice Appropriation Act of July 26, 1908. Originally called the Bureau of Investigation, the duties of this body were confined only to the Justice Department, until J. Edgar Hoover became Director in 1924. In 1933 Congress endowed the Bureau with greater powers; and on July 1, 1935, the organization became the Federal Bureau of Investigation, when it was given authority to investigate alleged violations of Federal laws, including sabotage, treason, and conspiracy.

Hoover's plea for public support of the eighteenth amendment was ignored by the majority, who refused to abide by the law and continued to patronize bootleggers and speak-easies of the metropolitan areas and to vie for local home-brew honors elsewhere. With such widespread flouting of an established law it was not surprising that local law enforcement in many cities crumbled before the avalanche of pay-off money in the hands of organized racketeers. Despite the number of prohibition convictions, about 80,000 in 1932, for every violator convicted two others seemed to come into being.

speedy justice is decreasing. I am not prepared to believe that this indicates any decay in the moral fiber of the American people. I am not prepared to believe that it indicates an impotence of the Federal Government to enforce its laws.

It is only in part due to the additional burdens imposed upon our judicial system by the eighteenth amendment. The problem is much wider than that. Many influences had increasingly complicated and weakened our law enforcement organization long before the adoption of the eighteenth amendment.

To reestablish the vigor and effectiveness of law enforcement we must critically consider the entire Federal machinery of justice, the redistribution of its functions, the simplification of its procedure, the provision of additional special tribunals, the better selection of juries, and the more effective organization of our agencies of investigation and prosecution that justice may be sure and that it may be swift. While the authority of the Federal Government extends to but part of our vast system of national, State, and local justice, yet the standards which the Federal Government establishes have the most profound influence upon the whole structure.

We are fortunate in the ability and integrity of our Federal judges and attorneys. But the system which these officers are called upon to administer is in many respects ill adapted to present-day conditions. Its intricate and involved rules of procedure have become the refuge of both big and little criminals. There is a belief abroad that by invoking technicalities, subterfuge, and delay, the ends of justice may be thwarted by those who can pay the cost.

Reform, reorganization and strengthening of our whole judicial and enforcement system both in civil and criminal sides have been advocated for years by statesmen, judges, and bar associations. First steps toward that end should not longer be delayed. Rigid and expeditious justice is the first safeguard of freedom, the basis of all ordered liberty, the vital force of progress. It must not come to be in our Republic that it can be defeated by the indifference of the citizen, by exploitation of the delays and entanglements of the law, or by combinations of criminals. Justice must not fail because the agencies of enforcement are either delinquent or inefficiently organized. To consider these evils, to find their remedy, is the most sore necessity of our times.

Enforcement of the Eighteenth Amendment

Of the undoubted abuses which have grown up under the eighteenth amendment, part are due to the causes I have just mentioned; but part are due to the failure of some States to accept their share of responsibiliy for concurrent enforcement and to the failure of many State and local officials to accept the obligation under their oath of office zealously to enforce the laws. With the failures from these many causes has come a dangerous expansion in the criminal elements who have found enlarged opportunities in dealing in illegal liquor.

But a large responsibility rests directly upon our citizens. There would be little traffic in illegal liquor if only criminals patronized it. We must awake to the fact that this patronage from large numbers of law-abiding citizens is supplying the rewards and stimulating crime.

I have been selected by you to execute and enforce the laws of the country. I propose to do so to the extent of my own abilities, but the measure of success that the Government shall attain will depend upon the moral support which you, as citizens, extend. The duty of citizens to support the laws of the land is coequal with the duty of their Government to enforce the laws which exist. No greater national service can be given by men and women of good will—who, I know, are not unmindful of the responsibilities of citizenship—than that they should, by their example, assist in stamping out crime and outlawry by refusing participation in and condemning all transactions with illegal liquor. Our whole system of self-government will crumble either if officials elect what laws they will enforce or citizens elect what laws they will support. The worst evil of disregard for some law is that it destroys respect for all law. For our citizens to patronize the violation of a particular law on the ground that they are opposed to it is destructive of the very basis of all that protection of life, of homes and property which they rightly claim under other laws. If citizens do not like a law, their duty as honest men and women is to discourage its violation; their right is openly to work for its repeal.

To those of criminal mind there can be no appeal but vigorous enforcement of the law. Fortunately they are but a small percentage of our people. Their activities must be stopped.

A National Investigation

I propose to appoint a national commission for a searching investigation of the whole structure of our Federal system of jurisprudence, to include the method of enforcement of the eighteenth amendment and the causes of abuse under it. Its purpose will be to make such recommendations for reorganization of the administration of Federal laws and court procedure as may be found desirable. In the meantime it is essential that a large part of the enforcement activities be transferred from the Treasury Department to the Department of Justice as a beginning of more effective organization.

The Relation of Government to Business

The election has again confirmed the determination of the American people that regulation of private enterprise and not Government ownership or operation is the course rightly to be pursued in our relation to business. In recent years we have established a differentiation in the whole method of business regulation between the industries which produce and distribute commodities on the one hand and public utilities on the other. In the former, our laws insist upon effective competition; in the latter, because we substantially confer a monopoly by limiting competition, we must regulate their services and rates. The rigid enforcement of the laws applicable to both groups is the very base of equal opportunity and freedom from domination for all our people, and it is just as essential for the stability and prosperity of business itself as for the protection of the public at large. Such regulation should be extended by the Federal Government within the limitations of the Constitution and only when the individual States are without power to protect their citizens through their own authority. On the other hand, we should be fearless when the authority rests only in the Federal Government.

Cooperation by the Government

The larger purpose of our economic thought should be to establish more firmly stability and security of business and employment and thereby remove poverty still further from our borders. Our

Hoover's analysis of the problem of enforcing the eighteenth amendment had resulted in the conclusion that Treasury agents were unable to do the job alone and needed help. By increasing J. Edgar Hoover's powers and giving his Bureau the responsibility of bringing liquor-dealing gangsters to justice much progress was made. But a thirsting nation soon clamored for repeal of the obnoxious law. Enforcement had cut to a trickle what used to be a flood of illicit liquor and beer. Repeal would come in 1933, with 3.2 beer permitted by April and hard liquor made legal by December.

people have in recent years developed a new-found capacity for cooperation among themselves to effect high purposes in public welfare. It is an advance toward the highest conception of self-government. Self-government does not and should not imply the use of political agencies alone. Progress is born of cooperation in the community—not from governmental restraints. The Government should assist and encourage these movements of collective self-help by itself cooperating with them. Business has by cooperation made great progress in the advancement of service, in stability, in regularity of employment and in the correction of its own abuses. Such progress, however, can continue only so long as business manifests its respect for law.

There is an equally important field of cooperation by the Federal Government with the multitude of agencies, State, municipal and private, in the systematic development of those processes which directly affect public health, recreation, education, and the home. We have need further to perfect the means by which Government can be adapted to human service.

Education

Although education is primarily a responsibility of the States and local communities, and rightly so, yet the Nation as a whole is vitally concerned in its development everywhere to the highest standards and to complete universality. Self-government can succeed only through an instructed electorate. Our objective is not simply to overcome illiteracy. The Nation has marched far beyond that. The more complex the problems of the Nation become, the greater is the need for more and more advanced instruction. Moreover, as our numbers increase and as our life expands with science and invention, we must discover more and more leaders for every walk of life. We can not hope to succeed in directing this increasingly complex civilization unless we can draw all the talent of leadership from the whole people. One civilization after another has been wrecked upon the attempt to secure sufficient leadership from a single group or class. If we would prevent the growth of class distinctions and would constantly refresh our leadership with the ideals of our people, we must draw constantly from the general mass. The full opportunity for every boy and girl to rise through the selective processes of education can alone secure to us this leadership.

Public Health

In public health the discoveries of science have opened a new era. Many sections of our country and many groups of our citizens suffer from diseases the eradication of which are mere matters of administration and moderate expenditure. Public health service should be as fully organized and as universally incorporated into our governmental system as is public education. The returns are a thousand fold in economic benefits, and infinitely more in reduction of suffering and promotion of human happiness.

World Peace

The United States fully accepts the profound truth that our own progress, prosperity and peace are interlocked with the progress, prosperity and peace of all humanity. The whole world is at peace. The dangers to a continuation of this peace to-day are largely the fear and suspicion which still haunt the world. No suspicion or fear can be rightly directed toward our country.

In attempting to provide better education and health for the nation—and particularly for the youth of America—in each year of his administration Hoover would increase appropriations for the children's and women's bureaus in the Department of Labor. He also would help draft and support a bill to provide Federal aid to states, so that they could build up rural health agencies for children. This measure eventually died in the Senate.

Later the Roosevelt administration, with a Democratic majority in both houses, would be able to enact measures providing Federal aid for the protection and health of the nation's children.

In the opening sentence of this section of his address Hoover advanced a philosophy which is the cornerstone of today's United Nations.

[226]

Those who have a true understanding of America know that we have no desire for territorial expansion, for economic or other domination of other peoples. Such purposes are repugnant to our ideals of human freedom. Our form of government is ill adapted to the responsibilities which inevitably follow permanent limitation of the independence of other peoples. Superficial observers seem to find no destiny for our abounding increase in population, in wealth and power except that of imperialism. They fail to see that the American people are engrossed in the building for themselves of a new economic system, a new social system, a new political system—all of which are characterized by aspirations of freedom of opportunity and thereby are the negation of imperialism. They fail to realize that because of our abounding prosperity our youth are pressing more and more into our institutions of learning; that our people are seeking a larger vision through art, literature, science, and travel; that they are moving toward stronger moral and spiritual life—that from these things our sympathies are broadening beyond the bounds of our Nation and race toward their true expression in a real brotherhood of man. They fail to see that the idealism of America will lead it to no narrow or selfish channel, but inspire it to do its full share as a nation toward the advancement of civilization. It will do that not by mere declaration but by taking a practical part in supporting all useful international undertakings. We not only desire peace with the world, but to see peace maintained throughout the world. We wish to advance the reign of justice and reason toward the extinction of force.

The recent treaty for the renunciation of war as an instrument of national policy sets an advanced standard in our conception of the relations of nations. Its acceptance should pave the way to greater limitation of armament, the offer of which we sincerely extend to the world. But its full realization also implies a greater and greater perfection in the instrumentalities for pacific settlement of controversies between nations. In the creation and use of these instrumentalities we should support every sound method of conciliation, arbitration, and judicial settlement. American statesmen were among the first to propose and they have constantly urged upon the world, the establishment of a tribunal for the settlement of controversies of a justiciable character. The Permanent Court of International Justice in its major purpose is thus peculiarly identified with American ideals and with American statesmanship. No more potent instrumentality for this purpose has ever been conceived and no other is practicable of establishment. The reservations placed upon our adherence should not be misinterpreted. The United States seeks by these reservations no special privilege or advantage but only to clarify our relation to advisory opinions and other matters which are subsidiary to the major purpose of the court. The way should, and I believe will, be found by which we may take our proper place in a movement so fundamental to the progress of peace.

Our people have determined that we should make no political engagements such as membership in the League of Nations, which may commit us in advance as a nation to become involved in the settlements of controversies between other countries. They adhere to the belief that the independence of America from such obligations increases its ability and availability for service in all fields of human progress.

I have lately returned from a journey among our sister Republics of the Western Hemisphere. I have received unbounded hos-

In his Memoirs Hoover stated that his over-all hope was "to pull the people of the United States out of the extreme mental and spiritual isolationism which for years had made impossible a proper American participation in the constructive building of peace in the world." In this segment of his address he attempted to further this hope by speaking of our broadening sympathies, which were developing into "a real brotherhood of man." But world-wide depression would crush Hoover's hopes before his term had expired.

The Kellogg-Briand Pact of 1928 grew out of an agreement for outlawing war first proposed by French Foreign Minister Aristide Briand to Secretary of State Frank B. Kellogg. Kellogg helped to extend the treaty to include all nations. On August 27, 1928, the pact was signed in Paris by 15 nations, condemning "recourse to war for the solution of international controversies." 62 nations ultimately ratified the pact, but it was soon proved virtually meaningless by the rash of undeclared wars: Japan's invasion of Manchuria in 1931, Italy's invasion of Ethiopia in 1935, and Germany's invasion of Austria in 1938.

During the four months between election and inauguration President-elect and Mrs. Hoover made a journey of about six weeks to Latin American countries to build up relations between our "good neighbors." This policy would be continued by Hoover's successor.

Even as Hoover delivered this plea for peace there were forces in other nations working to transmute a virtually universal desire for peace into an equally widespread lust for war.

Hoover's hope that the Democrats would put country above party would soon be buried. Bill after bill would be introduced by the Republicans only to be voted down by the majority.

Hoover would carry out this pledge by calling a special session of Congress in April, 1929. As a result the Agricultural Marketing Act of June 15, 1929, was passed, authorizing the creation of a Federal Farm Board, with a revolving fund of $500,-000,000 to provide low-interest loans to farm agencies.

pitality and courtesy as their expression of friendliness to our country. We are held by particular bonds of sympathy and common interest with them. They are each of them building a racial character and a culture which is an impressive contribution to human progress. We wish only for the maintenance of their independence, the growth of their stability, and their prosperity. While we have had wars in the Western Hemisphere, yet on the whole the record is in encouraging contrast with that of other parts of the world. Fortunately the New World is largely free from the inheritances of fear and distrust which have so troubled the Old World. We should keep it so.

It is impossible, my countrymen, to speak of peace without profound emotion. In thousands of homes in America, in millions of homes around the world, there are vacant chairs. It would be a shameful confession of our unworthiness if it should develop that we have abandoned the hope for which all these men died. Surely civilization is old enough, surely mankind is mature enough so that we ought in our own lifetime to find a way to permanent peace. Abroad, to west and east, are nations whose sons mingled their blood with the blood of our sons on the battle fields. Most of these nations have contributed to our race, to our culture, our knowledge, and our progress. From one of them we derive our very language and from many of them much of the genius of our institutions. Their desire for peace is as deep and sincere as our own.

Peace can be contributed to by respect for our ability in defense. Peace can be promoted by the limitation of arms and by the creation of the instrumentalities for peaceful settlement of controversies. But it will become a reality only through self-restraint and active effort in friendliness and helpfulness. I covet for this administration a record of having further contributed to advance the cause of peace.

Party Responsibilities

In our form of democracy the expression of the popular will can be effected only through the instrumentality of political parties. We maintain party government not to promote intolerant partisanship but because opportunity must be given for expression of the popular will, and organization provided for the execution of its mandates and for accountability of government to the people. It follows that the government both in the executive and the legislative branches must carry out in good faith the platforms upon which the party was intrusted with power. But the government is that of the whole people; the party is the instrument through which policies are determined and men chosen to bring them into being. The animosities of elections should have no place in our Government, for government must concern itself alone with the common weal.

Special Session of the Congress

Action upon some of the proposals upon which the Republican Party was returned to power, particularly further agricultural relief and limited changes in the tariff, cannot in justice to our farmers, our labor, and our manufacturers be postponed. I shall therefore request a special session of Congress for the consideration of these two questions. I shall deal with each of them upon the assembly of the Congress.

Other Mandates From the Election

It appears to me that the more important further mandates from the recent election were the maintenance of the integrity of the Constitution; the vigorous enforcement of the laws; the continuance of economy in public expenditure; the continued regulation of business to prevent domination in the community; the denial of ownership or operation of business by the Government in competition with its citizens; the avoidance of policies which would involve us in the controversies of foreign nations; the more effective reorganization of the departments of the Federal Government; the expansion of public works; and the promotion of welfare activities affecting education and the home.

These were the more tangible determinations of the election, but beyond them was the confidence and belief of the people that we would not neglect the support of the embedded ideals and aspirations of America. These ideals and aspirations are the touchstones upon which the day-to-day administration and legislative acts of government must be tested. More than this, the Government must, so far as lies within its proper powers, give leadership to the realization of these ideals and to the fruition of these aspirations. No one can adequately reduce these things of the spirit to phrases or to a catalogue of definitions. We do know what the attainments of these ideals should be: The preservation of self-government and its full foundations in local government; the perfection of justice whether in economic or in social fields; the maintenance of ordered liberty; the denial of domination by any group or class; the building up and preservation of equality of opportunity; the stimulation of initiative and individuality; absolute integrity in public affairs; the choice of officials for fitness to office; the direction of economic progress toward prosperity for the further lessening of poverty; the freedom of public opinion; the sustaining of education and of the advancement of knowledge; the growth of religious spirit and the tolerance of all faiths; the strengthening of the home; the advancement of peace.

There is no short road to the realization of these aspirations. Ours is a progressive people, but with a determination that progress must be based upon the foundation of experience. Ill-considered remedies for our faults bring only penalties after them. But if we hold the faith of the men in our mighty past who created these ideals, we shall leave them heightened and strengthened for our children.

Conclusion

This is not the time and place for extended discussion. The questions before our country are problems of progress to higher standards; they are not the problems of degeneration. They demand thought and they serve to quicken the conscience and enlist our sense of responsibility for their settlement. And that responsibility rests upon you, my countrymen, as much as upon those of us who have been selected for office.

Ours is a land rich in resources; stimulating in its glorious beauty; filled with millions of happy homes; blessed with comfort and opportunity. In no nation are the institutions of progress more advanced. In no nation are the fruits of accomplishment more secure. In no nation is the government more worthy of respect. No country is more loved by its people. I have an abiding faith in their capacity, integrity and high purpose. I have no fears for the future of our country. It is bright with hope.

In the presence of my countrymen, mindful of the solemnity of this occasion, knowing what the task means and the responsibility which it involves, I beg your tolerance, your aid, and your cooperation. I ask the help of Almighty God in this service to my country to which you have called me.

Hoover's successor, Roosevelt, was to be fully supported in both houses. During the first hundred days of Roosevelt's administration every New Deal measure would be passed without opposition.

[229]

THE PRESIDENT

Franklin Delano Roosevelt came to the White House at the height of the nation's economic crisis. A graduate of Harvard, Roosevelt had served in the New York state senate, where his campaign for Woodrow Wilson's election in 1912 had won him an appointment as Assistant Secretary of the Navy. A year after his defeat as vice-presidential candidate in 1920 Roosevelt was stricken with polio and dropped out of the public eye, until he nominated Alfred E. Smith for the presidency in 1924 and again in 1928. He went on to win the governorship of New York, and his success there culminated in nomination and subsequent election to the presidency.

THE NATION

In the stock market crash of October, 1929, President Hoover's administration received a blow from which it never recovered. 1930 saw a population count of 122,775,046 registered by the census takers. Although crippled by polio Franklin D. Roosevelt was reëlected Governor of New York, and began to fight back at the deepening depression by creating jobs within the state for the growing number of unemployed. 1930 was a bad year, 1931 was worse; but 1932, an election year, was black, indeed: 13,000,000 men were unemployed and a "bonus army" marched on Washington to plead for help from the president.

Despite Hoover's plans for government spending on public works, the establishment of the Reconstruction Finance Corporation, and other measures to ease the unemployment problem the voters clamored for a change of administration. Election returns showed a landslide for Democrat Franklin D. Roosevelt, who polled 22,821,857 popular votes (472 electoral) to Hoover's 15,761,841 popular votes (59 electoral). Socialist Norman Thomas polled 881,951 votes, Communist William Z. Foster 102,785, Socialist Laborite Verne L. Reynolds 33,276, Prohibitionist William D. Upshaw 81,869, Liberty Party William H. Harvey 53,425, and Farmer-Laborite Jacob S. Coxey 7,309. John Nance Garner was elected vice-president.

THE WORLD

Repercussions from the disastrous Wall Street crash in October, 1929, were felt throughout the world. Almost unnoticed was Admiral Richard E. Byrd's flight over the South Pole. And in India a virtual unknown, Mahatma Gandhi, touched off a bitter controversy by demanding India's complete independence from England. On January 21, 1930, King George of England opened the London Naval Conference between the Big Five naval powers: the United States, Great Britain, France, Japan, and Italy. In May Premier Mussolini of Italy announced Italy would build ship for ship with France. In September the Hitler-led Nazi party won a surprising total of 107 seats in the Reichstag. 1931 witnessed Japan's invasion of Manchuria. In Spain King Alfonso XIII fled the throne and a republic was proclaimed. In other countries, hard-pressed by the deepening depression, the gold standard was abandoned and exportation of gold was prohibited. 1932 saw the Japanese gain control of Manchuria, renamed Manchukuo. Henry Pu-yi was installed as puppet Emperor, despite League of Nations' orders to withdraw all troops.

SITTING BY THE FIRE AT HYDE PARK on the night of February 27, 1933, you write the first draft of your address in your own hand, knowing that the nation's banks are closing and business and industry have declined to their lowest levels. And so you seek to dispel the nation's general feeling of helplessness, as well as the fear of the present and of the future which are stifling American initiative. So strongly do you feel the nation needs reassurance against fear itself that you later add the sentence which will become the high point of the address you deliver over a nationwide radio network on a day blessed with sunny skies a quirk of weather which many take as a good omen of brighter days ahead. . . .

Franklin Delano Roosevelt

[1933–1937]

FIRST INAUGURAL ADDRESS, MARCH 4, 1933

Capitol Steps, Washington, D.C.

I am certain that my fellow Americans expect that on my induction into the Presidency I will address them with a candor and a decision which the present situation of our Nation impels. This is preeminently the time to speak the truth, the whole truth, frankly and boldly. Nor need we shrink from honestly facing conditions in our country to-day. This great Nation will endure as it has endured, will revive and will prosper. So, first of all, let me assert my firm belief that the only thing we have to fear is fear itself—nameless, unreasoning, unjustified terror which paralyzes needed efforts to convert retreat into advance. In every dark hour of our national life a leadership of frankness and vigor has met with that understanding and support of the people themselves which is essential to victory. I am convinced that you will again give the support to leadership in these critical days.

Roosevelt's famous reference to fear, which was added to his address after he had completed the first draft, may well have been developed from an entry in Thoreau's Journal. *On September 7, 1851, Thoreau wrote, "Nothing is so much to be feared as fear."*

In such a spirit on my part and on yours we face our common difficulties. They concern, thank God, only material things. Values have shrunken to fantastic levels; taxes have risen; our ability to pay has fallen; government of all kinds is faced by serious curtailment of income; the means of exchange are frozen in the currents of trade; the withered leaves of industrial enterprise lie on every side; farmers find no markets for their produce; the savings of many years in thousands of families are gone.

Roosevelt's imagery was at its superb best in his reference to "the withered leaves of industrial enterprise."

More important, a host of unemployed citizens face the grim problem of existence, and an equally great number toil with little return. Only a foolish optimist can deny the dark realities of the moment.

Yet our distress comes from no failure of substance. We are stricken by no plague of locusts. Compared with the perils which our forefathers conquered because they believed and were not afraid, we have still much to be thankful for. Nature still offers her bounty and human efforts have multiplied it. Plenty is at our door-steps, but a generous use of it languishes in the very sight of the supply. Primarily this is because the rulers of the exchange of mankind's goods have failed, through their own stubbornness and their own incompetence, have admitted their failure, and abdicated. Practices of the unscrupulous money changers stand indicted in the court of public opinion, rejected by the hearts and minds of men.

Here, for the first time, the nation heard the term "money changers" used by a president in reference to a class.

True they have tried, but their efforts have been cast in the pattern of an outworn tradition. Faced by failure of credit they have proposed only the lending of more money. Stripped of the lure of profit by which to induce our people to follow their false leadership, they have resorted to exhortations, pleading tearfully for restored confidence. They know only the rules of a generation of self-seekers. They have no vision, and when there is no vision the people perish.

The money changers have fled from their high seats in the temple of our civilization. We may now restore that temple to the ancient truths. The measure of the restoration lies in the extent to which we apply social values more noble than mere monetary profit.

Happiness lies not in the mere possession of money; it lies in the joy of achievement, in the thrill of creative effort. The joy and moral stimulation of work no longer must be forgotten in the mad chase of evanescent profits. These dark days will be worth all they cost us if they teach us that our true destiny is not to be ministered unto but to minister to ourselves and to our fellow men.

Recognition of the falsity of material wealth as the standard of success goes hand in hand with the abandonment of the false belief that public office and high political position are to be valued only by the standards of pride of place and personal profit; and there must be an end to a conduct in banking and in business which too often has given to a sacred trust the likeness of callous and selfish wrongdoing. Small wonder that confidence languishes, for it thrives only on honesty, on honor, on the sacredness of obligations, on faithful protection, on unselfish performance; without them it can not live.

To the confused men and women of America huddled close to their radio sets these stirring words seemed to possess an irresistible magnetism that at once castigated and comforted, revitalized and reassured, scolded and sympathized.

Restoration calls, however, not for changes in ethics alone. This Nation asks for action, and action now.

Our greatest primary task is to put people to work. This is no unsolvable problem if we face it wisely and courageously. It can be accomplished in part by direct recruiting by the Government itself, treating the task as we would treat the emergency of a war, but at the same time, through this employment, accomplishing greatly needed projects to stimulate and reorganize the use of our natural resources.

Hand in hand with this we must frankly recognize the overbalance of population in our industrial centers and, by engaging on a national scale in a redistribution, endeavor to provide a better use of the land for those best fitted for the land. The task can be helped by definite efforts to raise the values of agricultural products and with this the power to purchase the output of our cities. It can be helped by preventing realistically the tragedy of the growing loss through foreclosure of our small homes and our farms. It can be helped by insistence that the Federal, State, and local governments act forthwith on the demand that their cost be drastically reduced. It can be helped by the unifying of relief activities which to-day are often scattered, uneconomical, and unequal. It can be helped by national planning for and supervision of all forms of transportation and of communications and other utilities which have a definitely public character. There are many ways in which it can be helped, but it can never be helped merely by talking about it. We must act and act quickly.

Finally, in our progress toward a resumption of work we require two safeguards against a return of the evils of the old order; there must be a strict supervision of all banking and credits and investments; there must be an end to speculation with other people's money, and there must be provision for an adequate but sound currency.

There are the lines of attack. I shall presently urge upon a new Congress in special session detailed measures for their fulfillment, and I shall seek the immediate assistance of the several States.

Through this program of action we address ourselves to putting our own national house in order and making income balance outgo. Our international trade relations, though vastly important, are in point of time and necessity secondary to the establishment of a sound national economy. I favor as a practical policy the putting of first things first. I shall spare no effort to restore world trade by international economic readjustment, but the emergency at home can not wait on that accomplishment.

In his address Roosevelt twice referred to an unbalanced budget as reprehensible.

The basic thought that guides these specific means of national recovery is not narrowly nationalistic. It is the insistence, as a first consideration, upon the interdependence of the various elements in and parts of the United States—a recognition of the old and permanently important manifestation of the American spirit of the pioneer. It is the way to recovery. It is the immediate way. It is the strongest assurance that the recovery will endure.

The word recovery, here introduced by Roosevelt to his nationwide radio audience for the first time, would become one of the key words of the Roosevelt era.

In the field of world policy I would dedicate this Nation to the policy of the good neighbor—the neighbor who resolutely respects himself and, because he does so, respects the rights of others—the neighbor who respects his obligations and respects the sanctity of his agreements in and with a world of neighbors.

If I read the temper of our people correctly, we now realize as we have never realized before our interdependence on each other; that we can not merely take but we must give as well; that if we are to go forward, we must move as a trained and loyal army willing to sacrifice for the good of a common discipline, because without such discipline no progress is made, no leadership becomes effective. We are, I know, ready and willing to submit our lives and property to such discipline, because it makes possible a leadership which aims at a larger good. This I propose to offer, pledging that the larger purposes will bind upon us all as a sacred obligation with a unity of duty hitherto evoked only in time of armed strife.

With this pledge taken, I assume unhesitatingly the leadership of this great army of our people dedicated to a disciplined attack upon our common problems.

Action in this image and to this end is feasible under the form of government which we have inherited from our ancestors. Our Constitution is so simple and practical that it is possible always to meet extraordinary needs by changes in emphasis and arrangement without loss of essential form. That is why our constitutional system has proved itself the most superbly enduring political mechanism the modern world has produced. It has met every stress of vast expansion of territory, of foreign wars, of bitter internal strife, of world relations.

It is to be hoped that the normal balance of executive and legislative authority may be wholly adequate to meet the unprecedented task before us. But it may be that an unprecedented demand and need for undelayed action may call for temporary departure from that normal balance of public procedure.

I am prepared under my constitutional duty to recommend the measures that a stricken nation in the midst of a stricken world may require. These measures, or such other measures as the Congress may build out of its experience and wisdom, I shall seek, within my constitutional authority, to bring to speedy adoption.

But in the event that the Congress shall fail to take one of these two courses, and in the event that the national emergency is still critical, I shall not evade the clear course of duty that will then confront me. I shall ask the Congress for the one remaining instrument to meet the crisis—broad Executive power to wage a war against the emergency, as great as the power that would be given to me if we were in fact invaded by a foreign foe.

For the trust reposed in me I will return the courage and the devotion that befit the time. I can do no less.

We face the arduous days that lie before us in the warm courage of the national unity; with the clear consciousness of seeking old and precious moral values; with the clean satisfaction that comes from the stern performance of duty by old and young alike. We aim at the assurance of a rounded and permanent national life.

We do not distrust the future of essential democracy. The people of the United States have not failed. In their need they have registered a mandate that they want direct, vigorous action. They have asked for discipline and direction under leadership. They have made me the present instrument of their wishes. In the spirit of the gift I take it.

In this dedication of a Nation we humbly ask the blessing of God. May He protect each and every one of us. May He guide me in the days to come.

During the first hundred days of his administration Roosevelt would deliver the action he promised in his address. On March 3, 1933, the CCC (Civilian Conservation Corps) would be created by the Reforestation Unemployment Act to ease unemployment; on March 6 legislation would be passed forbidding the export of gold except when approved by the Treasury; on May 12, the AAA (Agricultural Adjustment Act) would become law, although it would later be ruled unconstitutional by the Supreme Court. A flood of alphabetical agencies would follow, including the FERA, TVA, FCA, PWA, WPA, SEC, NLB, CWA, FCC, FHA, and the NRA. Some of these were scuttled by Supreme Court action.

Roosevelt promised the nation action and action he delivered. On March 5 Roosevelt made plans for a special session of Congress; On the 6th he closed all banks and prohibited all gold payments and exports; on the 12th of March he delivered the first of his famous fireside chats over the radio networks. "It has been wonderful to me to catch the note of confidence from all over the country. . . . Confidence and Courage are the essentials of success in carrying out our plan. . . . Together, we cannot fail."

F.D.R. delivering his first inaugural address.

THE PRESIDENT

Franklin D. Roosevelt discarded the Big Stick policy introduced by Theodore Roosevelt. In its place came the doctrine of the Good Neighbor and the New Deal. Recovery from the depression was slow and costly, but even opponents of the New Deal had to agree it was better than the dictatorships spawned by the depression in other countries. The era saw the birth of the Townsend Plan, Reverend Charles E. Coughlin's National Union for Social Justice, the German-American Bund, and Huey Long's share-our-wealth plan.

THE NATION

The ratification of the twentieth amendment, February 6, 1933, moved the traditional March 4 presidential inauguration date up to January 20, and also specified that if the president-elect should die before inauguration the vice-president-elect was to become president.

With the change of administration on March 4 President Roosevelt began activating his inaugural promises of action. He closed the nation's banks and successfully allayed the fears of depositors. A gold embargo in April was the first step in abandoning the gold standard. The N.R.A. set up in June was only one of many Federal agencies created by Roosevelt in his all-out bid to start the nation on the road to recovery.

But social reform occupied only part of the nation's interest in 1933. On December 5 the twenty-first amendment was ratified, repealing the eighteenth amendment. Roosevelt continued his fight against the depression, but in May, 1935, the N.R.A. was declared unconstitutional by the Supreme Court.

The election year of 1936 saw the national income upped $30,000,000, and despite continued drought in the southwest dust bowl the Democrats claimed recovery was well on its way. The nation responded with another Democratic landslide: Roosevelt, 27,751,597 popular votes (523 electoral); Republican Alfred M. Landon, 16,-679,583 popular votes (8 electoral); the Union party's William Lemke, 882,479; Socialist Norman Thomas, 187,720; Communist Earl Browder, 80,159; Prohibitionist D. Leigh Colvin, 37,847; Socialist Laborite John W. Aiken, 12,777. John Nance Garner was reëlected vice-president.

THE WORLD

Adolf Hitler, now Chancellor of Germany, began in earnest his drive for power by establishing a ten-year nonaggression pact with Poland. With the death of President von Hindenburg, August 2, 1934, the offices of president and chancellor were assumed by Der Führer. In 1935 Mussolini flouted the restraining demands of the League of Nations and invaded helpless Ethiopia. King George V of England died, January 20, 1936, succeeded by King Edward VIII, who resigned in less than a year. German troops goose-stepped into a demilitarized Rhineland on March 7th, in defiance of the Locarno pacts. On May 9th Mussolini announced the annexation of Ethiopia, with Italy's King Victor Emmanuel as emperor. In July bitter civil war broke out between the Insurgents and Loyalists in Spain, and the world previewed many new tactics and weapons destined for world-wide use within three years.

[236]

IN PREPARING THE SECOND INAUGURAL ADDRESS you have at your disposal the help of Judge Samuel I. Rosenman and other members of the "Brain Trust," as the young men who surround you have been dubbed by your Republican opponents. With the help of the Brain Trust you prepare a comprehensive review of the past four years and outline in broad strokes a blueprint for future social reforms to come. On inauguration day, held for the first time on January 20th, you deliver your address over a national radio hookup, as thousands of citizens fill the Capitol steps and plaza despite the cold and rain . . . .

Franklin Delano Roosevelt

[1937–1941]

SECOND INAUGURAL ADDRESS, JANUARY 20, 1937

Capitol Steps, Washington, D.C.

When four years ago we met to inaugurate a President, the Republic, single-minded in anxiety, stood in spirit here. We dedicated ourselves to the fulfillment of a vision—to speed the time when there would be for all the people that security and peace essential to the pursuit of happiness. We of the Republic pledged ourselves to drive from the temple of our ancient faith those who had profaned it; to end by action, tireless and unafraid, the stagnation and despair of that day. We did those first things first.

Our covenant with ourselves did not stop there. Instinctively we recognized a deeper need—the need to find through government the instrument of our united purpose to solve for the individual the ever-rising problems of a complex civilization. Repeated attempts at their solution without the aid of government had left us baffled and bewildered. For, without that aid, we had been unable to create those moral controls over the services of science which are necessary to make science a useful servant instead of a ruthless master of mankind. To do this we knew that we must find practical controls over blind economic forces and blindly selfish men.

We of the Republic sensed the truth that democratic government has innate capacity to protect its people against disasters once considered inevitable, to solve problems once considered unsolvable. We would not admit that we could not find a way to master economic epidemics just as, after centuries of fatalistic suffering, we had

Two of the government's first answers to the nation's need for employment aid were the Civil Works Administration, which absorbed 4,000,000 unemployed, and the Civilian Conservation Corps, which took 500,000 more off the relief rolls. The Agricultural Adjustment Act aided the farmers by placing a floor under prices and a ceiling on acreage under cultivation. The Social Security Act was designed to help the aged. When the wings of the NIRA Blue Eagle had been clipped by the Supreme Court other measures were devised to control business and industry.

[237]

found a way to master epidemics of disease. We refused to leave the problems of our common welfare to be solved by the winds of chance and the hurricanes of disaster.

In this we Americans were discovering no wholly new truth; we were writing a new chapter in our book of self-government.

This year marks the one hundred and fiftieth anniversary of the Constitutional Convention which made us a nation. At that Convention our forefathers found the way out of the chaos which followed the Revolutionary War; they created a strong government with powers of united action sufficient then and now to solve problems utterly beyond individual or local solution. A century and a half ago they established the Federal Government in order to promote the general welfare and secure the blessings of liberty to the American people.

Today we invoke those same powers of government to achieve the same objectives.

Four years of new experience have not belied our historic instinct. They hold out the clear hope that government within communities, government within the separate States, and government of the United States can do the things the times require, without yielding its democracy. Our tasks in the last four years did not force democracy to take a holiday.

Nearly all of us recognize that as intricacies of human relationships increase, so power to govern them also must increase—power to stop evil; power to do good. The essential democracy of our Nation and the safety of our people depend not upon the absence of power, but upon lodging it with those whom the people can change or continue at stated intervals through an honest and free system of elections. The Constitution of 1787 did not make our democracy impotent.

In fact, in these last four years, we have made the exercise of all power more democratic; for we have begun to bring private autocratic powers into their proper subordination to the public's government. The legend that they were invincible—above and beyond the processes of a democracy—has been shattered. They have been challenged and beaten.

Our progress out of the depression is obvious. But that is not all that you and I mean by the new order of things. Our pledge was not merely to do a patchwork job with secondhand materials. By using the new materials of social justice we have undertaken to erect on the old foundations a more enduring structure for the better use of future generations.

The public debt had risen to an unprecedented $31,000,000,000 during this period.

In that purpose we have been helped by achievements of mind and spirit. Old truths have been relearned; untruths have been unlearned. We have always known that heedless self-interest was bad morals; we know now that it is bad economics. Out of the collapse of a prosperity whose builders boasted their practicality has come the conviction that in the long run economic morality pays. We are beginning to wipe out the line that divides the practical from the ideal; and in so doing we are fashioning an instrument of unimagined power for the establishment of a morally better world.

This new understanding undermines the old admiration of worldly success as such. We are beginning to abandon our tolerance of the abuse of power by those who betray for profit the elementary decencies of life.

In this process evil things formerly accepted will not be so easily condoned. Hard-headedness will not so easily excuse hard-heartedness. We are moving toward an era of good feeling. But we realize that there can be no era of good feeling save among men of good will.

For these reasons I am justified in believing that the greatest change we have witnessed has been the change in the moral climate of America.

Among men of good will, science and democracy together offer an ever-richer life and ever-larger satisfaction to the individual. With this change in our moral climate and our rediscovered ability to improve our economic order, we have set our feet upon the road of enduring progress.

Shall we pause now and turn our back upon the road that lies ahead? Shall we call this the promised land? Or, shall we continue on our way? For "each age is a dream that is dying, or one that is coming to birth."

A quotation from Arthur O'Shaughnessy's "The Music Makers."

Many voices are heard as we face a great decision. Comfort says, "Tarry a while." Opportunism says, "This is a good spot." Timidity asks, "How difficult is the road ahead?"

True, we have come far from the days of stagnation and despair. Vitality has been preserved. Courage and confidence have been restored. Mental and moral horizons have been extended.

But our present gains were won under the pressure of more than ordinary circumstances. Advance became imperative under the goad of fear and suffering. The times were on the side of progress.

To hold to progress today, however, is more difficult. Dulled conscience, irresponsibility, and ruthless self-interest already reappear. Such symptoms of prosperity may become portents of disaster! Prosperity already tests the persistence of our progressive purpose.

Let us ask again: Have we reached the goal of our vision of that fourth day of March, 1933? Have we found our happy valley?

I see a great nation, upon a great continent, blessed with a great wealth of natural resources. Its hundred and thirty million people are at peace among themselves; they are making their country a good neighbor among the nations. I see a United States which can demonstrate that, under democratic methods of government, national wealth can be translated into a spreading volume of human comforts hitherto unknown, and the lowest standard of living can be raised far above the level of mere subsistence.

But here is the challenge to our democracy: In this nation I see tens of millions of its citizens—a substantial part of its whole population—who at this very moment are denied the greater part of what the very lowest standards of today call the necessities of life.

I see millions of families trying to live on incomes so meager that the pall of family disaster hangs over them day by day.

I see millions whose daily lives in city and on farm continue under conditions labeled indecent by a so-called polite society half a century ago.

I see millions denied education, recreation, and the opportunity to better their lot and the lot of their children.

I see millions lacking the means to buy the products of farm and factory and by their poverty denying work and productiveness to many other millions.

I see one-third of a nation ill-housed, ill-clad, ill-nourished.

It is not in despair that I paint you that picture. I paint it for you in hope—because the Nation, seeing and understanding the injustice in it, proposes to paint it out. We are determined to make every American citizen the subject of his country's interest and concern; and we will never regard any faithful law-abiding group within our borders as superfluous. The test of our progress is not

[239]

whether we add more to the abundance of those who have much; it is whether we provide enough for those who have too little.

If I know aught of the spirit and purpose of our Nation, we will not listen to Comfort, Opportunism, and Timidity. We will carry on.

Overwhelmingly, we of the Republic are men and women of good will; men and women who have more than warm hearts of dedication; men and women who have cool heads and willing hands of practical purpose as well. They will insist that every agency of popular government use effective instruments to carry out their will.

Government is competent when all who compose it work as trustees for the whole people. It can make constant progress when it keeps abreast of all the facts. It can obtain justified support and legitimate criticism when the people receive true information of all that government does.

If I know aught of the will of our people, they will demand that these conditions of effective government shall be created and maintained. They will demand a nation uncorrupted by cancers of injustice and, therefore, strong among the nations in its example of the will to peace.

Today we reconsecrate our country to long-cherished ideals in a suddenly changed civilization. In every land there are always at work forces that drive men apart and forces that draw men together. In our personal ambitions we are individualists. But in our seeking for economic and political progress as a nation, we all go up, or else we all go down, as one people.

To maintain a democracy of effort requires a vast amount of patience in dealing with differing methods, a vast amount of humility. But out of the confusion of many voices rises an understanding of dominant public need. Then political leadership can voice common ideals, and aid in their realization.

In taking again the oath of office as President of the United States, I assume the solemn obligation of leading the American people forward along the road over which they have chosen to advance.

While this duty rests upon me I shall do my utmost to speak their purpose and to do their will, seeking Divine guidance to help us each and every one to give light to them that sit in darkness and to guide our feet into the way of peace.

When members of Roosevelt's own party followed the lead of Democrat Burton K. Wheeler and rose in opposition to the President's Supreme Court "packing" effort Roosevelt turned against Congressmen who opposed him. But many would be returned to office in the 1938 mid-term election, despite all the President could do.

President Roosevelt taking the oath of office at his second inaugural.

THE PRESIDENT

As the war in Europe continued to progress in favor of Hitler, Mussolini, and Hirohito during Roosevelt's second term, the President had to change the nation's predominantly noninterventionist attitude by convincing the people of the ominous danger to the American way of life if England succumbed. At the same time he had to do all in his power to aid the sorely beset Allies not only with guns, ships, and supplies but also with the moral support of speeches and public pronouncements, as exemplified in the third inaugural address.

Photo by Leon Perskie,
Franklin D. Roosevelt Library

THE NATION

After Roosevelt's smashing victory in the 1936 election he sent a message to Congress on February 5, 1937, recommending revisions in the statutes governing appointment of members of the Supreme Court. But the President was given an abrupt setback when his "court packing" program was decisively defeated in a battle led, strangely enough, by a Democrat: Senator Burton K. Wheeler, a man who had the courage to place his country's welfare above party politics. This marked the ending of the New Deal.

In 1937–8 sit-down strikes at home and the rising threat of war in Europe dominated the news. In 1939 a war-stimulated prosperity began to be felt in the United States, as orders from abroad flooded in. When Congress passed the Neutrality Act of 1939 permitting "cash and carry" sales of arms overseas the economy was helped even more.

The census of 1940 disclosed a population of 131,669,275. In September, despite the nation's professed neutrality, 50 overage destroyers were given to Great Britain in return for 99-year leases on West Indies and Newfoundland air and naval bases. On September 16 the first peace-time selective service was enacted by Congress.

In the election year of 1940 Roosevelt broke the unwritten precedent set by George Washington when he accepted nomination for a third term. Democrat Roosevelt polled 27,244,160 popular votes (449 electoral), Republican Wendell Willkie received 22,305,198 popular votes (82 electoral), Socialist Norman Thomas 99,557, Prohibitionist Roger W. Babson 57,812, Communist Earl Browder 46,251, Socialist Laborite John W. Aiken 10,164. Henry A. Wallace was elected vice-president.

THE WORLD

In 1937 the war in Spain continued unabated; Japan occupied Shanghai; Stalin purged still more of his opposition; Edward VIII abdicated; and King George VI and Queen Elizabeth were crowned. After Austria was seized, Hitler's demands for the Czech Sudetenland in 1938 forced a conference at Munich. In 1939 Hitler took Czechoslovakia and Poland in a display of power that brought a new word into the language: blitzkrieg! France and England declared war on Germany. Russia attempted to roll over little Finland, but met heroic resistance. In Rome Cardinal Pacelli became Pope Pius XII, but his pleas for peace were lost in the sounds of world conflict. Hitler's goose-stepping legions trampled Denmark, Norway, the Netherlands, Luxemburg, Belgium, and France underfoot in 1940; but he was frustrated at Dunkirk when the British Expeditionary Force escaped annihilation.

YOU HAVE DETERMINED that the general theme of your third inaugural address shall be that nations, like humans, possess a soul, a spirit, a faith, a sacred fire—and if Hitler, Stalin, and Mussolini are allowed to continue, this vital force may well be destroyed. After you complete your longhand version, Justice Felix Frankfurter, Judge Samuel I. Rosenman, Archibald MacLeish, and Robert Sherwood all help revise and polish what you have written, until the seventh draft is considered acceptable. On inauguration day, which is sunny but cold, you deliver your address well, but are to be surprised and disappointed at the nation's apathetic reaction to your painstakingly fashioned philosophical phrases . . . .

Franklin Delano Roosevelt

[1941–1945]

THIRD INAUGURAL ADDRESS, JANUARY 20, 1941

Capitol Steps, Washington, D.C.

On each national day of inauguration since 1789, the people have renewed their sense of dedication to the United States.

In Washington's day the task of the people was to create and weld together a nation.

In Lincoln's day the task of the people was to preserve that Nation from disruption from within.

In this day the task of the people is to save that Nation and its institutions from disruption from without.

To us there has come a time, in the midst of swift happenings, to pause for a moment and take stock—to recall what our place in history has been, and to rediscover what we are and what we may be. If we do not, we risk the real peril of inaction.

Lives of nations are determined not by the count of years, but by the lifetime of the human spirit. The life of a man is three-score years and ten: A little more, a little less. The life of a nation is the fullness of the measure of its will to live.

There are men who doubt this. There are men who believe that democracy, as a form of Government and a frame of life, is limited or measured by a kind of mystical and artificial fate—that, for some unexplained reason, tyranny and slavery have become the surging wave of the future—and that freedom is an ebbing tide.

But we Americans know that this is not true.

Eight years ago, when the life of this Republic seemed frozen by a fatalistic terror, we proved that this is not true. We were in the midst of shock—but we acted. We acted quickly, boldly, decisively.

These later years have been living years—fruitful years for the people of this democracy. For they have brought to us greater security and, I hope, a better understanding that life's ideals are to be measured in other than material things.

Most vital to our present and our future is this experience of a democracy which successfully survived crisis at home; put away many evil things; built new structures on enduring lines; and, through it all, maintained the fact of its democracy.

When delivering this part of his address Roosevelt made one of his rare errors. He misread the word "inaction" as "isolation." On his copy of the address he later noted, "I misread this word as 'isolation,' then added 'and inaction.' All of which improved it!" Improved or not this address was one of the few times Roosevelt talked over the heads of the masses with whom he had established such an intimate rapport through his fire-side chats and studiously plain, neighborly style of delivery.

[243]

For action has been taken within the three-way framework of the Constitution of the United States. The coordinate branches of the Government continue freely to function. The Bill of Rights remains inviolate. The freedom of elections is wholly maintained. Prophets of the downfall of American democracy have seen their dire predictions come to nought.

Democracy is not dying.

We know it because we have seen it revive—and grow.

We know it cannot die—because it is built on the unhampered initiative of individual men and women joined together in a common enterprise—an enterprise undertaken and carried through by the free expression of a free majority.

We know it because democracy alone, of all forms of government, enlists the full force of men's enlightened will.

We know it because democracy alone has constructed an unlimited civilization capable of infinite progress in the improvement of human life.

We know it because, if we look below the surface, we sense it still spreading on every continent—for it is the most humane, the most advanced, and in the end the most unconquerable of all forms of human society.

A nation, like a person, has a body—a body that must be fed and clothed and housed, invigorated and rested, in a manner that measures up to the objectives of our time.

A nation, like a person, has a mind—a mind that must be kept informed and alert, that must know itself, that understands the hopes and the needs of its neighbors—all the other nations that live within the narrowing circle of the world.

And a nation, like a person, has something deeper, something more permanent, something larger than the sum of all its parts. It is that something which matters most to its future—which calls forth the most sacred guarding of its present.

It is a thing for which we find it difficult—even impossible—to hit upon a single, simple word.

And yet we all understand what it is—the spirit—the faith of America. It is the product of centuries. It was born in the multitudes of those who came from many lands—some of high degree, but mostly plain people, who sought here, early and late, to find freedom more freely.

The democratic aspiration is no mere recent phase in human history. It *is* human history. It permeated the ancient life of early peoples. It blazed anew in the middle ages. It was written in Magna Carta.

In the Americas its impact has been irresistible. America has been the New World in all tongues, to all peoples, not because this continent was a new-found land, but because all those who came here believed they could create upon this continent a new life—a life that should be new in freedom.

Its vitality was written into our own Mayflower Compact, into the Declaration of Independence, into the Constitution of the United States, into the Gettysburg Address.

Those who first came here to carry out the longings of their spirit, and the millions who followed, and the stock that sprang from them—all have moved forward constantly and consistently toward an ideal which in itself has gained stature and clarity with each generation.

The hopes of the Republic cannot forever tolerate either undeserved poverty or self-serving wealth.

[244]

We know that we still have far to go; that we must more greatly build the security and the opportunity and the knowledge of every citizen, in the measure justified by the resources and the capacity of the land.

But it is not enough to achieve these purposes alone. It is not enough to clothe and feed the body of this Nation, and instruct and inform its mind. For there is also the spirit. And of the three, the greatest is the spirit.

Without the body and the mind, as all men know, the Nation could not live.

But if the spirit of America were killed, even though the Nation's body and mind, constricted in an alien world, lived on, the America we know would have perished.

That spirit—that faith—speaks to us in our daily lives in ways often unnoticed, because they seem so obvious. It speaks to us here in the Capital of the Nation. It speaks to us through the processes of governing in the sovereignties of 48 States. It speaks to us in our countries, in our cities, in our towns, and in our villages. It speaks to us from the other nations of the hemisphere, and from those across the seas—the enslaved, as well as the free. Sometimes we fail to hear or heed these voices of freedom because to us the privilege of our freedom is such an old, old story.

The destiny of America was proclaimed in words of prophecy spoken by our first President in his first inaugural in 1789—words almost directed, it would seem, to this year of 1941: "The preservation of the sacred fire of liberty and the destiny of the republican model of government are justly considered * * * deeply, * * * finally, staked on the experiment intrusted to the hands of the American people."

If we lose that sacred fire—if we let it be smothered with doubt and fear—then we shall reject the destiny which Washington strove so valiantly and so triumphantly to establish. The preservation of the spirit and faith of the Nation does, and will, furnish the highest justification for every sacrifice that we may make in the cause of national defense.

In the face of great perils never before encountered, our strong purpose is to protect and to perpetuate the integrity of democracy.

For this we muster the spirit of America, and the faith of America.

We do not retreat. We are not content to stand still. As Americans, we go forward, in the service of our country, by the will of God.

Note the use of the words "and will" in this key sentence. By their use Roosevelt seemed to imply many sacrifices were ahead for the nation "in the cause of national defense." It is doubtful if many realized at the time how prophetic Roosevelt's statement was.

The third inauguration of President Franklin D. Roosevelt, January 20, 1941.

THE PRESIDENT

While saying "I hate war" Roosevelt was at the same time doing all he could to prepare the nation for the conflict he evidently considered inescapable. A keen student of history, he evidently had early determined not to make Wilson's mistake of committing the nation to foreign entanglements before the people had been conditioned to accept such responsibilities. And so, step by step, the war drew closer, until the country was shocked into action by the attack on Pearl Harbor. Once committed, Roosevelt ordered a number of calculated risks that, fortunately for the Allies, carried through to ultimate success. But the toll of advancing age, the debilitating effects of polio, and the crushing burden of war proved too much for Roosevelt, whose health began to ebb as his fourth inauguration approached.

Franklin D. Roosevelt Library

THE NATION

March 11, 1941, President Roosevelt signed the Lend-Lease Bill, making America, in the words of the President, the "arsenal of democracy." This was followed by the announcement on May 27 that an unlimited national emergency existed, and on September 11 an order to the Navy and Air Force to "shoot at sight" all German or Italian submarines or ships encountered in American defensive waters. The Japanese attack on Pearl Harbor December 7 brought forth an immediate declaration of war against Japan on December 8, and three days later against Germany and Italy. 1942 witnessed the beginning of rationing, rent ceilings, and price controls, as the nation's war machine ground slowly into action. 1943 saw the first American victories in the Pacific, and round-the-clock bombing of Germany by Flying Fortresses based in England.

In the election year of 1944 the success of the D-Day landing in Normandy made the reëlection of President Roosevelt for a fourth term a predictable certainty. The election returns showed Roosevelt polled 25,602,504 popular votes (432 electoral), while Republican Thomas E. Dewey received 22,006,285 popular votes (99 electoral). Socialist Norman Thomas polled 80,518, Prohibitionist Claude A. Watson 74,758, Socialist Laborite Edward A. Teichert 45,336. Harry S. Truman was elected vice-president.

THE WORLD

On June 22, 1941, Hitler turned on Stalin and invaded Russia. President Roosevelt and Prime Minister Churchill issued the Atlantic Charter, August 14th. In July of 1941 Great Britain and Russia had become allies. December 7, 1941, the Japanese attacked Pearl Harbor, plunging the United States into the global conflict. 1943 brought defeat to Hitler in Stalingrad, and also to the Fascists in Sicily. Italy surrendered to the Allies on September 8th, and declared war against Germany on October 13th. In late November Roosevelt, Churchill, and Stalin met at Teheran and agreed on the invasion of fortress Europe. General Dwight D. Eisenhower was named Supreme Commander of the invasion forces. D-Day for the invasion of Europe was June 6, 1944. In the Pacific American forces under General Douglas MacArthur were slowly overcoming stubborn Japanese resistance. The tide of war definitely had turned.

[246]

YOU REQUEST A SIMPLE CEREMONY for your fourth inaugural. It is a bitter, cold day with snow on the ground, but you brave the weather in a lightweight suit, without a hat or overcoat. A small crowd gathers at the south portico of the White House to hear you read a short address, lasting about five minutes, prepared by Judge Rosenman, Archibald MacLeish, Robert Sherwood, and yourself, in which you plead for understanding, confidence, and courage . . . .

Franklin Delano Roosevelt

[1945]

FOURTH INAUGURAL ADDRESS, JANUARY 20, 1945
White House, Washington, D.C.

Mr. Chief Justice, Mr. Vice President, my friends, you will understand and, I believe, agree with my wish that the form of this inauguration be simple and its words brief.

We Americans of today, together with our allies, are passing through a period of supreme test. It is a test of our courage—of our resolve—of our wisdom—of our essential democracy.

If we meet that test—successfully and honorably—we shall perform a service of historic importance which men and women and children will honor throughout all time.

As I stand here today, having taken the solemn oath of office in the presence of my fellow countrymen—in the presence of our God—I know that it is America's purpose that we shall not fail.

In the days and in the years that are to come we shall work for a just and honorable peace, a durable peace, as today we work and fight for total victory in war.

We can and we will achieve such a peace.

We shall strive for perfection. We shall not achieve it immediately—but we still shall strive. We may make mistakes—but they must never be mistakes which result from faintness of heart or abandonment of moral principle.

I remember that my old schoolmaster, Dr. Peabody, said, in days that seemed to us then to be secure and untroubled: "Things in life will not always run smoothly. Sometimes we will be rising toward the heights—then all will seem to reverse itself and start downward. The great fact to remember is that the trend of civilization itself is forever upward; that a line drawn through the middle of the peaks and the valleys of the centuries always has an upward trend."

Our Constitution of 1787 was not a perfect instrument; it is not perfect yet. But it provided a firm base upon which all manner of men, of all races and colors and creeds, could build our solid structure of democracy.

A reference to Dr. Endicott Peabody, who founded Groton, a school for boys in Groton, Massachusetts. Described as "a large, vigorous, uncomplicated man with blond hair and an athletic frame," Dr. Peabody served as headmaster at Groton from its founding until 1940, four years before his death.

And so today, in this year of war, 1945, we have learned lessons—at a fearful cost—and we shall profit by them.

We have learned that we cannot live alone, at peace; that our own well-being is dependent on the well-being of other nations far away. We have learned that we must live as men, not as ostriches, nor as dogs in the manger.

We have learned to be citizens of the world, members of the human community.

We have learned the simple truth, as Emerson said, that "The only way to have a friend is to be one."

We can gain no lasting peace if we approach it with suspicion and mistrust or with fear. We can gain it only if we proceed with the understanding, the confidence, and the courage which flow from conviction.

The Almighty God has blessed our land in many ways. He has given our people stout hearts and strong arms with which to strike mighty blows for freedom and truth. He has given to our country a faith which has become the hope of all peoples in an anguished world.

So we pray to Him now for the vision to see our way clearly—to see the way that leads to a better life for ourselves and for all our fellow men—to the achievement of His will, to peace on earth.

Franklin D. Roosevelt Library

President Roosevelt making his fourth inaugural address on the White House porch.

[248]

The shocking news of President Roosevelt's death was withheld from the public until Vice-President Truman could be called to the White House. Shortly before eight o'clock, April 12, 1945, Chief Justice Harlan Fiske Stone administered the oath of office to the plain and humble Missouri ex-farmer, who had been carried to the presidency by unpredictable circumstance.

Harry S. Truman
[1945–1949]

THE PRESIDENT

Harry S. Truman's middle initial was the result of a family disagreement as to which grandfather's name he should carry: Shippe or Solomon. To settle the matter neither name was used. Instead the initial was allowed to stand for both names.

A farmer from 1906 to 1916, Truman served in World War I in the field artillery, emerging as a major in 1919. When his postwar haberdashery failed, Truman entered politics, studying law at night. With the backing of "Boss" Tom Pendergast, Truman became a judge in the Jackson County Court, serving from 1922 to 1924. First elected to the U.S. Senate in 1934, Truman was reëlected in 1940 and entered the last stage of his climb to fame.

National prominence was accorded Truman when he was chairman of the Special Committee to Investigate National Defense, which kept a careful check on the national defense program. At the Democratic nominating convention of 1944, when President Roosevelt decided not to back Vice-President Henry A. Wallace for reëlection, the names of William O. Douglas and Harry S. Truman were suggested, and Truman was eventually selected.

The day after being sworn in, still dazed by the tremendous responsibilities he had inherited, a truly humble Truman told reporters: "Boys, when they told me yesterday what had happened, I felt like the moon and stars and all the planets had fallen on me . . . I've got the most awful responsibility a man ever had. If you fellows ever pray, pray for me."

Harry S. Truman was the 7th vice-president to accede to the presidency. Like others before him, Truman had the misfortune to be thrust into the presidency at a critical time, when he was faced with grave problems he was virtually unprepared to meet. But the American public would rally to the emergency and accord the new President a long political honeymoon, in which he would enjoy the nation's sympathy and support until he had time to prove his true worth.

THE PRESIDENT

The humility with which Truman accepted the responsibilities of the presidency after Roosevelt's death was still apparent during his grueling whistle-stop campaign, as he toured the nation in 1948, speaking wherever and whenever he could. This helped bring about his surprising defeat of Thomas E. Dewey and his election to the presidency.

Courtesy of the artist Greta Kempton, in the White House Collection

THE NATION

In 1945 one momentous event followed another: February 19, Iwo Jima was invaded by United States Marines; March 16, organized resistance on Iwo Jima was declared at an end; April 1– June 30, American troops fought on Okinawa; April 12, President Roosevelt died at Warm Springs, Georgia, with Vice-President, Harry S. Truman being sworn in at 3:35 P.M.; June 21, Japanese on Okinawa surrendered; July 5, the Philippine Islands were liberated; July 16, an atomic bomb was exploded at Los Alamos, New Mexico, testing grounds; August 14, President Truman announced unconditional surrender of Japan.

Americans wanted to forget the war and return to their peacetime pursuits as quickly as possible. Before the end of 1946 nearly all price and wage controls had been removed, and inflationary forces began pushing prices upwards.

1947 witnessed the creation of the Marshall Plan, the need for which became more and more apparent as the nation—and the world—slowly realized that although the shooting war had ended, another kind of conflict had begun. And a new phrase was added to the language—cold war.

1948, another election year, was good for business and industry, due to increased foreign aid spending and large defense outlays. The Foreign Assistance Act—otherwise known as the Marshall Plan—authorized $6,098,000,000 for overseas aid. Americans were suddenly made aware of a new menace: Communists in government. Confronted by the increasingly alarming revelations of Soviet-inspired espionage President Truman still chose to ignore the reports, some of which he dismissed as red herrings.

In the 1948 election the Republicans felt so sure of victory that millions of Republican voters stayed home. The result was a smashing upset in favor of Truman, who was reëlected by a popular vote of 24,105,695 (303 electoral) to Republican Thomas E. Dewey's 21,969,170 (189 electoral). States' Rights Democrat Governor J. Strom Thurmond polled 1,169,021 (39 electoral), Progressive Henry A. Wallace 1,156,103, Socialist Norman M. Thomas, 139,009, Prohibitionist Claude A. Watson, 103,216. Senator Alben W. Barkley was elected vice-president.

THE WORLD

April, 1945, witnessed the passing of three world figures: President Roosevelt (April 12), Mussolini (April 28), Adolph Hitler (April 30). Germany surrendered unconditionally on May 7th. June 26th brought the signing of the Charter of the United Nations in San Francisco. General MacArthur announced July 5th that the Philippines were liberated. Hiroshima was devastated by an atomic bomb on August 6th, followed by Nagasaki on August 9th. On September 2nd Japan surrendered unconditionally.

[250]

IN PREPARING YOUR INAUGURAL ADDRESS you determine to use it to introduce a four point program to which your administration will be dedicated. Before you begin your address to the huge crowd standing in the cold sunlight you cannot know your fourth point will take hold and become known the world over as the Point Four program, which will later rank in importance with the United Nations and the Marshall Plan . . . .

Harry S. Truman

[1949–1953]

INAUGURAL ADDRESS, JANUARY 20, 1949

Capitol Steps, Washington, D.C.

Mr. Vice President, Mr. Chief Justice, and fellow citizens, I accept with humility the honor which the American people have conferred upon me. I accept it with a deep resolve to do all that I can for the welfare of this Nation and for the peace of the world.

In performing the duties of my office, I need the help and prayers of every one of you. I ask for your encouragement and your support. The tasks we face are difficult, and we can accomplish them only if we work together.

Each period of our national history has had its special challenges. Those that confront us now are as momentous as any in the past. Today marks the beginning not only of a new administration, but of a period that will be eventful, perhaps decisive, for us and for the world.

It may be our lot to experience, and in large measure to bring about, a major turning point in the long history of the human race. The first half of this century has been marked by unprecedented and brutal attacks on the rights of man, and by the two most frightful wars in history. The supreme need of our time is for men to learn to live together in peace and harmony.

The peoples of the earth face the future with grave uncertainty, composed almost equally of great hopes and great fears. In this time of doubt, they look to the United States as never before for good will, strength, and wise leadership.

It is fitting, therefore, that we take this occasion to proclaim to the world the essential principles of the faith by which we live, and to declare our aims to all peoples.

The American people stand firm in the faith which has inspired this Nation from the beginning. We believe that all men have a right to equal justice under law and equal opportunity to share in the common good. We believe that all men have the right to freedom of thought and expression. We believe that all men are created equal because they are created in the image of God.

From this faith we will not be moved.

The American people desire, and are determined to work for, a

Truman's humility, expressed in his opening remarks, was to be gradually eroded during his next four years in office, until his likable unpretentiousness would be supplanted by a "give 'em hell" attitude he would cultivate with jaunty insouciance.

[251]

world in which all nations and all peoples are free to govern themselves as they see fit and to achieve a decent and satisfying life. Above all else, our people desire, and are determined to work for, peace on earth—a just and lasting peace—based on genuine agreement freely arrived at by equals.

In the pursuit of these aims, the United States and other likeminded nations find themselves directly opposed by a regime with contrary aims and a totally different concept of life.

That regime adheres to a false philosophy which purports to offer freedom, security, and greater opportunity to mankind. Misled by this philosophy, many peoples have sacrificed their liberties only to learn to their sorrow that deceit and mockery, poverty and tyranny, are their reward.

That false philosophy is communism.

Communism is based on the belief that man is so weak and inadequate that he is unable to govern himself, and therefore requires the rule of strong masters.

Democracy is based on the conviction that man has the moral and intellectual capacity, as well as the inalienable right, to govern himself with reason and justice.

Communism subjects the individual to arrest without lawful cause, punishment without trial, and forced labor as the chattel of the state. It decrees what information he shall receive, what art he shall produce, what leaders he shall follow, and what thoughts he shall think.

Democracy maintains that government is established for the benefit of the individual, and is charged with the responsibility of protecting the rights of the individual and his freedom in the exercise of his abilities.

Communism maintains that social wrongs can be corrected only by violence.

Democracy has proved that social justice can be achieved through peaceful change.

Communism holds that the world is so deeply divided into opposing classes that war is inevitable.

Democracy holds that free nations can settle differences justly and maintain lasting peace.

These differences between communism and democracy do not concern the United States alone. People everywhere are coming to realize that what is involved is material well-being, human dignity, and the right to believe in and worship God.

I state these differences, not to draw issues of belief as such, but because the actions resulting from the Communist philosophy are a threat to the efforts of free nations to bring about world recovery and lasting peace.

Since the end of hostilities, the United States has invested its substance and its energy in a great constructive effort to restore peace, stability, and freedom in the world.

We have sought no territory and we have imposed our will on none. We have asked for no privileges we would not extend to others.

We have constantly and vigorously supported the United Nations and related agencies as a means of applying democratic principles to international relations. We have consistently advocated and relied upon peaceful settlement of disputes among nations.

We have made every effort to secure agreement on effective international control of our most powerful weapon, and we have worked steadily for the limitation and control of all armaments.

We have encouraged, by precept and example, the expansion of world trade on a sound and fair basis.

Almost a year ago, in company with 16 free nations of Europe, we launched the greatest cooperative economic program in history. The purpose of that unprecedented effort is to invigorate and strengthen democracy in Europe, so that the free people of that continent can resume their rightful place in the forefront of civilization and can contribute once more to the security and welfare of the world.

The program to which Truman referred was the Foreign Assistance Act of April 3, 1948, soon more popularly known as the Marshall Plan.

Our efforts have brought new hope to all mankind. We have beaten back despair and defeatism. We have saved a number of countries from losing their liberty. Hundreds of millions of people all over the world now agree with us, that we need not have war —that we can have peace.

The initiative is ours.

We are moving on with other nations to build an even stronger structure of international order and justice. We shall have as our partners countries which, no longer solely concerned with the problem of national survival, are now working to improve the standards of living of all their people. We are ready to undertake new projects to strengthen the free world.

The "structure" mentioned here was the United Nations. With this as an introduction Truman presented his bold new four-point program for peace and freedom.

In the coming years, our program for peace and freedom will emphasize four major courses of action.

First. We will continue to give unfaltering support to the United Nations and related agencies, and we will continue to search for ways to strengthen their authority and increase their effectiveness. We believe that the United Nations will be strengthened by the new nations which are being formed in lands now advancing toward self-government under democratic principles.

Point One of Truman's program would be carried out without interruption.

Second. We will continue our programs for world economic recovery.

This means, first of all, that we must keep our full weight behind the European recovery program. We are confident of the success of this major venture in world recovery. We believe that our partners in this effort will achieve the status of self-supporting nations once again.

Point Two—the Marshall Plan—would also continue to be implemented throughout Truman's administration.

In addition, we must carry out our plans for reducing the barriers to world trade and increasing its volume. Economic recovery and peace itself depend on increased world trade.

Third. We will strengthen freedom-loving nations against the dangers of aggression.

We are now working out with a number of countries a joint agreement designed to strengthen the security of the North Atlantic area. Such an agreement would take the form of a collective defense arrangement within the terms of the United Nations Charter.

We have already established such a defense pact for the Western Hemisphere by the treaty of Rio de Janeiro.

The primary purpose of these agreements is to provide unmistakable proof of the joint determination of the free countries to resist armed attack from any quarter. Each country participating in these arrangements must contribute all it can to the common defense.

Point Three would result in the North Atlantic Treaty, which would be signed by 12 nations in Washington, D.C., April 4, 1949. The signatories would be Belgium, Canada, Denmark, England, France, Iceland, Italy, Luxembourg, the Netherlands, Norway, Portugal, and the United States. The Senate would ratify the pact July 21, 1949, thus giving substance to the treaty operating as a regional agreement under the United Nations Charter.

If we can make it sufficiently clear, in advance, that any armed attack affecting our national security would be met with overwhelming force, the armed attack might never occur.

I hope soon to send to the Senate a treaty respecting the North Atlantic security plan.

Point Four would become effective on June 5, 1950, when the Act for International Development would be passed by Congress. In the first two years following passage of this act more than 200 projects involving technical assistance would be instituted in 35 nations.

Among the projects to grow out of Truman's Point Four were these: a campaign in Burma to control diseases of young children; an educational program in India where the natives would be taught to read and write, as well as methods of modern irrigation and farming; a technical school in Libya, where plumbing and other trades would be taught; programs of like nature in Israel, Brazil, Saudi Arabia, Ecuador, and many other United Nations member countries.

In addition, we will provide military advice and equipment to free nations which will cooperate with us in the maintenance of peace and security.

Fourth. We must embark on a bold new program for making the benefits of our scientific advances and industrial progress available for the improvement and growth of underdeveloped areas.

More than half the people of the world are living in conditions approaching misery. Their food is inadequate. They are victims of disease. Their economic life is primitive and stagnant. Their poverty is a handicap and a threat both to them and to more prosperous areas.

For the first time in history humanity possesses the knowledge and the skill to relieve the suffering of these people.

The United States is preeminent among nations in the development of industrial and scientific techniques. The material resources which we can afford to use for the assistance of other peoples are limited. But our imponderable resources in technical knowledge are constantly growing and are inexhaustible.

I believe that we should make available to peace-loving peoples the benefits of our store of technical knowledge in order to help them realize their aspirations for a better life. And, in cooperation with other nations, we should foster capital investment in areas needing development.

Our aim should be to help the free peoples of the world, through their own efforts, to produce more food, more clothing, more materials for housing, and more mechanical power to lighten their burdens.

We invite other countries to pool their technological resources in this undertaking. Their contributions will be warmly welcomed. This should be a cooperative enterprise in which all nations work together through the United Nations and its specialized agencies wherever practicable. It must be a world-wide effort for the achievement of peace, plenty, and freedom.

With the cooperation of business, private capital, agriculture, and labor in this country, this program can greatly increase the industrial activity in other nations and can raise substantially their standards of living.

Such new economic developments must be devised and controlled to benefit the peoples of the areas in which they are established. Guaranties to the investor must be balanced by guaranties in the interest of the people whose resources and whose labor go into these developments.

The old imperialism—exploitation for foreign profit—has no place in our plans. What we envisage is a program of development based on the concepts of democratic fair dealing.

All countries, including our own, will greatly benefit from a constructive program for the better use of the world's human and natural resources. Experience shows that our commerce with other countries expands as they progress industrially and economically.

Greater production is the key to prosperity and peace. And the key to greater production is a wider and more vigorous application of modern scientific and technical knowledge.

Only by helping the least fortunate of its members to help themselves can the human family achieve the decent, satisfying life that is the right of all people.

Democracy alone can supply the vitalizing force to stir the peoples of the world into triumphant action, not only against their human oppressors, but also against their ancient enemies—hunger, misery, and despair.

On the basis of these four major courses of action we hope to help create the conditions that will lead eventually to personal freedom and happiness for all mankind.

If we are to be successful in carrying out these policies, it is clear that we must have continued prosperity in this country and we must keep ourselves strong.

Slowly but surely we are weaving a world fabric of international security and growing prosperity.

We are aided by all who wish to live in freedom from fear—even by those who live today in fear under their own governments.

We are aided by all who want relief from the lies of propaganda —who desire truth and sincerity.

We are aided by all who desire self-government and a voice in deciding their own affairs.

We are aided by all who long for economic security—for the security and abundance that men in free societies can enjoy.

We are aided by all who desire freedom of speech, freedom of religion, and freedom to live their own lives for useful ends.

Our allies are the millions who hunger and thirst after righteousness.

In due time, as our stability becomes manifest, as more and more nations come to know the benefits of democracy and to participate in growing abundance, I believe that those countries which now oppose us will abandon their delusions and join with the free nations of the world in a just settlement of international differences.

Events have brought our American democracy to new influence and new responsibilities. They will test our courage, our devotion to duty, and our concept of liberty.

But I say to all men, what we have achieved in liberty, we will surpass in greater liberty.

Steadfast in our faith in the Almighty, we will advance toward a world where man's freedom is secure.

To that end we will devote our strength, our resources, and our firmness of resolve. With God's help, the future of mankind will be assured in a world of justice, harmony, and peace.

Truman's optimistic outlook on world peace would soon be forgotten, when North Korean troops would invade the Republic of South Korea. The President would order American forces to the aid of South Korea and the United Nations Security Council would approve a resolution for armed intervention.

THE PRESIDENT

Dwight David Eisenhower's progress up the Army's promotion ladder was slow until the attack on Pearl Harbor. Thereafter he rose quickly, achieving the post of Supreme Commander, Allied Expeditionary Forces, December 31, 1943, which led to the permanent rank of five-star General of the Army in 1944. General Eisenhower served as Chief of Staff from November 19, 1945, to February 7, 1948. He became president of Columbia University on June 7, 1948. In December, 1950, he was granted a leave of absence to serve as Supreme Allied Commander in Europe while coördinating the forces of N.A.T.O.—the North Atlantic Treaty Organization. Resigning from the Army in July of 1952, Eisenhower was nominated by the Republicans and elected to the presidency.

THE NATION

The census of 1950 showed a population of 150,697,361. An analysis of the United States at mid-century revealed the nation was concerned with three issues of primary importance: a slowly spiraling inflation, a growing undercurrent of internal Communist subversion, and a foreign policy which seemed incapable of providing a stable bulwark against the active spread of global communism under the implementation of the cold war. The entry of America into the unpopular Korean War; the recall of General MacArthur, which contributed to the ultimate Korean stalemate; the revelation of subversive elements in high places of government; and the "5-percenter" scandals combined to effect a Republican victory in the next election.

In 1952 Republican presidential candidate Dwight D. Eisenhower polled 33,824,351 popular votes (442 electoral) to Democrat Adlai Stevenson's 27,314,987 popular votes (89 electoral). Progressive Vincent Hallinan polled 132,608, Prohibitionist Stuart Hamblen received 72,768, Socialist Darlington Hoopes polled 18,322 votes, and Socialist Labor candidate Eric Hass 29,333. Richard M. Nixon was elected vice-president.

THE WORLD

On April 4, 1949, the United States and eleven western European powers adopted the North Atlantic Defense Pact. In September it was reported that the Russians exploded their first atomic bomb, ending the brief monopoly enjoyed by the United States. In December Chiang Kai-shek's Nationalist government was forced by the Communists to flee to Formosa. Secretary of State Dean Acheson's White Paper of August 6th had cut off all further American aid to the beleaguered Nationalists. On June 25, 1950, the Republic of South Korea was invaded by North Korean Communist forces. General Douglas MacArthur was placed in command of American and United Nations troops. For three years the struggling armies surged back and forth across the 38th parallel dividing North and South Korea.

ON THE NIGHT BEFORE YOUR INAUGURATION, at a meeting of the men you have selected as members of your cabinet, you look over the finished draft of your address and say, "One flame seems to be missing. Perhaps it is a feeling of prayer." Next day, standing bareheaded in the unseasonably warm sunshine bathing the vast inaugural crowd, you take the oath of office and soberly turn toward the assembly to begin your address. But you are interrupted by a roar of applause, causing you to flash your well-known smile and spontaneously fling your arms up in your familiar V gesture until the cheers die down. Then you seek to supply the flame you feel is missing from your address by asking the assembly present, including the television and radio audience, to bow their heads, while you utter "a little private prayer" of your own as a preface to your formal address . . . .

Dwight D. Eisenhower

[1953–1957]

FIRST INAUGURAL ADDRESS, JANUARY 20, 1953

Capitol Steps, Washington, D.C.

My friends, before I begin the expression of those thoughts that I deem appropriate to this moment, would you permit me the privilege of uttering a little private prayer of my own. And I ask that you bow your heads.

Almighty God, as we stand here at this moment my future associates in the executive branch of government join me in beseeching that Thou will make full and complete our dedication to the service of the people in this throng, and their fellow citizens everywhere.

Give us, we pray, the power to discern clearly right from wrong, and allow all our words and actions to be governed thereby, and by the laws of this land. Especially we pray that our concern shall be for all the people regardless of station, race, or calling.

May cooperation be permitted and be the mutual aim of those who, under the concepts of our Constitution, hold to differing political faiths; so that all may work for the good of our beloved country and Thy glory. Amen.

My fellow citizens:

The world and we have passed the midway point of a century of continuing challenge. We sense with all our faculties that forces of good and evil are massed and armed and opposed as rarely before in history.

This fact defines the meaning of this day. We are summoned by this honored and historic ceremony to witness more than the act of one citizen swearing his oath of service, in the presence of God. We are called as a people to give testimony in the sight of the world to our faith that the future shall belong to the free.

Since this century's beginning, a time of tempest has seemed to come upon the continents of the earth. Masses of Asia have awakened to strike off shackles of the past. Great nations of Europe have fought their bloodiest wars. Thrones have toppled and their vast empires have disappeared. New nations have been born.

As the Republicans took over control of the government for the first time since 1932 the nation heard a conservative, middle-of-the-road approach to world and domestic problems expressed by Eisenhower in his inaugural address. Due to the bitterness of the recent presidential campaign a man of lesser stature might have been expected to strike back at his vanquished opponent's supporters. But instead, the address revealed Eisenhower's humility.

For our own country, it has been a time of recurring trial. We have grown in power and in responsibility. We have passed through the anxieties of depression and of war to a summit unmatched in man's history. Seeking to secure peace in the world, we have had to fight through the forests of the Argonne, to the shores of Iwo Jima, and to the cold mountains of Korea.

In the swift rush of great events, we find ourselves groping to know the full sense and meaning of these times in which we live. In our quest of understanding, we beseech God's guidance. We summon all our knowledge of the past and we scan all signs of the future. We bring all our wit and all our will to meet the question:

How far have we come in man's long pilgrimage from darkness toward light? Are we nearing the light—a day of freedom and of peace for all mankind? Or are the shadows of another night closing in upon us?

Great as are the preoccupations absorbing us at home, concerned as we are with matters that deeply affect our livelihood today and our vision of the future, each of these domestic problems is dwarfed by, and often even created by, this question that involves all human kind.

This trial comes at a moment when man's power to achieve good or to inflict evil surpasses the brightest hopes and the sharpest fears of all ages. We can turn rivers in their courses, level mountains to the plains. Oceans and land and sky are avenues for our colossal commerce. Disease diminishes and life lengthens.

Yet the promise of this life is imperiled by the very genius that has made it possible. Nations amass wealth. Labor sweats to create —and turns out devices to level not only mountains but also cities. Science seems ready to confer upon us, as its final gift, the power to erase human life from this planet.

At such a time in history, we who are free must proclaim anew our faith.

This faith is the abiding creed of our fathers. It is our faith in the deathless dignity of man, governed by eternal moral and natural laws.

This faith defines our full view of life. It establishes, beyond debate, those gifts of the Creator that are man's inalienable rights, and that make all men equal in His sight.

In the light of this equality, we know that the virtues most cherished by free people—love of truth, pride of work, devotion to country—all are treasures equally precious in the lives of the most humble and of the most exalted. The men who mine coal and fire furnaces and balance ledgers and turn lathes and pick cotton and heal the sick and plant corn—all serve as proudly, and as profitably, for America as the statesmen who draft treaties and the legislators who enact laws.

This faith rules our whole way of life. It decrees that we, the people, elect leaders not to rule but to serve. It asserts that we have the right to choice of our own work and to the reward of our own toil. It inspires the initiative that makes our productivity the wonder of the world. And it warns that any man who seeks to deny equality among all his brothers betrays the spirit of the free and invites the mockery of the tyrant.

It is because we, all of us, hold to these principles that the political changes accomplished this day do not imply turbulence, upheaval or disorder. Rather this change expresses a purpose of strengthening our dedication and devotion to the precepts of our founding documents, a conscious renewal of faith in our country and in the watchfulness of a Divine Providence.

The enemies of this faith know no god but force, no devotion but its use. They tutor men in treason. They feed upon the hunger of others. Whatever defies them, they torture, especially the truth.

Here, then, is joined no argument between slightly differing philosophies. This conflict strikes directly at the faith of our fathers and the lives of our sons. No principle or treasure that we hold, from the spiritual knowledge of our free schools and churches to the creative magic of free labor and capital, nothing lies safely beyond the reach of this struggle.

Freedom is pitted against slavery; lightness against the dark.

The faith we hold belongs not to us alone but to the free of all the world. This common bond binds the grower of rice in Burma and the planter of wheat in Iowa, the shepherd in southern Italy and the mountaineer in the Andes. It confers a common dignity upon the French soldier who dies in Indo-China, the British soldier killed in Malaya, the American life given in Korea.

We know, beyond this, that we are linked to all free peoples not merely by a noble idea but by a simple need. No free people can for long cling to any privilege or enjoy any safety in economic solitude. For all our own material might, even we need markets in the world for the surpluses of our farms and our factories. Equally, we need for these same farms and factories vital materials, and products of distant lands. This basic law of interdependence, so manifest in the commerce of peace, applies with thousand-fold intensity in the event of war.

So we are persuaded by necessity and by belief that the strength of all free peoples lies in unity; their danger, in discord.

To produce this unity, to meet the challenge of our time, destiny has laid upon our country the responsibility of the free world's leadership.

So it is proper that we assure our friends once again that, in the discharge of this responsibility, we Americans know and we observe the difference between world leadership and imperialism; between firmness and truculence; between a thoughtfully calculated goal and spasmodic reaction to the stimulus of emergencies.

We wish our friends the world over to know this above all: we face the threat—not with dread and confusion—but with confidence and conviction.

We feel this moral strength because we know that we are not helpless prisoners of history. We are free men. We shall remain free, never to be proven guilty of the one capital offense against freedom, a lack of stanch faith.

In pleading our just cause before the bar of history and in pressing our labor for world peace, we shall be guided by certain fixed principles.

These principles are:

(1) Abhorring war as a chosen way to balk the purposes of those who threaten us, we hold it to be the first task of statesmanship to develop the strength that will deter the forces of aggression and promote the conditions of peace. For, as it must be the supreme purpose of all free men, so it must be the dedication of their leaders, to save humanity from preying upon itself.

In the light of this principle, we stand ready to engage with any and all others in joint effort to remove the causes of mutual fear and distrust among nations, so as to make possible drastic reduc-

Here Eisenhower set forth in his own words the underlying thought expressed by Jefferson when he stated, ". . . every difference of opinion is not a difference of principle. We have called by different names brethren of the same principle. We are all Republicans, we are all Federalists."

In Jefferson's day the people expected turbulence, upheaval, and disorder, but Jefferson's philosophy of moderation quickly cooled hot tempers and restored the ship of state to a relatively even keel. So, too, did Eisenhower's calm appraisal of national and world conditions.

The intriguing difference between Jefferson's first inaugural address and Eisenhower's is that Jefferson was speaking to liberty-loving Americans only, whereas Eisenhower's reassurances were directed to freedom-loving men and women everywhere in the world. The threat of world communism had forced the United States to become involved in "entangling alliances" with foreign nations, in spite of contrary advice suggested by George Washington and later adopted as a policy by Thomas Jefferson in his first inaugural address. In place of this policy Eisenhower advanced nine principles or "rules of conduct," as he called them, by which the United States would be guided in its unceasing efforts to achieve world peace during his administration.

tion of armaments. The sole requisites for undertaking such effort are that—in their purpose—they be aimed logically and honestly toward secure peace for all; and that—in their result—they provide methods by which every participating nation will prove good faith in carrying out its pledge.

(2) Realizing that common sense and common decency alike dictate the futility of appeasement, we shall never try to placate an aggressor by the false and wicked bargain of trading honor for security. Americans, indeed all free men, remember that in the final choice a soldier's pack is not so heavy a burden as a prisoner's chains.

(3) Knowing that only a United States that is strong and immensely productive can help defend a freedom in our world, we view our Nation's strength and security as a trust upon which rests the hope of free men everywhere. It is the firm duty of each of our free citizens and of every free citizen everywhere to place the cause of his country before the comfort, the convenience of himself.

(4) Honoring the identity and the special heritage of each nation in the world, we shall never use our strength to try to impress upon another people our own cherished political and economic institutions.

(5) Assessing realistically the needs and capacities of proven friends of freedom, we shall strive to help them to achieve their own security and well-being. Likewise, we shall count upon them to assume, within the limits of their resources, their full and just burdens in the common defense of freedom.

(6) Recognizing economic health as an indispensable basis of military strength and the free world's peace, we shall strive to foster everywhere, and to practice ourselves, policies that encourage productivity and profitable trade. For the impoverishment of any single people in the world means danger to the well-being of all other peoples.

(7) Appreciating that economic need, military security and political wisdom combine to suggest regional groupings of free peoples, we hope, within the framework of the United Nations, to help strengthen such special bonds the world over. The nature of these ties must vary with the different problems of different areas.

In the Western Hemisphere, we enthusiastically join with all our neighbors in the work of perfecting a community of fraternal trust and common purpose.

In Europe, we ask that enlightened and inspired leaders of the Western nations strive with renewed vigor to make the unity of their peoples a reality. Only as free Europe unitedly marshals its strength can it effectively safeguard, even with our help, its spiritual and cultural heritage.

(8) Conceiving the defense of freedom, like freedom itself, to be one and indivisible, we hold all continents and peoples in equal regard and honor. We reject any insinuation that one race or another, one people or another, is in any sense inferior or expendable.

(9) Respecting the United Nations as the living sign of all people's hope for peace, we shall strive to make it not merely an eloquent symbol but an effective force. And in our quest for an honorable peace, we shall neither compromise, nor tire, nor ever cease.

By these rules of conduct, we hope to be known to all peoples.

By their observance, an earth of peace may become not a vision but a fact.

This hope—this supreme aspiration—must rule the way we live.

We must be ready to dare all for our country. For history does not long entrust the care of freedom to the weak or the timid. We must acquire proficiency in defense and display stamina in purpose.

We must be willing, individually and as a Nation, to accept whatever sacrifices may be required of us. A people that values its privileges above its principles soon loses both.

These basic precepts are not lofty abstractions, far removed from matters of daily living. They are laws of spiritual strength that generate and define our material strength. Patriotism means equipped forces and a prepared citizenry. Moral stamina means more energy and more productivity, on the farm and in the factory. Love of liberty means the guarding of every resource that makes freedom possible—from the sanctity of our families and the wealth of our soil to the genius of our scientists.

And so each citizen plays an indispensable role. The productivity of our heads, our hands, and our hearts is the source of all the strength we can command, for both the enrichment of our lives and the winning of the peace.

No person, no home, no community can be beyond the reach of this call. We are summoned to act in wisdom and in conscience, to work with industry, to teach with persuasion, to preach with conviction, to weigh our every deed with care and with compassion. For this truth must be clear before us: whatever America hopes to bring to pass in the world must first come to pass in the heart of America.

The peace we seek, then, is nothing less than the practice and fulfillment of our whole faith among ourselves and in our dealings with others. This signifies more than the stilling of guns, easing the sorrow of war. More than escape from death, it is a way of life. More than a haven for the weary, it is a hope for the brave.

This is the hope that beckons us onward in this century of trial. This is the work that awaits us all, to be done with bravery, with charity, and with prayer to Almighty God.

Eisenhower summed up his reading of history in one passage: "We must be ready to dare all for our country. For history does not long entrust the care of freedom to the weak or the timid. . . . A people that values its privileges above its principles soon loses both."

U.S. Army Photograph

Chief Justice Fred M. Vinson swears in Dwight D. Eisenhower as President of the United States on the east steps of the Capitol on January 20, 1953.

THE PRESIDENT

President Eisenhower's first term was marred by a heart attack on September 24, 1955, and an ileitis operation, June 9, 1956. Despite these interruptions the President continued to carry out his plans for countering the spread of communism throughout the world, by maintaining aid to friendly European countries under the Marshall Plan and striving to bring about unity among the nations outside the Iron Curtain. The apparent containment of Soviet efforts abroad, plus a rising wave of domestic prosperity, sufficed to see the President reëlected over his Democratic opponent by an even greater margin than before.

THE NATION

President Eisenhower, after his inauguration, turned his attention to the final signing of the armistice in Korea, which was brought about July 27, 1953. With this accomplished, the President and his Secretary of State, John Foster Dulles, were able to turn their attention to the pressing problem of offsetting the spread of communism throughout the world. In 1955 the campaign against communism in America was intensified, with more than 3000 federal employees discharged between 1953 and 1955 as security risks.

On February 2, 1954, President Eisenhower revealed to Congress that the first hydrogen bomb had been exploded, November 1, 1952. This thermonuclear explosion over Eniwetok was the AEC's first step in the United States' hydrogen weapon program.

In 1956 Republican Dwight D. Eisenhower was reëlected, polling 35,582,236 popular votes (457 electoral). Democrat Adlai Stevenson received 26,028,887 popular votes (73 electoral). Socialist Laborite Eric Hass polled 44,368, Prohibitionist Enoch A. Holtwick received 41,547, the Social Workers party's Farrell Dobbs polled 7,805 popular votes, T. Coleman Andrews of the States' Rights party 275,915, and Independent Harry F. Byrd 134,157. Walter B. Jones received 1 electoral vote. Richard M. Nixon was reëlected vice-president.

THE WORLD

The death of Joseph Stalin in Moscow, March 5, 1953, touched off a scramble among his subordinates for the position of premier. Egypt was proclaimed a republic, June 18th. In Korea an armistice was signed, July 27, 1953. On August 20, 1953, the Soviet Union announced the testing of a hydrogen bomb. On July 20, 1954, an armistice ended more than seven years of war in Indo-China. On July 18-23, 1955, a summit meeting between the heads of state of the United States, Great Britain, France, and the Soviet Union was held in Geneva, Switzerland. Unconditional cease-fire agreements were announced by Israel, Egypt, Jordan, Lebanon, and Syria on May 10, 1956. On October 23rd freedom-loving Hungarians revolted against Soviet rule; the uprising was crushed early in November. On March 6, 1957, Ghana became an independent nation. In July Nikita S. Khrushchev took another step toward becoming Soviet premier by ousting V. M. Molotov and Georgi Malenkov. Khrushchev was elected premier replacing Nicolai A. Bulganin, March 27, 1958. On October 4, 1957, the Soviet satellite Sputnik I was launched into orbit around the earth, marking the birth of a new era—the Space Age.

IN YOUR FIRST INAUGURAL ADDRESS you carefully avoided using the word "communism" in any form, although beneath the cloak of your rhetoric the thoughtful observer could distinguish the red garb of the "aggressor" to whom you referred. Now, four years later, the Cold War has lost its nebulous lines and has reached the point where you decide to pull no punches and eschew diplomatic double talk in your second inaugural address. And so you stand under sullen gray clouds, pierced by occasional shafts of sunlight, to spell out slowly—and firmly—the price of peace in today's communism-threatened world . . . .

Dwight D. Eisenhower

[1957–1961]

SECOND INAUGURAL ADDRESS, JANUARY 20, 1957

Capitol Steps, Washington, D.C.

THE PRICE OF PEACE

Mr. Chairman, Mr. Vice President, Mr. Chief Justice, Mr. Speaker, members of my family and friends, my countrymen, and the friends of my country, wherever they may be, we meet again, as upon a like moment 4 years ago, and again you have witnessed my solemn oath of service to you.

I, too, am a witness, today testifying in your name to the principles and purposes to which we, as a people, are pledged.

Before all else, we seek, upon our common labor as a nation, the blessings of Almighty God. And the hopes in our hearts fashion the deepest prayers of our whole people.

May we pursue the right without selfrighteousness.

May we know unity without conformity.

May we grow in strength without pride in self.

May we, in our dealings with all peoples of the earth, ever speak truth and serve justice.

And so shall America—in the sight of all men of good will—prove true to the honorable purposes that bind and rule us as a people in all this time of trial through which we pass.

II

We live in a land of plenty, but rarely has this earth known such peril as today.

In our Nation work and wealth abound. Our population grows. Commerce crowds our rivers and rails, our skies, harbors, and highways. Our soil is fertile, our agriculture productive. The air rings with the song of our industry—rolling mills and blast furnaces, dynamos, dams, and assembly lines—the chorus of America the bountiful.

This is our home—yet this is not the whole of our world. For our world is where our full destiny lies—with men, of all peoples, and all nations, who are or would be free. And for them—and so for us—this is no time of ease or of rest.

In too much of the earth there is want, discord, danger. New forces and new nations stir and strive across the earth, with power

Eisenhower was quoting from his personal conservative philosophy which he followed in dealing with domestic as well as global problems. He once described the basic creed of his administration in this way: "We should conserve everything that is basic to our system," he said. "We should be dynamic in applying it to the problems of the day." Thus was born the term "dynamic conservatism," two words to which Eisenhower attached great importance.

[263]

to bring, by their fate, great good or great evil to the free world's future. From the deserts of North Africa to the islands of the South Pacific one-third of all mankind has entered upon a historic struggle for a new freedom; freedom from grinding poverty. Across all continents, nearly a billion people seek, sometimes almost in desperation, for the skills and knowledge and assistance by which they may satisfy from their own resources, the material wants common to mankind.

No nation, however old or great, escapes this tempest of change and turmoil. Some, impoverished by the recent World War, seek to restore their means of livelihood. In the heart of Europe, Germany still stands tragically divided. So is the whole Continent divided. And so, too, is all the world.

The divisive force is international communism and the power that it controls.

The designs of that power, dark in purpose, are clear in practice. It strives to seal forever the fate of those it has enslaved. It strives to break the ties that unite the free. And it strives to capture —to exploit for its own greater power—all forces of change in the world, especially the needs of the hungry and the hopes of the oppressed.

Yet the world of international communism has itself been shaken by a fierce and mighty force: the readiness of men who love freedom to pledge their lives to that love. Through the night of their bondage, the unconquerable will of heroes has struck with the swift, sharp thrust of lightning. Budapest is no longer merely the name of a city; henceforth it is a new and shining symbol of man's yearning to be free.

Applause interrupted the President when he made this reference to the 1956 Hungarian uprising, which had been quelled by the use of Soviet tanks.

Thus across all the globe there harshly blow the winds of change. And, we—though fortunate be our lot—know that we can never turn our back to them.

III

We look upon this shaken earth, and we declare our firm and fixed purpose—the building of a peace with justice in a world where moral law prevails.

The building of such a peace is a bold and solemn purpose. To proclaim it is easy. To serve it will be hard. And to attain it, we must be aware of its full meaning—and ready to pay its full price.

We know clearly what we seek, and why.

We seek peace, knowing that peace is the climate of freedom. And now, as in no other age, we seek it because we have been warned, by the power of modern weapons, that peace may be the only climate possible for human life itself.

Yet this peace we seek cannot be born of fear alone: it must be rooted in the lives of nations. There must be justice, sensed and shared by all peoples, for, without justice the world can know only a tense and unstable truce. There must be law, steadily invoked and respected by all nations, for without law, the world promises only such meager justice as the pity of the strong upon the weak. But the law of which we speak, comprehending the values of freedom, affirms the equality of all nations, great and small.

Splendid as can be the blessings of such a peace, high will be its cost, in toil patiently sustained, in help honorably given, in sacrifice calmly borne.

We are called to meet the price of this peace.

To counter the threat of those who seek to rule by force, we must pay the costs of our own needed military strength, and help to build the security of others.

We must use our skills and knowledge and, at times, our substance, to help others rise from misery, however far the scene of suffering may be from our shores. For wherever in the world a people knows desperate want, there must appear at least the spark of hope, the hope of progress—or there will surely rise at last the flames of conflict.

We recognize and accept our own deep involvement in the destiny of men everywhere. We are accordingly pledged to honor, and to strive to fortify, the authority of the United Nations. For in that body rests the best hope of our age for the assertion of that law by which all nations may live in dignity.

And, beyond this general resolve, we are called to act a responsible role in the world's great concerns or conflicts—whether they touch upon the affairs of a vast region, the fate of an island in the Pacific, or the use of a canal in the Middle East. Only in respecting the hopes and cultures of others will we practice the equality of all nations. Only as we show willingness and wisdom in giving counsel, in receiving counsel, and in sharing burdens, will we wisely perform the work of peace.

For one truth must rule all we think and all we do. No people can live to itself alone. The unity of all who dwell in freedom is their only sure defense. The economic need of all nations—in mutual dependence—makes isolation an impossibility; not even America's prosperity could long survive if other nations did not prosper. No nation can longer be a fortress, lone and strong and safe. And any people, seeking such shelter for themselves, can now build only their own prison.

IV

Our pledge to these principles is constant, because we believe in their rightness.

We do not fear this world of change. America is no stranger to much of its spirit. Everywhere we see the seeds of the same growth that America itself has known. The American experiment has, for generations, fired the passion and the courage of millions elsewhere seeking freedom, equality, and opportunity. And the American story of material progress has helped excite the longing of all needy peoples for some satisfaction of their human wants. These hopes that we have helped to inspire, we can help to fulfill.

In this confidence, we speak plainly to all peoples.

We cherish our friendship with all nations that are or would be free. We respect, no less, their independence. And when, in time of want or peril, they ask our help, they may honorably receive it; for we no more seek to buy their sovereignty than we would sell our own. Sovereignty is never bartered among freemen.

We honor the aspirations of those nations which, now captive, long for freedom. We seek neither their military alliance nor any artificial imitation of our society. And they can know the warmth of the welcome that awaits them when, as must be, they join again the ranks of freedom.

We honor, no less in this divided world than in a less tormented time, the people of Russia. We do not dread, rather do we welcome, their demands for more intellectual freedom, greater security in their demands for more intellectual freedom, greater security before their own laws, fuller enjoyment of the rewards of their own toil.

These blunt words of Eisenhower's left no room for doubt as to America's future role in striving to maintain world peace. Isolationism, once the accepted panacea for threats to America's security, had been permanently junked, and the perimeter of our defenses had been expanded far beyond the continental limits of the nation.

Extending the hand of friendship to the people of Russia in an attempt to penetrate the Iron Curtain and end the cold war produced some remarkable results. Premier Nikita S. Khrushchev, after his tour of the United States, said, "the cold war ice has cracked and peaceful coexistence must emerge unless we want the madness of a world nuclear war." Whether this indicated a genuine gesture toward world peace or simply another coldly calculated maneuver toward world domination only time will reveal.

For as such things come to pass, the more certain will be the coming of that day when our peoples may freely meet in friendship.

So we voice our hope and our belief that we can help to heal this divided world. Thus may the nations cease to live in trembling before the menace of force. Thus may the weight of fear and the weight of arms be taken from the burdened shoulders of mankind.

This, nothing less, is the labor to which we are called and our strength dedicated.

And so the prayer of our people carries far beyond our own frontiers, to the wide world of our duty and our destiny.

May the light of freedom, coming to all darkened lands, flame brightly—until at last the darkness is no more.

May the turbulence of our age yield to a true time of peace, when men and nations shall share a life that honors the dignity of each, the brotherhood of all.

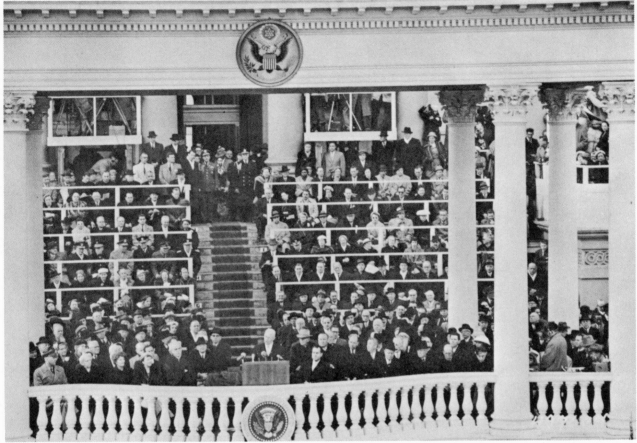

President Eisenhower making his inaugural address on January 21, 1957, after swearing-in ceremonies conducted by Chief Justice Earl Warren. Vice-President Nixon is to the President's left.

THE PRESIDENT

After the most costly campaign in U.S. history, highlighted by the use of the television medium to carry a series of *Great Debates*, Senator John F. Kennedy became the youngest man ever to be elected to the presidency.

THE NATION

President Eisenhower suffered a mild stroke November 25, 1957, but recovered quickly. The United States made news in 1958 with the first undersea crossings of the North Pole by two U.S. Navy atomic submarines: the *Nautilus* on August 3rd and the *Skate* on August 11th. January 3, 1959, Alaska was admitted as the 49th state, to be followed on August 21st by Hawaii as the 50th state. Secretary of State John Foster Dulles died of cancer May 24, 1959; he was succeeded on his April 15th resignation by Christian A. Herter. September 15th Premier Nikita S. Khrushchev arrived by air to visit the United States in search of peace. But the warm atmosphere of cultivated cordiality was to grow increasingly colder between the U.S. and the U.S.S.R., until the incident of the U-2 "spy plane" in mid-1960. There

followed Premier Khrushchev's dissolution of the Paris summit meeting, a move that presaged the return to cold war tactics and served to aid Senator Kennedy's campaign claims that U.S. prestige abroad was at an all-time low. In the 1960 election Democrat John F. Kennedy polled 34,221,485 popular votes (303 electoral) and Republican Richard M. Nixon received 34,108,684 popular votes (219 electoral). Socialist Workers Party candidate Farrell Dobbs polled 39,692; Prohibitionist Dr. Rutherford B. Decker received 46,197; Socialist Labor Party candidate Eric Haas polled 48,031; and Orville Faubus of the National States Rights party polled 227,881 popular votes. Senator Lyndon B. Johnson was elected vice-president.

THE WORLD

The U.S.S.R.'s Sputnik II, carrying a live dog, was orbited on November 3, 1957. America's answer was Explorer I, launched into orbit by the U.S. Army on January 31, 1958. This was followed by the Navy's Vanguard I, successfully orbited on March 17th, and Explorer III on March 26th. The race for space continued with the almost 3,000-pound Sputnik III, launched on May 15th, and the Explorer IV on July 26, 1958. Pope Pius XII died on October 9th; Angelo Guiseppe Cardinal Roncalli became Pope John XXIII on October 28th. General Charles de Gaulle was elected the first president of the Fifth French Republic on December 21st. The victorious rebel forces in Cuba named Fidel Castro as commander in chief on January 3, 1959, a move that was to produce far-reaching effects, for the next 24 months saw Cuba move ever closer to the doctrine of communism.

*THROUGHOUT THE GRUELING PREELECTION CAMPAIGN you have consistently man-
aged to project an image of youthful vigor, unshakeable self-confidence, and great personal magnetism. In this
respect television has proved to be a tremendous asset. For you have mastered this relatively new medium of
mass communication as adroitly as Franklin D. Roosevelt mastered the use of radio before you. Like Roosevelt you have promised much to many during the heat of the campaign—promises accepted at face value by
those who voted for you. But now the election fervor has cooled. And as you take your place on the inaugural
platform to deliver your address your audience of millions throughout the nation—and indeed the world—
cannot help but wonder how you will begin your attack on the infinitely complex regional, national, and
global problems with which you now must cope. . . .*

John F. Kennedy

[1961–1963]

INAUGURAL ADDRESS, JANUARY 20, 1961

Capitol Steps, Washington, D.C.

Fellow citizens:

We observe today not a victory of party but a celebration of freedom—symbolizing an end as well as a beginning—signifying renewal as well as change. For I have sworn before you and
Almighty God the same solemn oath our forebears prescribed
nearly a century and three-quarters ago.

The world is very different now. For man holds in his mortal
hands the power to abolish all forms of human poverty and all
forms of human life. And yet the same revolutionary beliefs for
which our forebears fought are still at issue around the globe—the
belief that the rights of man come not from the generosity of the
state but from the hand of God.

We dare not forget today that we are the heirs of that first revolution. Let the word go forth from this time and place, to friend
and foe alike, that the torch has been passed to a new generation
of Americans—born in this century, tempered by war, disciplined
by a hard and bitter peace, proud of our ancient heritage—and
unwilling to witness or permit the slow undoing of those human
rights to which this nation has always been committed, and to
which we are committed today at home and around the world.

Let every nation know, whether it wishes us well or ill, that we
shall pay any price, bear any burden, meet any hardship, support
any friend, oppose any foe to assure the survival and the success of
liberty.

This much we pledge—and more.

To those old allies whose cultural and spiritual origins we share,
we pledge the loyalty of faithful friends. United, there is little we
cannot do in a host of cooperative ventures. Divided, there is
little we can do—for we dare not meet a powerful challenge at
odds and split asunder.

*From this forceful statement to which all
true Americans must subscribe—and which
drew loud applause—President Kennedy
went on to make specific pledges to carefully
detailed groups around the globe.*

*The President's original manuscript as re-
leased to the press contained the word "new"
in the phrase ". . . there is little we cannot
do in a host of new cooperative ventures. . . ."
In his actual delivery the word was omitted.*

[269]

In this reference to "iron tyranny" the President did not specifically mention communism, but his meaning was unmistakable.

This phrase, which created a ripple of amused applause from the more than 20,000 persons witnessing the inaugural ceremonies, was an oblique reference to an old limerick:

> There was a young lady of Niger
> Who smiled as she rode on a tiger;
> They returned from the ride
> With the lady inside,
> And the smile on the face of the tiger.

In this paragraph President Kennedy made his only reference to the Communists by name. He concluded with a sentence which again touched off applause from the quiet, attentive throng.

In this clear-cut reaffirmation of the Monroe Doctrine the President reached one of the high points of an address noteworthy for its ringing rhetoric. Like Lincoln, who sought to unite a nation split asunder by the slavery question, Kennedy was speaking to all the peoples of the world, faced everywhere with the choice between a free world and communism. The new President sought to give reassurance to lovers of freedom around the globe, knowing full well the impact of his words.

In leaving the door open for new disarmament negotiations to avert "mankind's final war," President Kennedy was yet careful to point out that we must keep our arms at full strength until we have brought ". . . the absolute power to destroy other nations under the absolute control of all nations"; a phrase which was applauded, as were his words, "Let us never negotiate out of fear. But let us never fear to negotiate."

The full quotation from Isaiah 58:6 reads: "Is not this the fast that I have chosen? to loose the bands of wickedness, to undo the heavy burdens, and to let the oppressed go free, and that ye break every yoke?"

The President's original manuscript read "jungles," but he actually said "jungle" when delivering his address.

To those new states whom we welcome to the ranks of the free, we pledge our word that one form of colonial control shall not have passed away merely to be replaced by a far more iron tyranny. We shall not always expect to find them supporting our view. But we shall always hope to find them strongly supporting their own freedom—and to remember that, in the past, those who foolishly sought power by riding the back of the tiger ended up inside.

To those peoples in the huts and villages of half the globe struggling to break the bonds of mass misery, we pledge our best efforts to help them help themselves, for whatever period is required—not because the Communists may be doing it, not because we seek their votes, but because it is right. If a free society cannot help the many who are poor, it can not save the few who are rich.

To our sister republics south of our border, we offer a special pledge—to convert our good words into good deeds—in a new alliance for progress—to assist free men and free governments in casting off the chains of poverty. But this peaceful revolution of hope cannot become the prey of hostile powers. Let all our neighbors know that we shall join with them to oppose aggression or subversion anywhere in the Americas. And let every other power know that this hemisphere intends to remain the master of its own house.

To that world assembly of sovereign states, the United Nations, our last best hope in an age where the instruments of war have far outpaced the instruments of peace, we renew our pledge of support —to prevent it from becoming merely a forum for invective—to strengthen its shield of the new and the weak—and to enlarge the area in which its writ may run.

Finally, to those nations who would make themselves our adversary, we offer not a pledge but a request: that both sides begin anew the quest for peace, before the dark powers of destruction unleashed by science engulf all humanity in planned or accidental self-destruction.

We dare not tempt them with weakness. For only when our arms are sufficient beyond doubt can we be certain beyond doubt that they will never be employed.

But neither can two great and powerful groups of nations take comfort from our present course—both sides overburdened by the cost of modern weapons, both rightly alarmed by the steady spread of the deadly atom, yet both racing to alter that uncertain balance of terror that stays the hand of mankind's final war.

So let us begin anew—remembering on both sides that civility is not a sign of weakness, and sincerity is always subject to proof. Let us never negotiate out of fear. But let us never fear to negotiate.

Let both sides explore what problems unite us instead of belaboring those problems which divide us.

Let both sides, for the first time, formulate serious and precise proposals for the inspection and control of arms—and bring the absolute power to destroy other nations under the absolute control of all nations.

Let both sides seek to invoke the wonders of science instead of its terrors. Together let us explore the stars, conquer the deserts, eradicate disease, tap the ocean depths and encourage the arts and commerce.

Let both sides unite to heed in all corners of the earth the command of Isaiah—to "undo the heavy burdens . . . [and] let the oppressed go free."

And if a beach-head of cooperation may push back the jungle of suspicion, let both sides join in creating a new endeavor not a new balance of power, but a new world of law, where the strong are just and the weak secure and the peace preserved.

All this will not be finished in the first 100 days. Nor will it be finished in the first 1,000, nor in the life of this Administration, nor even perhaps in our lifetime on this planet. But let us begin.

This apparent reference to the first 100 days of Franklin D. Roosevelt's first term drew an enthusiastic response from the crowd of listeners.

In your hands, my fellow citizens, more than mine, will rest the final success or failure of our course. Since this country was founded, each generation of Americans has been summoned to give testimony to its national loyalty. The graves of young Americans who answered the call to service surround the globe.

Now the trumpet summons us again—not as a call to bear arms, though arms we need—not as a call to battle, though embattled we are—but a call to bear the burden of a long twilight struggle year in and year out, "rejoicing in hope, patient in tribulation"—a struggle against the common enemies of man: tyranny, poverty, disease and war itself.

The quotation referred to is from The Epistle of Paul the Apostle to the Romans 12:12: "Rejoicing in hope; patient in tribulation; continuing instant in prayer."

Can we forge against these enemies a grand and global alliance, north and south, east and west, that can assure a more fruitful life for all mankind? Will you join in that historic effort?

This appeal brought forth scattered cries of "yes!" mingled with cheers and applause, as the audience belatedly realized the President had actually asked a question.

In the long history of the world, only a few generations have been granted the role of defending freedom in its hour of maximum danger. I do not shrink from this responsibility—I welcome it. I do not believe that any of us would exchange places with any other people or any other generation. The energy, the faith, the devotion which we bring to this endeavor will light our country and all who serve it—and the glow from that fire can truly light the world.

Pumping his right hand alongside the podium in a characteristic, vigorous motion seen often during the heat of the pre-election campaign, the new President drove home his point; forthrightly accepted his responsibility.

And so, my fellow Americans: ask not what your country can do for you—ask what you can do for your country.

My fellow citizens of the world: ask not what America will do for you, but what together we can do for the freedom of man.

Finally, whether you are citizens of America or citizens of the world, ask of us here the same high standards of strength and sacrifice which we ask of you. With a good conscience our only sure reward, with history the final judge of our deeds, let us go forth to lead the land we love, asking His blessing and His help, but knowing that here on earth God's work must truly be our own.

In a climactic final passage President Kennedy made a blunt attack on self-centered ambition and those who put personal interest above national interest.

[271]

John F. Kennedy being sworn in as President, January 20, 1961, with former President Eisenhower on the left and, to the right, future Presidents Johnson and Nixon.

Wide World Photos

In the cabin of the presidential plane, Lyndon B. Johnson is sworn in as President on November 22, 1963, by Judge Sarah T. Hughes.

Wide World Photos

United Press International Photo

Lyndon Baines Johnson

[1963–1965]

THE PRESIDENT

Lyndon Baines Johnson was born on a small farm near Stonewall, Texas, August 27, 1908. When he was five, his parents, Sam and Rebekah Johnson, moved to Johnson City where he completed his high school education in 1924, going on to obtain a Bachelor of Science degree at Southwest Texas State Teachers College in 1930. He then attended Georgetown University Law School in Washington, D.C.

In 1937 he entered politics, taking over a representative's seat vacated due to death, and winning a full term a year later. After four terms in the House, he was elected Senator in 1948. He became Democratic whip in 1951 and leader in 1953.

When John F. Kennedy asked Johnson to run for vice-president in the 1960 campaign against Richard M. Nixon, Johnson accepted and campaigned vigorously. He was with President Kennedy on the political fence-mending trip to Dallas, which ended in the tragedy that made Lyndon Baines Johnson the 8th vice-president to accede to the presidency.

At Johnson's request, U.S. District Court Judge Sarah T. Hughes of Dallas administered the oath of office to him at 2:39 p.m. (CST) in the heavily guarded presidential plane at Dallas' Love Field. The new President then flew to Washington, D.C., where he addressed the stunned American people via radio and television, telling them: "I will do my best. That is all I can do. I ask for your help, and God's."

Three days later, Monday, November 25, 1963, President Johnson was joined by national leaders and world statesmen to follow the martyred President and his grieving family from the Capitol to St. Matthew's Cathedral for Requiem Mass, and then to the grave in Arlington National Cemetery. Wednesday, November 27, President Johnson asked a somber Congress to honor John F. Kennedy's memory with swift action on the slain leader's legislative program, topped by civil rights and tax reduction. He called for: "an end to the teaching and preaching of hate and evil and violence in the land" . . . a plea that was increasingly ignored the longer he remained in office.

[273]

THE PRESIDENT

Lyndon B. Johnson filled out President John Kennedy's term by carrying out legislation for welfare, civil rights, tax reduction, and poverty relief, in an all-out attempt to create what Johnson named in his Inaugural Address a "Great Society." His popularity rose as he emerged from Kennedy's nimbus, and he was swept into office for a full term on November 3, 1964.

THE NATION

January 3, 1961, two years to the day from the date Fidel Castro was named commander-in-chief of the rebel forces in Cuba, the United States severed diplomatic relations with Cuba. Three months later, on April 17, Cuban exiles attempted to invade Cuba but they were repulsed with a heavy loss of life in what has since become known as the Bay of Pigs defeat, blame for which was laid by many on President Kennedy and the CIA for withdrawal of allegedly promised support.

May 5, 1961, Commander Alan B. Shepard, Jr., made the first U.S. manned sub-orbital space flight 116.5 miles above the earth in a Mercury capsule. July 21, Captain Virgil I. Grissom completed a similar flight, to be followed on February 20, 1962, by Lt. Colonel John H. Glenn, Jr., who circled the earth 3 times in orbit. This feat was the first of many: Lt. Commander Scott Car-penter, 3-orbit flight, May 24, 1962; Lt. Commander Walter M. Schirra, Jr., 6-orbit flight, October 3, 1962; Major Leroy Gordon Cooper, 22-orbit flight, May 15–16, 1963.

Meanwhile, back on earth, unresolved civil rights inequities and rising poverty combined to produce a demonstration on August 28, 1963, in Washington, D.C., where Negro leader Dr. Martin Luther King delivered his now-famous "I have a dream" speech. On October 20, 1964, former President Herbert Hoover died in New York City.

In the 1964 election incumbent President Lyndon B. Johnson rolled up the greatest popular vote cast to date—43,126,506 (486 electoral)—to defeat Republican Barry M. Goldwater who received 27,176,799 votes (52 electoral). Hubert H. Humphrey was elected vice-president.

THE WORLD

Russia's Major Yuri Gagarin became the first human in orbit on April 12, 1961, in *Vostok I*, followed by Major Gherman S. Titov who made 17 orbits on August 6–7 in *Vostok II*. A week later, the border was closed between East and West Berlin and a wall was built by the East Germans without forcible remonstrance by President Kennedy. On August 11, 1962, Soviet Cosmonaut Major Andrian G. Niko-layev began 64 orbits and on August 12, Soviet Lt. Colonel Pavel R. Popovich began 48 orbits, at times in sight of each other. On October 22, 1962, the existence of Soviet missile bases in Cuba was revealed by President Kennedy, who set up a naval and air blockade until the crisis was resolved on November 2 by removal of the missiles.

More space firsts were tallied by Russia. On June 16, 1963, Soviet Jr. Lt. Valentina V. Tereshkova was launched into orbit aboard *Vostok VI*, making 48 orbits. This feat was followed by the first space-craft with more than one astronaut aboard when the *Voshod I* was launched October 12, 1964, for 16 orbits, carrying Colonel V. M. Komarov, Dr. B. B. Yegerov, and K. P. Feoktistov. Soviet Premier Khrushchev was removed on October 14–15, 1964; Aleksei N. Kosygin became Premier; Leonard I. Brezhnev became party leader. The following day, October 16, Communist China successfully exploded its first atomic bomb.

The conflict in Vietnam continued to grow and spread despite the warning that President Kennedy had uttered in the fourth paragraph of his Inaugural Address.

NOW ELECTED AS PRESIDENT IN YOUR OWN RIGHT by an overwhelming majority, you appear to have at last come into your own heritage. You have admirably fulfilled the late President Kennedy's unexpired term and carried out as many of his unfinished projects as a sorrowfully pliant Congress could enact into law. But now—now you have won the presidency by a far greater margin than your predecessor. You step forward on the inaugural platform built over the Capitol's east steps to be sworn in on this clear, cold, occasionally sunny day, as the 36th President of the United States by Chief Justice Earl Warren, with Mrs. Johnson setting a precedent by becoming the first woman to hold the Bible for the ceremony. The Bible used was given to you by your mother, the late Rebekah Baines Johnson, thirteen years ago. After you have repeated the oath of office, you usher your wife to her seat, return, and pause briefly as though to savor your victory before beginning your address, which will be carried to a global audience via radio and satellite television....

Lyndon Baines Johnson

[1965–1969]

INAUGURAL ADDRESS, JANUARY 20, 1965

Capitol Steps, Washington, D.C.

My fellow countrymen: On this occasion, the oath I have taken before you and before God, is not mine alone, but ours together. We are one nation and one people. Our fate as a nation and our future as a people rest not upon one citizen but upon all citizens.

That is the majesty and the meaning of this moment.

For every generation, there is a destiny. For some, history decides. For this generation, the choice must be our own.

Even now, a rocket moves toward Mars. It reminds us that the world will not be the same for our children, or even for ourselves in a short span of years. The next man to stand here will look out on a scene that is different from our own, because ours is a time of change—rapid and fantastic change—baring the secrets of nature—multiplying the nations—placing in uncertain hands new weapons for mastery and destruction—shaking old values and uprooting old ways.

Our destiny in the midst of change will rest on the unchanged character of our people and on their faith.

They came here—the exile and the stranger, brave but frightened—to find a place where a man could be his own man. They made a covenant with this land. Conceived in justice, written in liberty, bound in union, it was meant one day to inspire the hopes of all mankind, and it binds us still. If we keep its terms we shall flourish.

First, justice was the promise that all who made the journey would share in the fruits of the land.

In a land of great wealth, families must not live in hopeless poverty.

In a land rich in harvest, children just must not go hungry.

In a land of healing miracles, neighbors must not suffer and die untended.

The President began his address with a blunt appeal for national unity.

In less than four years, the wonder of a rocket moving toward Mars would be relegated to the commonplace by one space exploit after another as Russia and America leap-frogged from one "first" to another in their all-out race to the moon—and beyond.

The President apparently built much of his address around a "covenant" made by the Pilgrims—the so-called Mayflower Compact that was executed between the members of the first Pilgrim settlers of the Massachusetts colony who agreed to: "solemnly and mutually in the presence of God and one another, covenant and combine ourselves together into a civil body politick, for our better order and preservation."

In a great land of learning and scholars, young people must be taught to read and write.

For the more than thirty years that I have served this nation, I have believed that this injustice to our people, this waste of our resources, was our real enemy. For thirty years or more, with the resources I have had, I have vigilantly fought against it. I have learned and I know that it will not surrender easily.

But change has given us new weapons. Before this generation of Americans is finished, this enemy will not only retreat—it will be conquered.

Justice requires us to remember: when any citizen denies his fellow, saying: His color is not mine or his beliefs are strange and different, in that moment he betrays America, though his forebears created this nation.

Liberty was the second article of our covenant. It was self-government, it was our Bill of Rights. But it was more. America would be a place where each man could be proud to be himself: stretching his talents, rejoicing in his work, important in the life of his neighbors and his nation.

This has become more difficult in a world where change and growth seem to tower beyond the control and even the judgment of men. We must work to provide the knowledge and the surroundings which can enlarge the possibilities of every citizen.

The American covenant called on us to help show the way for the liberation of man, and that is our goal. Thus, if as a nation, there is much outside our control, as a people no stranger is outside our hope.

Change has brought new meaning to that old mission. We can never again stand aside prideful in isolation. Terrific dangers and troubles that we once called "foreign" now constantly live among us. If American lives must end, and American treasure be spilled, in countries that we barely know, then that is the price that change has demanded of conviction and of our enduring covenant.

Think of our world as it looks from that rocket that is heading toward Mars. It is like a child's globe, hanging in space, the continent stuck to its side like colored maps. We are all fellow passengers on a dot of earth. And each of us, in the span of time, has really only a moment among his companions.

How incredible it is that in this fragile existence we should hate and destroy one another. There are possibilities enough for all who will abandon mastery over others to pursue mastery over nature. There is world enough for all to seek their happiness in their own way.

Our nation's course is abundantly clear. We aspire to nothing that belongs to others. We seek no dominion over our fellow man, but man's dominion over tyranny and misery.

But more is required. Men want to be a part of a common enterprise—a cause greater than themselves. And each of us must find a way to advance the purpose of the nation, thus finding new purpose for ourselves. Without this, we will simply become a nation of strangers.

The third article is union. To those who were small and few against the wilderness, the success of liberty demanded the strength of the union. Two centuries of change have made this true again.

No longer need capitalist and worker, farmer and clerk, city and countryside, struggle to divide our bounty. By working shoulder to shoulder together we can increase the bounty of all.

[276]

We have discovered that every child who learns, and every man who finds work, and every sick body that is made whole—like a candle added to an altar—brightens the hope of all the faithful.

So let us reject any among us who seek to reopen old wounds and rekindle old hatreds. They stand in the way of a seeking nation.

Let us now join reason to faith and action to experience, to transform our unity of interest into a unity of purpose. For the hour and the day and the time are here to achieve progress without strife, to achieve change without hatred; not without difference of opinion but without the deep and abiding divisions which scar the union for generations.

Under this covenant of justice, liberty, and union, we have become a nation; prosperous, great, and mighty. And we have kept our freedom. But we have no promise from God that our greatness will endure.

We have been allowed by Him to seek greatness with the sweat of our hands and the strength of our spirit.

I do not believe that the Great Society is the ordered, changeless, and sterile battalion of the ants.

It is the excitement of becoming—always becoming, trying, probing, falling, resting, and trying again—but always trying and always gaining.

In each generation—with toil and tears—we have had to earn our heritage again.

If we fail now, then we will have forgotten in abundance what we learned in hardship: that democracy rests on faith, that freedom asks more than it gives, and that the judgment of God is harshest on those who are most favored.

If we succeed, it will not be because of what we have, but it will be because of what we are; not because of what we own, but rather because of what we believe.

For we are a nation of believers. Underneath the clamor of building and the rush of our day's pursuits, we are believers in justice and liberty and union. And in our own Union we believe that every man must someday be free. And we believe in ourselves.

That is the mistake that our enemies have always made. In my lifetime—in depression and in war—they have awaited our defeat. Each time, from the secret places of the American heart, came forth the faith that they could not see or that they could not even imagine, and it brought us victory. And it will again.

For this is what America is all about. It is the uncrossed desert and the unclimbed ridge. It is the star that is not reached and the harvest that is sleeping in the unplowed ground.

Is our world gone? We say farewell. Is a new world coming? We welcome it—and we will bend it to the hopes of man.

To these trusted public servants and to my family, and those close friends of mine who have followed me down a long winding road, and to all the people of this Union and the world—I will repeat today what I said on that sorrowful day in November last year: I will lead and I will do the best I can.

But you, you must look within your own hearts to the old promises and to the old dreams. They will lead you best of all.

For myself, I ask only in the words of an ancient leader: "Give me now wisdom and knowledge that I may go out and come in before this people: for who can judge this, thy people, that is so great?"

From Johnson's reference to "the Great Society" grew the term by which his administration will be remembered. His administration was indeed marked by "trying, probing, falling, resting, and trying again." In delivering this passage relating to his concept of a "Great Society," the President raised clenched fists as if to pummel home the importance with which he regarded this philosophy.

In this, perhaps the most moving passage of his address, the President recalls his words of November 22, 1963, when he had addressed the shocked nation on his return to Washington following President Kennedy's assassination.

The "ancient leader" Johnson quotes here was Solomon. The complete quotation appears in Second Chronicles, 1:6 to 1:12...

6 And Solomon went up thither to the brasen altar before the LORD, which *was* at the tabernacle of the congregation, and offered a thousand burnt offerings upon it.

7 In that night did God appear unto Solomon, and said unto him, Ask what I shall give thee.

8 And Solomon said unto God, Thou hast shewed great mercy unto David my father, and hast made me to reign in his stead.

9 Now, O LORD God, let thy promise unto David my father be established: for thou hast made me king over a people like the dust of the earth in multitude.

10 Give me now wisdom and knowledge, that I may go out and come in before this people: for who can judge this thy people, *that is* so great?

11 And God said to Solomon, Because this was in thine heart, and thou hast not asked riches, wealth, or honour, nor the life of thine enemies, neither yet hast asked long life; but hast asked wisdom and knowledge for thyself, that thou mayest judge my people, over whom I have made thee king:

12 Wisdom and knowledge *is* granted unto thee; and I will give thee riches, and wealth, and honour, such as none of the kings have had that *have been* before thee, neither shall there any after thee have the like.

[277]

THE PRESIDENT

In a dramatic comeback from his narrow defeat by John F. Kennedy in the 1960 campaign, Richard M. Nixon successfully fought off the Democratic candidate, Hubert H. Humphrey, and the third party candidate, George C. Wallace, to become the 37th President.

THE NATION

February 7, 1965, President Johnson ordered the bombing of North Vietnam in retaliation for Viet Cong attacks on Pleiku. On June 3, U.S. Major Edward H. White was the first American to "space-walk"; on December 4, Lt. Colonel Frank Borman and Commander James A. Lovell, Jr., orbited for 14 days in *Gemini 7,* to hold the first manned space rendezvous December 15 with *Gemini 6,* piloted by Captain Walter M. Schirra, Jr., and Major Thomas P. Stafford.

August 11–16, 1965, Negroes in Los Angeles' Watts area rioted. October 4, Pope Pius visited New York City and the United Nations to plead and pray for peace. On July 1, 1966, President Johnson signed the Medicare bill, living up to his Inaugural Address pledge to implement a Great Society in which "neighbors must not suffer and die untended." November 8, Edward Brooke (R., Mass.) was elected U.S. Senator—the first Negro Senator in 85 years. January 27, 1967, astronauts Grissom, White, and Chaffee perished in a fire aboard the spacecraft, Apollo I, at Cape Kennedy, Florida. July 12–17, riots in Newark, New Jersey, killed at least 26. July 23–30, at least 40 died in riots in Detroit, Michigan. October 2, 1967, Thurgood Marshall became the first Negro U.S. Supreme Court justice. January 19, 1968, Clark Clifford replaced Robert McNamara as Secretary of Defense. Four days later the U.S. Navy's electronic intelligence ship U.S.S. *Pueblo* was seized in international waters by 4 North Korean vessels. March 31, 1968, President Johnson announced his decision not to seek a second term. April 4, Dr. Martin Luther King was assassinated in Memphis, Tennessee. June 6, Senator Robert F. Kennedy (D., N.Y.) died of an assassin's bullet in Los Angeles, California. 1968 saw the spread of student and civil rights rioting, culminating in the Chicago riots during the Democratic convention.

In the 1968 election Republican Richard M. Nixon polled 31,770,237 popular votes (301 electoral). Democrat Hubert H. Humphrey polled 31,270,533 (191 electoral). Third party candidate George C. Wallace polled 9,906,141 (46 electoral). Spiro T. Agnew was elected vice-president.

THE WORLD

March 18, 1965, Soviet Lt. Colonel Aleksei A. Leonov was the first man to "walk" in space outside his capsule. November 11, minority whites proclaimed for Rhodesia independence from Britain. February 3, 1966, Russia's *Luna 9* was the first unmanned spacecraft to make a soft landing on the moon; U.S.A.'s *Surveyor I* duplicated the feat on June 2. Ghana's President Kwame Nkrumah was overthrown February 24, 1967. In a smashing 6-day attack, June 5–10, 1967, Israel conquered the forces of the United Arab Republic. December 3, the first human heart was transplanted by Dr. Christian N. Barnard in Capetown, South Africa, to usher in a new era in surgery. May 2, 1968, student riots challenged the regime of French President Charles de Gaulle. May 3, preliminary Vietnam peace talks opened in Paris. August 24, France exploded a fusion bomb, the 5th nation to do so. In mid-December, surgeons performed history's 100th human heart transplant, a few days more than a year from Dr. Barnard's pioneering breakthrough. To close out the year, 3 American astronauts, Frank Borman, James Lovell, Jr., and William Anders, looped around the moon in *Apollo 8* on Christmas Eve and returned to earth safely.

EIGHT YEARS AGO, AFTER YOUR HEART-BREAKING LOSS OF THE PRESIDENCY by only 118,550 votes, you told reporters they had seen the last of you. But after the shock wears off, you recover your poise and your determination and, although defeated in your bid to become governor of California, you persist with the same doggedness that first brought you into national prominence when you unraveled the tangled trail leading to the "pumpkin papers" and the conviction of an enemy of the nation. When the votes are in, the victory—so bitterly twice contested—is finally yours and doubly relished. Now, thanks to world-wide television and radio, you have an audience of hundreds of millions who are watching and listening as the oath of office is administered on a cold, raw day by Chief Justice Earl Warren, with your wife, Patricia, holding your two leather-bound family Bibles, dated 1828 and 1873, one on top of the other and both opened to Isaiah 2:4. After being sworn in, you help your wife to her seat, turn back to the lectern, and begin to deliver your address to the nation and to the waiting world whose future is now so inextricably bound to yours . . . .

Richard Milhous Nixon

[1969–   ]

INAUGURAL ADDRESS, JANUARY 20, 1969

Capitol Steps, Washington, D.C.

Senator Dirksen, Mr. Chief Justice, Mr. Vice-President, President Johnson, Vice-President Humphrey, My Fellow Americans—and my fellow citizens of the world community:

I ask you to share with me today the majesty of this moment. In the orderly transfer of power, we celebrate the unity that keeps us free.

Each moment in history is a fleeting time, precious and unique. But some stand out as moments of beginning, in which courses are set that shape decades or centuries.

This can be such a moment.

Forces now are converging that make possible, for the first time, the hope that many of man's deepest aspirations can at last be realized. The spiraling pace of change allows us to contemplate, within our own lifetime, advances that once would have taken centuries.

In throwing wide the horizons of space, we have discovered new horizons on earth.

For the first time, because the people of the world want peace, and the leaders of the world are afraid of war, the times are on the side of peace.

Eight years from now America will celebrate its 200th Anniversary as a nation. Within the lifetime of most people now living, mankind will celebrate that great new year which comes only once in a thousand years—the beginning of the Third Millennium.

What kind of a nation we will be, what kind of a world we will live in, whether we shape the future in the image of our hopes, is ours to determine by our actions and our choices.

The greatest honor history can bestow is the title of peacemaker. This honor now beckons America—the chance to help lead the world at last out of the valley of turmoil and onto that high ground of peace that man has dreamed of since the dawn of civilization.

If we succeed, generations to come will say of us now living that we mastered our moment, that we helped make the world safe for mankind.

This is our summons to greatness.

I believe the American people are ready to answer this call.

In his opening words addressed to "my fellow citizens of the world community," President Nixon followed the lead of President Eisenhower who, in his second Inaugural Address of January 20, 1957, was the first to address his Inaugural remarks specifically to listeners other than American. Eisenhower put it thus: "Mr. Chairman, Mr. Vice-President, Mr. Chief Justice, Mr. Speaker, members of my family and friends, my countrymen, and the friends of my country, wherever they may be . . ."

Woodrow Wilson's hope was to "make the world safe for democracy" . . . a desire that Nixon updated in the spirit of this era of mass-destruction to include not only democracy but the whole human race.

[279]

The second third of this century has been a time of proud achievement. We have made enormous strides in science and industry and agriculture. We have shared our wealth more broadly than ever. We have learned at last to manage a modern economy to assure its continued growth.

We have given freedom new reach. We have begun to make its promise real for black as well as for white.

We see the hope of tomorrow in the youth of today. I know America's youth. I believe in them. We can be proud that they are better educated, more committed, more passionately driven by conscience than any generation in our history.

No people has ever been so close to the achievement of a just and abundant society, or so possessed of the will to achieve it. And because our strengths are so great, we can afford to appraise our weaknesses with candor and to approach them with hope.

A quotation from the second paragraph of President Franklin D. Roosevelt's first Inaugural Address, delivered March 4, 1933.

Standing in this same place a third of a century ago, Franklin Delano Roosevelt addressed a nation ravaged by depression and gripped in fear. He could say in surveying the nation's troubles: "They concern, thank God, only material things."

Our crisis today is in reverse.

We have found ourselves rich in goods, but ragged in spirit; reaching with magnificent precision for the moon, but falling into raucous discord here on earth.

We are caught in war, wanting peace. We are torn by division, wanting unity. We see around us empty lives, wanting fulfillment. We see tasks that need doing, waiting for hands to do them.

To a crisis of the spirit, we need an answer of the spirit.

And to find that answer, we need only look within ourselves.

Nixon's address is marked by references to the spiritual crisis confronting the nation, which he sums up here, followed by a paraphrase from Shakespeare's Julius Caesar, *Act I, Scene II: "... the fault, my dear Brutus, is not in our stars, but in ourselves, that we are underlings."*

On March 4, 1861, Lincoln concluded his first Inaugural Address with this stirring sentence here quoted in part by Nixon: "The mystic chords of memory, stretching from every battlefield and patriot grave to every living heart and hearthstone all over this broad land, will yet swell the chorus of the Union, when again touched, as surely as they will be, by the better angels of our nature."

When we listen to "the better angels of our nature," we find that they celebrate the simple things, the basic things—such as goodness, decency, love, kindness.

Greatness comes in simple trappings.

The simple things are the ones most needed today if we are to surmount what divides us, and cement what unites us.

To lower our voices would be a simple thing.

In these difficult years, America has suffered from a fever of words; from inflated rhetoric that promises more than it can deliver; from angry rhetoric that fans discontents into hatreds; from bombastic rhetoric that postures instead of persuading.

We cannot learn from one another until we stop shouting at one another—until we speak quietly enough so that our words can be heard as well as our voices.

For its part, government will listen. We will strive to listen in new ways—to the voices of quiet anguish, the voices that speak without words, the voices of the heart—to the injured voices, the anxious voices, the voices that have despaired of being heard.

Nixon's theme was similar to Lincoln's: "let us bind up the wounds." Faced with dissident factions at home, Nixon praised his former political foes and offered reconciliation, compassion, understanding, equality, and help to the young, the needy, and to all clamoring minorities.

Those who have been left out, we will try to bring in.

Those left behind, we will help to catch up.

For all our people, we will set as our goal the decent order that makes progress possible and our lives secure.

As we reach toward our hopes, our task is to build on what has gone before—not turning away from the old, but turning toward the new.

In this past third of a century, government has passed more laws, spent more money, initiated more programs, than in all our previous history.

In pursuing our goals of full employment, better housing, excellence in education; in rebuilding our cities and improving our

[280]

rural areas; in protecting our environment and enhancing the quality of life; in all these and more, we will and must press urgently forward.

We shall plan now for the day when our wealth can be transferred from the destruction of war abroad to the urgent needs of our people at home.

The American dream does not come to those who fall asleep.

But we are approaching the limits of what government alone can do.

Our greatest need now is to reach beyond government, to enlist the legions of the concerned and the committed.

What has to be done, has to be done by government and people together or it will not be done at all. The lesson of past agony is that without the people we can do nothing; with the people we can do everything.

To match the magnitude of our tasks, we need the energies of our people—enlisted not only in grand enterprises, but more importantly in those small, splendid efforts that make headlines in the neighborhood newspaper instead of the national journal.

With these, we can build a great cathedral of the spirit—each of us raising it one stone at a time, as he reaches out to his neighbor, helping, caring, doing.

I do not offer a life of uninspiring ease. I do not call for a life of grim sacrifice. I ask you to join in a high adventure—one as rich as humanity itself, and exciting as the times we live in.

The essence of freedom is that each of us shares in the shaping of his own destiny.

Until he has been part of a cause larger than himself, no man is truly whole.

The way to fulfillment is in the use of our talents. We achieve nobility in the spirit that inspires that use.

As we measure what can be done, we shall promise only what we know we can produce, but as we chart our goals, we shall be lifted by our dreams.

No man can be fully free while his neighbor is not. To go forward at all is to go forward together.

This means black and white together, as one nation, not two. The laws have caught up with our conscience. What remains is to give life to what is in the law: to insure at last that as all are born equal in dignity before God, all are born equal in dignity before man.

As we learn to go forward together at home, let us also seek to go forward together with all mankind.

Let us take as our goal: where peace is unknown, make it welcome; where peace is fragile, make it strong; where peace is temporary, make it permanent.

After a period of confrontation, we are entering an era of negotiation.

Let all nations know that during this Administration our lines of communication will be open.

We seek an open world—open to ideas, open to the exchange of goods and people, a world in which no people, great or small, will live in angry isolation.

We cannot expect to make everyone our friend, but we can try to make no one our enemy.

Those who would be our adversaries, we invite to a peaceful competition—not in conquering territory or extending dominion, but in enriching the life of man.

The phrase "black and white together" is the first line of the second verse of the civil rights anthem "We Shall Overcome."

Nixon here carries on the thought expressed by President Kennedy in his Inaugural Address of January 20, 1961, when he said: ". . . to those nations who would make themselves our adversary, we offer not a pledge but a request: that both sides begin anew the quest for peace, before the dark powers of destruction unleashed by science engulf all humanity in planned or accidental self-destruction."

[281]

Again Nixon carries on an ideal expressed by Kennedy thus: "We dare not tempt them with weakness. For only when our arms are sufficient beyond doubt can we be certain beyond doubt that they will never be employed."

As we explore the reaches of space, let us go to the new worlds together—not as new worlds to be conquered, but as a new adventure to be shared.

With those who are willing to join, let us cooperate to reduce the burden of arms, to strengthen the structure of peace, to lift up the poor and the hungry.

But to all who would be tempted by weakness, let us leave no doubt that we will be as strong as we need to be for as long as we need to be.

Over the past 20 years, since I first came to this Capital as a freshman Congressman, I have visited most of the nations of the world. I have come to know the leaders of the world, and the great forces, the hatreds, the fears that divide the world.

I know that peace does not come through wishing for it—that there is no substitute for days and even years of patient and prolonged diplomacy.

I also know the people of the world.

I have seen the hunger of a homeless child, the pain of a man wounded in battle, the grief of a mother who has lost her son. I know these have no ideology, no race.

I know America. I know the heart of America is good.

I speak from my own heart, and the heart of my country, the deep concern we have for those who suffer, and those who sorrow.

I have taken an oath today in the presence of God and my countrymen to uphold and defend the Constitution of the United States. To that oath I now add this sacred commitment: I shall consecrate my office, my energies, and all the wisdom I can summon to the cause of peace among nations.

Once again Nixon paraphrases Kennedy's Inaugural words, which were: "Let the word go forth from this time and place, to friend and foe alike . . ."

Let this message be heard by strong and weak alike:

The peace we seek—the peace we seek to win—is not victory over any other people, but the peace that comes "with healing in its wings"; with compassion for those who have suffered; with understanding for those who have opposed us; with the opportunity for all the peoples of this earth to choose their own destiny.

The complete quotation from the Book of Malachi 4:2, reads: "But unto you that fear my name shall the Sun of righteousness arise with healing in his wings; and ye shall go forth, and grow up as calves of the stall."

Only a few short weeks ago we shared the glory of man's first sight of the world as God sees it, as a single sphere reflecting light in the darkness.

As the Apollo Astronauts flew over the moon's gray surface on Christmas eve, they spoke to us of the beauty of earth—and in that voice so clear across the lunar distance, we heard them invoke God's blessing on its goodness.

In that moment, their view from the moon moved poet Archibald MacLeish to write: "To see the earth as it truly is, small and blue and beautiful in that eternal silence where it floats, is to see ourselves as riders on the Earth together, brothers in that bright loveliness in the eternal cold—brothers who know now they are truly brothers."

Quoted from the last paragraph of an essay written by Archibald MacLeish that appeared on the front page of The New York Times, *Christmas Day, December 25th, 1968.*

In that moment of surpassing technological triumph, men turned their thoughts toward home and humanity—seeing in that far perspective that man's destiny on earth is not divisible, telling us that however far we reach into the cosmos, our destiny lies not in the stars but on earth itself, in our own hands, in our own hearts.

We have endured a long night of the American spirit. But as our eyes catch the dimness of the first rays of dawn, let us not curse the remaining dark. Let us gather the light.

In his final sentence Nixon paraphrased Lincoln, who closed his second Inaugural Address with these now-famous words: "With malice toward none, with charity for all, with firmness in the right as God gives us to see the right, let us strive on to finish the work we are in . . ."

Our destiny offers not the cup of despair, but the chalice of opportunity. So let us seize it not in fear, but in gladness—and, "riders on the Earth together," let us go forward, firm in our faith, steadfast in our purpose, cautious of the dangers; but sustained by our confidence in the will of God and the promise of man.

Richard M. Nixon, receiving the oath of office from Chief Justice Earl Warren, has his left hand on two brown, leather-covered family Bibles held one atop the other by his wife, Patricia. This was a precedent set when Mrs. Johnson held the family Bible for her husband. Both Bibles are opened to Isaiah 2:4, which reads: "And He shall judge among the nations, and shall rebuke many people: and they shall beat their swords into plowshares and their spears into pruning-hooks: nation shall not lift up sword against nation, neither shall they learn war any more."

United Press
International Photo

Richard M. Nixon, 37th President of the United States, delivers his Inaugural Address, January 20th, 1969.

Wide World Photos

APPENDIX

Declaration of Independence

IN CONGRESS, JULY 4, 1776.

The unanimous Declaration of the thirteen united States of America,

When in the Course of human events, it becomes necessary for one people to dissolve the political bands which have connected them with another, and to assume among the Powers of the earth, the separate and equal station to which the Laws of Nature and of Nature's God entitle them, a decent respect to the opinions of mankind requires that they should declare the causes which impel them to the separation.—We hold these truths to be self-evident, that all men are created equal, that they are endowed by their Creator with certain unalienable Rights, that among these are Life, Liberty and the pursuit of Happiness.—That to secure these rights, Governments are instituted among Men, deriving their just powers from the consent of the governed,—That whenever any Form of Government becomes destructive of these ends, it is the Right of the People to alter or to abolish it, and to institute new Government, laying its foundation on such principles and organizing its powers in such form, as to them shall seem most likely to effect their Safety and Happiness. Prudence, indeed, will dictate that Governments long established should not be changed for light and transient causes; and accordingly all experience hath shewn, that mankind are more disposed to suffer, while evils are sufferable, than to right themselves by abolishing the forms to which they are accustomed. But when a long train of abuses and usurpations, pursuing invariably the same Object evinces a design to reduce them under absolute Despotism, it is their right, it is their duty, to throw off such Government, and to provide new Guards for their future security.—Such has been the patient sufferance of these Colonies; and such is now the necessity which constrains them to alter their former Systems of Government. The history of the present King of Great Britain is a history of repeated injuries and usurpations, all having in direct object the establishment of an absolute Tyranny over these States. To prove this, let Facts be submitted to a candid world.—He has refused his Assent to Laws, the most wholesome and necessary for the public good.—He has forbidden his Governors to pass Laws of immediate and pressing importance, unless suspended in their operation till his Assent should be obtained; and when so suspended, he has utterly neglected to attend to them.—He has refused to pass other Laws for the accommodation of large districts of people, unless those people would relinquish the right of Representation in the Legislature, a right inestimable to them and formidable to tyrants only.—He has called together legislative bodies at places unusual, uncomfortable, and distant from the depository of their public Records, for the sole purpose of fatiguing them into compliance with his measures.—He has dissolved Representative Houses repeatedly, for opposing with manly firmness his invasions on the rights of the people.—He has refused for a long time, after such dissolutions, to cause others to be elected; whereby the Legislative powers, incapable of Annihilation, have returned to the People at large for their exercise; the State remaining in the mean time exposed to all the dangers of invasion from without, and convulsions within.—He has endeavoured to prevent the population of these States; for that purpose obstructing the Laws for Naturalization of Foreigners; refusing to pass others to encourage their migrations hither, and raising the conditions of new Appropriations of Lands.—He has obstructed the Administration of Justice, by refusing his Assent to Laws for establishing Judiciary powers.—He has made Judges dependent on his Will alone, for the tenure of their offices, and the amount and payment of their salaries.—He has erected a multitude of New Offices, and sent hither swarms of Officers to harrass our people, and eat out their substance. —He has kept among us, in times of peace, Standing Armies without the Consent of our legislatures.—He has affected to render the Military independent of and superior to the Civil power.—He has combined with others to subject us to a jurisdiction foreign to our constitution, and unacknowledged by our laws; giving his Assent to their Acts of pretended Legislation:— For quartering large bodies of armed troops among us:—For protecting them, by a mock Trial, from punishment for any Murders which they should commit on the Inhabitants of these States:—For cutting off our Trade with all parts of the world:—For imposing Taxes on us without our Consent:—For depriving us in many cases, of the benefits of Trial by Jury:—For transporting us beyond Seas to be tried for pretended offences:—For abolishing the free System of English Laws in a neighbouring Province, establishing therein an Arbitrary government, and enlarging its Boundaries so as to render it at once an example and fit instrument for introducing the same absolute rule into these Colonies:—For taking away our Charters, abolishing our most valuable Laws, and altering fundamentally the Forms of our Governments:—For suspending our own Legislatures, and declaring themselves invested with power to legislate for us in all cases whatsoever.—He has abdicated Government here, by declaring us out of his Protection and waging War against us.—He has plundered our seas, ravaged our Coasts, burnt our towns, and destroyed the Lives of our people.—He is at this time transporting large Armies of foreign Mercenaries to compleat the works of death, desolation and tyranny, already begun with circumstances of Cruelty & perfidy scarcely paralleled in the most barbarous ages, and totally unworthy the Head of a civilized nation.—He has constrained our fellow Citizens taken Captive on the high Seas to bear Arms against their Country, to become the executioners of their friends and Brethren, or to fall themselves by their Hands. —He has excited domestic insurrections amongst us, and has endeavoured to bring on the inhabitants of our frontiers, the merciless Indian Savages, whose known rule of warfare, is an undistinguished destruction of all ages, sexes and conditions. In every stage of these Oppressions We have Petitioned for Redress in the most humble terms: Our repeated Petitions have been answered only by repeated injury. A Prince, whose character is thus marked by every act which may define a Tyrant, is unfit to be the ruler of a free people. Nor have We been wanting in attentions to our Brittish brethren. We have warned them from time to time of attempts by their legislature to extend an unwarrantable jurisdiction over us. We have reminded them of the circumstances of our emigration and settlement here. We have appealed to their native justice and magnanimity, and we have conjured them by the ties of our common kindred to disavow these usurpations, which, would inevitably interrupt our connec-

tions and correspondence. They too have been deaf to the voice of justice and of consanguinity. We must, therefore, acquiesce in the necessity, which denounces our Separation, and hold them, as we hold the rest of mankind, Enemies in War, in Peace Friends.—

We, therefore, the Representatives of the *united States of America,* in General Congress, Assembled, appealing to the Supreme Judge of the world for the rectitude of our intentions, do, in the Name, and by Authority of the good People of these Colonies, solemnly publish and declare, That these United Colonies are, and of Right ought to be *Free and Independent States;* that they are Absolved from all Allegiance to the British Crown, and that all political connection between them and the State of Great Britain, is and ought to be totally dissolved; and that as Free and Independent States, they have full Power to levy War, conclude Peace, contract Alliances, establish Commerce, and to do all other Acts and Things which Independent States may of right do.—And for the support of this Declaration, with a firm reliance on the protection of divine Providence, we mutually pledge to each other our Lives, our Fortunes and our sacred Honor.

JOHN HANCOCK

Josiah Bartlett
Wm Whipple
Saml Adams
John Adams
Robt Treat Paine
Elbridge Gerry
Step. Hopkins
William Ellery
Roger Sherman
Samel Huntington
Wm Williams
Oliver Wolcott
Matthew Thornton
Wm Floyd
Phil. Livingston
Frans. Lewis
Lewis Morris
Richd Stockton
Jno Witherspoon
Fras. Hopkinson
John Hart
Abra Clark
Robt Morris
Benjamin Rush

Benja. Franklin
John Morton
Geo Clymer
Jas. Smith.
Geo. Taylor
James Wilson
Geo. Ross
Cæsar Rodney
Geo Read
Tho M:Kean
Samuel Chase
Wm. Paca
Thos. Stone
Charles Carroll of Carrollton
George Wythe
Richard Henry Lee.

Th Jefferson
Benja Harrison
Thos Nelson jr.
Francis Lightfoot Lee
Carter Braxton
Wm Hooper
Joseph Hewes
John Penn
Edward Rutledge
Thos Heyward, Junr.
Thomas Lynch Junr.
Arthur Middleton
Button Gwinnett
Lyman Hall
Geo Walton

Note: In the foregoing the exact spelling and punctuation as shown in the original draft have been reproduced.

Act of Confederation of the United States of America

ARTICLES OF CONFEDERATION

To all to Whom these Presents shall come, we the undersigned Delegates of the States affixed to our Names send greeting. Whereas the Delegates of the United States of America in Congress assembled did on the fifteenth day of November in the Year of Our Lord One thousand seven Hundred and Seventy seven, and in the second Year of the Independence of America agree to certain articles of Confederation and perpetual Union between the States of Newhampshire, Massachusetts-bay, Rhodeisland and Providence Plantations, Connecticut, New York, New Jersey, Pennsylvania, Delaware, Maryland, Virginia, North-Carolina, South-Carolina, and Georgia in the Words following, viz. "Articles of Confederation and perpetual Union between the States of Newhampshire, Massachusetts-bay, Rhodeisland and Providence Plantations, Connecticut, New-York, New-Jersey, Pennsylvania, Delaware, Maryland, Virginia, North-Carolina, South-Carolina and Georgia.

Article I. The Stile of this confederacy shall be "The United States of America."

Article II. Each state retains its sovereignty, freedom and independence, and every Power, Jurisdiction and right, which is not by this confederation expressly delegated to the United States, in Congress assembled.

Article III. The said states hereby severally enter into a firm league of friendship with each other, for their common defence, the security of their Liberties, and their mutual and general welfare, binding themselves to assist each other, against all force offered to, or attacks made upon them, or any of them, on account of religion, sovereignty, trade, or any other pretence whatever.

Article IV. The better to secure and perpetuate mutual friendship and intercourse among the people of the different states in this union, the free inhabitants of each of these states, paupers, vagabonds and fugitives from Justice excepted, shall be entitled to all privileges and immunities of free citizens in the several states; and the people of each state shall have free ingress and regress to and from any other state, and shall enjoy therein all the privileges of trade and commerce, subject to the same duties, impositions and restrictions as the inhabitants thereof respectively, provided that such restriction shall not extend so far as to prevent the removal of property imported into any state, to any other state of which the Owner is an inhabitant; provided also that no imposition, duties or restriction shall be laid by any state, on the property of the united states, or either of them.

If any Person be guilty of, or charged with treason, felony, or other high misdemeanor in any state, shall flee from Justice, and be found in any of the united states, he shall upon demand of the Governor or executive power, of the state from which he fled, be delivered up and removed to the state having jurisdiction of his offence.

Full faith and credit shall be given in each of these states to the records, acts and judicial proceedings of the courts and magistrates of every other state.

Article V. For the more convenient management of the general interests of the united states, delegates shall be annually appointed in such manner as the legislature of each state shall direct, to meet in Congress on the first Monday in November, in every year, with a power reserved to each state, to recal its delegates, or any of them, at any time within the year, and to send others in their stead, for the remainder of the Year.

No state shall be represented in Congress by less than two, nor by more than seven Members; and no person shall be capable of being a delegate for more than three years in any term of six years; nor shall any person, being a delegate, be capable of holding any office under the united states, for which he, or another for his benefit receives any salary, fees or emolument of any kind.

Each state shall maintain its own delegates in a meeting of the states, and while they act as members of the committee of the states.

In determining questions in the united states, in Congress assembled, each state shall have one vote.

Freedom of speech and debate in Congress shall not be impeached or questioned in any Court, or place out of Congress, and the members of Congress shall be protected in their persons from arrests and imprisonments, during the time of their going to and from, and attendance on congress, except for treason, felony, or breach of the peace.

Article VI. No state without the consent of the united states in congress assembled, shall send any embassy to, or receive any embassy from, or enter into any conference, agreement, alliance or treaty with any King prince or state; nor shall any person holding any office of profit or trust under the united states, or any of them, accept of any present, emolument, office or title of any kind whatever from any king, prince or foreign state; nor shall the united states in congress assembled, or any of them, grant any title of nobility.

No two or more states shall enter into any treaty, confederation or alliance whatever between them, without the consent of the united states in congress assembled, specifying accurately the purpose for which the same is to be entered into, and how long it shall continue.

No state shall lay any imposts or duties, which may interfere with any stipulations in treaties, entered into by the united states in congress assembled, with any king, prince or state, in pursuance of any treaties already proposed by congress, to the courts of France and Spain.

No vessels of war shall be kept up in time of peace by any state, except such number only, as shall be deemed necessary by the united states in congress assembled, for the defence of such state, or its trade; nor shall any body of forces be kept up by any state, in time of peace, except such number only, as in the judgment of the united states, in congress assembled, shall be deemed requisite to garrison the forts necessary for the defence of such state; but every state shall always keep up a well regulated and disciplined militia, sufficiently armed and accoutred, and shall provide and constantly have ready for use, in public stores, a due number of field pieces and tents, and a proper quantity of arms, ammunition and camp equipage.

No state shall engage in any war without the consent of the united states in congress assembled, unless such state be actually invaded by enemies, or shall have received certain advice of a resolution being formed by some nation of Indians to invade such state, and the danger is so imminent as not to admit of a delay, till the united states in congress assembled can be consulted: nor shall any state grant commissions to any ships or vessels of war, nor letters of marque or reprisal, except it be after a declaration of war by the united states in congress assembled, and then only against the kingdom or state and the subjects thereof, against which war has been so declared, and under such regulations as shall be established by the united states in congress assembled, unless such state be infested by pirates, in which case vessels of war may be fitted out for that occasion, and kept so long as the danger shall continue, or until the united states in congress assembled shall determine otherwise.

Article VII. When land-forces are raised by any state for the common defence, all officers of or under the rank of colonel, shall be appointed by the legislature of each state respectively by whom such forces shall be raised, or in such manner as such state shall direct, and all vacancies shall be filled up by the state which first made the appointment.

Article VIII. All charges of war, and all other expenses that shall be incurred for the common defence or general welfare, and allowed by the united states in congress assembled, shall be defrayed out of a common treasury, which shall be supplied by the several states, in proportion to the value of all land within each state, granted to or surveyed for any Person, as such land and the buildings and improvements thereon shall be estimated according to such mode as the united states in congress assembled, shall from time to time direct and appoint. The taxes for paying that proportion shall be laid and levied by the authority and direction of the legislatures of the several states within the time agreed upon by the united states in congress assembled.

Article IX. The united states in congress assembled, shall have the sole and exclusive right and power of determining on peace and war, except in the cases mentioned in the sixth article —of sending and receiving ambassadors—entering into treaties and alliances, provided that no treaty of commerce shall be made whereby the legislative power of the respective states shall be restrained from imposing such imposts and duties on foreigners, as their own people are subjected to, or from prohibiting the exportation or importation of any species of goods or commodities whatsoever—of establishing rules for deciding in all cases, what captures on land or water shall be legal, and in what manner prizes taken by land or naval forces in the service of the united states shall be divided or appropriated—of granting letters of marque and reprisal in times of peace—appointing courts for the trial of piracies and felonies committed on the high seas and establishing courts for receiving and determining finally appeals in all cases of captures, provided that no member of congress shall be appointed a judge of any of the said courts.

The united states in congress assembled shall also be the last resort on appeal in all disputes and differences now subsisting or that hereafter may arise between two or more states concerning boundary, jurisdiction or any other cause whatever; which authority shall always be exercised in the manner following. Whenever the legislative or executive authority or lawful agent of any state in controversy with another shall present a petition to congress, stating the matter in question and praying for a hearing, notice thereof shall be given by order of congress to the legislative or executive authority of the other state in controversy, and a day assigned for the appearance of the parties by their lawful agents, who shall then be directed to appoint by joint consent, commissioners or judges to constitute a court for hearing and determining the matter in question: but if they cannot agree, congress shall name three persons out of each of the united states, and from the list of such persons each party shall alternately strike out one, the petitioners beginning, until the number shall be reduced to thirteen; and from that number not less than seven, nor more than nine names as congress shall direct, shall in the presence of congress be drawn out by lot, and the persons whose names shall be so drawn or any five of them, shall be commissioners or judges, to hear and finally determine the controversy, so always as a major part of the judges who shall hear the cause shall agree in the determination: and if either party shall neglect to attend at the day appointed, without shewing reasons, which congress shall judge sufficient, or being present shall refuse to strike, the congress shall proceed to nominate three persons out of each state, and the secretary of congress shall strike in behalf of such party absent or refusing; and the judgment and sentence of the court to be appointed, in the manner before prescribed, shall be final and conclusive; and if any of the parties shall refuse to submit to the authority of such court, or to appear or defend their claim or cause, the court shall nevertheless proceed to pronounce sentence, or judgment, which shall in like manner be final and decisive, the judgment or sentence and other proceedings being in either case transmitted to congress, and lodged among the acts of congress for the security of the parties concerned: provided that every commissioner, before he sits in judgment, shall take an oath to be administered by one of the judges of the supreme or superior court of the state, where the cause shall be tried, "well and truly to hear and determine the matter in question, according to the best of his judgment, without favour, affection or hope of reward:" provided also that no state shall be deprived of territory for the benefit of the united states.

All controversies concerning the private right of soil claimed under different grants of two or more states, whose jurisdictions as they may respect such lands, and the states which passed such grants are adjusted, the said grants or either of them being at the same time claimed to have originated antecedent to such settlement of jurisdiction, shall on the petition of either party to the congress of the united states, be finally determined as near as may be in the same manner as is before prescribed for deciding disputes respecting territorial jurisdiction between different states.

The united states in congress assembled shall also have the sole and exclusive right and power of regulating the alloy and value of coin struck by their own authority, or by that of the respective states—fixing the standard of weights and measures throughout the united states—regulating the trade and manageing all affairs with the Indians, not members of any of the states, provided that the legislative right of any state within its own limits be not infringed or violated—establishing and regulating post-offices from one state to another, throughout all the united states, and exacting such postage on the papers passing thro' the same as may be requisite to defray the expences of the said office—appointing all officers of the land forces, in the service of the united states, excepting regimental officers. —appointing all the officers of the naval forces, and commissioning all officers whatever in the service of the united states—making rules for the government and regulation of the said land and naval forces, and directing their operations.

The united states in congress assembled shall

have authority to appoint a committee, to sit in the recess of congress, to be denominated "A Committee of the States," and to consist of one delegate from each state; and to appoint such other committees and civil officers as may be necessary for manageing the general affairs of the united states under their direction—to appoint one of their number to preside, provided that no person be allowed to serve in the office of president more than one year in any term of three years; to ascertain the necessary sums of Money to be raised for the service of the united states, and to appropriate and apply the same for defraying the public expences—to borrow money, or emit bills on the credit of the united states, transmitting every half year to the respective states an account of the sums of money so borrowed or emitted,—to build and equip a navy—to agree upon the number of land forces, and to make requisitions from each state for its quota, in proportion to the number of white inhabitants in such state; which requisition shall be binding, and thereupon the legislature of each state shall appoint the regimental officers, raise the men and cloath, arm and equip them in a soldier like manner, at the expence of the united states, and the officers and men so cloathed, armed and equipped shall march to the place appointed, and within the time agreed on by the united states in congress assembled: But if the united states in congress assembled shall, on consideration of circumstances judge proper that any state should not raise men, or should raise a smaller number than its quota, and that any other state should raise a greater number of men than the quota thereof, such extra number shall be raised, officered, cloathed, armed and equipped in the same manner as the quota of such state, unless the legislature of such state shall judge that such extra number cannot be safely spared out of the same, in which case they shall raise officer, cloath, arm and equip as many of such extra number as they judge can be safely spared. And the officers and men so cloathed, armed and equipped, shall march to the place appointed, and within the time agreed on by the united states in congress assembled.

The united states in congress assembled shall never engage in a war, nor grant letters of marque and reprisal in time of peace, nor enter into any treaties or alliances, nor coin money, nor regulate the value thereof, nor ascertain the sums and expences necessary for the defence and welfare of the united states, or any of them, nor emit bills, nor borrow money on the credit of the united states, nor appropriate money, nor agree upon the number of vessels of war, to be built or purchased, or the number of land or sea forces to be raised, nor appoint a commander in chief of the army or navy, unless nine states assent to the same: nor shall a question on any other point, except for adjourning from day to day be determined, unless by the votes of a majority of the united states in congress assembled.

The congress of the united states shall have power to adjourn to any time within the year, and to any place within the united states, so that no period of adjournment be for a longer duration than the space of six months, and shall publish the Journal of their proceedings monthly, except such parts thereof relating to treaties, alliances or military operations, as in their judgment require secrecy; and the yeas and nays of the delegates of each state on any question shall be entered on the Journal, when it is desired by any delegate; and the delegates of a state, or any of them, at his or their request shall be furnished with a transcript of the said Journal, except such parts as are above excepted, to lay before the legislatures of the several states.

Article X. The committee of the states, or any nine of them, shall be authorized to execute, in the recess of congress, such of the powers of congress as the united states in congress assembled, by the consent of nine states, shall from time to time think expedient to vest them with; provided that no power be delegated to the said committee, for the exercise of which, by the articles of confederation, the voice of nine states in the congress of the united states assembled is requisite.

Article XI. Canada acceding to this confederation, and joining in the measures of the united states, shall be admitted into, and entitled to all the advantages of this union: but no other colony shall be admitted into the same, unless such admission be agreed to by nine states.

Article XII. All bills of credit emitted, monies borrowed and debts contracted by, or under the authority of congress, before the assembling of the united states, in pursuance of the present confederation, shall be deemed and considered as a charge against the united states, for payment and satisfaction whereof the said united states, and the public faith are hereby solemnly pledged.

Article XIII. Every state shall abide by the determinations of the united states in congress assembled, on all questions which by this confederation are submitted to them. And the Articles of this confederation shall be inviolably observed by every state, and the union shall be perpetual; nor shall any alteration at any time hereafter be made in any of them; unless such alteration be agreed to in a congress of the united states, and be afterwards confirmed by the legislatures of every state.

And Whereas it hath pleased the Great Governor of the World to incline the hearts of the legislatures we respectively represent in congress, to approve of, and to authorize us to ratify the said articles of confederation and perpetual union. Know Ye that we the under-signed delegates, by virtue of the power and authority to us given for that purpose, do by these presents, in the name and in behalf of our respective constituents, fully and entirely ratify and confirm each and every of the said articles of confederation and perpetual union, and all and singular the matters and things therein contained: And we do further solemnly plight and engage the faith of our respective constituents, that they shall abide by the determinations of the united states in congress assembled, on all questions, which by the said confederation are submitted to them. And that the articles thereof shall be inviolably observed by the states we repectively represent, and that the union shall be perpetual. In Witness whereof we have hereunto set our hands in Congress. Done at Philadelphia in the state of Pennsylvania the ninth Day of July in the Year of Our Lord one Thousand seven Hundred and Seventy eight, and in the third year of the independence of America.

THOS M:KEAN Feb 12. 1779
JOHN DICKINSON, May 5th 1779   } On the part & behalf of the State of Delaware
NICHOLAS VANDYKE

JOHN HANSON March 1st 1781
DANIEL CARROLL. do   } on the part and behalf of the State of Maryland

RICHARD HENRY LEE
JOHN BANNISTER
THOMAS ADAMS   } On the Part and Behalf of the State of Virginia
JNO HARVIE
FRANCIS LIGHTFOOT LEE

JOHN PENN July 21st 1778
CORNS HARNETT   } on the part and Behalf of the State of No. Carolina
JNO. WILLIAMS

HENRY LAURENS
WILLIAM HENRY DRAYTON
JNO. MATHEWS   } On the part and behalf of the State of South-Carolina
RICHD. HUDSON
THOS. HEYWARD JUNR.

JNO WALTON 24th July 1778
EDWD. TELFAIR.   } On the part and behalf of the State of Georgia
EDWD. LANGWORTHY.

JOSIAH BARTLETT
JOHN WENTWORTH JUNR.
        august 8th 1778   } on the part & behalf of the State of New Hampshire

JOHN HANCOCK.
SAMUEL ADAMS
ELBRIDGE GERRY.
FRANCIS DANA
JAMES LOVELL
SAMUEL HOLTEN.   } on the part and behalf of the State of Massachusetts Bay

WILLIAM ELLERY
HENRY MARCHANT
JOHN COLLINS   } On the part and behalf of the State of Rhode-Island and Providence Plantations

ROGER SHERMAN
SAMUEL HUNTINGTON
OLIVER WOLCOTT
TITUS HOSMER
ANDREW ADAMS   } on the Part and behalf of the State of Connecticut

JAS. DUANE.
FRAS. LEWIS
WM DUER
GOUV. MORRIS   } On the Part and Behalf of the State of New York

JNO WITHERSPOON
NATH. SCUDDER   } On the Part and in Behalf of the State of New Jersey. Novr. 26. 1778

ROBT MORRIS.
DANIEL ROBERDEAU
JON. BAYARD SMITH
WILLIAM CLINGAN
JOSEPH REED. 22d July 1778   } On the part and behalf of the State of Pennsylvania

Note: In the foregoing the exact spelling and punctuation as shown in the original draft have been reproduced.

The Constitution of the United States of America

[ADOPTED SEPTEMBER 17, 1787, AND BECAME EFFECTIVE MARCH 4, 1789]

We the People of the United States, in Order to form a more perfect Union, establish Justice, insure domestic Tranquility, provide for the common defence, promote the general Welfare, and secure the Blessings of Liberty to ourselves and our Posterity, do ordain and establish this Constitution for the United States of America.

ARTICLE I.

Section. 1. All legislative Powers herein granted shall be vested in a Congress of the United States, which shall consist of a Senate and House of Representatives.

Section. 2. The House of Representatives shall be composed of Members chosen every second Year by the People of the several States, and the Electors in each State shall have the Qualifications requisite for Electors of the most numerous Branch of the State Legislature.

No Person shall be a Representative who shall not have attained to the Age of twenty five Years, and been seven Years a Citizen of the United States, and who shall not, when elected, be an Inhabitant of that State in which he shall be chosen.

Representatives and direct Taxes shall be apportioned among the several States which may be included within this Union, according to their respective Numbers, which shall be determined by adding to the whole Number of free Persons, including those bound to Service for a Term of Years, and excluding Indians not taxed, three fifths of all other Persons.[1] The actual Enumeration shall be made within three Years after the first Meeting of the Congress of the United States, and within every subsequent Term of ten Years, in such Manner as they shall by Law direct. The Number of Representatives shall not exceed one for every thirty Thousand, but each State shall have at Least one Representative; and until such enumeration shall be made, the State of New Hampshire shall be entitled to chuse three, Massachusetts eight, Rhode-Island and Providence Plantations one, Connecticut five, New-York six, New Jersey four, Pennsylvania eight, Delaware one, Maryland six, Virginia ten, North Carolina five, South Carolina five, and Georgia three.

When vacancies happen in the Representation from any State, the Executive Authority thereof shall issue Writs of Election to fill such Vacancies.

The House of Representatives shall chuse their Speaker and other Officers; and shall have the sole Power of Impeachment.

Section. 3. The Senate of the United States shall be composed of two Senators from each State, *chosen by the Legislature thereof,*[2] for six Years; and each Senator shall have one Vote.

Immediately after they shall be assembled in Consequence of the first Election, they shall be divided as equally as may be into three Classes. The Seats of the Senators of the first Class shall be vacated at the Expiration of the second Year, of the second Class at the Expiration of the fourth Year, and of the third Class at the Expiration of the sixth Year, so that one third may be chosen every second Year; and if Vacancies happen by Resignation, or otherwise, during the Recess of the Legislature of any State, the Executive thereof may make temporary Appointments until the next Meeting of the Legislature, which shall then fill such Vacancies.[2]

No Person shall be a Senator who shall not have attained to the Age of thirty Years, and been nine Years a Citizen of the United States, and who shall not, when elected, be an inhabitant of that State for which he shall be chosen.

The Vice President of the United States shall be President of the Senate, but shall have no Vote, unless they be equally divided.

The Senate shall chuse their other Officers, and also a President pro tempore, in the Absence of the Vice President, or when he shall exercise the Office of President of the United States.

The Senate shall have the sole Power to try all Impeachments. When sitting for that Purpose, they shall be on Oath or Affirmation. When

---

1. See 14th and 16th Amendments.

2. See 17th Amendment.

the President of the United States is tried, the Chief Justice shall preside: And no Person shall be convicted without the Concurrence of two thirds of the Members present.

Judgment in Cases of Impeachment shall not extend further than to removal from Office, and disqualification to hold and enjoy any Office of honor, Trust or Profit under the United States: but the Party convicted shall nevertheless be liable and subject to Indictment, Trial, Judgment and Punishment, according to Law.

Section. 4. The Times, Places and Manner of holding Elections for Senators and Representatives, shall be prescribed in each State by the Legislature thereof; but the Congress may at any time by Law make or alter such Regulations, except as to the Places of chusing Senators.

The Congress shall assemble at least once in every Year, and such Meeting shall be on the first Monday in December, unless they shall by Law appoint a different Day.[3]

Section. 5. Each House shall be the Judge of the Elections, Returns and Qualifications of its own Members, and a Majority of each shall constitute a Quorum to do Business; but a smaller Number may adjourn from day to day, and may be authorized to compel the Attendance of absent Members, in such Manner, and under such Penalties as each House may provide.

Each House may determine the Rules of its Proceedings, punish its Members for disorderly Behaviour, and, with the Concurrence of two thirds, expel a Member.

Each House shall keep a Journal of its Proceedings, and from time to time publish the same, excepting such Parts as may in their Judgment require Secrecy; and the Yeas and Nays of the Members of either House on any question shall, at the Desire of one fifth of those Present, be entered on the Journal.

Neither House, during the Session of Congress, shall, without the Consent of the other, adjourn for more than three days, nor to any other Place than that in which the two Houses shall be sitting.

Section. 6. The Senators and Representatives shall receive a Compensation for their Services, to be ascertained by Law, and paid out of the Treasury of the United States. They shall in all Cases, except Treason, Felony and Breach of the Peace, be privileged from Arrest during their Attendance at the Session of their respective Houses, and in going to and returning from the same; and for any Speech or Debate in either House, they shall not be questioned in any other Place.

No Senator or Representative shall, during the Time for which he was elected, be appointed to any civil Office under the Authority of the United States which shall have been created, or the Emoluments whereof shall have been encreased during such time; and no Person holding any Office under the United States, shall be a Member of either House during his Continuance in Office.

Section. 7. All Bills for raising Revenue shall originate in the House of Representatives; but the Senate may propose or concur with Amendments as on other Bills.

Every Bill which shall have passed the House of Representatives and the Senate, shall, before it become a Law, be presented to the President of the United States; If he approve he shall sign it, but if not he shall return it, with his Objections to that House in which it shall have originated, who shall enter the Objections at large on their Journal, and proceed to reconsider it. If after such Reconsideration two thirds of that House shall agree to pass the Bill, it shall be sent, together with the Objections, to the other House, by which it shall likewise be reconsidered, and if approved by two thirds of that House, it shall become a Law. But in all such Cases the Votes of both Houses shall be determined by yeas and Nays, and the Names of the Persons voting for and against the Bill shall be entered on the Journal of each House respectively. If any Bill shall not be returned by the President within ten Days (Sundays excepted) after it shall have been presented to him, the Same shall be a Law, in like Manner as if he had signed it, unless the Congress by their Adjournment prevent its Return, in which Case it shall not be a Law.

Every Order, Resolution, or Vote to which the Concurrence of the Senate and House of Representatives may be necessary (except on a question of Adjournment) shall be presented to the President of the United States; and before the Same shall take Effect, shall be approved by him, or being disapproved by him, shall be repassed by two thirds of the Senate and House of Representatives, according to the Rules and Limitations prescribed in the Case of a Bill.

---

3. See 20th Amendment.

Section. 8. The Congress shall have Power To lay and collect Taxes, Duties, Imposts and Excises, to pay the Debts and Provide for the common Defence and general Welfare of the United States; but all Duties, Imposts and Excises shall be uniform throughout the United States;

To borrow Money on the credit of the United States;

To regulate Commerce with foreign Nations, and among the several States, and with the Indian Tribes;

To establish an uniform Rule of Naturalization, and uniform Laws on the subject of Bankruptcies throughout the United States;

To coin Money, regulate the Value thereof, and of foreign Coin, and fix the Standard of Weights and Measures;

To provide for the Punishment of counterfeiting the Securities and current Coin of the United States;

To establish Post Offices and post Roads;

To promote the Progress of Science and useful Arts, by securing for limited Times to Authors and Inventors the exclusive Right to their respective Writings and Discoveries;

To constitute Tribunals inferior to the supreme Court;

To define and punish Piracies and Felonies committed on the high Seas, and Offences against the Law of Nations;

To declare War, grant Letters of Marque and Reprisal, and make Rules concerning Captures on Land and Water;

To raise and support Armies, but no Appropriation of Money to that Use shall be for a longer Term than two Years;

To provide and maintain a Navy;

To make Rules for the Government and Regulation of the land and naval Forces;

To provide for calling forth the Militia to execute the Laws of the Union, suppress Insurrections and repel Invasions;

To provide for organizing, arming, and disciplining, the Militia, and for governing such Part of them as may be employed in the Service of the United States, reserving to the States respectively, the Appointment of the Officers, and the Authority of training the Militia according to the discipline prescribed by Congress;

To exercise exclusive Legislation in all Cases whatsoever, over such District (not exceeding ten Miles square) as may, by Cession of Particular States, and the Acceptance of Congress, become the Seat of the Government of the United States, and to exercise like Authority over all Places purchased by the Consent of the Legislature of the State in which the Same shall be, for the Erection of Forts, Magazines, Arsenals, dock-Yards, and other needful Buildings;—And

To make all Laws which shall be necessary and proper for carrying into Execution the foregoing Powers, and all other Powers vested by this Constitution in the Government of the United States, or in any Department or Officer thereof.

Section. 9. The Migration of Importation of such Persons as any of the States now existing shall think proper to admit, shall not be prohibited by the Congress prior to the Year one thousand eight hundred and eight, but a Tax or duty may be imposed on such Importation, not exceeding ten dollars for each Person.

The Privilege of the Writ of Habeas Corpus shall not be suspended, unless when in Cases of Rebellion or Invasion the public Safety may require it.

No Bill of Attainder or ex post facto Law shall be passed.

No Capitation, or other direct, Tax shall be laid, unless in Proportion to the Census or Enumeration herein before directed to be taken.[4]

No Tax or Duty shall be laid on Articles exported from any State.

No Preference shall be given by any Regulation of Commerce or Revenue to the Ports of one State over those of another: nor shall Vessels bound to, or from, one State, be obliged to enter, clear, or pay Duties in another.

No Money shall be drawn from the Treasury, but in Consequence of Appropriations made by Law; and a regular Statement and Account of the Receipts and Expenditures of all public Money shall be published from time to time.

No Title of Nobility shall be granted by the United States: And no Person holding any Office of Profit or Trust under them, shall, without the Consent of the Congress, accept of any present, Emolument, Office, or Title, of any kind whatever, from any King, Prince, or foreign State.

Section. 10. No State shall enter into any Treaty, Alliance, or Confederation; grant Letters of Marque and Reprisal; coin Money; emit Bills of

4. See 16th Amendment.

Credit; make any Thing but gold and silver Coin a Tender in Payment of Debts; pass any Bill of Attainder, ex post facto Law, or Law impairing the Obligation of Contracts, or grant any Title of Nobility.

No State shall, without the Consent of the Congress, lay any Imposts or Duties on Imports or Exports, except what may be absolutely necessary for executing it's inspection Laws: and the net Produce of all Duties and Imposts, laid by any State on Imports or Exports, shall be for the Use of the Treasury of the United States; and all such Laws shall be subject to the Revision and Controul of the Congress.

No State shall, without the Consent of Congress, lay any Duty of Tonnage, keep Troops, or Ships of War in time of Peace, enter into any Agreement or Compact with another State, or with a foreign Power, or engage in War, unless actually invaded, or in such imminent Danger as will not admit of delay.

ARTICLE II.

Section. 1. The executive Power shall be vested in a President of the United States of America. He shall hold his Office during the Term of four Years, and, together with the Vice President, chosen for the same Term, be elected, as follows

Each State shall appoint, in such Manner as the Legislature thereof may direct, a Number of Electors, equal to the whole Number of Senators and Representatives to which the State may be entitled in the Congress: but no Senator or Representative, or Person holding an Office of Trust or Profit under the United States, shall be appointed an Elector.

The Electors shall meet in their respective States, and vote by Ballot for two Persons, of whom one at least shall not be an Inhabitant of the same State with themselves. And they shall make a List of all the Persons voted for, and of the Number of Votes for each; which List they shall sign and certify, and transmit sealed to the Seat of the Government of the United States, directed to the President of the Senate. The President of the Senate shall, in the Presence of the Senate and House of Representatives, open all the Certificates, and the Votes shall then be counted. The Person having the greatest Num-

ber of Votes shall be the President, if such Number be a Majority of the whole Number of Electors appointed; and if there be more than one who have such Majority, and have an equal Number of Votes, then the House of Representatives shall immediately chuse by Ballot one of them for President; and if no Person have a Majority, then from the five highest on the List the said House shall in like Manner chuse the President. But in chusing the President, the Votes shall be taken by States, the Representation from each State having one Vote; A quorum for this Purpose shall consist of a Member or Members from two thirds of the States, and a Majority of all the States shall be necessary to a Choice. In every Case, after the Choice of the President, the Person having the greatest Number of Votes of the Electors shall be the Vice President. But if there should remain two or more who have equal Votes, the Senate shall chuse from them by Ballot the Vice President.[5]

The Congress may determine the Time of chusing the Electors, and the Day on which they shall give their Votes; which Day shall be the same throughout the United States.

No Person except a natural born Citizen, or a Citizen of the United States, at the time of the Adoption of this Constitution, shall be eligible to the Office of President; neither shall any Person be eligible to that Office who shall not have attained to the Age of thirty five Years, and been fourteen Years a Resident within the United States.

In Case of the Removal of the President from Office, or of his Death, Resignation, or Inability to discharge the Powers and Duties of the said Office, the Same shall devolve on the Vice President, and the Congress may by Law provide for the Case of Removal, Death, Resignation or Inability, both of the President and Vice President, declaring what Officer shall then act as President, and such Officer shall act accordingly, until the Disability be removed, or a President shall be elected.

The President shall, at stated Times, receive for his Services, a Compensation, which shall neither be encreased nor diminished during the Period for which he shall have been elected, and he shall not receive within that Period any other Emolument from the United States, or any of them.

5. See 12th and 20th Amendments.

Before he enter on the Execution of his Office, he shall take the following Oath of Affirmation:—"I do solemnly swear (or affirm) that I will faithfully execute the Office of President of the United States, and will to the best of my Ability, preserve, protect and defend the Constitution of the United States."

Section. 2. The President shall be Commander in Chief of the Army and Navy of the United States, and of the Militia of the several States, when called into the actual Service of the United States; he may require the Opinion, in writing, of the principal Officer in each of the executive Departments, upon any Subject relating to the Duties of their respective Offices, and he shall have Power to grant Reprieves and Pardons for Offences against the United States, except in Cases of Impeachment.

He shall have Power, by and with the Advice and Consent of the Senate, to make Treaties, provided two thirds of the Senators present concur; and he shall nominate, and by and with the Advice and Consent of the Senate, shall appoint Ambassadors, other public Ministers and Consuls, Judges of the supreme Court, and all other Officers of the United States, whose appointments are not herein otherwise provided for, and which shall be established by Law: but the Congress may by Law vest the Appointment of such inferior Officers, as they think proper, in the President alone, in the Courts of Law, or in the Heads of Departments.

The President shall have Power to fill up all Vacancies that may happen during the Recess of the Senate, by granting Commissions which shall expire at the End of their next Session.

Section. 3. He shall from time to time give to the Congress Information of the State of the Union, and recommend to their consideration such Measures as he shall judge necessary and expedient; he may, on extraordinary Occasions, convene both Houses, or either of them, and in Case of Disagreement between them, with Respect to the Time of Adjournment, he may adjourn them to such Time as he shall think proper; he shall receive Ambassadors and other public Ministers; he shall take Care that the Laws be faithfully executed, and shall Commission all the Officers of the United States.

Section. 4. The President, Vice President and all civil Officers of the United States, shall be removed from Office on Impeachment for, and Conviction of, Treason, Bribery, or other high Crimes and Misdemeanors.

ARTICLE III.

Section. 1. The judicial Power of the United States, shall be vested in one supreme Court, and in such inferior Courts as the Congress may from time to time ordain and establish. The Judges, both of the supreme and inferior Courts, shall hold their Offices during good Behaviour, and shall, at stated Times, receive for their Services, a Compensation, which shall not be diminished during their Continuance in Office.

Section. 2. The judicial Power shall extend to all Cases, in Law and Equity, arising under this Constitution, the Laws of the United States, and Treaties made, or which shall be made, under their Authority;—to all Cases affecting Ambassadors, other public Ministers and Consuls;—to all Cases of admiralty and maritime Jurisdiction;—to Controversies to which the United States shall be a Party;—to Controversies between two or more States;—between a State and Citizens of another State;[6]—between Citizens of different States,—between Citizens of the same State claiming Lands under Grants of different States, and between a State, or the Citizens thereof, and foreign States, Citizens or Subjects.

In all Cases affecting Ambassadors, other public Ministers and Consuls, and those in which a State shall be Party, the supreme Court shall have original Jurisdiction. In all the other Cases before mentioned, the supreme Court shall have appellate Jurisdiction, both as to Law and Fact, with such Exceptions, and under such Regulations as the Congress shall make.

The Trial of all Crimes, except in Cases of Impeachment, shall be by Jury; and such Trial shall be held in the State where the said Crimes shall have been committed; but when not committed within any State, the Trial shall be at such Place or Places as the Congress may by Law have directed.

Section. 3. Treason against the United States, shall consist only in levying War against them, or in adhering to their Enemies, giving them Aid and Comfort. No Person shall be convicted of Treason unless on the Testimony of two Witnesses

6. See 11th Amendment.

to the same overt Act, or on Confession in open Court.

The Congress shall have Power to declare the Punishment of Treason, but no Attainder of Treason shall work Corruption of Blood, or Forfeiture except during the Life of the Person attainted.

ARTICLE IV.

Section. 1. Full Faith and Credit shall be given in each State to the public Acts, Records, and judicial Proceedings of every other State. And the Congress may by general Laws prescribe the Manner in which such Acts, Records and Proceedings shall be proved, and the Effect thereof.

Section. 2. The Citizens of each State shall be entitled to all Privileges and Immunities of Citizens in the several States.[7]

A Person charged in any State with Treason, Felony, or other Crime, who shall flee from Justice, and be found in another State, shall on Demand of the executive Authority of the State from which he fled, be delivered up, to be removed to the State having Jurisdiction of the Crime.

No Person held to Service or Labour in one State, under the Laws thereof, escaping into another, shall, in Consequence of any Law or Regulation therein, be discharged from such Service or Labour, but shall be delivered up on Claim of the Party to whom such Service or Labour may be due.[8]

Section. 3. New States may be admitted by the Congress into this Union; but no new State shall be formed or erected within the Jurisdiction of any other State; nor any State be formed by the Junction of two or more States, or Parts of States, without the Consent of the Legislatures of the States concerned as well as of the Congress.

The Congress shall have Power to dispose of and make all needful Rules and Regulations respecting the Territory or other Property belonging to the United States; and nothing in this Constitution shall be so construed as to Prejudice any Claims of the United States, or of any particular State.

Section. 4. The United States shall guarantee to every State in this Union a Republican Form of Government, and shall protect each of them against Invasion; and on Application of the Legislature, or of the Executive (when the Legislature cannot be convened) against domestic Violence.

ARTICLE V.

The Congress, whenever two thirds of both Houses shall deem it necessary, shall propose Amendments to this Constitution, or, on the Application of the Legislatures of two thirds of the several States, shall call a Convention for proposing Amendments, which, in either Case, shall be valid to all Intents and Purposes, as Part of this Constitution, when ratified by the Legislatures of three fourths of the several States, or by Conventions in three fourths thereof, as the one or the other Mode of Ratification may be proposed by the Congress; Provided that no Amendment which may be made prior to the Year One thousand eight hundred and eight shall in any Manner affect the first and fourth Clauses in the Ninth Section of the first Article; and that no State, without its Consent, shall be deprived of its equal Suffrage in the Senate.

ARTICLE VI.

All Debts contracted and Engagements entered into, before the Adoption of this Constitution, shall be as valid against the United States under this Constitution, as under the Confederation.[9]

This Constitution, and the Laws of the United States which shall be made in Pursuance thereof; and all Treaties made, or which shall be made, under the Authority of the United States, shall be the supreme Law of the Land; and the Judges in every State shall be bound thereby, any Thing in the Constitution or Laws of any State to the Contrary notwithstanding.

The Senators and Representatives before mentioned, and the Members of the several State Legislatures, and all executive and judicial Officers, both of the United States and of the several States, shall be bound by Oath or Affirmation, to support this Constitution; but no religious Test shall ever be required as a Qualification to any Office or public Trust under the United States.

7. See Section 1, 14th Amendment.
8. See 13th Amendment.

9. See Section 4, 14th Amendment.

ARTICLE VII.

The Ratification of the Conventions of nine States, shall be sufficient for the Establishment of this Constitution between the States so ratifying the Same.

Done in Convention by the Unanimous Consent of the States present the Seventeenth Day of September in the Year of our Lord one thousand seven hundred and Eighty seven and of the Independance of the United States of America the Twelfth *In witness* whereof We have hereunto subscribed our Names,

Geo. WASHINGTON—Presidt.
and deputy from Virginia.

The Word "the," being interlined between the seventh and eighth Lines of the first Page, the word "Thirty" being partly written on an Erasure in the fifteenth Line of the first Page. The words "is tried" being interlined between the thirty-second and thirty-third Lines of the first Page and the Word "the" being interlined between the forty-third and forty-fourth Lines of the second Page.

Attest WILLIAM JACKSON, SECRETARY.

New Hampshire { JOHN LANGDON
NICHOLAS GILMAN

Delaware { GEO READ
GUNNING BEDFORD JUN
JOHN DICKINSON
RICHARD BASSETT
JACO: BROOM

Massachusetts { NATHANIEL GORHAM
RUFUS KING

Maryland { JAMES MCHENRY
DAN OF ST THOS. JENIFER
DANL. CARROLL.

Connecticut { WM. SAML. JOHNSON
ROGER SHERMAN

New York . . . { ALEXANDER HAMILTON

Virginia { JOHN BLAIR—
JAMES MADISON JR.

New Jersey { WIL. LIVINGSTON
DAVID BREARLEY
WM. PATERSON
JONA: DAYTON

North Carolina { WM. BLOUNT
RICHD. DOBBS SPAIGHT
HU WILLIAMSON

South Carolina { J. RUTLEDGE
CHARLES COTESWORTH PINCKNEY
CHARLES PINCKNEY
PIERCE BUTLER.

Pennsylvania { B FRANKLIN
THOMAS MIFFLIN
ROBT MORRIS
GEO. CLYMER
THOS. FITZSIMONS
JARED INGERSOLL
JAMES WILSON
GOUV MORRIS

Georgia { WILLIAM FEW
ABR BALDWIN

Note: In the foregoing the exact spelling and punctuation as shown in the original draft have been reproduced.

Articles in addition to and Amendment of the Constitution of the United States of America, proposed by Congress, and ratified by the Legislatures of the several States, pursuant to the fifth Article of the original Constitution.*

[ARTICLE I.]

Congress shall make no law respecting an establishment of religion, or prohibiting the free exercise thereof; or abridging the freedom of speech, or of the press; or the right of the people peaceably to assemble, and to petition the Government for a redress of grievances.

[ARTICLE II.]

A well regulated Militia, being necessary to the security of a free State, the right of the people to keep and bear Arms, shall not be infringed.

[ARTICLE III.]

No Soldier shall, in time of peace be quartered in any house, without the consent of the Owner, nor in time of war, but in a manner to be prescribed by law.

[ARTICLE IV.]

The right of the people to be secure in their persons, houses, papers, and effects, against unreasonable searches and seizures, shall not be violated, and no Warrants shall issue, but upon probable cause, supported by Oath or affirmation, and particularly describing the place to be searched, and the persons or things to be seized.

[ARTICLE V.]

No person shall be held to answer for a capital, or otherwise infamous crime, unless on a presentment or indictment of a Grand Jury, except in cases arising in the land or naval forces, or in the Militia, when in actual service in time of War or public danger; nor shall any person be subject for the same offence to be twice put in jeopardy of life or limb; nor shall be compelled in any criminal case to be a witness against himself, nor be deprived of life, liberty, or property, without due process of law; nor shall private property be taken for public use, without just compensation.

[ARTICLE VI.]

In all criminal prosecutions the accused shall enjoy the right to a speedy and public trial, by an impartial jury of the State and district wherein the crime shall have been committed, which district shall have been previously ascertained by law, and to be informed of the nature and cause of the accusation; to be confronted with the witnesses against him; to have compulsory process for obtaining witnesses in his favor, and to have the Assistance of Counsel for his defence.

[ARTICLE VII.]

In Suits at common law, where the value in controversy shall exceed twenty dollars, the right of trial by jury shall be preserved, and no fact tried by a jury shall be otherwise re-examined in any Court of the United States, than according to the rules of the common law.

[ARTICLE VIII.]

Excessive bail shall not be required, nor excessive fines imposed, nor cruel and unusual punishments inflicted.

[ARTICLE IX.]

The enumeration in the Constitution, of certain rights, shall not be construed to deny or disparage others retained by the people.

* [Articles I through X passed by Congress Sept. 25, 1789, and ratified by three-fourths of the States, December 15, 1791.]

[Article X.]

The powers not delegated to the United States by the Constitution, nor prohibited by it to the States, are reserved to the States respectively, or to the people.

[Article XI.]

[Passed by Congress March 5, 1794, and ratified January 8, 1798]

The judicial power of the United States shall not be construed to extend to any suit in law or equity, commenced or prosecuted against one of the United States by citizens of another State, or by citizens or subjects of any foreign State.

[Article XII.]

[Passed by Congress December 12, 1803, and ratified September 25, 1804]

The electors shall meet in their respective States, and vote by ballot for President and Vice-President, one of whom, at least, shall not be an inhabitant of the same State with themselves; they shall name in their ballots the person voted for as President, and in distinct ballots, the person voted for as Vice-President, and they shall make distinct lists of all persons voted for as President and of all persons voted for as Vice-President, and of the number of votes for each, which lists they shall sign and certify, and transmit sealed to the seat of the government of the United States, directed to the President of the Senate;—The President of the Senate shall, in the presence of the Senate and House of Representatives, open all the certificates and the votes shall then be counted;—The person having the greatest number of votes for President, shall be the President, if such number be a majority of the whole number of electors appointed; and if no person have such majority, then from the persons having the highest numbers not exceeding three on the list of those voted for as President, the House of Representatives shall choose immediately, by ballot, the President. But in choosing the President, the votes shall be taken by states, the representation from each state having one vote; a quorum for this purpose shall consist of a member or members from two-thirds of the states, and a majority of all the states shall be necessary to a choice. And if the House of Representatives shall not choose a President whenever the right of choice shall devolve upon them, before the fourth day of March next following, then the Vice-President shall act as President, as in the case of the death or other constitutional disability of the President. The person having the greatest number of votes as Vice-President, shall be the Vice-President, if such number be a majority of the whole number of Electors appointed, and if no person have a majority, then from the two highest numbers on the list, the Senate shall choose the Vice-President; a quorum for the purpose shall consist of two-thirds of the whole number of Senators, and a majority of the whole number shall be necessary to a choice. But no person constitutionally ineligible to the office of President shall be eligible to that of Vice-President of the United States.

[Article XIII.]

[Passed by Congress February 1, 1865, and ratified December 18, 1865]

Section 1. Neither slavery nor involuntary servitude, except as a punishment for crime whereof the party shall have been duly convicted, shall exist within the United States, or any place subject to their jurisdiction.

Section 2. Congress shall have power to enforce this article by appropriate legislation.

[Article XIV.]

[Passed by Congress June 16, 1866, and ratified July 28, 1868]

Section 1. All persons born or naturalized in the United States, and subject to the jurisdiction thereof, are citizens of the United States and of the State wherein they reside. No State shall make or enforce any law which shall abridge the privileges or immunities of citizens of the United States; nor shall any State deprive any person of life, liberty, or property, without due process of law; nor deny to any person within its jurisdiction the equal protection of the laws.

Section 2. Representatives shall be apportioned among the several States according to their respective numbers, counting the whole number of persons in each State, excluding Indians not taxed. But when the right to vote at any election for the choice of electors for President and Vice-President of the United States, Representatives in Congress, the Executive and Judicial officers of a State, or the members of the Legislature thereof, is denied to any of the male inhabitants of such State, being twenty-one years of age, and citizens of the United States, or in any way abridged, except for participation in rebellion, or other crime, the basis of representation therein shall be reduced in the proportion which the number of such male citizens shall bear to the whole number of male citizens twenty-one years of age in such State.

SECTION 3. No person shall be a Senator or Representative in Congress, or elector of President and Vice President, or hold any office, civil or military, under the United States, or under any State, who, having previously taken an oath, as a member of Congress, or as an officer of the United States, or as a member of any State legislature, or as an executive or judicial officer of any State, to support the Constitution of the United States, shall have engaged in insurrection or rebellion against the same, or given aid or comfort to the enemies thereof. But Congress may by a vote of two-thirds of each House, remove such disability.

SECTION 4. The validity of the public debt of the United States, authorized by law, including debts incurred for payment of pensions and bounties for services in suppressing insurrection or rebellion, shall not be questioned. But neither the United States nor any State shall assume or pay any debt or obligation incurred in aid of insurrection or rebellion against the United States, or any claim for the loss or emancipation of any slave; but all such debts, obligations and claims shall be held illegal and void.

SECTION 5. The Congress shall have power to enforce, by appropriate legislation, the provisions of this article.

[ARTICLE XV.]
[Passed by Congress February 27, 1869, and ratified March 30, 1870]

SECTION 1. The right of citizens of the United States to vote shall not be denied or abridged by the United States or by any State on account of race, color, or previous condition of servitude.—

SECTION 2. The Congress shall have power to enforce this article by appropriate legislation.—

[ARTICLE XVI.]
[Passed by Congress July 12, 1909, and ratified February 25, 1913]

The Congress shall have power to lay and collect taxes on incomes, from whatever source derived, without apportionment among the several States, and without regard to any census or enumeration.

[ARTICLE XVII.]
[Passed by Congress May 16, 1912, and ratified May 31, 1913]

The Senate of the United States shall be composed of two Senators from each state, elected by the people thereof, for six years; and each Senator shall have one vote. The electors in each State shall have the qualifications requisite for electors of the most numerous branch of the State legislatures.

When vacancies happen in the representation of any State in the Senate, the executive authority of such State shall issue writs of election to fill such vacancies: *Provided,* That the legislatures of any State may empower the executive thereof to make temporary appointment until the people fill the vacancies by election as the legislature may direct.

This amendment shall not be so construed as to affect the election or term of any Senator chosen before it becomes valid as part of the Constitution.

[ARTICLE XVIII.]
[Passed by Congress December 17, 1917, and ratified January 29, 1919]

SECTION 1. After one year from the ratification of this article the manufacture, sale, or transportation of intoxicating liquors within, the importation thereof into, or the exportation thereof from the United States and all territory subject to the jurisdiction thereof for beverage purposes is hereby prohibited.

SECTION 2. The Congress and the several States shall have concurrent power to enforce this article by appropriate legislation.

SECTION 3. The article shall be inoperative unless it shall have been ratified as an amendment to the Constitution by the legislatures of the several States, as provided in the Constitution, within seven years from the date of the submission hereof to the States by Congress.

[ARTICLE XIX.]
[Passed by Congress June 5, 1919, and ratified August 26, 1920]

The right of citizens of the United States to vote shall not be denied or abridged by the United States or by any State on account of sex. Congress shall have power to enforce this article by appropriate legislation.

[Passed by Congress March 3, 1932, and ratified February 6, 1933]

SECTION 1. The terms of the President and Vice-President shall end at noon on the 20th day of January, and the terms of Senators and Representatives at noon on the 3d day of January, of the years in which such terms would have ended if this article had not been ratified; and the terms of their successors shall then begin.

SECTION 2. The Congress shall assemble at least once in every year, and such meeting shall begin at noon on the 3d day of January, unless they shall by law appoint a different day.

SECTION 3. If, at the time fixed for the beginning of the term of the President, the President-elect shall have died, the Vice-President-elect shall become President. If a President shall not have been chosen before the time fixed for the beginning of his term, or if the President-elect shall have failed to qualify, then the Vice-President-elect shall act as President until a President shall have qualified; and the Congress may by law provide for the case wherein neither a President-elect nor a Vice-President-elect shall have qualified, declaring who shall then act as President, or the manner in which one who is to act shall be selected, and such person shall act accordingly until a President or Vice-President shall have qualified.

SECTION 4. The Congress may by law provide for the case of the death of any of the persons from whom the House of Representatives may choose a President whenever the right of choice shall have devolved upon them, and for the case of the death of any of the persons from whom the Senate may choose a Vice-President whenever the right of choice shall have devolved upon them.

SECTION 5. Sections 1 and 2 shall take effect on the 15th day of October following the ratification of this article.

SECTION 6. This article shall be inoperative unless it shall have been ratified as an amendment to the Constitution by the legislatures of three-fourths of the several States within seven years from the date of its submission.

[ARTICLE XXI.]
[Passed by Congress February 20, 1933, and ratified December 5, 1933]

SECTION 1. The Eighteenth Article of amendment to the Constitution of the United States is hereby repealed.

SECTION 2. The transportation or importation into any State, Territory, or possession of the United States for delivery or use therein of intoxicating liquors, in violation of the laws thereof, is hereby prohibited.

SECTION 3. This article shall be inoperative unless it shall have been ratified as an amendment to the Constitution by conventions in the several States, as provided in the Constitution, within seven years from the date of the submission hereof to the States by the Congress.

[ARTICLE XXII.]
[Passed by Congress March 12, 1947, and ratified February 26, 1951]

No person shall be elected to the office of the President more than twice, and no person who has held the office of President, or acted as President, for more than two years of a term to which some other person was elected President shall be elected to the office of the President more than once.

But this article shall not apply to any person holding the office of President when this article was proposed by the Congress, and shall not prevent any person who may be holding the office of President, or acting as President, during the term within which this article becomes operative from holding the office of President or acting as President during the remainder of such term.

PRESIDENTS OF THE UNITED STATES

	President	Party Affiliation	Years in Office	Age took office	Birthplace	Born	Died	Age at Death
1	George Washington	Federalist	1789–1797	57	Virginia	1732	1799	67
2	John Adams	Federalist	1797–1801	61	Massachusetts	1735	1826	90
3	Thomas Jefferson	Democrat-Republican	1801–1809	57	Virginia	1743	1826	83
4	James Madison	Democrat-Republican	1809–1817	57	Virginia	1751	1836	85
5	James Monroe	Democrat-Republican	1817–1825	58	Virginia	1758	1831	73
6	John Quincy Adams	Democrat-Republican	1825–1829	57	Massachusetts	1767	1848	80
7	Andrew Jackson	Democrat	1829–1837	61	So. Carolina	1767	1845	78
8	Martin Van Buren	Democrat	1837–1841	54	New York	1782	1862	79
9	William Henry Harrison	Whig	1841	68	Virginia	1773	1841	68
10	John Tyler	Whig	1841–1845	51	Virginia	1790	1862	71
11	James K. Polk	Democrat	1845–1849	49	No. Carolina	1795	1849	53
12	Zachary Taylor	Whig	1849–1850	64	Virginia	1784	1850	65
13	Millard Fillmore	Whig	1850–1853	50	New York	1800	1874	74
14	Franklin Pierce	Democrat	1853–1857	48	New Hampshire	1804	1869	64
15	James Buchanan	Democrat	1857–1861	65	Pennsylvania	1791	1868	77
16	Abraham Lincoln	Republican	1861–1865	52	Kentucky	1809	1865	56
17	Andrew Johnson	Republican	1865–1869	56	No. Carolina	1808	1875	66
18	Ulysses S. Grant	Republican	1869–1877	46	Ohio	1822	1885	63
19	Rutherford B. Hayes	Republican	1877–1881	54	Ohio	1822	1893	70
20	James A. Garfield	Republican	1881	49	Ohio	1831	1881	49
21	Chester A. Arthur	Republican	1881–1885	50	Vermont	1830	1886	56
22	Grover Cleveland	Democrat	1885–1889	47	New Jersey	1837	1908	71
23	Benjamin Harrison	Republican	1889–1893	55	Ohio	1833	1901	67
24	Grover Cleveland	Democrat	1893–1897	55	New Jersey	1837	1908	71
25	William McKinley	Republican	1897–1901	54	Ohio	1843	1901	58
26	Theodore Roosevelt	Republican	1901–1909	43	New York	1858	1919	60
27	William Howard Taft	Republican	1909–1913	51	Ohio	1857	1930	72
28	Woodrow Wilson	Democrat	1913–1921	56	Virginia	1856	1924	67
29	Warren G. Harding	Republican	1921–1923	55	Ohio	1865	1923	57
30	Calvin Coolidge	Republican	1923–1929	51	Vermont	1872	1933	60
31	Herbert Hoover	Republican	1929–1933	54	Iowa	1874	1964	90
32	Franklin Delano Roosevelt	Democrat	1933–1945	51	New York	1882	1945	63
33	Harry S. Truman	Democrat	1945–1953	60	Missouri	1884	....	....
34	Dwight D. Eisenhower	Republican	1953–1961	62	Texas	1890	1969	78
35	John F. Kennedy	Democrat	1961–1963	43	Massachusetts	1917	1963	46
36	Lyndon B. Johnson	Democrat	1963–1969	55	Texas	1908	....	....
37	Richard M. Nixon	Republican	1969–	56	California	1913	....	....

VICE-PRESIDENTS OF THE UNITED STATES

		Vice-President	Party Affiliation	Year took office
*	1	John Adams	Federalist	1789
*	2	Thomas Jefferson	Republican	1797
	3	Aaron Burr	Republican	1801
	4	George Clinton	Republican	1805
	5	Elbridge Gerry	Republican	1813
	6	Daniel D. Tompkins	Republican	1817
	7	John C. Calhoun	Republican	1825
*	8	Martin Van Buren	Democrat	1833
	9	Richard M. Johnson	Democrat	1837
*	10	John Tyler	Whig	1841
	11	George M. Dallas	Democrat	1845
*	12	Millard Fillmore	Whig	1849
	13	William R. King	Democrat	1853
	14	John C. Breckinridge	Democrat	1857
	15	Hannibal Hamlin	Republican	1861
*	16	Andrew Johnson	Republican	1865
	17	Schuyler Colfax	Republican	1869
	18	Henry Wilson	Republican	1873
	19	William A. Wheeler	Republican	1877
*	20	Chester A. Arthur	Republican	1881
	21	Thomas A. Hendricks	Democrat	1885
	22	Levi P. Morton	Republican	1889
	23	Adlai E. Stevenson	Democrat	1893
	24	Garrett A. Hobart	Republican	1897
*	25	Theodore Roosevelt	Republican	1901
	26	Charles W. Fairbanks	Republican	1905
	27	James S. Sherman	Republican	1909
	28	Thomas R. Marshall	Democrat	1913
*	29	Calvin Coolidge	Republican	1921
	30	Charles G. Dawes	Republican	1925
	31	Charles V. Curtis	Republican	1929
	32	John Nance Garner	Democrat	1933
	33	Henry Agard Wallace	Democrat	1941
*	34	Harry S. Truman	Democrat	1945
	35	Alben W. Barkley	Democrat	1949
	36	Richard M. Nixon	Republican	1953
*	37	Lyndon B. Johnson	Democrat	1961
	38	Hubert H. Humphrey	Democrat	1965
	39	Spiro T. Agnew	Republican	1969

* Succeeded to presidency